THE TERROR MATRIX

Decoding Terrorism

THE TERROR MATRIX

Decoding Terrorism

Vikas Katheria, IPS

PENTAGON PRESS LLP

First published in 2025 by
PENTAGON PRESS LLP
206, Peacock Lane, Shahpur Jat
New Delhi-110049, India
Contact: 011-26490600

Typeset in AGaramond, 11.5 Point
Printed at Thomson Press India Limited

ISBN 978-81-991162-0-7

Disclaimer: The views and opinions expressed in the book is the individual assertion of the Author. The Publisher does not take any responsibility for the same in any manner whatsoever. The same shall solely be the responsibility of the Author.

www.pentagonpress.in

CONTENTS

Preface *ix*

Acknowledgements *xv*

1. Terrorism: Past, Present, and Future 1
Terrorism in Antiquity to Now: A Concise History 1
Evolution of Terrorism as a Political Tool in the 20th Century 5
Terror's Peak: A Look Back at the 1970s and 1980s 6
India's Battle against Terror: A Historical Overview 7
Revolutionary Fire: India's Armed Struggle for Freedom 10
The Evolution of Terrorism: From Concept to Universally Condemned Political Weapon 12
Employing Violent Tactics to Achieve Political Goals: A Short History 13
Western Perspectives on the History of Terrorism 15
Religion and Terrorism: A Dangerous Cocktail 17
Terrorism Now: 21st Century 18
Emergence of the Tech-savvy Terrorist 19

2. The Problem of Defining Terrorism: A Complex Web of Politics, Law, and Ethics 22
Defining Terrorism: An Elusive Quest 23
Customary Terrorism Law in Focus: The Lebanon Tribunal's Legacy 32
The Perils of Ambiguity: Implications of Undefined Terrorism in International Law 34
Comprehensive Convention on International Terrorism & other Efforts on the UN Forum 35
Navigating the Gray Area: Approaches to Defining Terrorism 38
Regional and Multilateral Approaches to Adopt Definition 39
Terrorism: Is It What We Say It Is? Perils of a Commonsense Approach 42
The Case against a Universal Definition of Terrorism 43
Hostages Case: Nuremberg Trial: Implications for Terrorism Definition 44
Balancing Act: Global Consensus vs. National Interests in Defining Terrorism 46
The Perils of Precision: Pitfalls of a Global Terrorism Definition 47
Evolving Perspectives on Defining Terrorism: Ongoing Struggle 51
Conclusion 51

3. The Invisible Enemy: The Rise of Cyber Terrorism 54
A Short History of Cyber-Terrorism 55

Cyber-terrorism: Meaning and Issues 58
The Cyber-terrorism Hype? Perspective with a Difference 64
Motivations for Cyber-Terrorism 65
Digital Dark Matter: The Hidden Dangers of Cyber-Terrorism 66
Challenges in Encountering Threats from Cyber-Terrorism 70
Legal and Policy Aspects in addressing Cyber-terrorism 75
Cyber-Terrorism and Cyber-Warfare: Legal Complexities 80
Cyber-Terrorism and Information Security: The Global Response 82

4. Protecting the Skies: The Fight against Aviation Terrorism 86
Impact of Aviation Terrorism: From Psychological to Physical 86
The Threat from Above: A Look at Indian Aviation Hijackings 87
International Legal Regime Governing Aviation Terrorism: Issues and Concerns 89
No Safe Haven: Criminalizing Aircraft Seizure and Related Offences 93
A United Front: The Global Imperative to Combat Aviation Terrorism 96
Beyond Hijacking: The Evolving Threat of Aviation Terrorism 96
Intelligence Blindspots and Aviation Terrorism: Bojinka Plot, 9/11 failure and more 101
Drones in the Sky: A New Threat to Aviation 101
United Against Drone Threats: The Berlin Memorandum 103
Use of Unmanned Aerial Vehicles as a Counter-terrorism Tool 105
Balancing Sovereignty and Global Air Connectivity 106
Safeguarding Our Skies: A Blueprint for Preventing Aviation Terrorism 107

5. Counter-Terrorism Legislation in India: Evolution, Issues, and Trends 109
Indian Experience with Special Counter-Terrorism Laws: Issues and Challenges 109
Persistence of 'Special Circumstances': Secessionism in Post-Independent India 112
Tackling Terror Through Cyclic Legislation? Compulsions of Governance? 113
The Role of Emergency Powers in Counter-Terrorism Legislation 117
The Armed Forces (Special Powers) Act, 1958 118
Combating Terrorism: The Role of Terrorist and Disruptive Activities (Prevention) Act 123
Prevention of Terrorism Act, 2002 (POTA) 129
Unlawful Activities (Prevention) Act, 1967 132
Summing up India's Counter-Terrorism Legislative Journey 135

6. Balancing Security and Justice: Procedural Aspects of Anti-Terror Laws 137
The Nature of Terrorist Crimes and the Need for 'Special' Procedures 140
Special Procedures Related to Seizure of Property 144
Special Procedures for Arrest, Detention, and Bail 152
Special Courts and Trial Process in Terrorism Cases 159
Conclusion 163

7. Counter-Terrorism and Human Rights Law 164
National Security, Torture and Human Rights Imperatives 166

Surveillance Capitalism and Human Right Concerns: The Right to Privacy and to Live with Dignity 167
The International Human Rights Law and its Implications for Countering Terrorism 169
Counter-Terrorism: Human Rights vs. National Security Considerations 173
The Extraterritorial Application of Human Rights Law: Implications for Counter-Terror Strategy 173
The Impact of International Human Rights Regime on Counter-Terrorism Measures 175
Incitement, Glorification and Support to Terrorist Activities: Human Rights Concerns 177
Big Brother is Watching: The Implications of Mass Surveillance on Human Rights 181
The Digital Transformation of Intelligence: Privacy Implications and Human Rights Concerns 182
Conclusion 189

8. Preparatory Acts of Terrorism, Prevention and Counter-Radicalisation 190
Criminalisation of Preparatory Acts of Terrorism: Principle of Pre-emption, Precaution and Preventative Paradigm 190
The Evolution of Counter-terrorism: Criminalizing Preparatory Acts of Terrorism 194
Preventative Measures in Counter-Terrorism Legislation: The Unlawful Activities (Prevention) Act 197
Navigating the Legal Terrain of Terrorism Prevention in India 197
Preventing Radicalisation: Promoting Counter-radicalization 200
Countering Support and Promotion of Terrorism and Violent Ideologies 204
First Line of Defence Against Preparation: Target Recruitment and Training 209
Closing the Gaps: Legal Framework against Preparatory Acts of Terror 210
Legal Limitations: Tackling Modern Terrorism 211
Conclusion 214

9. The Poppy Fields of Terror: The Narco-Terrorism Threat 215
Narco-terrorism: Emotive Undertones 215
Drugs, Guns, and Fear: The Menace of Narco-Terrorism 217
The Silent Enemy: India's Battle Against Narco-Terrorism 222
Money-Laundering and Narco-Terrorism 225
Investigative Complexity in Narco-terrorism Cases 229
Conclusion 234

10. Cashing in on Chaos: The Business of Terror-Funding 236
What is Terrorist Financing? 236
How do Terrorists Finance Themselves? A Case Study of Aum Shinrikyo 240
Distinguishing Features of Terror Finance 241
Stages of Terror Financing 244
Strategic versus Tactical Terror Financing 246
Stages in Terror Financing 247
Terrorist Financing: Web of Ideology and Operations 249
Combating Terror Finance: International Institutional and Legal Framework 249

FATF: A Standard-Setter, not a Lone Watchdog 254
FATF's 40 Recommendations: Standard Protocols to Combat Money Laundering and Terrorist Financing 255
Shifting Sands of Terrorist Financing: New Challenges, New Opportunities 258
Strengthening the Global Fight Against Terrorist Financing: Preventing Terror Financing 261
A Ticking Time Bomb: Emerging Trends in Terrorist Financing 263
Conclusion 266

11. The Silent Arsenal: The Menace of CBRN Terror 268
A Toxic Timeline: CBRN Attacks Through History 268
A Short History of CBRN Terrorism 269
CBRN Ambition: What Drives Terrorists to the Brink? 271
The Role of State-Sponsored Terrorism in the Acquisition of CBRN Capabilities by Terrorist Organisations 273
World's Most Dangerous Gamble: Pakistan's Nuclear Weapons 275
CBRN Catastrophe: Preventing Weaponization by Terrorists 277
Axis of Evil: Nations Fuelling the CBRN Threat 279
Defending Against Doom: Global Cooperation on CBRN Terrorism 282
Future Trends and Emerging Technologies in CBRN Terrorism 288
From Backyard to Battlefield: The Risks of DIY Technology 291

12. The Digital Caliphate: Emerging Tech and the Terrorist Nexus 293
The Ethics of Innovation: Technology and Terrorism 293
The Rise of Big Tech and the Erosion of State Control 294
Skies under Threat: The Drone Terrorism Challenge 297
From Lab to Weapon: The Rise of Synthetic Biology Threats 302
From Recruitment to Rampage: AI's Potential Role in Terrorism of the Future 307
Artificial Intelligence and Effective Counter-terrorism: Public Policy and the Compliance Conundrum 314
Crypto Currency and Funding of Terrorism: The Dark Web Economy 315
Printing Terror: The Looming Threat of 3D-Printed Weapons 321
Conclusion 325

13. The Psychology of Fear: How Perception Shapes Our Understanding of Terrorism 326
Public Opinion: The Silent Architect of Counter-terrorism Policy 326
How Bias Guides Notions About Terrorism 330
How Emotions such as Motivations Sustain Terrorism 336
Social Media: Propaganda's Perfect Playground 339
Social Media and Terrorist Propaganda: Is BigTech Acting Responsibly? 345
The Digital Horde: AI, Perception Control, and Mass Manipulation 351
Where Does All This Leave Us? 355

Notes 360

Index 383

PREFACE

In a world that seems more interconnected than ever before, terrorism remains a shadowy force that continues to haunt the global stage. It is a term that is frequently thrown around in political debates, newsrooms, social media platforms, and even casual conversations, yet its understanding is often shrouded in a fog of jargon and emotive undertones. The very mention of the word 'terrorism' can provoke strong reactions, leading to heated discussions that seldom reach clear conclusions. It is this muddled dialogue—clouded by complex terminology and emotional biases—that not only confuses the public but also obscures the real issues at the heart of terrorism.

This book, aims precisely to cut through the noise and offer a clearer, more precise understanding of one of the most misunderstood topics of our time. We will delve deep into the complexities of terrorism, examining its various definitions, historical contexts, and the different types of terrorism that have emerged throughout history. We will explore the motivations behind terrorist acts, the strategies they employ, and the impact they have on societies, economies, and international relations.

By examining terrorism from a variety of perspectives, we will challenge the simplistic narratives that often dominate public discourse. We will explore the ways in which terrorism is shaped by political, social, economic, and cultural factors, and how it is influenced by the broader geopolitical landscape. We will also consider the role of technology, globalization, and the spread of information in facilitating and countering terrorist activities.

One of the key challenges in understanding terrorism is the subjective nature of the term itself. What constitutes terrorism can vary depending on the perspective of the observer. Governments, media outlets, and individuals may have different interpretations of what constitutes a terrorist act. This can lead to confusion and disagreement, making it difficult to develop a unified response to the threat of terrorism.

The concept of terrorism has evolved significantly over time, shaped by political, legal, and cultural factors. What was once considered a relatively straightforward act of violence against civilians has become a complex and multifaceted phenomenon. To understand the contemporary challenges posed by terrorism, it is essential to trace its historical roots and examine how its definition has shifted over the centuries.

During the 19th and early 20th centuries, terrorism was often associated with nationalist movements seeking to overthrow colonial powers. Many national movements used violence to achieve their political goals whose targets were often restricted to those who were working for the colonial powers. However, these early forms of terrorism were often characterized by a degree of selectivity and restraint. Targets were typically limited to government officials, military personnel, and symbols of colonial authority.

The post-World War II era witnessed a significant shift in the nature of terrorism. The emergence of transnational terrorist organizations, such as al-Qaeda and the Islamic State, marked a new era of global terrorism. These groups often employed indiscriminate violence against civilians, targeting both military and civilian targets. They also sought to use media to spread their message and inspire acts of violence around the world.

In recent years, the definition of terrorism has become even more complex. The rise of cyber terrorism, environmental terrorism, and lone-wolf attacks has challenged traditional notions of what constitutes terrorism. These new forms of terrorism often blur the lines between state-sponsored violence and non-state violence, making it difficult to assign responsibility and develop effective counter-measures.

By understanding the historical evolution of the concept of terrorism, we can better appreciate the complexities and challenges associated with addressing this global threat. It is essential to recognize that terrorism is not a monolithic phenomenon but rather a diverse set of activities that have been shaped by a variety of factors. By examining the different perspectives on terrorism, we can develop a more nuanced and comprehensive understanding of the phenomenon and the challenges it poses to our societies.

The discussions on terrorism are not only complicated by the use of jargon but also by the fact that such issues are often debated with intense passion where reason becomes an obvious casualty. Indeed, terrorism is one of the most frequently discussed issues in public discourse, yet it remains one of the least understood. Why is that? A significant reason for this widespread misunderstanding lies in the subjectivity of those who engage in these debates. Opinions about terrorism are often coloured by personal experience, cultural background, and even professional involvement. For example, the viewpoint of someone directly affected by terrorism—either as a victim or as someone living in a region plagued by violent acts—differs greatly from that of a scholar or a policymaker studying the phenomenon from a distance.

Those most equipped to offer a dispassionate perspective on terrorism often come from professions that require a more analytical approach, such as law enforcement, academics, journalists, or individuals directly involved in counter-terrorism efforts. These professionals are trained to look beyond the immediate emotional reactions and examine the structural, social, and political factors that drive terrorism. Yet, their voices are frequently overshadowed in the public domain by those who speak from a place of fear, anger, or ideological bias. This book seeks to amplify these dispassionate voices, shedding light on the realities of terrorism without succumbing to the emotional currents that so often steer the conversation off course.

One of the most pressing concerns in the fight against terrorism today is the lack of effective international cooperation. In recent years, we have witnessed a disturbing trend towards unilateralism, especially by powerful nations such as the United States and its allies. This tendency to act independently, without seeking broader consensus or support from the international community, has weakened the global effort to counter terrorism. The notion that terrorism can only be countered through the use of military force has led to a spate of unilateral actions that often do more harm than good. When the response to terrorism is framed solely in terms of violence, it not only perpetuates the cycle of bloodshed but also risks alienating entire communities, fostering resentment, and inadvertently nurturing the very ideologies that fuel terrorism.

The belief that 'evil can never be countered by evil' is not merely a moral stance; it is a pragmatic approach that recognizes the limitations of violence as a sole tool against terrorism. Lasting peace and stability require more than just the application of force; they require addressing the underlying causes of terrorism such as easy availability of arms, an atmosphere of criminality and defective law and order maintenance, corruption, political disenfranchisement, religious extremism, and the further accentuated by lack of socio-economic justice. In this book, we will explore how a comprehensive approach that includes diplomacy, development, and dialogue is essential to counter-terrorism strategies.

The threat of terrorism transcends national borders and requires a concerted global effort to address. The international community must move beyond fragmented and often conflicting approaches and work together in good faith to build a united front against this insidious threat. Terrorism cannot be viewed through a parochial lens of self-interest, as its consequences are felt around the world.

The interconnectedness of a globalized world has made it increasingly difficult to isolate terrorist threats. Reinforced by internet, terrorists now are much more organized and able to sustain their operations over a wider geographical landscape. They now often operate across multiple borders, exploiting vulnerabilities in international systems and leveraging technological advancements to spread their message and plan attacks. In the face of such a complex and adaptable adversary, fragmented approaches in counter-terrorism are simply not sufficient.

Despite the international community's longstanding recognition of the need for cooperation, intelligence sharing, and strengthened institutions, the global response to terrorism has been far from comprehensive. While mechanisms and institutions have been established, their effectiveness has been hindered by a lack of political will, divergent interests, and the complex nature of the threat itself.

A key challenge lies in the reluctance of some states to condemn terrorism in all its forms. Double standards and selective condemnation have undermined efforts to build a united front against this global threat. Without a clear and consistent approach, it has been difficult to establish effective international mechanisms to address terrorist financing and cross-border linkages, which are essential for disrupting terrorist operations.

While there is no doubt that the United Nations and regional security organizations have played important roles in the fight against terrorism, however their effectiveness has been limited by their mandates and resources. To truly make a difference, these organizations need to be equipped with the necessary tools and authority to address the evolving nature of terrorist threats, including their financing networks and cross-border activities.

As we move forward into the 21st century, the challenges posed by terrorism are set to become even more complex due to the advent of emergent technologies. Innovations in artificial intelligence, biotechnology, 3D printing, and other fields are transforming how people interact, live, and even wage war. While these technologies hold tremendous potential for good, they also have a darker side when exploited by those with malicious intent. Terrorists have historically been quick to adapt and employ new technologies to their advantage, and there is every indication that they will continue to do so. The potential for these tools to be weaponized in ways that we are only beginning to understand poses a serious threat to global security.

Imagine a future where terrorists use AI to create sophisticated cyber-attacks that can cripple a nation's infrastructure or use biotechnology to develop deadly pathogens that could spark pandemics. The terrifying reality is that these scenarios are no longer confined to the realm of science fiction; they are genuine possibilities that demand our immediate attention. In this book, we will explore how these emergent technologies are reshaping the landscape of terrorism and what steps must be taken to mitigate these risks. Understanding this evolving threat is crucial for developing strategies that are both effective and forward-looking.

Another factor that has profoundly influenced the spread of terrorism in recent years is the rise of social media. Platforms like Facebook, Twitter, and YouTube have become not only tools for communication but also powerful instruments for propaganda. Terrorist groups such as ISIS, al-Qaeda, and others have harnessed these platforms to spread their ideologies, recruit new members, and even coordinate attacks. The power of social media lies in its ability to reach vast audiences instantaneously and create virtual communities that transcend geographical boundaries. For terrorists, it provides a cost-effective way to radicalize individuals and mobilize support on a global scale.

The role of social media in enabling the spread of terror has two-sides. While it gives extremists a voice, it also provides authorities with new ways to track and disrupt terrorist networks. In this book, we will explore the dual nature of social media—both as a tool for spreading hate and violence and as a potential asset in counter-terrorism efforts. We will examine the challenges that governments and tech companies face in regulating online content without infringing on free speech, and how they can work together to curb the misuse of these platforms by terrorist organizations.

The purpose of this book is not merely to add another voice to the already noisy discourse on terrorism but to provide a clear and balanced perspective that cuts through the fog of confusion and misinformation. It seeks to equip readers with a nuanced understanding of what terrorism truly is, why it persists, and how it can be countered effectively. By breaking down the complexities of terrorism into comprehensible concepts and exploring the roles of international cooperation, types of terrorism, emergent technologies, and social media, this book aims to foster a deeper awareness of the threats we face and the strategies required to confront them.

Terrorism is not a problem that can be solved by any single nation or through military might alone; it requires a collective effort, innovative thinking, and a commitment to address the underlying real causes of violence. As we move forward, it is crucial to remember that understanding the nature of terrorism is the first step toward combating it. We must strive to look beyond the rhetoric, the fear, and the anger, to see the true dynamics at play. Only then can we hope to develop strategies that are not only effective but also just and humane.

This book is a call to action for all those who seek a world free from the scourge of terrorism—a world where peace, justice, and human dignity prevail over hatred and violence. It is my hope that this humble attempt will serve as a valuable resource for anyone interested in understanding this complex issue, and that it will inspire thoughtful dialogue and meaningful action in the pursuit of a safer, more peaceful world.

Vikas Katheria

ACKNOWLEDGEMENTS

A project of this scale can never be the achievement of an individual alone. Without the guidance, support, and insights of those with deep experience and wisdom, such an undertaking would have remained an unfulfilled ambition. In the field of counter-terrorism, there is no substitute for hands-on experience; it is a domain where learning principally occurs through action rather than theory.

I have had the privilege of working across the triad that forms the backbone of counter-terrorism efforts, intelligence, operations, and investigation—each informing and reinforcing the others, shaping a holistic understanding of the national security landscape. Another stroke of fortune was the nature of my professional assignments, which took me through nearly all major theatres of counter-terrorism and counter-insurgency: from the North-East to Jammu & Kashmir, from Left Wing Extremism to Jihadi terrorism and Khalistani disturbances among others. These engagements offered not only operational exposure but also a constant need to stay updated and alert to evolving threats and strategies.

Writing a book on a subject as complex and sensitive as terrorism, while simultaneously serving in some of the country's most demanding conflict zones, was both an intense challenge and a deeply enriching experience. This endeavor would not have been possible without the steady support of my seniors, the encouragement of colleagues and friends, and, above all, the unwavering understanding and sacrifice of my family.

At the heart of it all stands my mother, to whom I owe my life, my education, and every step of the journey that brought me here. Her strength, values, and silent resilience shaped the man I am today.

Most professionals in the counter-terrorism and national security community choose to remain unnamed, and I fully respect that preference.

Yet, I must express my heartfelt gratitude to a few individuals who graciously permitted their mention. Above all, my deepest and most enduring appreciation goes to my wife, Rashmi. With infinite patience, she read through the manuscript, offering thoughtful suggestions—most notably, encouraging me to reduce the jargon and make the narrative more accessible without compromising its depth and seriousness.

More than that, her unwavering support, quiet strength, and countless sacrifices, especially during my remote postings and relentless schedule—allowed me to focus on both my duties and this writing project, mostly free from the burden of domestic concerns. Her love, along with the affection of our children, remains my greatest source of joy and strength, making me not just a better officer, but the happiest man.

Prolific writer and much respected national security expert Mr. Bharat Karnad offered thoughtful suggestions on several themes, and Dr. Gulshan Rai (Distinguished Fellow at ORF) provided critical inputs on emerging technologies and their implications.

I extend my deepest respect and gratitude to Mr. Gyanendra Pratap Singh, Mr. Anand Jain, Mr. Rupin Sharma, Mrs. Sonia Narang, and Mr. Saket Kumar Singh of the Indian Police Service. Their unwavering guidance, patient mentorship, and steady supervision played a pivotal role in shaping a raw probationer into a committed professional. I remain indebted to them for the values and direction they instilled in me.

Vikas Katheria

1

Terrorism: Past, Present, and Future

> *"All attempts to destroy democracy by terrorism will fail. It must be business as usual."*
>
> **—Margaret Thatcher**

This chapter aims to provide a general, non-linear overview of the nature, history, and evolution of terrorism, especially its journey from a bit of legal perspective, rather than delve into a detailed timeline progression of an historical account of terrorism itself. Analysing the complex history of the evolution of terrorism is a vast undertaking that has filled entire books by experts and practitioners. Therefore, this chapter will focus specifically on the historical development of terrorism law, with relevant emphasis on the Indian subcontinent.

Terrorism in Antiquity to Now: A Concise History

Zealots aka Sicarii

Western academicians customarily begin their introduction to the history of terrorism from *Zealots,* who were also known as *Sicarii.*

The Sicarii were a radical offshoot of the first-century Jewish Zealots, known for their violent resistance against Roman rule. Armed with hidden daggers called *sicae,* they targeted Roman officials and Jewish collaborators. Unlike other Zealot groups, the Sicarii acted without religious approval and were condemned by Jewish religious leaders for their extreme violence.

Though their actions reflected the desperation of a people under harsh occupation, they were later blamed for worsening the Roman crackdown, leading to the fall of Jerusalem and the destruction of the Second Temple. Tensions rose further when their leader, Menachem, ordered the assassination of the high priest, Ananias, sparking conflict with other Jewish factions.

The Sicarii became feared for their brutality. Eventually, most were wiped out, but some retreated to the fortress of Masada in the Herodian Mountains. There, in 73 CE, Roman governor Lucius Flavius Silva led a siege with 10,000 soldiers, ending the Sicarii's violent legacy.

For the Sicarii, every action carried deep religious and apocalyptic meaning. They believed they were morally justified in their violence, often targeting fellow Jews who disagreed with them. Their use of terror was intense and focused, especially against their own people—something rare in ancient times.

While other uprisings against Rome occurred in places like North Africa, Britain, and Germany during the first century, none matched the Sicarii in intensity or extremism. They saw anyone who opposed them—even fellow Jews—as enemies.

The Sicarii share striking similarities with modern terrorist groups like al-Qaeda and ISIS. Like these groups, they combined political and religious goals, used fear as a weapon, and targeted civilians to break their trust in ruling powers and stir rebellion.

In the end, their violent ideology isolated them from the wider Jewish community and limited their support. Their rise was fuelled by the tense political and social climate of Judaea before 70 CE. Without those conditions, the movement faded. Yet, the Sicarii were not the last example of a radical group emerging from a mix of religion and politics—similar patterns have continued into the modern era.

The Hashashians

The Hashashians, later known in the West as the '*assassins*,' were a radical group active between the 11th and 13th centuries. Their name likely comes from the Arabic word *hashish*, though there's little evidence they used drugs—this label was probably used to discredit them. They are best known for targeting and killing powerful Muslim leaders, spreading fear across the Islamic world.

The group used intense psychological and religious training to create highly loyal and fanatical killers. These assassinations were carefully planned for maximum impact, both strategically and psychologically. Historian Bernard Lewis even called them 'the first terrorist group in history.'[1]

Originating from the Nizari branch of Isma'ili Shi'ism, the group was founded by Hasan-i Sabbah in 1081. From his stronghold at the mountain fortress of Alamut in Persia, Hasan led a rebellion against the dominant Sunni Seljuk Empire. He promoted absolute loyalty to the Imam, which clashed with mainstream Islamic beliefs and drew widespread condemnation.

One of their earliest and most famous victims was Nizam-ul-Mulk, the Seljuk prime minister. The Hashashians' reputation for ruthless, targeted killings earned them notoriety. Western Crusaders encountered them and passed on distorted accounts, calling them names like '*Al-Hachichine*' or '*Assassins*,' which stuck in European culture.

Though feared and demonized, the Hashashians were highly organized and disciplined. Their legacy endures in history and popular culture as one of the earliest examples of organized, ideologically driven political violence.

The *Naziris*, also known as the Assassins, became one of the most hated groups of their time due to their strategic use of terror, especially political assassinations. Their most famous victims included powerful leaders like Nizam-ul-Mulk, Fatimid Caliph al-Amir, and two Sunni Abbasid caliphs, al-Mustarshid and al-Rashid. They carefully selected high-profile targets to create fear and gain maximum political impact. The term 'Hashashians' was likely a derogatory label used to portray them as criminals.

The Naziris' assassins, called *fedayeen*, used daggers—not poison or other weapons—and carried out their killings openly, often in public places like mosques, courts, or military camps. They disguised themselves as Sufis or beggars and chose moments like prayer days or Ramadan to make their attacks more shocking. Their goal wasn't just to kill but to make bold, unforgettable statements and intimidate enemies.

They also targeted Western leaders, with Count Raymond of Tripoli being the first known victim in 1152. Western writers, unfamiliar with their beliefs, often exaggerated or misunderstood their practices, focusing on rumours of drug use, secret training, and brainwashing. Some chroniclers claimed young recruits were raised in isolation, taught multiple languages, and trained to obey their leader without question, even killing princes on command.

Later stories, like those from Arnold of Lübeck, suggested that the group used narcotics to manipulate followers with dreams of paradise, though this is likely an exaggeration. Interestingly, while the Naziris killed many Muslim leaders, they were responsible for only five Crusader deaths. Despite their relatively low impact on Christians, Western accounts heavily sensationalized their actions.

In the 13th century, the Old Man of the Mountain—leader of the Assassins—became the focus of many European conspiracy theories. These stories were so influential that in 1245, the Church banned killings by Assassins, with Pope Innocent IV declaring that anyone using them would lose all titles and privileges. The Assassins' loyalty to their leader was believed to be absolute, with tales of them sacrificing their lives at his command.

Over time, the Naziris became just one of many Shiite sub-sects. Their influence faded as they failed to achieve lasting political goals. The Mongols destroyed their base at Alamut in 1256, and by 1271 the Mamluks forced their surrender in Syria. By the late 13th century, the Naziris had lost all power, though stories about them lived on.

Comparing ancient groups like the Sicarii and Assassins to modern terrorists' risks applying modern ideas to a different era. Still, these groups show that terrorism-like tactics—organized violence and psychological fear—existed long before today's media and weapons. Their rarity in the past, however, shows that terrorism hadn't yet become a widespread method. Unlike today, no other groups copied their tactics back then, marking a clear difference between the ancient and modern use of terror.

Among Christians, some sects actively employed terrorism against their adversaries. Foremost among these were the *Taborites* of Bohemia, the *Anabaptists*, and fiercely anti-Semitic factions during the *First Crusade*. Throughout the Middle Ages, various Christian denominations, and the Church itself adopted terror tactics as official policies, including the notorious Inquisitions.

The Inquisition: Terror from Above

The Inquisition was an institutional setup to inquire and punish any activity that was considered blasphemous or heresy or in any way opposed to the Gospel of Jesus and other symbols of the Church. In effect, this was anything that the Church adjudged as a threat to its domination and power. This was an act of extreme psychological war on the territories where the writ of the Church ran. The Church through the Inquisitions dominated the elites, and commons alike. During the later period of Islamic history, similarly the Mongols employed varied terror tactics on the subjects of vanquished empires.

They chiefly targeted the elites of the vanquished empires and their methods were brutal to the extreme. Mongol armies used scorched earth policy on a large scale and indiscriminately destroyed hundreds of cities and killed millions of people while imposing their own rule. There is even an estimate of killing the world's 11 per cent population in several Mongol invasions. Mongol invasions are counted as some of the worst and deadliest acts of mass killing and destruction in recorded history.

Evolution of Terrorism as a Political Tool in the 20th Century

Up to World War I, terrorism was primarily individual and left-wing. After the war, it also included right-wing and separatist elements. State-led terrorism became prominent in totalitarian regimes, especially during the 1930s–40s, where certain groups were labelled enemies and targeted, leading to genocide in World War II.

In the 20th century, terrorism became a major political tool used by various groups to challenge authority. Russian Anarchists and the Social Democratic Party (later split into Bolsheviks and Mensheviks) used violence to fight the Tsarist regime, leading to the 1917 Bolshevik Revolution.

Bombing became a common tactic because it caused mass fear and casualties. Italian anarchists used it early on, followed by groups in the Spanish Civil War. The Algerian National Liberation Front used bombings to fight French colonial rule, and Germany's Red Army Faction used them against capitalist systems.

In Ireland, the IRA used guerrilla warfare, assassinations, and bombings during the Irish War of Independence. Later, the Provisional IRA resumed bombing campaigns during the 'Troubles' to seek Irish unification.

In India, revolutionaries used terrorism to fight British rule. Groups like Anushilan Samiti, Jugantar, and the Hindustan Socialist Republican Association, with figures like Bhagat Singh, carried out bombings and assassinations. The Ghaddar Party, formed by Indians abroad, tried to spark armed rebellion in India.

In the 1970s, Northern Ireland's *"Troubles"* began, with the Provisional IRA using bombings to push for Irish unification. A major attack was the 1984 bombing targeting British Prime Minister Margaret Thatcher.

In Latin America, groups like the Tupamaros in Uruguay and the Shining

Path in Peru used terror to fight authoritarian rule and promote Marxism. The Shining Path's extreme violence in the 1980s–90s led to its downfall.

Later in the century, religious terrorism grew. After the 1979 Iranian Revolution, Islamist groups like Hezbollah and Hamas emerged. Hezbollah, backed by Iran, attacked Israeli and Western targets, including the 1983 U.S. Marine barracks bombing in Beirut.

The 1990s brought a new wave of terrorism with the emergence of al-Qaeda, founded by Osama bin Laden. Al-Qaeda's ideology combined militant Islamism with anti-Western sentiments. The group's 1998 bombings of U.S. embassies in Kenya and Tanzania marked their operational capabilities and global reach. The decade culminated in the 2000 *USS Cole* bombing in Yemen, foreshadowing the catastrophic attacks of September 11, 2001.

Throughout these five decades, terrorism evolved in its methods, motivations, and impacts. The interplay of political ideologies, nationalist aspirations, and religious fervour drove the actions of various groups, shaping global security dynamics. The legacy of terrorism from 1950 to 2000 underscores the complexity of addressing this persistent threat in the international arena.

Terror's Peak: A Look Back at the 1970s and 1980s

The "*Golden Age of Terrorism*" is a term used to describe a tumultuous period spanning the 1970s and 1980s when terrorism experienced a marked increase in frequency, intensity, and global impact. This era saw the emergence of numerous radical groups employing a variety of tactics to advance their political, ideological, and nationalist agendas.[2]

The 1970s and 1980s saw major global changes, such as the end of colonialism, Cold War tensions, and rising inequality. These factors fuelled the rise of terrorism as a way to challenge existing powers. Radical groups like the PLO, Red Brigades, Baader-Meinhof Gang (Red Army Faction), ETA, IRA, and Japanese Red Army used tactics like hijackings, bombings, assassinations, kidnappings, and guerrilla warfare. Famous events included the 1970 Dawson's Field hijackings and the 1976 Entebbe raid.

Terrorist attacks targeted government sites, public spaces, and key figures to spread fear and weaken authority. These groups operated across borders, making terrorism a global issue and prompting international cooperation in counter-terrorism.

Governments responded with stronger intelligence sharing, airport security, anti-terror laws, and sometimes negotiations. This period highlighted the need to tackle the real causes of terrorism and work together globally to prevent it.

India's Battle against Terror: A Historical Overview

As discussed earlier, Western notions of terrorism significantly differ from the experiences of other cultures. However, in India, terrorism by non-state actors cannot be understood without discussing certain disparate groups that used violent means to spread unprecedented terror and fear among populations across different states and kingdoms during British Raj. These groups were a cause of concern for the British authorities for a long time. Studying the history of counter-measures against such disparate groups, as recorded primarily by British civil servants and military officers, is relevant for understanding the recent history of terrorism in India.

Thugs and Thugee

From ancient times, India had a feared underground community known as the 'Thugs' or 'Phansigar.' A rough translation of 'Phansigar' would be someone who kills by tightening a noose around the neck. These were organized bands of robbers and assassins, targeting travellers to steal their possessions. The Thugs added a layer of religiosity to their actions, believing their victims were offerings to the goddess of death and destruction, Kali, and that by killing them, they were liberating their souls.

Membership began early, often passed from father to son, but sometimes through the kidnapping of children. By the age of ten or eleven, boys would accompany the killers to observe and learn the sect's trade. They actively participated as they grew older.

The Thugs had a peculiar approach to killing—they did so without spilling blood. Their method involved using a cloth noose called 'Roomal' or 'Phansi,' which is why they were also called 'Phansigar.' They worshipped Kali, the Hindu goddess of death. According to tradition, she created two men from her perspiration to aid her in battling demons and allowed them to kill without remorse as long as no blood was spilled.[3]

According to Thugee's garbled mythology, the goddess Kali was initially responsible for the disposal of the deceased. However, after witnessing this macabre task, she became overwhelmed and abdicated her duties. In lieu of her direct involvement, Kali commanded her devotees to undertake the gruesome ritual of dismemberment and burial. This divine mandate transformed a personal obligation into a collective, religious duty, imbuing the Thugs with a profound sense of sacred purpose as they carried out their murderous rites.[4]

The Thugee phenomenon offers a lens to examine the complexities of colonial knowledge production. The British Raj, represented by its European officers, confronted with India's vast and unfamiliar landscape, created a narrative of the Thugs as a secretive, monolithic cult operating freely. This narrative was shaped more by colonial anxieties than by actual evidence.

While the Thugs were real and dangerous, their activities were exaggerated to fit the colonial framework. The "information panic" surrounding them stemmed from several factors. First, the British faced a radically different social and cultural landscape, leading to misunderstandings. Second, the Thugs' secretive nature and ability to act with impunity challenged colonial control. Finally, the Thugs were used as proof of India's 'inherent barbarity,' justifying colonialism as a civilizing mission. The eradication of Thugee was portrayed as a divine task aimed at uplifting people oppressed by 'pagan' cults like the Thugs.

Examining the Thugee phenomenon reveals how power and knowledge intersected in colonial contexts. The construction of the Thugs as a unified threat justified British intervention while obscuring the complex social and economic factors behind such criminal activities.[5]

Thugee was responsible for the disappearance of thousands of travellers every year. However, Thuggee as an organised activity was on the wane during the third decade of the 19th century by the concerted efforts of British authorities who took stern action against the terrorist group. Seen from the angle of the modern conception of terrorism, *Thuggee* appears to be quite close to our perception of a highly organized terrorist group.

Pindaris

The Pindaris were a formidable irregular cavalry force that caused widespread havoc across the Indian subcontinent from the 17th to the 19th centuries. Acting as mercenaries, they offered their services to the highest bidder, plundering with impunity. Initially employed by Mughal and later Maratha rulers, the Pindaris eventually became independent marauders. Their reign of terror ended with the Pindari War of 1817-19, which led to their suppression.

Regular armies, including those of the Mughals and Marathas, used the Pindaris as shock troops and intelligence assets, taking advantage of their knowledge of the terrain and local populations. Despite originating from different religious backgrounds, the Pindaris formed a unified identity that transcended sectarian divisions.

The Pindaris rose to prominence during the Mughal era (late 17th to early 18th century) and expanded during the Maratha period. Initially employed in Mughal Deccan campaigns, they later became essential to Maratha military strategy. Their tactics—swift raids, intelligence gathering, and scorched-earth methods—made them highly effective in subduing enemy territories. The Marathas, through the Chauth tax, indirectly supported the growth of these irregular forces, creating a relationship that proved devastating for the region.[6]

The Pindaris' terror tactics made them highly effective auxiliaries while keeping their allies in check through serious abuses. At their peak during the 'Gardi-ka-waqt' (times of unrest) in north and north-central India, their forces numbered about 50,000. They pillaged villages, killing indiscriminately and enslaving survivors. For much of the early 19th century, they were a major challenge to law and order.

During the Third Anglo-Maratha War, British Governor-General Francis Rawdon-Hastings led a 120,000-strong force against the Pindaris, resulting in the Pindari War. Labelling them as terrorists is anachronistic, as they were more auxiliary forces used for raids on enemy territories. By this logic, much of British colonial history could be viewed as a study of European-inflicted terrorism on the 'oriental world.'

Maratha scholar G.S. Sardesai noted:

> '*Their true history has perhaps not yet been written. The profuse British accounts suffer from a natural bias created by the last years of their activities perpetuating the impression that the Pindaris were the enemies of society and such loathsome pests as deserved to be exterminated.*'

The Pindaris' history remains obscured due to the lack of their own written records. Historians like S.N. Sen and G.S. Sardesai have examined limited primary sources, but their findings offer few conclusive answers. British accounts, often prejudiced, make it difficult to fully understand this elusive group. A complete history remains unattainable until new evidence emerges.

Revolutionary Fire: India's Armed Struggle for Freedom

The idea that India's independence was solely the result of non-violent resistance is increasingly challenged, even by Western historians. While Mahatma Gandhi's leadership is undeniable, the freedom struggle was a complex mix of both non-violent and violent resistance.

Revolutionary groups, driven by nationalism, used armed struggle as a counter as well as a supplement to Gandhi's methods. The Arms Act of 1878 further fuelled this radical element. The British attempt to disarm Indians was rightly considered a ploy to helplessly colonize India for ages. Although influenced by external revolutionary ideas, the core of this resistance was deeply rooted in India.

Indian historians have used terms like 'militant nationalism,' 'revolutionary terrorism,' or simply 'terrorism' to describe this violent resistance.

Political terrorism in India began in the early 20th century, with notable activity in Bengal, the United Provinces, Bombay, Punjab, and Madras. The first major act of political terrorism occurred in the Bombay Presidency on June 22, 1897, when two brothers assassinated Walter Rand, the Plague Commissioner, and another British officer, Lieutenant Ayerst. These killings were acts of retaliation against British policies during a bubonic plague outbreak in Pune. Public resentment against these oppressive measures was widespread. Revolutionary leader Bal Gangadhar Tilak was falsely implicated, with his alleged seditious activities used to link him to the killings.

A more radical movement emerged in Bengal in 1902, led by Bengali barrister Parmatha Nath Mitra, with Sister Nivedita's involvement[7] and Jatindranath Banerji, a Bengali expatriate serving in the Indian state of Baroda's army, established the Calcutta Anushilan Samiti. This organization served as the precursor to two main terrorist groups in Bengal: Anushilan and Yugantar.

Their primary objective was to engage in terrorism by targeting government officials, with the aim of paralyzing and ultimately toppling the colonial government. They funded their activities through extortion from the wealthy and affluent, and robbing post offices soon became a common practice, giving rise to the concept of 'political dacoities' as a distinctive hallmark of Bengal's terrorists.

An official British government report indicated more than 200 'revolutionary outrages' and about 100 terrorist attempts involving more than

1,000 terrorists between 1906 and 1917. Between 1930 and 1934, Bengal saw intense terrorist activity wherein more than 180 terrorist incidents were reported.[8] Also called the Rowlatt Report). Bengal terrorists extensively used print media to propagate their ideas of independence and the methods to achieve their goals. The first such newspaper was *Jugantar* (the new age), and *Sandhya* ('Evening or the period of transition').

The militant nationalists and the 'extremist' faction of the Indian National Congress shared a powerful term: 'Swaraj,' meaning self-rule. This term was interpreted differently by leaders, ranging from the demand for full independence to seeking dominion status within the British Commonwealth, similar to Australia or Canada.

Key figures like Aurobindo Ghosh, Sachin Sanyal, and Bal Gangadhar Tilak advocated for direct action to achieve independence, opposing what they saw as the futile 'constitutional mendicancy' of asking the British for token participation in Indian legislative bodies. They believed that direct action would mobilize the masses and challenge British authority, contrasting with the moderate leaders who favoured gradual reform.

Tilak's declaration, "Swaraj is my birthright and I shall have it," captured the movement's spirit. These revolutionaries were driven by urgency and the belief in their cause's righteousness, seeking to inspire mass resistance against colonial rule.

However, their radical tactics clashed with more moderate leaders who feared British repression could weaken the broader struggle. Despite these differences, Swaraj became a unifying force symbolizing self-determination and national pride in India's freedom movement.

Revolutionary activities, including terror tactics, gained momentum amid the unpopular division of Bengal and Britain's economic exploitation of India. Many nationalist groups grew frustrated with the Indian Congress's slow, constitutional approach. These activities were a recurring feature of early 20th-century Indian politics, culminating in the Chittagong Armoury Raid of April 18, 1930, led by Surya Sen, which mirrored the 1916 Dublin Easter Rising.

Despite later historians minimizing the role of these revolutionary movements, their violent actions remained a constant in India's freedom struggle, particularly in Bengal and northern India. The history of the movement is marked by simultaneous, diverse efforts—some violent, some peaceful. Debates on their contributions often focus on the superiority of one method over the other, which may not offer the most rational understanding of history.

The Evolution of Terrorism: From Concept to Universally Condemned Political Weapon

The word 'terrorism' originates from the Latin verb 'terrere,' meaning 'to make tremble.' The first formal use of the term appeared in the 1798 supplement of the *Dictionary of the Académie Française* as *"système, régime de la terreur."* In a French dictionary published in 1796, the Jacobins used terrorism positively. The term spread to Britain when Edmund Burke, in a 1795 passage, referred to '*thousands of those hell-hounds called terrorists.*' Initially describing the "reign of terror" in France between March 1793 and July 1794, terrorism later came to describe the use of coercive intimidation to achieve political aims.

Terror as a political tool has a long history. During Sargon of Akkad's reign (23rd century BCE),[9] the first identifiable empire used terror to control subject populations. The Romans, Greeks, and nearly all ancient and medieval empires employed terror to maintain authority, using it as a tool to keep people in constant fear of reprisal.

Similarly, the Mongols and Tamerlane (Timur Lang) used terror by destroying cities, instilling fear in nearby populations. These historical examples demonstrate how terror has consistently been used to achieve political goals. The modern understanding of terrorism stems from the French Revolution's Reign of Terror, where perceived opponents of the revolution were ruthlessly executed.

Terrorism in Contemporary History

In contemporary discussions, terrorism is primarily viewed as the illegitimate use of violence by non-state actors, often linked to private entities rather than state institutions. However, historical records show that terrorism has often been rooted in ideological foundations, whether religious or otherwise. In recent times, many of the most violent forms of terrorism, such as Islamic or jihadi terrorism have had a religious dimension, regardless of their political goals. Terrorism, in its various forms, is often tied to religious fanaticism, aiming to create terror through selective violence and foster uncertainty and confusion.

From the terrorist's perspective, the primary target is the mind. Terrorism is a powerful form of psychological warfare, and its psychological impact far outweighs its physical effects. Using seemingly insignificant means, terrorists aim to gain power from below, in contrast to the authority the state wields from above.

Employing Violent Tactics to Achieve Political Goals: A Short History

In her book, *Political Violence in Ancient India*, Dr. Upinder Singh argues that violence is central to the State. Dominant control over force was crucial in the transition from pre-state to state societies. Modern states tend to claim a monopoly on the legitimate use of violence, with any unsanctioned violence being addressed by state agencies, including the criminal justice system.

When states criminalize terrorism internationally, some resist this principle, questioning the legitimacy of the state's use of force rather than its monopoly on violence. Objections often stem from ideas like the 'rights of minorities' or 'the inherent right of persecuted communities to express their national consciousness.'

Emperor Ashoka's XIIIth Major Rock Edict reflects his adoption of Buddhist principles, marking a shift away from using violence as a state tool. This represents one of the earliest examples of a sovereign renouncing violence and advocating peaceful cultural assimilation without forceful annexation.

The idea that the state holds exclusive authority over physical force is not new; it defines modern states. Max Weber, in his 1918 lecture *Politics as a Vocation*, described the state as a community that asserts a monopoly on legitimate force within its territory. Weber suggested that the modern state arose by controlling political organization and violence while establishing legitimacy. However, legitimacy doesn't mean the state is the only entity allowed to use force—it can delegate this authority but must retain control over its use.[10]

In essence, this legitimacy endures as long as the overwhelming majority of the populace maintains faith in the institutional integrity of their State and its benevolent objectives. Similarly, righteousness is indeed hailed as the quintessential component of the legitimacy of a regime. In his XIIIth rock edict, Ashoka, while abjuring violence as a state policy, nevertheless retains his right to use every means, including violence, to tame the wicked on the grounds of an inherent right to maintain law and order.

In the '*Encyclopaedia of Violence, Peace, & Conflict*,' Jon D. Wiseman astutely observes that the state's monopoly on violence is conferred by the citizenry of the state in exchange for the safeguarding of their person and property. In return, this bestows upon states the capacity to exert coercion and control over individuals, often through mechanisms such as taxation and other lawful exactions. An authority deemed legitimate frequently possesses both the right and rationale to exercise power.

Evolution of Terrorism in the 20th Century: From Top to Bottom

Historically, terrorism gained its negative connotation mainly in the second half of the 20th century. Though it always had a negative association, it was often seen as a political tactic by groups unable to confront state power directly. The distinction between being called an 'extremist,' 'revolutionary,' or 'terrorist' was often blurred, depending on the perspective. The term remains highly emotive, designed to evoke fear.

In *The History of Terrorism from Antiquity to ISIS*, Gerard Chaliand and others argue that terrorism can be divided into Top and Bottom approaches. 'Top-down' terrorism refers to the use of terror by states to establish and maintain dominance over their subjects, making state apparatus the primary source of terrorism in history.[11]

The Western tradition upholds the belief that the State possesses an exclusive monopoly on coercive methods, including the use of violence. An essential corollary to this principle is that anyone else resorting to violence commits a criminal act and will face prosecution. Considerable literature has been dedicated to critiquing this Western perspective, arguing that it inadequately addresses the concept of terrorism. According to this viewpoint, the conventional definition of terrorism fails to account for the terror inflicted by those who lack lawful avenues to alleviate oppression.[12]

Under British Raj, the tyranny of autocratic rule seemed justifiable due to the lack of legitimate recourse beyond 'constitutional' means. This was a key argument of revolutionaries fighting for Indian independence. Bal Gangadhar Tilak, Bipin Chandra Pal, and Lala Lajpat Rai coined the term 'Constitutional Mendicancy' to criticize the futility of the moderates' gradual approach. They rejected begging colonial rulers for political participation without self-determination, an inherent right of Indians.

In the context of national liberation movements in the 1950s and 1960s, terrorist activities were often romanticized, as they accelerated the fight for freedom from colonial powers. Those once labelled terrorists in places like Algeria, Indo-China, and India are now celebrated as heroes. This trend continues in separatist movements worldwide. Democratic societies have shifted to constitutional and legal means of addressing grievances, reducing violent protest, yet terrorism still appeals to those facing perceived persecution and ideological or religious oppression. In mature democracies, terrorism becomes a potent political strategy as media amplifies the grievances of marginalized groups, fostering the rise of terrorist organizations.

An illustrative example is the Khalistan movement in Canada. Canada appears to adopt a soft approach towards overt calls for the assassination of Indian diplomats by Khalistani activists. Despite numerous intelligence reports and information shared by Indian authorities providing evidence of Khalistani activities in Canada, Canadian authorities portray these activities as 'freedom of expression,' seemingly because the violent actions do not take place within Canada's borders. This lenient approach to Khalistani terrorism is likely to yield adverse consequences, as history has consistently demonstrated that terrorists ultimately destroy the tranquillity of any country that offers them refuge.[13]

Seen from the angle of a 'persecuted' community, political terrorism would appear to be a mode of warfare. Insurgencies, it has been argued are dictated by circumstances wherein they employ terrorism as one of the potent modes of political strategy besides other means. Terrorism seen in this way would be the easiest form of insurgency. Today the concept has generally metamorphosed into the employment of terrorist non-state actors by certain States which is called 'State-Sponsored' terrorism. This type of terrorism gained traction during the second part of the 20th century which saw its apogee during the 9/11 episode and War on Terror. This type of terrorism has many manifestations and is generally understood to be a significant cause of recrimination during the debates in the United Nations and sectoral conventions on the subject of international terrorism.

Western Perspectives on the History of Terrorism

As discussed above, the etymological evolution of terrorism reveals it as a relatively recent concept. This primarily arose due to a conceptual change in the structure of the state. Previously, the state was never a defined unit, and several armed factions led by their own leaders could claim constantly changing territories. Territorial limits were never defined on the ground; instead, a mix of landmarks, such as villages, forts, and rivers, kept changing hands between different warlords who could switch loyalties to different sovereigns depending on circumstances. This changed when nation-states largely became territorially fixed entities (at least in theory) after the Treaty of Westphalia in 1648.

Treaty of Westphalia and the New World Order

The Treaty of Westphalia, signed in 1648, marked a turning point in European and international relations, laying the foundations for the modern nation-state. It ended the Thirty Years' War and introduced the principle of state sovereignty, affirming that each state has authority over its territory and affairs without external interference. This principle also established territorial integrity, where states govern within their borders.

The treaty also recognized the legal equality of states, giving even the smallest nations the same standing as the largest. Non-interference was another crucial principle, preventing states from meddling in each other's internal affairs. Additionally, the treaty allowed religious tolerance by granting rulers the right to determine their state's religion, reducing religious conflicts.

While not directly related to nation-states, the treaty also contributed to modern diplomacy, encouraging permanent diplomatic missions. It marked the decline of the Catholic Church's political power, reinforcing secular governance and the state's authority. Over time, the treaty's principles solidified the state's role in governance, centralizing power and creating more stable political units.

Establishment of Permanent State: Emergence of the Idea of Non-state Actors

The principles of state sovereignty and legal equality laid the foundation for international law, leading to organized treaties, conventions, and diplomatic norms. Sovereignty also fuelled nationalism, as states became more defined and autonomous, forming nation-states where political and cultural boundaries aligned.

As strong, centralized states emerged, violence by non-state actors for political purposes increasingly became labelled as terrorism. This development highlighted the tension between state sovereignty and the actions of groups outside traditional state power, with terrorism serving as a tool for non-state actors to challenge authority and disrupt the status quo.

Religion and Terrorism: A Dangerous Cocktail

Karen Armstrong in her magisterial work titled, '*Fields of Blood: Religion and the History of Violence*,' vociferously argues the Western misconception of the notion of religion and the role of religion in wars. She succinctly explains the apparent irony ingrained in the Western thought which takes the idea for granted that religion is inherently violent: that there is a recurring narrative that religion has been cruel and aggressive, a view repeatedly expressed in strikingly similar terms whenever religion is cited as the cause of major historical wars. While experts in political violence and terrorism acknowledge that atrocities arise from a complex array of factors, the perception of religious faith as inherently violent remains deeply ingrained in secular consciousness. As a result, the violent conflicts of the twentieth century are often simplistically attributed to religion, marginalizing it within political discourse.

The Western view on the history and causes of terrorism has evolved through historical events, ideological shifts, and geopolitical dynamics, shaped by religious and sectarian differences. From its origins in the French Revolution to contemporary struggles against jihadist extremism, Western nations have developed their own understanding of terrorism, often validating terrorist themes in other cultures that differ significantly from their own.

Recognizing the interplay of ideological, socioeconomic, and political factors, Western countries have developed counter-terrorism strategies to address both the symptoms and real causes of terrorism.

Critics argue that Western powers imposing their tactics on other cultures raises ethical, legal, and practical concerns. They claim that such actions violate sovereignty, cause civilian casualties, erode human rights, and fuel radicalization, highlighting the challenges of Western foreign policy in counterterrorism and military interventions. As the global landscape evolves, understanding Western perspectives on terrorism remains key to crafting effective policies and fostering international cooperation.[14]

Western tradition has a distinctive understanding of violence that is quite unique to it. It considers violence legitimate only when it is practiced by the State and hence all violence that is not sanctioned by the State is *ipso facto* illegitimate if not outright criminal. Some would argue that the legitimacy of terrorist acts lies in the objectives of its agents.

In numerous interviews given by terrorist leaders, they try to justify their means by justifying the end that it would produce. Seen in this light, terrorist actions in support of certain national liberation movements such as those in the 1950s and 1960s were often regarded positively as they were primarily against the occupiers and not against the civilian populations. This was due to the fact that they were hailed as hastening the liberation of 'oppressed communities.' It is also a fact that those agents of terrorism- be it Algeria, or Indochina-are now heroes.

In his book, '*A History of Terrorism*,' Walter Laqueur succinctly argues how having written about terrorism for over twenty years, it became increasingly difficult to avoid the conclusion that, by and large, terrorism was largely futile—its loud spectacle often inversely related to its actual political impact. It was, of course, understood that terrorism has always been heavily tied to public relations and propaganda—*"Propaganda by Deed"* was the nineteenth-century slogan. Yet even two decades ago, it was evident that technological advances would soon place unprecedented destructive power into the hands of small groups.

This notion had long been explored by science fiction writers, whose imaginative scenarios often eventually materialized, albeit sometimes later than expected. This foresight applies not only to weapons of mass destruction—nuclear, biological, and chemical—but also to society's growing vulnerability to cyber-terrorism. The concern extends beyond casualties and physical damage to include profound psychological effects, such as widespread panic, triggered by the use or even mere threat of these new forms of terror.

In the same book, Walter Laqueur again raises a significant issue, by arguing that ideas of enlightenment and its appeal of nationalism were significant determinants of intolerance of oppressive regimes and autocratic governance. The employment of coercive action to suppress dissent and organized opposition that was an acceptable domain of the State became increasingly unacceptable. This was a sufficiently important cause of the emergence of several organizations during the late part of the nineteenth century that employed terrorist methods to reach their goals of self-determination and other political objectives.

Terrorism Now: 21st Century

In the early 21st century, terrorism evolved into a global security challenge, marked by major events and shifts in tactics. The 21st century saw the use of technology to inflict serious harm. The period began with the September 11, 2001 attacks, orchestrated by the Islamist extremist group al-Qaeda. These coordinated attacks on the World Trade Centre in New York and the Pentagon in Washington, D.C., caused nearly 3,000 deaths and reshaped global perceptions of terrorism. The attacks triggered the U.S.-led War on Terror, aiming to dismantle al-Qaeda and its supporters, leading to military interventions in Afghanistan and later Iraq.

In response to increased security and military actions, terrorist groups adapted their strategies. Al-Qaeda decentralized its operations, leading to the rise of affiliated groups like al-Qaeda in the Arabian Peninsula (AQAP) and al-Qaeda in Iraq (AQI). These groups focused on local insurgencies, using suicide bombings and kidnappings to destabilize governments.

The period also saw the rise of new terrorist organizations. In Iraq, opposition to U.S. occupation fuelled the insurgency, with groups like the Islamic State of Iraq (ISI) emerging from AQI. This eventually evolved into the Islamic State of Iraq and Syria (ISIS), later known as the Islamic State (IS).

By the end of the decade, terrorist activities spread beyond the Middle East, with attacks in Europe, Asia, and Africa by both Islamist and nationalist extremist groups. These events highlighted the decentralized and diverse nature of modern terrorism, driven by ideological, political, and religious motives.

Emergence of the Tech-savvy Terrorist

Of late, the understanding that terrorism might metamorphose into newer methods and tactics is dawning upon the experts on the subject. Terrorists are notorious for using advanced technologies and their ability to surprise by improvisation is what gives an edge to their methodologies.

A new challenge has come in the shape of Artificial Intelligence (AI) which has arrived on the scene after a significant period of technological pessimism. Regardless of intense optimism during the 80s and the early 2000s, AI remained an elusive dream and passing the Turing Test[15] remained a tough nut to crack for any apparently 'intelligent' machine.

Even supposedly 'intelligent' computer systems like 'Deep Blue' and 'Deep Thought' remained nothing more than curiosities for a long time. In many ways, the history of the emergence of Artificial Intelligence has many similarities with the quest for flying. Flying for a long time remained a dream, of consistent failure and experimentation and eventual realization by the Wright brothers. For a long time even experts in the field of engineering sneered at the possibility of human flight and declared any attempt to be futile. It is another matter that an aeroplane was engineered by Wright brothers whose only experience with engineering was bi-cycle repair and printing business.

The horrors that AI can bring about became eerily evident in 2020, 'Collaboration Pharmaceuticals' a company which specializes in looking for new drug candidates for rare and communicable diseases experimentally tested an AI-based MegaSyn software to work generating a compendium of toxic molecules that were similar to VX, a notorious nerve agent when it came up with more than 40,000 new chemical combinations hitherto undiscovered! The only thing that was required was a bit of programming, open-source data, a 2015 Mac computer, and less than six hours of machine time.[16]

In their study, the scoring method used by the company revealed that many of the novel molecules MegaSyn generated were predicted to be more toxic than VX. Despite several objections to the research methodologies pointed out by peer review groups one thing remains certain, the fact that AI can rapidly generate a vast quantity of potentially hazardous substances and can phenomenally speed up the process of creating lethal bio-weapons. The dark side of AI technologies and their potential misuse by terrorist groups would be the subject of a subsequent chapter on 'Cyber-terrorism and Emerging Technologies'. For now, we may remind ourselves that we are living in a very important epoch of human history where technology seems to have unleashed an insidious egalitarianism for the development and acquisition of weapons of mass destruction.

The dark side of AI has attracted significant attention recently, fuelled by apocalyptic portrayals in movies like the *Terminator* series and numerous books. These often depict a bleak future where AI dominates humanity. Despite such fictional narratives, the core challenge remains real: in the wrong hands, AI has immense potential as a weapon. For terrorists, any technology that is affordable, can be developed covertly, and deployed discreetly offers a major advantage—and AI promises exactly that.

Drones can now be programmed with lethal precision. Recent incidents alongside of India-Pakistan border have shown that cheaply made drones can be easily used for the delivery of weapons, and narcotics across borders. Such drones can easily be programmed and modified to attack a target across borders or can be easily manufactured inland by a sleeper cell for use against targets. Self-driving vehicles can be weaponised or significant quantities of explosives can be laden on such vehicles for the manufacturer of Autonomous Vehicles Based-Improvised Explosive Devices (AVB-IED).

In several ways, it can be argued that AI has the potential to become the future of terrorism. The evolution of AI technologies will be surely used by terrorists as every emerging technology has already been used by them with devastating effect. Kamikaze attacks were re-invented during 9/11 when no one could even predict such an eventuality. Surprise and shock are quintessential characteristics of terrorism.

The history of terrorism demonstrates that terrorists continually find ways to challenge the might of the state. Although the state legitimately claims the use of violence for its preservation, it does not hold an exclusive monopoly on this force. Non-state actors, unable to directly confront the organized power of the state, nevertheless find various methods to undermine its effectiveness and disrupt its policies. These actors use terrorism as a means to keep the state on edge and enable disproportionately small entities to confront even the most powerful governments through acts of raw power, such as large explosions. From the Sicarii of ancient times to contemporary terrorists, their primary motive has always been to destabilize the state and assert their presence through dramatic and violent actions.

2

The Problem of Defining Terrorism: A Complex Web of Politics, Law, and Ethics

"*To stand against terrorism is to stand with its victims everywhere.*"

—Gadha Fathi Waly

The legal definition of terrorism has long been a subject of global debate. Legal practitioners worldwide struggle to craft a comprehensive, universally accepted definition, largely due to the influence of cultural, socio-economic, and political contexts on national legal systems. This complexity helps explain why the phrase "one person's terrorist is another person's freedom fighter" remains relevant. Political considerations—both immediate and long-term, significantly shape how terrorism is understood and classified.

Regardless of differing definitions, terrorism clearly threatens global peace and stability. It is not only a violent act but also a powerful political weapon. History shows how attacks by non-state actors have sparked international crises. One such example is the assassination of Archduke Franz Ferdinand by Gavrilo Princip on June 28, 1914, which triggered World War I. Though deeper tensions existed, this single act ignited a chain of events that drew Europe's powers into war. The early 20th century also saw a rise in international terrorism from communist and anarchist groups.

Terrorism, in all its forms, remains a major threat to global security. Yet, despite its seriousness, international law still lacks a unified definition, complicating collective efforts to combat it.

Defining Terrorism: An Elusive Quest

The international community continues to grapple with a major challenge: the absence of a universally accepted definition of terrorism. While the threat of terrorism has endured for decades, efforts to define it began early. After the assassinations of King Alexander I of Yugoslavia and the French Foreign Minister in 1934, the League of Nations initiated a pioneering effort. The resulting 1937 Convention on the Prevention and Punishment of Terrorism broadly defined terrorism as:

> "*All criminal acts directed against a state and intended and calculated to create a state of terror in the minds of particular persons or a group of persons or the general public.*"[1]

This early definition focused on non-state actors, reflecting the political realities of the time. However, the Convention saw limited support, with only a few signatories and a single ratification by India—likely due to concerns over its broad scope.

The United Nations later adopted a more targeted strategy. Instead of a single definition, it developed conventions addressing specific terrorist acts, such as hijackings, hostage-taking, and terrorist financing. These instruments created strong legal frameworks but deliberately avoided defining terrorism in general terms.

This definitional gap continues to pose challenges. Without consensus, nations interpret and respond to terrorism differently, leading to inconsistent policies and enforcement. Although there is broad agreement on the urgency of addressing terrorism, the lack of clarity undermines coordinated global action and increases the risk of misinterpretation.

Defining terrorism remains difficult due to many factors. Cultural, political, and historical differences have led to varied understanding of the term. The term is also highly politicized—states often label opposing groups as terrorists to delegitimize them, while others view those same groups as freedom fighters. Furthermore, terrorism's evolving tactics and goals have made it even harder to craft a definition acceptable to all.

Let us now explore the main reasons behind these divergences and the obstacles to achieving consensus.

Subjectivity and Perspective

"One person's freedom fighter may be another person's terrorist." This adage has often been used by states to justify the actions of favoured non-state actors and avoid labelling them as "terrorists." China, for example, has repeatedly exercised its UN Security Council veto to block India's efforts to designate individuals from Pakistan as terrorists. Similarly, many Arab nations view Hamas and other Palestinian groups as freedom fighters, opposing their designation as terrorists by Western countries, despite acts of sabotage and violence.

Such polarization understandably stems from apparent political motivations. Yet, history shows that views on terrorism are also shaped by cultural, political, and historical contexts. Nelson Mandela, once branded a terrorist for his role in the African National Congress's anti-apartheid movement, is now celebrated as a global icon. His journey illustrates how the meaning of "terrorism" can shift with societal values and political change.

Likewise, Yasser Arafat, long considered a terrorist due to his leadership of the Palestine Liberation Organization (PLO), was once targeted by Israeli and Western agencies. Yet, he is now honoured by many as a prominent Arab leader and was jointly awarded the Nobel Peace Prize in 1994 with Shimon Peres. This transformation highlights the subjective and often controversial nature of the term. What one party calls terrorism, another may see as legitimate resistance or self-defence, fuelling disputes over how incidents are classified.

The label "terrorist" carries serious legal and political weight, potentially leading to sanctions, prosecution, or military action. As a result, both state and non-state actors use language strategically, branding their opponents as terrorists while defending their allies. In this contested space, defining terrorism involves not just legal and academic debate but also political, moral, and strategic considerations.

Subjectivity and perspective remain key barriers to a globally accepted definition of terrorism. Achieving consensus demands careful navigation of contemporary conflicts, grounded in justice, human rights, and international law.

Political Motivation Fuelling Subjectivity

Some non-state actors carry out terrorist acts beyond their countries of residence. Often, they establish fronts such as charities, religious, or cultural organizations to conceal illicit activities aimed at other nations. These groups build ties with expatriate communities, exploiting grievances to further their political agendas. Local politicians may mistakenly view them as community leaders, overlooking concerns raised by affected states and Diaspora voices. This pattern is evident in the rise of Khalistan-linked terror networks in Canada.

These organizations harness Diaspora sympathy to fund raise, recruit, and coordinate, creating challenges for local law enforcement and global security. Their operations include spreading propaganda, raising funds through legitimate channels, and conducting covert activities that threaten regional and international stability.

The Khalistan movement's radical factions illustrate how extremist ideologies can thrive abroad, exploiting democratic freedoms to incite violence in their homelands. Such cases of transnational terrorism highlight the difficulties of addressing threats that cross borders and legal systems.

The absence of a universally accepted definition of terrorism reflects its complex legal and political nature. Far from being merely a legal term, it is frequently politicized to advance national interests. This flexibility obstructs the creation of consistent counter terrorism norms.

Definitional ambiguity is shaped by broader geopolitical dynamics, where states brand certain groups as terrorists to discredit them or justify intervention. This subjectivity causes inconsistencies in global responses and legal standards, complicating prosecution efforts and hindering international cooperation.

A telling example is the reclassification of Osama bin Laden, who was once hailed as CIA-supported mujahideen resisting Soviet forces, now requiring no introduction as the all-time number one terrorist.

The United Nations currently tends to view the Palestinian cause through the lens of resistance to occupation, whereas Israel characterizes such actions as acts of terrorism. This divergence in political framing, in the absence of universally accepted legal standards, contributes to inconsistencies in global counter terrorism efforts, thereby diminishing their coherence, objectivity, and overall effectiveness.

Cultural and Contextual Differences

Terrorist organizations often exploit cultural and contextual differences to justify their actions and advance harmful agendas. They often present acts of terror as self-defence or responses to perceived state injustice, down-playing their own violence while exaggerating the actions of security forces. What is considered terrorism in one context may be framed as resistance in another, reflecting the term's subjectivity.

These groups use sophisticated strategies, particularly social media, to manipulate narratives and win sympathy. They depict themselves as defenders of marginalized communities or as freedom fighters. For example, the Communist Party of India (Maoist) claims to represent impoverished tribal populations, casting state responses as human rights abuses, thus portraying law enforcement as oppressive.

This narrative manipulation blurs the line between terrorism and political dissent, complicating efforts to uphold the rule of law. By exploiting grievances and historical injustices, terrorist groups justify violence and seek legitimacy. Social media amplifies their messages, enabling recruitment, fundraising, and international attention. Their online prominence is often mistaken for public support.

Through these platforms, terrorist groups shape public opinion and frame conflict in ways that serve their aims. Countering such propaganda requires strategies that operate both online and offline, promote alternative voices, and support vulnerable communities.

This evolving digital landscape complicates global counter terrorism efforts and the development of shared legal frameworks. By presenting lawful state actions as illegitimate, terrorist groups undermine government authority and deepen social divisions.

Effectively addressing the contemporary terrorism landscape necessitates a comprehensive approach that extends beyond coercive measures such as military action. It is equally important to counter extremist narratives, address underlying contextual drivers—including the easy availability of weapons and financing, as well as perceived political injustices—and foster community resilience to prevent radicalisation. Saying that terrorism is just a result of 'socio-economic' injustice oversimplifies the issue—and can be more harmful than helpful, as it overlooks the deeper ideological, political, and strategic factors at play.

International cooperation is vital to disrupt funding and combat radicalization online. Attempts to define terrorism universally face challenges due to geopolitical interests and cultural differences. Historical experience, ideology, and societal values shape each nation's view of violence. While one state sees terrorism, another may see a just cause.

States also use the label strategically to discredit opponents or justify force, politicizing the concept and hindering consensus. This not only obstructs clear legal frameworks but also weakens global efforts to tackle extremism at its roots.

Political Manipulation: How Certain States Use Terrorism as an Instrument of Policy

Political dishonesty sees certain states backing non-state actors to foment conflict with neighbours, advancing their strategic agendas. This tactic undermines the targeted state's military capability by embroiling it in prolonged low-intensity and proxy wars. Over time, such conflicts erode public trust in institutions and weaken leadership credibility.

Nations such as Pakistan, Syria, Iran, and China have allegedly supported non-state actors via covert programmes run by intelligence agencies. These actions, constituting forms of low-intensity conflict, represent a disturbing use of terrorism as a tool of state policy. Such practices threaten global stability and undermine human rights, diplomacy, and international cooperation.

Some states institutionalize terrorism as a long-term strategic instrument. However, these policies often backfire. For example, Pakistan's support for terrorist groups has severely damaged its international reputation, isolating it diplomatically and hindering efforts to gain economic aid from global financial bodies.[2]

Even more troubling is the state use of terrorism. When governments support such groups, the impact on civilians is devastating and can destabilize entire regions. These actions may fuel conflicts, trigger refugee flows, and strain international relations. Moreover, state sponsorship blurs distinctions between official and non-state violence, complicating global counter terrorism efforts.[3]

Complexities of Modern Conflict

The complexity of modern conflict has greatly contributed to the difficulty of defining terrorism. Contemporary conflicts are no longer confined to traditional battlefields between states but have evolved into ever-present, asymmetric struggles involving non-state actors, global networks, and a wide range of tactics. This complexity often challenges our ability to arrive at a universally accepted definition of terrorism. Unlike the era of the Hiroshima atomic bomb, states today seldom engage in direct traditional forms of warfare. Instead, terrorism has provided certain states with a means to support groups within enemy territory, offering them sustenance in the form of money, political backing, and other assistance.

When analysing the complexity of modern conflicts, it becomes increasingly evident that the lines between terrorism and other forms of violence are blurring. For certain states like Pakistan, terrorism has become both a home-grown industry and a low-cost method of waging proxy warfare against India. Many foreign policy experts make it plain that Pakistan has fostered radicalized armed groups to harass Indian military forces, destabilize its political leadership, and keep the Kashmir issue on the international agenda.[4]

Oppositional Violence: A Complex Issue of Definition

One key factor contributing to this complexity is the blurred distinction between terrorism and other forms of oppositional violence. In many modern conflicts, armed groups employ a mix of guerrilla warfare, insurgency tactics, and sporadic acts of terrorism. Distinguishing between acts of terrorism and acts of insurgency can be challenging, as both often involve attacks on civilian targets. This ambiguity can lead to political manipulation and varying interpretations of events, complicating efforts to reach a consensus on what constitutes terrorism. Terming every act of oppositional violence such as large-scale riots against an oppressive regime is a complex issue in defining acts of terrorism.

Moreover, the use of state-sponsored terrorism further muddies the waters, as it involves the deliberate support and utilization of non-state actors by governments to achieve strategic objectives. Such actions not only cause immense suffering to innocent civilians but also destabilize entire regions, leading to conflicts, refugee crises, and strained international relations. State-sponsored terrorism undermines global counter-terrorism efforts by blurring the lines between state and non-state actors, making it difficult to address its causes effectively.

Globalization of Conflicts and its Effect on Defining Terrorism

The globalization of conflict has intensified the difficulty of defining terrorism. As extremist groups operate across borders, their actions evade clear categorization under national legal frameworks. Transnational networks, shaped by global ideologies, economic inequalities, and regional tensions, make a universal definition of terrorism elusive.

Organizations such as al-Qaeda, Hezbollah, Hamas, and ISIS operate across continents, requiring unprecedented international cooperation in intelligence, law enforcement, and counter-terrorism. However, divergent political and legal systems hinder a unified global response. Some Middle Eastern countries portray groups like Hamas and Hezbollah as defenders against Western aggression, complicating their global designation as terrorist entities.

Radical ideologies, often rooted in historical narratives, transcend borders and fuel terrorism. These ideologies are exploited to radicalize youth, with some national elites supporting such groups for political reasons. Countries including Pakistan, Iran, and Saudi Arabia have faced criticism for harbouring such sympathies. Many in these regions view Western definitions of terrorism as ideologically biased, resisting a shared global understanding.

Extremist propaganda spreads via social media, enabling global radicalization. Groups like ISIS have incited attacks far beyond the Middle East. In Pakistan, elites often justify terrorism by citing the Kashmir dispute, transforming a political issue into a supposed moral cause, despite weak logical foundations.

Economic inequality and global disruptions further aid terrorist recruitment. Promises of justice and prosperity appeal to marginalized populations. Meanwhile, international financial networks help sustain terrorist operations, adding complexity to defining and tackling terrorism.

Regional conflicts and historical grievances also shape terrorist narratives. The Israel–Palestine conflict, for example, fuels international support for actors on both sides, blurring the line between terrorism and resistance.

Ethical Conundrum

Defining terrorism also involves significant ethical considerations. Balancing the need to protect human rights and civil liberties with the imperative of countering terrorism can be a delicate and contentious task, even for those with an advanced understanding of the law. One of the primary ethical challenges is the inherent subjectivity of the term "terrorism." This is fundamentally an epistemological challenge rather than a purely legalistic issue.

How does one define an act of terror? What should we think if state forces, acting with impunity, attack innocent civilians who have done nothing other than reside in an area of conflict? How would you classify Holocaust by Nazi Germany? How would your perspective shift if someone in your own family were a victim of terrorism? These questions highlight the complexity of defining terrorism in terminologies that can be legally fastened universally.

The subjectivity of terrorism is evident in the varying perspectives on violent acts. For some, an attack might be seen as a legitimate act of resistance against oppression, while others view it as an unjustifiable act of terror. This disparity in perception underscores the difficulty in formulating a universally accepted definition.

Moreover, whenever state forces engage in counter-terrorism measures such as operations against insurgents and terrorists, the issue becomes further complicated. Every action of state forces is scrutinized, whereas the actions of militants are often ignored, even when they involve extreme violations of the human rights of security personnel. Opprobrium against violence is often restricted to state forces, despite their actions generally being intended to uphold the rule of law. The line between state-sanctioned violence and terrorism can appear to blur, leading to debates on the legitimacy and morality of such actions. These situations demand a nuanced understanding of context, intent, and impact.

Personal experiences with terrorism also influence individual standpoints. Victims of terrorism and their families may have a more visceral and immediate understanding of its impact, potentially leading to a more stringent definition. Conversely, those who have not been directly affected might approach the issue from a more detached, analytical perspective.

An Analogy of Cancer: Problem of Defining Terrorism

Problems and issues in defining terrorism can also be illustrated by an analogy with cancer. Terminologically, it is difficult to characterize cancer as a single disease. However, there is a central characteristic: the 'uncontrolled' multiplication of certain cells that do not adhere to the genetic kill-switch that every normal cell contains. These are cells that have gone rogue and divide without any restrictions. They are not detected by our immune system because they do not cause any adverse effects until they have reached a critical state (variously called Stage III and IV).

Like terrorism, cancer has a central characteristic: some kind of violence or threat of violence that has a tendency, perceived or otherwise, to cause unacceptable harm. Like cancer, terrorism is a malignancy that does not restrict itself to the target but spreads its tentacles into the otherwise healthy political climate of its host country. In its early stages, terrorism remains benign as non-state actors apply an ersatz patina of legitimacy by projecting their sinister organizations with a philanthropic, cultural, or otherwise altruistic façade. Like cancer, terrorism often begins as an imperceptible, benign-seeming growth. It infiltrates the socio-political landscape under the guise of legitimate socio-cultural activities, cloaking itself in the mantle of humanitarian or charitable causes.

Like cancer, the host realizes too late that the terror it cultivated for its enemy has become the enemy. Terrorism is extremely hard to detect in its early stages, and its symptoms are generally misinterpreted as political, cultural, and socio-economic disaffection. Each type of terrorism has its own architectural makeup that is unique to itself.

Conversely, many medical professionals view cancer as internal terrorism that wreaks havoc on the body and is an indiscriminate killer. Epithets like, '*Cancer is a bloodthirsty killer deep inside you, presiding over a vast terror network, and secretly plotting schemes of mass murder with a mushrooming army of malignant cells,*' illustrate this comparison. Replace the image of the terrorist with that of a devastating disease, and you will get a picture of how cancers operate and why they are so difficult to beat.

Several oncologists have equated the challenges of cancer pathology with the War on Terror, highlighting similar themes of malignancy, plasticity, creeping progression, relapse, and sleeper cells. These subjects of equivalence then superimpose a strong remedy of bombarding the malignancy. Radical treatment of malignant tissues in cancer is equated to the swift and radical eradication of terrorist groups and their leaders. On the whole, terror and terrorists are equated with cancer as a terminal condition that requires early detection and effective and radical interventions.[5]

Accordingly, the 'war on terror' often used such a medical analogy, comparing terrorists to cancer cells and counter-terrorism to treatment. This can be helpful in emphasizing the need for a multi-pronged approach, including dismantling networks (surgery), addressing grievances (immunotherapy), and promoting peace (prevention). While the analogy between terrorism and cancer is often used to convey the insidious and pervasive nature of the threat, it ultimately breaks down when defining the phenomenon. Cancer is a biological process, while terrorism is a political act driven by human motivations, ideologies, and social conditions. Unlike cancer cells, terrorist groups can rapidly evolve their ideologies, splinter into smaller factions, and adapt to changing circumstances.

Furthermore, unlike diseased cells, terrorists often justify their actions, however warped those justifications may be. This makes it difficult to apply the same kind of objective and impersonal approach to combating terrorism as one would to treating a biological disease. Understanding the motivations and ideologies of terrorist groups is crucial for developing effective counter-measures, but it also requires a more nuanced and complex analysis than simply eradicating a disease-causing agent.

The analogy—comparing the elimination of terrorists to the removal of cancer cells—focuses narrowly on eradication, risking the neglect of deeper causes of terrorism. While socio-economic factors may play a peripheral role, core drivers often include the easy availability of weapons, external sponsorship, and intensified perceptions of political oppression. A more fitting analogy might be that of a chronic illness—one that demands not only immediate intervention but also sustained treatment and preventive measures to address underlying conditions. Unfortunately, definitions of terrorism are often influenced by irrational and politically motivated considerations, which tend to obscure the issues rather than clarify them.

Customary Terrorism Law in Focus: The Lebanon Tribunal's Legacy

There's broad agreement among experts that September 11, 2001, marked a watershed moment. Like Pearl Harbour, it propelled the USA to lead a global response against terrorism. Previously viewed primarily as a regional issue (except aviation hijackings), terrorism was now seen as a global threat demanding a forceful response. The ensuing 'War on Terror' had a significant worldwide impact, with both supporters and critics.

This period also witnessed the potential emergence of a universally recognized definition of terrorism. The controversial 2011 judgment by the Special Tribunal for Lebanon suggested the existence of a 'transnational terrorism' definition within customary international law, a legal system based on long-standing practices accepted by states.

Background

The Special Tribunal for Lebanon was established at Lebanon's request following the terrorist attack of 14 February 2005 in central Beirut, which killed 22 people, including former Prime Minister Rafik Hariri, and injured many others. Created under UN Security Council Resolution 1757, the Tribunal later convicted, in absentia, Ayyash, Merhi, and Oneissi, sentencing them to five concurrent life terms in the STL-11-01 case—the severest punishment under its Statute and Regulations—highlighting the grave impact of their crimes on Lebanon and its people.

Significantly, the Tribunal asserted that a definition of 'transnational terrorism' exists under customary international law, based on consistent state practice and *opinio juris*—a shared belief that certain actions are legally obligatory. In an interlocutory decision, the Tribunal conducted an extensive analysis of treaties, UN resolutions, and legal precedents, concluding that terrorism is prohibited under customary law, at least during peacetime. It defined terrorism by three core elements:

1. A criminal act (e.g., murder, arson, kidnapping) or threat thereof;
2. Intent to spread fear or coerce a national/international authority;
3. A transnational dimension to the act.[6]

The Tribunal relied primarily on UN policies and legal norms, asserting that elements required for other international crimes—war crimes and crimes against humanity—also apply to terrorism. While the latter two are widely accepted in treaty law and jurisprudence, terrorism as a peacetime international crime under customary law remains unsettled. References to terrorism in UN instruments, such as General Assembly resolutions, should not be assumed to reflect a universally accepted legal definition.

For instance, the General Assembly's Declaration on measures to eliminate international terrorism (Resolution 49/60) includes a political motive, while the draft Comprehensive Convention does not. Meanwhile, Security Council Resolution 1566 (2004) reiterates sector-specific crimes without offering a comprehensive or unified definition.

The Tribunal's assertion of a customary legal norm for terrorism drew significant criticism. Many argued that the cited state practice and *opinio juris* were insufficient. Legal scholar Ben Saul noted that despite many treaties addressing terrorist methods none offer a comprehensive definition of terrorism or establish it as a general international crime. At most, certain specific offences—like hijacking or hostage-taking—may be customary law. But the lack of a general treaty-based crime of terrorism prevents a corresponding customary rule from forming.

Ben Saul further noted that regional counter-terrorism instruments cited by the Tribunal do not show consensus on a definition. Broadly, while a customary norm may be evolving, the Tribunal's declaration was viewed as premature and innovative.

The Perils of Ambiguity: Implications of Undefined Terrorism in International Law

The quest for a universally accepted definition of terrorism remains a vexing challenge in the international arena. This absence, however, does not negate the existence of a core understanding of the term. At its essence, terrorism denotes the calculated use of violence or intimidation by non-state actors to achieve political objectives by sowing fear within a populace. While the precise parameters may be subject to debate, this core meaning remains crucial in fostering international cooperation against this global menace.

Why Do We Need a Clear Definition?

This is so much obvious a question. A universally agreed-upon definition would be a potent weapon in the fight against terrorism. It would streamline the critical exchange of intelligence between nations, paving the way for a more unified global response. Imagine a world where all countries approach counter-terrorism with a shared lexicon and understanding, leading to a more coordinated and effective effort. However, the pursuit of a legal definition has not been without its pitfalls.

In their zealous efforts to counter terrorism, certain jurisdictions might enact legislation criminalizing acts that may not demonstrably constitute acts of terror. The risk of overly broad definitions is counter-productive, as it can potentially suppress legitimate dissent and hinder progress in the global fight against terrorism. Consequently, a precise and universally accepted definition of terrorism that safeguards fundamental freedoms is imperative. Unfortunately, counter-terrorism measures such as the presumption of guilt and the utilization of military tribunals for civilian trials often undermine human rights protections, compounding the challenges of achieving a balanced approach.[7]

The absence of a universally accepted definition of terrorism carries far-reaching implications in legal contexts that one can imagine. One consequence imaginable is that this absence can inadvertently open the door to the politicization and misapplication of the term 'terrorism' to curtail activities that do not constitute acts of terrorism (and sometimes are not even criminal). Consequently, this situation may lead to states infringing upon the rights of their citizens or citizens of other nations, including those safeguarded by international human rights laws, during their counter-terrorism endeavours. This concept of 'overkill' is akin to oncological studies concerning cancer treatment wherein chemotherapy and intense radiological treatment often wreak havoc on the otherwise healthy tissues while attacking the malignancy.[8]

Certainty in Criminal Laws is Essential

When domestic legislation is similarly ambiguous in scope and implications regarding criminalized conduct, it risks contravening the fundamental legal principle of *nullum crimen, nulla poena sine lege*. This principle unequivocally mandates that individuals cannot be subjected to criminal prosecution or punishment for acts that were not criminalized at the time of their commission. Essential to this principle is the requirement for clarity and certainty in the law, demanding that prohibited acts and corresponding penalties be explicitly defined prior to their alleged occurrence. Such unequivocal articulation of penal provisions is a prerequisite for the characterization of an act as terrorism.

A significant challenge in the global counter-terrorism effort arises from the incongruence between national, regional, and international legal frameworks. While Security Council Resolution 1373 (2001) mandated the enactment of effective national counter terrorism legislation, the absence of a universally agreed-upon definition of terrorism has resulted in a disparate patchwork of national laws. This divergence in legal approaches has hindered international cooperation, as a single act of terrorism can be interpreted and prosecuted differently across jurisdictions. Such inconsistencies undermine the efficacy of global counter-terrorism strategies and create opportunities for terrorist organizations to exploit legal loopholes.

Comprehensive Convention on International Terrorism and other Efforts on the UN Forum

Within the United Nations framework, the absence of a universally accepted definition of "terrorism" has resulted in the use of various terminologies in its documents. These terms are not usually intended to imply a universally agreed-upon definition. Instead, they serve as reference points to help states implement actions specified or required by particular documents and instruments. The pursuit of a universally accepted definition of terrorism is one of the goals discussed in the ongoing negotiations for the Comprehensive Convention on International Terrorism. To illustrate this, let us examine the issue here.

The first instance is General Assembly resolution 49/60, which seeks to criminalize several armed activities considered "terrorist" in nature:

> *"[A]cts intended or calculated to provoke a state of terror in the general public, a group of persons, or particular persons for political purposes are in any circumstance unjustifiable, whatever the considerations of a political, philosophical, ideological, racial, ethnic, religious or any other nature that may be invoked to justify them."* (Paragraph 3)].

A noteworthy aspect of this approach is its unanimous adoption by the General Assembly without the need for a vote, which lends it a high level of legitimacy as the outcome of a fully representative forum. However, since it is a product of the General Assembly, it is not legally binding. This is reinforced by the fact that a universally accepted definition of terrorism has yet to be agreed upon in the ongoing negotiations for the draft Comprehensive Convention.

While General Assembly resolution 49/60 recognizes the need for the gradual development and codification of anti-terrorism norms, any potential role in lawmaking remains uncertain. On the 17th of December 1996, during a session of the United Nations General Assembly (UNGA), India introduced the Comprehensive Convention on International Terrorism (CCIT).[9]

The CCIT was designed to *"criminalize all forms of international terrorism, prevent the provision of safe havens, and block access to funds and arms for terrorists and their financiers."* As of 2021, the CCIT remains in a state of 'stalemate' due to disagreements among UN member-states regarding the definition of terrorism. Since the terrorist attacks in Dhaka in 2016, India has been advocating for the adoption of the treaty. The lack of consensus on the convention has impeded global efforts to combat terrorism. It nevertheless attempted to define terrorism in its solemn declaration number 3 as:

> *"3. Criminal acts intended or calculated to provoke a state of terror in the general public, a group of persons or particular persons for political purposes are in any circumstance unjustifiable, whatever the considerations of a political, philosophical, ideological, racial, ethnic, religious or any other nature that may be invoked to justify them."*[10]

Another example of suggested terminology related to terrorism is United Nations Resolution 1566 (2004), which aimed to assist states in fulfilling their obligations under Security Council Resolution 1373 (2001), to enact domestic legislative measures. It defines terrorism by recalling that:

> "*...criminal acts, including against civilians, committed with intent to cause death or serious bodily injury, or taking of hostages, with the purpose to provoke a state of terror in the general public or a group of persons or particular persons, intimidate a population, or compel a government or an international organization to do or to abstain from doing any act, which constitute offences within the scope of and as defined in the international conventions and protocols relating to terrorism, are under no circumstances justifiable by considerations of a political, philosophical, ideological, racial, ethnic, religious, or other similar nature, and calls upon all States to prevent such acts and, if not prevented, to ensure that such acts are punished by penalties consistent with their grave nature.*" (Paragraph 3).[11]

Adopted by the United Nations Security Council under Chapter VII, this Resolution could be argued to be legally binding on all member-states. However, in practice, the idea of an obligation to accept and implement a specific definition of terrorism is likely to be strongly rejected by states. Nonetheless, United Nations Security Council Resolution 1566 has been pivotal in influencing and harmonizing terrorism definitions within national legislation. It has also addressed gaps in domestic criminal frameworks regarding these offences and contributes to the body of norms shaping the categorization and treatment of terrorism offences today.

Financing of Terror: A Semblance of Agreed Universal Definition

In a broader context, as discussed below, most universal anti-terrorism instruments avoid defining terrorism due to its political sensitivities. A notable exception is Article 2 of the 1999 International Convention for the Suppression of the Financing of Terrorism, which criminalizes the financing of terrorism as follows:

> "*Any person commits an offence within the meaning of this Convention if that person by any means, directly or indirectly, unlawfully and wilfully, provides or collects funds with the intention that they should be used or in the knowledge that they are to be used, in full or in part, to carry out:*
>
> *(a) An act which constitutes an offence within the scope of and as defined in one of the treaties listed in the annex; or*

> *(b) Any other act intended to cause death or serious bodily injury to a civilian, or to any other person not taking an active part in the hostilities in a situation of armed conflict, when the purpose of such act, by its nature or context, is to intimidate a population or to compel a government or an international organization to do or to abstain from doing any act."*

This text was reaffirmed by Security Council Resolution 1373 (2001), which called upon all States to:

> *"[b]ecome parties as soon as possible to the relevant international conventions and protocols relating to terrorism, including the International Convention for the Suppression of the Financing of Terrorism of 9 December 1999."* (Paragraph 3(d)).

Navigating the Gray Area: Approaches to Defining Terrorism

The complex and multifaceted nature of terrorism has presented a significant challenge in formulating a universally accepted definition. Several approaches have emerged in response to this difficulty.[12]

The *comprehensive approach* endeavours to create a single, all-encompassing definition by identifying core elements common to terrorist acts. While ambitious, this approach has been fraught with disagreements over these core elements. Alternatively, the crime-based approach focuses on specific criminal acts often associated with terrorism, such as bombings or kidnappings. This method offers a more practical approach but may overlook the broader context of terrorist motivations and goals.

The *purpose-based approach* emphasizes the underlying intent of terrorist acts, concentrating on the desire to instil fear or coerce a government. This approach provides a clearer focus on the psychological impact of terrorism but may exclude acts that, while violent, do not explicitly aim to achieve these objectives.

The *sectoral approach* to defining terrorism eschews a comprehensive, universal definition in favour of a more granular approach. By focusing on specific terrorist acts, such as hijacking, bombings, or hostage-taking, this method facilitates the development of targeted legal frameworks and international cooperation. This approach circumvents the complexities and political sensitivities inherent in crafting a general definition of terrorism, enabling states to effectively address concrete terrorist threats without becoming embroiled in protracted definitional debates.

On the other hand, the *hybrid approach* to defining terrorism represents a pragmatic response to the complexities inherent in establishing a universally accepted definition. Recognizing the limitations of singular definitional frameworks, this approach amalgamates elements from various methodologies to provide a more comprehensive and nuanced understanding of the phenomenon.

By blending elements from comprehensive, crime-based, and purpose-driven definitions, the hybrid approach seeks to reflect the complex and evolving nature of terrorism. It recognizes that terrorist acts are not one-dimensional; they take many forms and carry varying motives and consequences. Viewing terrorism through this hybrid lens enables states to better pinpoint its core features while staying responsive to the changing tactics of terrorist groups.

However, this flexibility comes with its own set of challenges. The overlap and variations in definitions across different jurisdictions can lead to inconsistencies that complicate international cooperation. Despite these hurdles, the hybrid approach remains a promising path for states striving to effectively counter terrorism while upholding fundamental rights and abiding by international law.

Regional and Multilateral Approaches to Adopt Definition

Several influential regional multilateral organizations have developed distinct counter-terrorism legal frameworks, each with a definition of terrorism tailored to regional priorities. These varying definitions, however, have led to significant challenges. Differences between regional organizations hinder international cooperation, while inconsistencies with national frameworks create complex legal dilemmas.

Resolving these conflicts often requires determining whether treaty law takes precedence over domestic legislation. In practice, domestic law often prevails due to constitutional imperatives, reinforcing the principle of legal sovereignty over shared norms.

The following sections will explore the key definitional approaches used by various regional organizations. It is important to note that none of these approaches offer a universally accepted or comprehensive definition of terrorism.

Armed National Liberation or Self-Determination Struggle Exemption

This approach distinctly demarcates between what is considered unlawful and criminal acts of terrorism and acts of violence perpetrated as part of what is regarded as a legitimate struggle against foreign occupation, aggression, or foreign dominion. The latter is accorded an exemption from criminal prosecution. For instance:

The Arab Convention for the Suppression of Terrorism (adopted 22 April 1998, entered into force 7 May 1999), Article 2(a), stipulates that acts of struggle, including armed struggle, against foreign occupation and aggression for liberation and self-determination, in accordance with international law principles, are not considered offences. This provision does not apply to acts that jeopardize the territorial integrity of any Arab State.

Similarly, the Organization of the Islamic Conference (OIC) Convention on Combating International Terrorism (adopted 1 July 1999), entered into force 7 November 2002), Article 2(a), follows a similar approach, as does the Organization of African Unity (OAU) Convention on the Prevention and Combating ofTerrorism (adopted 14 July 1999, entered into force 6 December 2003), Article 3(1).

Reference to Sectoral Conventions against Terrorism

The approach of most other regional conventions has been to cross-reference sectoral conventions against terrorism. These sectoral conventions do not proffer explicit definitions of terrorism but rather allude to the criminal elements characterizing specific offences. Regional conventions adopting this approach include:

- Council of Europe Convention on the Prevention of Terrorism (adopted on 16 May 2005, entered into force 1 June 2007), Article 1(1).
- Inter-American Convention against Terrorism (adopted 3 June 2002, entered into effect 6 July 2003), Article 2(1).
- South Asia Association for Regional Cooperation Regional Convention on Suppression of Terrorism (adopted on 4 November 1987), Article 1.)
- Association of Southeast Asian Nations Convention on Counter-Terrorism (adopted on 13 January 2007, entered into force 27 May 2011), Article II.)

Hybrid Approach

The Shanghai Convention on Combating Terrorism, Separatism, and Extremism (adopted 15 June 2001, entered into effect 29 March 2003) embraces a hybrid approach. Article 1(a) refers to existing anti-sectoral treaties. Nevertheless, Article 1(b) furnishes a definition reflective of regional priorities, delineating:

> "*[A]ny other act intended to cause death or serious bodily injury to a civilian, or any other person not taking an active part in the hostilities in a situation of armed conflict or to cause major damage to any material facility, as well as to organize, plan, aid and abet such act, when the purpose of such act, by its nature or context, is to intimidate the population, violate public security or compel public authorities or an international organization to do or to abstain from doing any act, and prosecuted in accordance with the national laws of the Parties.*"

Adoption of Regional Definition Reflecting International Norms

This approach is exemplified by the European Union, which has defined terrorism. According to Article 1 of the European Convention on the Suppression of Terrorism:

> "*For the purposes of extradition between Contracting States, none of the following offences shall be regarded as a political offence or as an offence connected with a political offence or as an offence inspired by political motives:*
>
> *(a) an offence within the scope of the Convention for the Suppression of Unlawful Seizure of Aircraft, signed at The Hague on 16 December 1970;*
>
> *(b) an offence within the scope of the Convention for the Suppression of Unlawful Acts against the Safety of Civil Aviation, signed at Montreal on 23 September 1971;*
>
> *(c) a serious offence involving an attack against the life, physical integrity or liberty of internationally protected persons, including diplomatic agents;*
>
> *(d) an offence involving kidnapping, the taking of a hostage or serious unlawful detention;*
>
> *(e) an offence involving the use of a bomb, grenade, rocket, automatic firearm or letter or parcel bomb if this use endangers persons;*
>
> *(f) an attempt to commit any of the foregoing offences or participation as an accomplice of a person who commits or attempts to commit such an offence.*".

The definition of the offences listed at Article 1(c) to (e) emphasizes the danger represented by the use of certain means for committing a crime and it does not take into account the specific intention required for a terrorist offence. Hence, it does not represent a proper definition of terrorist acts.

As previously mentioned, numerous instances exist wherein the term terrorism has been defined at the national level in the absence of an agreement concerning a universal definition.

Terrorism: Is It What We Say It Is? Perils of a Commonsense Approach

The main obstacles to a universally accepted definition of terrorism do not appear to stem from disagreement on the need to criminalize such acts, but rather from the complex ideological and technical considerations surrounding its precise definition. As a result, the development of a cohesive global counter-terrorism strategy has been significantly impeded.

The lack of consensus on what constitutes terrorism complicates efforts to create unified legal frameworks and policies. While nations agree that terrorism is a serious threat warranting international action, differing views on the specifics of what qualifies as terrorism hinder the establishment of a universal definition. These differences often reflect deeper ideological divides and regional priorities, making compromise challenging.

The issue is further complicated by some commentators, especially within the human rights community, who invoke the phrase, 'I know it when I see it.' Originally used in defining obscenity, this phrase highlights the subjective nature of identifying terrorism. While it reflects the intuitive understanding many have of terrorism, it fails to provide a clear, legally-actionable definition necessary for legal and policy frameworks.

Regional multilateral organizations add to the complexity by developing counter-terrorism frameworks tailored to their priorities, resulting in varying definitions that can cause inter-regional discrepancies. These discrepancies present significant challenges to international cooperation, as actions considered terrorism in one region may not be recognized as such in another.

The phrase 'I know it when I see it,' first used by U.S. Supreme Court Justice Potter Stewart in 1964, referred to a threshold test for obscenity in the case of *Jacobellis vs. Ohio*. While it offers a subjective understanding, the international community has yet to establish a commonsense approach for a universally accepted definition of terrorism.

The Case against a Universal Definition of Terrorism

The need for a universal definition of terrorism is clear when considering the transnational nature of terrorist activities. Groups like al-Qaeda, Jaish-e-Muhammad, Hamas, ISIS, and FARC operate globally, targeting victims regardless of nationality or location, thus requiring a unified international response.

A universal definition is crucial for coordinating a global response to these transnational threats. Effective action against terrorist groups, even within friendly nations, depends on a shared understanding of what constitutes terrorism. The U.S. response to terrorist threats from Pakistan highlights the challenges of lacking a universal legal framework.

State practice in addressing terrorism has evolved in response to transnational non-state actors, unilateral military actions, and efforts by the United Nations and regional organizations. This evolution has highlighted key principles that terrorism undermines:

1. Basic human rights
2. National governance systems
3. International peace and stability
4. Unilateral and excessive counter-terrorism measures by powerful states

Countries such as India, Israel, the U.S.A., and EU members have consistently urged the international community to present a united front against terrorism. The push for a universally accepted definition stems from this effort. Nations generally agree that terrorism is a crime against humanity, not a specific nation, and that terrorist acts threaten global peace. However, there remains disagreement on whether terrorism should be defined exclusively as an international crime.

Shared Characteristics of Terror Offences

The justification for criminalizing certain acts at the international level stems from shared characteristics of transnational offences and the broader goals of international criminal policy. Defining these crimes is vital for international criminal law, distinct from other legal domains such as humanitarian law, human rights law, and refugee law. It is crucial to note that national governments misusing this terminology to suppress political dissent can severely undermine fundamental human rights.

An international crime refers to conduct deemed criminal by the international community. This simple positivist definition identifies a crime based on state consent in treaties or customary international law. However, it does not explain why the international community criminalizes certain acts or the policy rationale behind such decisions. The rapid expansion of criminal law has lacked a thorough discussion of principles such as individual autonomy, welfare, harm, and minimalism that justify or limit criminalization.

Hostages Case: Nuremberg Trial: Implications for Terrorism Definition

The '*Hostages Case*' at the Nuremberg Trials (1947–48) involved the prosecution of German officials for war crimes and crimes against humanity, including the unlawful seizure and execution of hostages in retaliation for partisan activities. The trial focused on war crimes, such as targeting civilians as a strategy of terror by the German occupying forces. The practice of executing hostages as reprisals for resistance was deemed a breach of international law, despite Nazi authorities' legal sanctions.

The *Hostages Case* established legal precedents in international criminal law regarding the protection of civilians during conflict. It highlighted that actions aimed at terrorizing civilian populations were unjustifiable under any circumstances and constituted severe violations of international humanitarian law. The case reinforced the principle that certain acts, universally recognized as criminal, must not remain solely within national jurisdiction due to their grave international concern.

While criminal conduct typically falls under domestic jurisdiction, international law steps in when actions have cross-border repercussions or threaten global peace, security, or well-being. International criminal law aims to protect shared values, carrying a higher moral reprehensibility. However, relying on universal values or natural law for criminalization introduces subjectivity, potentially undermining the law's authority. Despite cultural differences, there has been gradual convergence on core international crimes through an ad hoc process rather than a systematic approach.

Moral Compass: A Significant Determining Principle?

It is essential to recognize that international moral consensus is a dynamic construct influenced by evolving societal concerns about public safety and social order. Terrorism, unlike the physical acts that constitute it, is not inherently criminal but derives its criminal status from its historical and political context.

In the Hostages Case, the U.S. Military Tribunal established a crucial criterion for determining whether an act of terrorism constitutes a crime against humanity. The tribunal held that the nature of the conduct must be such that relying solely on domestic law for its suppression would prove inadequate. This principle has become an important determinant in international law when assessing whether an act of terrorism violates the comity of nations.

This principle highlights the importance of cooperation among nations in addressing the threat of terrorism. While domestic laws may be sufficient to deal with certain types of terrorism, international cooperation is essential for addressing transnational terrorism and ensuring that perpetrators are held accountable.

Judicial Sovereignty: Within the National Realm

Jurisdictional sovereignty however, does matter. It may be seen that neither the 1997 Terrorist Bombings Convention nor the 1999 Terrorist Financing Convention applies when an offence is committed within a single State, the alleged perpetrator is within the territory of that State, and no other State has a Convention basis to exercise jurisdiction. A similar provision is included in the Draft Comprehensive Convention, which also specifies that *the victims must not be nationals of the State where the offence occurs.*[13]

It is inaccurate to assume that prohibited conduct must invariably exhibit a physical or material transnational element. Domestic terrorism, for instance, can pose significant threats to regional peace and security through cross-border violence and refugee crises. Moreover, while often associated with state actions due to their scale and severity, crimes such as genocide, war crimes, and crimes against humanity can occur entirely within a single jurisdiction.

Furthermore, conduct need not necessarily threaten peace and security to be considered an international crime; if it violates international values or interests deserving of international protection, such as specific human rights; then both domestic and international forms should be equally subject to criminalization. This is the approach adopted regionally in the EU Framework Decision, which does not differentiate between the criminalization of domestic or international terrorism, as long as the motive elements of altering or destroying a State or intimidating a population are met. It is not the mere presence of a physical international element that invokes international jurisdiction, but rather the egregious nature of the affected interests. Conversely, the international consensus leans toward defining and criminalizing only international terrorism, while allowing States the discretion to handle crimes of domestic terrorism.

Balancing Act: Global Consensus vs. National Interests in Defining Terrorism

A domestic crime is aimed at protecting a specific community, while an international crime protects the global community. However, the similarity often ends there. International criminal justice struggles with coherence, despite growing awareness of terrorism's global threat. Powerful states often dominate international debates, and some countries strongly resist these legal and ideological pressures, even when they seem harmless.[14]

The international system, which promotes shared values and peace, has resisted a global governance dominated by powerful states. Efforts to create a world government have failed. Similarly, attempts to criminalize terrorism through a comprehensive convention, first led by the League of Nations and then the United Nations, have stalled. Major powers have focused on non-state actors, while smaller states have pushed for including state-sponsored terrorism. The term "freedom fighters" has also been used to exclude certain groups from the definition of terrorism.

Instead of using the broad term "community," it's more accurate to define the level of cohesion within a group based on a specific issue and time. Terrorism has created a global community united by shared vulnerability, highlighting the need for international cooperation against it.[15]

There is an inherent political element in the international criminal justice system especially when it comes to formulating a comprehensive convention on such a debated topic as the definition of terrorism. The international criminal justice system is not a 'technical-instrumental-oriented enterprise', but is densely implicated in international politics.[16]

The United Nations' commitment to inclusivity, considering all member states' views regardless of power, is key to its legitimacy. Although a universal definition of terrorism remains elusive, this approach has helped build a strong global consensus against such acts.

This achievement is significant. Even without a single definition, states have endorsed anti-terrorism conventions. The success of sector-specific measures against terrorism is notable. The next step is criminalizing terrorism within international law and creating a universally effective legal framework, reflecting a shared goal for progress.

The Perils of Precision: Pitfalls of a Global Terrorism Definition

While supporters of a universal definition of terrorism often highlight the dangers of not having one, it's important to consider the opposing view. Some argue that a single definition could be exploited by powerful states to settle political scores. The term 'War on Terror' has been criticized as a justification for military action, potentially prioritizing military measures over criminal justice, even if they cause civilian harm. Additionally, opponents worry that framing terrorism as an absolute threat could lead to unchecked counter-terrorism actions that infringe on fundamental rights.

There are also concerns that labelling opponents as terrorists can dehumanize them, hindering peaceful resolution. Some argue for a more nuanced approach that distinguishes between violent acts and legitimate dissent. The absence of a shared definition gives those in power more freedom to act without a clear, agreed-upon standard.

After the 9/11 attacks, the USA used unilateral action, bypassing the UN's broader consensus. The US Congress quickly passed the Authorization for Use of Military Force (AUMF), granting authority to target not just those responsible but also those supporting them. While the effectiveness of these actions is debated, the impact on civilians in the affected areas remains a significant concern.

The lack of a universal definition creates a double-edged sword. While some fear it could be used for imperialistic agendas, the lack of clarity also hinders effective condemnation. Following 9/11, the UN Security Council mandated counter-terrorism measures but intentionally avoided defining terrorism to avoid jeopardizing agreement. This left room for states to define terrorism on their own, with the UN Counter-Terrorism Committee opting for a pragmatic, ad hoc approach.

Ultimately, the absence of a shared definition makes resolving disputes over who qualifies as a terrorist difficult, leading to inevitable disagreements.

Even Scholars Don't Agree

The quest for a universally agreed-upon definition of terrorism is a challenge not just for governments, but for experts and scholars as well. In his seminal work, "*Political Terrorism: A Research Guide*," Alex Schmid meticulously examined over a hundred definitions, dedicating significant effort to finding a broadly accepted and comprehensive term. However, a revised edition published in 2005 revealed the ongoing struggle. The opening sentence itself acknowledged the *"quest for a suitable definition persists,"* highlighting the elusiveness of a universally accepted definition.[17]

Walter Laqueur, in both editions of his monumental work on the subject, despaired of unequivocally defining terrorism, asserting that such an endeavour is neither attainable nor worthwhile. In response to a survey on definitions conducted by Schmid, Laqueur opined, *"Ten years of debates on typologies and definitions have not appreciably enriched our understanding of the subject."* Laqueur's contention is underscored by the identification of twenty-two distinct word categories within the corpus of 109 diverse definitions discerned by Schmid during his survey. Upon the culmination of this exhaustive endeavour, Schmid poses the question of whether the aforementioned compendium encapsulates all the requisite elements for a judicious definition, and he cautiously suggests that the answer probably leans towards the negative.[18]

Throw in the Towel: No Need for Such a Definition?

Should we accept, as Laqueur and Schmid suggest, that a universally agreed-upon definition of terrorism may be elusive? Does this render the concept itself undefinable? Not necessarily.

Even without a single, perfect definition, we can identify unique characteristics that distinguish terrorism from other forms of political violence. By focusing on these distinctive traits – such as the targeting of civilians to instil fear and achieve political aims – we can still develop a shared understanding of what constitutes terrorism. This allows for more effective international cooperation in combating this global threat.

Bruce Hoffman in his seminal work '*Inside Terrorism*'[19] brilliantly posits the potential for the identification of key characteristics intrinsic to terrorism, thus proposing that:

1. *Terrorism is inherently political in its objectives and motives.*
2. *It involves the use of violence or, equally significantly, the threat of violence.*
3. *Its design aims at instigating profound psychological repercussions extending beyond the immediate victim or target.*
4. *It is executed either by an organization with a discernible chain of command or a conspiratorial cell structure, whose members do not don uniforms or identifying insignia, or by individuals or a small collective directly influenced, motivated, or inspired by the ideological objectives or example of an existing terrorist movement and/or its leaders.*
5. *Terrorism is perpetrated by a sub-national group or non-state entity.*

Carsten Bockstette (2008)[20] a German military officer and a scholar on terrorism studies, offers an interesting definition accentuating the psychological and tactical dimensions of terrorism:

> *Terrorism is defined as political violence within an asymmetrical conflict designed to instil terror and psychic fear, at times indiscriminately, through the violent victimization and destruction of non-combatant targets, occasionally of iconic significance. Such acts are intended to convey a message on behalf of an illicit clandestine organization. The purpose of terrorism is to leverage the media to maximize attainable publicity as an amplifying force multiplier, thereby influencing the targeted audience(s) to achieve short- and mid-term political objectives and/or desired long-term end states.*

Lumpers and Splitters!

Scholars and practitioners can be categorized based on the definitions of terrorism they employ, with a distinction arising between *"act-centric"* and *"actor-centric"* definitions. Actor-centric definitions of terrorism emphasize the characteristics of the groups or individuals employing terrorism, while act-centric definitions underscore the unique attributes of terrorism distinguishing it from other forms of violence.

Max Abrahms (2010) introduces the division between "terrorist lumpers" and "terrorist splitters." Lumpers define terrorism broadly, with no differentiation from guerrilla warfare or civil war, contending that terrorism can coerce major government concessions. In contrast, terrorist splitters define terrorism narrowly, specifically as the selective use of violence against civilians for putative political gains, rejecting the notion that it is an effective tactic for achieving political ends.[21]

In 2011, Alex Schmid published an updated academic consensus definition in *The Routledge Handbook of Terrorism Research*, which encompasses a discussion of the UN's struggle to establish a legal definition and incorporates 260 alternative definitions. The revised definition comprises 12 points, with the first being:

> *Terrorism encompasses both a doctrine concerning the presumed efficacy of a distinct form or tactic of fear-inducing coercive political violence and a conspiratorial practice characterized by calculated, demonstrative, direct violent actions devoid of legal or moral constraints. These actions mainly target civilians and non-combatants, serving propagandistic and psychological purposes for various audiences and parties in conflict.*

Multitude of 'Essential Ingredients' Definitions

A study by Schmid and Jongman in 1983 revealed 109 different interpretations of the term 'terrorism,' highlighting that the issue isn't technical, but political. The differences in definitions often lie in emphasis and wording rather than substance. Many definitions list various elements without clearly indicating which are essential for an act to be considered terrorism.

To create a legal definition, we need to understand the objectionable nature of terrorism, which should be reflected in the law. However, precision is crucial to avoid retroactive punishment. According to the principle of "*nullum crimen, nulla poena sine lege*," only the law can define a crime and prescribe a penalty. Criminal law must be clear to ensure fairness, allowing individuals to understand what actions make them liable. Ambiguity in defining crimes creates uncertainty and opens the door for misuse of power, especially when determining criminal responsibility and imposing penalties that affect fundamental freedoms.[22]

Disputes over the technicalities of defining terrorism have often overshadowed more important questions about its criminalization. Rather than focusing on competing definitions, it's more useful to look at the harmful nature of terrorism itself. This approach helps clarify the types of actions the international community condemns.

Terrorist acts clearly cause harm, often leading to political instability, fear, and suffering, even without violence. These acts are condemned because they harm civilians who are not involved in the political goals of the perpetrators. From an ordinary person's perspective, the debate over terminology seems less important, as the focus should be on addressing the suffering rather than getting caught up in legal details. The comparison to cancer is fitting; like cancer, terrorism takes different forms, making a single definition difficult to establish.

Evolving Perspectives on Defining Terrorism: Ongoing Struggle

The European Union and United Nations have both supported banning and criminalizing terrorism, calling it a violation of human rights, state integrity, peaceful politics, and global peace. Their shared view on the wrongfulness of terrorism helps in creating clear legal definitions and tackling the issue without interference from conflicting political agendas.

Criminalizing terrorism also offers additional benefits, such as helping standardize national laws and reducing differences in how terrorist acts are treated. This makes it easier to follow the double criminality principle in extradition cases and implement a "prosecute or extradite" policy. A clear definition can also limit political exceptions in extradition for terrorist acts and prevent terrorists from gaining refugee status, as it could be classified as a serious non-political crime.

Although these reasons may not be strong on their own, together they provide a solid basis for defining and criminalizing terrorism. Criminalizing terrorism serves as a symbol of unacceptable behaviour, even if it doesn't deter motivated offenders. A clear definition helps satisfy calls to bring terrorists to justice without resorting to vengeance or over criminalizing minor actions. By clearly defining terrorism, we can prevent its misuse as a political tool and limit its exploitation as a term for "evil.

Conclusion

The history of defining terrorism has made some progress, with treaties like the Special Tribunal for Lebanon and the Financing of Terrorism Convention offering functional definitions. However, a general definition still hasn't been agreed upon. While the Comprehensive Convention on International Terrorism hopes to address this by criminalizing all forms of international terrorism and cutting off support to terrorists, it is still afar.

Scholars have debated the balance between state interests and global ethics in defining terrorism. Despite these debates, there's widespread agreement that terrorism is universally condemned as a threat to the global community. While state practices can vary due to political interests, supporting terrorism is generally seen as unacceptable.

We don't need another major attack to realize that terrorism is a pressing issue that needs resolution. The only ones benefiting from the ongoing definitional confusion are terrorists and their supporters. Some states give exceptions to "freedom fighters," even if their actions harm civilians, which amounts to supporting terrorism and must be addressed.

In internal armed conflicts, defining terrorism under International Human Rights Law is difficult. These conflicts often involve armed groups within a state or between factions, but not law enforcement against non-state actors. While large-scale counter-terrorism efforts may harm civilians, this shouldn't be equated with terrorism. States opposing a universally accepted definition of terrorism to protect certain '*freedom fighters*' must reconsider their stance.[23]

The definition of terrorism in the Financing of Terrorism Convention does not allow exceptions based on who commits the act. It follows the 1994 UN General Assembly Declaration, which clearly condemns all forms of terrorism as criminal and unjustifiable, regardless of whether the perpetrator is a '*freedom fighter*' or a state actor.

The draft UN Comprehensive Convention builds on this by including not just violence against people, but also against property when it causes major economic damage. It is the most thorough attempt so far. However, it faces strong opposition from regional groups like the Organization of Islamic Cooperation, which insists on including exceptions for groups like Hamas, Islamic Jihad, and Hezbollah, labelling them as engaged in a legitimate resistance struggle against Israeli occupation.

The real challenge in defining terrorism lies not in the violent acts themselves, but in deciding who can be labelled a terrorist. Complications arise when acts by rebel groups overlap with international humanitarian law or when governments commit violence against their own civilians, raising issues of state responsibility. These grey areas make it harder to finalize a clear, comprehensive definition.

Still, drafting the convention offers a chance to clarify these issues and align different areas of international law. A clear and consistent definition would help the world agree on which acts are always unacceptable, no matter who commits them.[24]

Defining international terrorism is therefore not only elusive, but the entire exercise has also been condemned by certain states as entirely unnecessary. Regardless of the motives of interested parties, no one should ignore the pain and threat to the very existence of humankind that this progressive ailment entails. The conviction that terrorism is a cancer of the international community of nations must never be lost sight of, regardless of differences of opinion among states. Terrorists are no one's friends, as amply demonstrated by the experiences of Pakistan and other such states that harbour non-state actors engaged in terrorism against their adversaries.

3

The Invisible Enemy: The Rise of Cyber Terrorism

> *"If you spend more on coffee than on IT security, you will be hacked. What's more, you deserve to be hacked."*
>
> **—Richard Clarke**

The term 'terrorism' often conjures images of violent attacks, bombings, hijackings, and mass casualties. However, in the realm of Information Technology, terrorism also includes non-violent but politically driven acts that undermine governments, destabilize economies, and cause long-term disruption.

As our dependence on internet-connected infrastructure grows exponentially, malicious actors—including terrorists—have come to recognize the vast opportunities to disrupt our lives from afar. Despite widespread discussion about cyber security protocols, the harsh reality is that many Internet-facing systems remain fundamentally untrustworthy and highly vulnerable. It's a troubling truth that much of the internet was built on a flawed foundation—one never designed to support the critical infrastructure upon which 21st-century society now depends.

Today, computers make vital decisions, such as when and where to route electricity to maintain power grid stability. From national security systems and emergency services to hospitals and transportation networks, nearly every essential service is tied to digital infrastructure. And these systems are increasingly exposed. Adversaries understand this all too well and are prepared to exploit these vulnerabilities to cause widespread disruption, chaos, and harm.

One such vulnerable target is *SCADA (Supervisory Control and Data Acquisition)* systems that monitor and control industrial processes remotely. They collect real-time data from sensors and devices, process it, and display information for operators. SCADA enhances efficiency, safety, and automation in industries like energy, water, manufacturing, and transportation by enabling centralized supervision and decision-making. In everyday life, SCADA ensures reliable electricity, clean water, efficient traffic systems, and safe industrial operations. It supports the smooth functioning of critical infrastructure we depend on without even noticing.

Terrorist groups can target critical infrastructure by exploiting weaknesses in such SCADA systems. These systems, designed for remote monitoring with minimal human oversight, are vulnerable to cyber attacks. Their connection to the broader internet increases the risk of large-scale disruption, potentially triggering cascading failures and systemic breakdowns.

The Federal Bureau of Investigation has revealed that terrorist groups have long considered cyber attacks as a strategic method to target America's critical infrastructure. As early as 2001 the FBI investigation revealed that Al-Qaeda's operatives extensively used online research to plan their attacks.[1] In 2012, the FBI uncovered a video released by al-Qaeda's Al-Shahab media wing, in which the group urged its operatives to launch coordinated cyber assaults on U.S. facilities. Further intelligence investigations confirmed that al-Qaeda was actively conducting online reconnaissance, targeting key systems such as emergency communication networks, power plants, water distribution systems, nuclear facilities, and gas storage infrastructure across the USA.[2]

A Short History of Cyber-Terrorism

The term 'cyber-crime,' first introduced by William Gibson in 1982 through his novel *Neuromancer*, described a virtual world of networked computer activity and soon became associated with cyber security threats. In the mid-1980s, Barry C. Collin coined 'cyber-terrorism,' identifying it as the fusion of terrorism and digital networks. One of the first major incidents was 'Moonlight Maze' (1996–1997), where U.S. government and military networks were penetrated, allegedly by Russian actors, to steal sensitive data. In 1998, Sri Lankan embassies faced a daily deluge of threatening emails from the LTTE claiming to be the 'Black Internet Tigers,' marking an early instance of politically motivated cyber harassment.[3]

Other significant attacks followed. In 2000, a hacker in Australia caused sewage leaks by breaching Maroochy Shire's water system. 'Titan Rain' (2003) targeted U.S. defence contractors, likely from China. That year, Japan's Aum Shinrikyo cult accessed nuclear facility data across several countries. Estonia faced a massive DDoS (Distributed Denial-of-Service) attack overwhelms a server, network, or website with excessive traffic from multiple sources, causing disruption, slowdowns, or complete shutdown of targeted online services in 2007 after a political dispute with Russia. In 2009, Israeli systems were hit by a cyber-assault attributed to Hamas and Hezbollah. The 2010 Stuxnet worm, widely linked to U.S.-Israeli cooperation, damaged Iran's nuclear centrifuges. In 2012, pro-Palestinian groups, including 'Nightmare' and Anonymous's OpIsrael, launched cyber attacks on key Israeli institutions, protesting alleged violations of Palestinian rights.

In April 2013, the Izz al-Din al-Qassam Cyber Fighters, tied to Hamas's military wing, launched a two-hour DDoS attack on the American Express website, disrupting customer access. Unlike botnet-based attacks, they used compromised servers with higher bandwidth. This incident reflected Hamas's growing cyber capabilities, including efforts to spy on Israeli Defence Forces and target soldiers' phones.

In 2014, the '*Guardians of Peace*' hacked Sony Pictures, leaking sensitive data in response to *The Interview*, a satire on North Korea's leader. The breach, widely seen as North Korea-backed, raised national security concerns and was considered cyber-terrorism due to its coercive intent.[4]

In 2015, hackers allegedly linked to Russian intelligence attacked Ukraine's power grid, causing blackouts, the first known cyber attack to create physical damage. In 2017, Ukraine was hit by the NotPetya malware, which spread globally through compromised accounting software, disrupting critical sectors. Though severe, it is labelled a cyber attack, not cyber-terrorism. That year, WannaCry ransomware infected hundreds of thousands of Windows systems in over 150 countries, encrypting data and demanding Bitcoin ransom.

During the Syrian civil war, the pro-Assad Syrian Electronic Army (SEA) conducted DDoS attacks, misinformation campaigns, and website defacements. Their targets included Syrian opposition sites and major Western media such as *The Washington Post*, *Financial Times*, and *Al Arabiya*. In April 2013, they hacked the Associated Press Twitter account, falsely reporting a White House bombing, briefly crashing U.S. markets.

The SEA also attempted to breach infrastructure, such as Israel's irrigation systems, and defaced entertainment and news sites including E! Online and *The Onion*. In 2014, they took down 16 Saudi government websites, condemning Saudi Arabia for terrorism.

In November 2022, a ransomware attack targeted the servers of the All-India Institute of Medical Sciences (AIIMS) in Delhi, causing significant disruptions to their systems, which had to be operated manually for two weeks before being restored. This attack compromised 40 million records, including those of influential individuals in India, with the value of the data extending beyond monetary terms. Terrorists are capable of launching attacks inflicting massive casualties by orchestrating Bhopal gas leak tragedy-like situations just by manipulating SCADA of such critical manufacturing units that use dangerous chemicals as a precursor to their products. Considering the political context, cyber warfare and cyber terrorism are tangible challenges that our society is currently confronting.

Hezbollah Pager Attack: Supply Chain Cyber-attack by Israel?

On September 17, 2024, a devastating coordinated attack in Lebanon injured thousands and claimed nine lives when pagers used by Hezbollah operatives exploded simultaneously across the country. The unprecedented complexity of the incident has fuelled speculation that Israel was behind the attack.

Hezbollah, which has often accused Israel of orchestrating such operation, alleged that the pagers received communications appearing from the group's leadership shortly before the explosions. However, experts have surmised that these messages could be detonation commands disguised as pre-coded instructions into the very firmware of the device. The scale and precision of the attack shocked analysts, particularly given Hezbollah's stringent evasion manoeuvres.

Initial speculation pointed to a hacking incident, with some theories suggesting the devices' batteries were made to overheat. However, forensic analysis and CCTV footage have largely discredited this hypothesis. The leading theory now centres on a supply chain attack, a sophisticated form of sabotage where devices are tampered with during manufacturing or distribution.

Supply chain attacks, while common in software-based cyber operations, are far rarer in hardware. Successfully compromising Hezbollah's pagers would have required a highly coordinated effort, with access to manufacturing or shipping points, allowing for the devices to be modified without detection.

On September 18, just a day after a deadly pager attack, a series of explosions involving walkie-talkies used by Hezbollah members occurred in Beirut. The blasts, killed at least 20 people and injured hundreds more. One of the explosions took place near a funeral for victims of the previous day's attack.

Lebanese security officials suspect that the pagers and walkie-talkies were fitted with explosives months before their arrival in Lebanon. A former British Army munitions expert posited that the pagers could have been remotely detonated by the attackers.[5]

Although Israel has not officially claimed responsibility, the extraordinary coordination of the attack and the use of advanced sabotage techniques strongly point to the involvement of Mossad, Israel's intelligence agency. Known for its history of eliminating key figures within Hezbollah and Hamas, Israel's suspected role in this operation marks a significant escalation in its conflict with Hezbollah.[6]

While the precise mechanism of the attack remains under investigation, the consensus points toward tampered devices. Early evidence suggests the pagers in question were part of a new shipment, produced by a manufacturer whose supply chain may have been compromised, likely in a covert operation.

Cyber-terrorism: Meaning and Issues

Despite entering the Information Technology revolution relatively late, India has exceeded expectations and emerged as a prominent leader in software development, contributing significantly to the expanding IT landscape. Along with these positive strides in internet accessibility, India also experienced a surge in cybercrimes, including internet fraud, financial crimes, illicit online sales, online gambling, digital forgery, cyber defamation, cyber stalking, phishing, cyber conspiracy, cyber pornography, web defacement, and cyber-terrorism.

Among these cybercrimes, cyber-terrorism stands out as particularly menacing, capable of causing severe and insidious harm, as exemplified by the AIIMS ransomware attack. The proliferation of anonymous communication and the terrorists' ability to conceal their locations and identities add a covert, and some might argue, *Machiavellian* dimension to the threat.

What is Cyber-terrorism? Definitional Challenge Revisited

Cyber-terrorism is fusion of terrorist actions and cyber-space. It is generally understood as unlawful, criminal, and offensive intrusion into a computer resource to intimidate or coerce a government or people in general in furtherance of objectives of the one mounting the attack whether it's a lone attacker or representative of a group.

The concept of cyber terrorism involves utilizing the Internet to execute violent or severely disruptive actions that either lead to or pose a threat of causing loss of life or significant physical harm. The aim is to achieve political or ideological objectives through intimidation or the use of threats. Various methods, including deliberate large-scale disruptions of computer networks and attacks on personal computers connected to the Internet, employ tools like computer viruses, worms, phishing, malicious software, hardware techniques, and programming scripts, making them forms of internet terrorism.

The term *cyber terrorism* is contentious, with some defining it narrowly as disruption attacks by known terrorist organizations against information systems to create alarm or physical disruption. Conversely, others adopt a broader definition that encompasses cybercrime, blurring the lines between the two. Determining whether certain online activities constitute cyber terrorism or cybercrime can be challenging by some definitions.[7]

Another definition of cyber terrorism involves the deliberate use of computers, networks, and the public internet to inflict destruction and harm for personal objectives. Skilled cyber terrorists, adept at hacking, can inflict extensive damage on government systems, leaving a nation apprehensive of potential future attacks. These cyber terrorists may be motivated by political or ideological objectives, effectively making it a form of terror with far-reaching consequences.

The Federal Bureau of Investigation defines Cyber-Terrorism as:

> '*The unlawful use of force or violence against persons or property to intimidate or coerce a government, the civilian population, or any segment thereof, in furtherance of political or social objectives through the exploitation of systems deployed by the target*'.

It is important to emphasize that amidst the multitude of available definitions, two crucial criteria must be met for an activity to be categorized as 'cyber-terrorism.' Firstly, the activity must occur within or be related to cyberspace, and secondly, the intention or *mens rea* must be to propagate terror.

Consequently, the term specifically denotes any malicious attempt or act carried out through a computer resource and/or on a computer resource with the aim of causing terror.

Barry C. Collin, a senior research fellow at the Institute for Security and Intelligence in California, is credited with introducing the term '*cyberterrorism*' in the mid-1980s. Collin initially defined cyber terrorism as the intersection of cybernetics and terrorism. The term gained widespread acceptance, particularly within the United States Armed Forces. Cyber terrorism encompasses premeditated, politically motivated attacks by subnational groups, clandestine agents, or individuals against information and computer systems, computer programs, and data, resulting in violence against non-combatant targets.[8]

Before the emergence of the term 'cyber terrorism,' there existed a term known as '*information warfare*':

> '*Information warfare is defined as a planned attack by nations or their agents against information and computer systems, computer programs, and data that result in enemy losses.*'[9]

The practical distinction between these two terms lies in the fact that cyber terrorism aims to instil fear and harm in anyone within proximity (i.e., bystanders), whereas information warfare targets a defined objective in a war, whether ideological or officially declared. Law enforcement agencies frequently use the term cybercrime, which refers to crimes committed through the use of information technology. It is crucial to note that the physical manifestations of cyber terrorism, information warfare, and cybercrime often exhibit striking similarities, leading to an understandable yet avoidable inclination to confuse these terms.

Cyber-Crime vs. Cyber-Terrorism: Explanation by Illustration

Suppose an individual surreptitiously gains control of a computer resource within a government organization where his female friend works, and he discovers that a particular setting can trigger the fire alarm, ensuring that the office will be temporarily closed, and his female friend will then be free for the rest of the day. He uses that switch remotely from the comfort of his home and sets off the fire alarm to achieve his objective. Will this be classified as terrorism? The government facility in this case is a crucial organization that serves the defence forces. Is it a regular cybercrime?

The defence counsel defending the accused in this case can argue that the mechanics of the crime in this case would hardly be a determinant to classify it as cyber-terrorism, or the fact that the facility was a crucial government entity, unless the *intent* was to affect the functioning of the facility for a purpose, such as declaring it with an intention to denounce a government policy or harm security forces. On the other hand, the Government prosecutor will always point to the fact that the facility in question had a public face that distinguished it to be a government facility serving the critical national security architecture. Hence, the prosecutor may substantiate that the accused committed an act of cyber-terrorism by malicious interference of a defence organisation regardless whether his intent was to inflict violent damage or not.

The most important aspect of a cyber-attack that has physical consequences, therefore, is determining the intention of the attacker. Without attempting in any way, the philosophical, political, or historical analysis of the terminologies, it must be emphasized that societal and cultural orientation and their resulting motivations are important in resolving the people component of such attacks. Just because the issues in cyber-terrorism primarily involve technological matters, the society and cultural landscape under which it occurs should not be disregarded, much less ignored.

Like Terrorism, Its Sub-variant Also Does not Have a Universally Agreed Definition

There is no universal definition of terrorism or cyber terrorism, just as there is none for cybercrime. Interpretations of cyberterrorism range from broad views, including all online terrorist activity, to narrow definitions focused only on violent acts committed through the Internet. The latter, often called 'pure cyberterrorism,' refers to politically motivated, cyber-dependent crimes intended to instil fear, intimidate governments or populations, and cause harm, such as sabotage.

Under this narrower view, cyberterrorism includes attacks that lead to death, injuries, explosions, infrastructure failures, or severe economic loss. However, disruptions to non-essential services or financially damaging but politically neutral incidents may not qualify. In contrast, a non-violent hack of a sensitive site used to spread fear-inducing political messages could still be classified as cyberterrorism.

Cyber-terrorism Hyperbole?

The inconsistent definitions of Cyber-Terrorism across jurisdictions stem from its origins in varied fields such as law enforcement, international relations, counter-terrorism, and information security. Media coverage further complicates matters by emphasizing the criminal angle over the nature of the act. Many definitions also fail to account for the evolving scope of Information and Communication Technologies (ICT), including those embedded in critical infrastructure, vehicles, and medical systems. Consider, for instance, the FBI's revised 2004 definition of Cyber-Terrorism.

> *'A criminal act perpetrated by the use of computers and telecommunications capabilities, resulting in violence, destruction and/or disruption of services, where the intended purpose is to create fear by causing confusion and uncertainty within a given population, with the goal of influencing a government or population to conform to a particular political, social or ideological agenda.'*

While initial definitions tend to emphasize the criminal aspect, they narrowly focus on instilling fear and uncertainty, disregarding the potential impacts of terrorism on the economy, environment, international relations, and governance. In essence, the majority of these definitions are constrained by a security-centric policy-legislative mindset.

International Efforts Towards Defining and Penalising Cyber-Terrorism

Several countries, such as India, Australia, Pakistan, and Kenya, have national laws addressing cyber terrorism. However, international law still lacks a clear definition or direct prohibition of it. Instead, global frameworks focus on protecting critical infrastructure, such as aviation, nuclear facilities, and government systems, through various UN conventions and protocols.

UN Security Council Resolutions 1373 (2001) and 2370 (2017) urge member states to criminalize terrorism-related cyber activity, enhance coordination, and foster public-private partnerships, while respecting human rights and international law. Resolution 2370 specifically highlights the threat of terrorists acquiring weapons, including through cyber means, and calls for greater collaboration via platforms like INTERPOL.

Media hype often labels every cyber disruption as 'cyber-terror', yet most of these incidents fades from memory and are later seen as cybercrime or activism. The term 'cyber-terrorism' is frequently overused to describe any online activity by terrorists. While terrorist groups do leverage cyberspace for planning, propaganda, and recruitment, not all such actions qualify as cyber-terrorism.

The clarity of defining *Cyber-terrorism* depends on several prerequisites, including:

- The *intent* behind the act: Is it explicitly intended to cause terror, or is it merely a secondary activity of the terrorist? This intent should also align with long-term goals such as societal or political change, or influencing political decision-making, which drive the terrorist or terrorist groups.
- Whether the cyber-space facility was deliberately *employed as a weapon* to cause harm?
- The *objective* of the malicious cyberspace act, which may include violence with profound psychological effects on the targeted audience.

The UK's Terrorism Act, 2000, defines cyber-terrorism broadly, categorizing any disruption of electronic systems affecting the public as terrorism, even without violence or harm. This approach considers any disruption, regardless of intent, as terrorism. Based on the definitions from Western democracies, we can identify key components that define cyber-terrorism in a broader context of cyberspace.

These components include violence, suffering, or death of individuals; significant damage to property; major risks to public health and safety; severe economic loss; ecological harm; and threats to the social and political stability of a nation. This broader understanding of cyber-terrorism emphasizes the far-reaching consequences that cyber attacks can have on public safety and national security.

No Dearth of Definitions

Despite hundreds of competing definitions and extensive literature on cyber-terrorism, distinguishing between cyber-crime and cyber-terrorism remains challenging. This ambiguity, especially given the rapid emergence of new threats, can undermine counter-cyber-terrorism strategies and blur the lines between violent and non-violent online acts.[10]

Because each country applies its own criteria, mislabelling cyber-crimes as cyber-terrorism can result in disproportionate penalties. Counter-terrorism laws should therefore be strictly limited to offenses defined by international conventions, UN Security Council resolutions (including the intent standards in Resolution 1556 (2001)), or other globally recognized protocols. Serious cyber-crimes without a terrorism nexus must remain under ordinary criminal law.

The Cyber-terrorism Hype? Perspective with a Difference

The term '*cyber terrorism*' often evokes visions of shadowy hackers crippling critical infrastructure and endangering national security. In reality, this sensationalized image overstates the threat. Without a clear definition, almost any malicious cyber intrusion is hastily branded 'cyber terrorism,' inflating perceived risks and obscuring genuine dangers.

While cyber terrorism is a real component of modern network warfare, it must be distinguished from other online threats. Media hype and public fear frequently blur the lines between hacktivism, ordinary cybercrime, and true terrorism. Clarifying these distinctions is essential to avoid unnecessary panic and ensure that countermeasures target only acts that genuinely aim to instil terror through violence or large-scale disruption.[11]

The novelty and complexity of cyber threats are key drivers behind the hype surrounding cyberterrorism. Rapid technological advancement has outpaced our ability to effectively address these risks, fuelling fear of the unknown and the potential catastrophic consequences of cyber-attacks. While most of the nearly 5 billion Internet users engage in positive, legitimate activities, even a small fraction of malicious actors can cause significant harm.[12]

For example, if just 0.01% of Internet users act maliciously, it would total half a million people. Even with just 1 in a million users engaging in nefarious activities, it still amounts to 5,000 individuals. When such people collaborate, they can cause significant disruption to societies reliant on computer systems and networks, affecting both major global economies and developing nations like India. With so many potential threats, cyberterrorism risks cannot be overlooked.

As noted earlier, media sensationalism fuels the hype around cyberterrorism. News outlets often exaggerate cyber-attacks, portraying them as sophisticated, insurmountable threats. This sensationalism boosts viewership, supports political agendas, and justifies increased cyber security spending. Moreover, confusion between groups like cyber-criminals, hacktivists, cyber-terrorists, and cyber-warriors arises due to their similar methods and tactics in using the internet to further their goals and create disruption.[13]

Terrorists use similar tactics for financing and recruitment as cyber actors. While hacktivists have clear targets and ideologies to protest and raise awareness, cyber-terrorists aim to instil fear, uncertainty, and cause disruption. Despite differing goals, hacktivists often collaborate and share information more than cyber-terrorists.

Governments and security agencies may use the threat of cyber terrorism to justify expanded surveillance and restrictive cyber security policies. This approach can pressure security forces to remain on high alert, hindering their ability to respond calmly. Not every cyber-intrusion is a cyber-terrorist attack, and lowering the threshold for identifying them could lead to misuse of legal powers. By framing cyber threats as existential risks, agencies may feel compelled to act, even when the threat is minimal, potentially infringing on civil liberties.

It is important to distinguish between genuine cyber security concerns and exaggerated fears of cyber terrorism. While cyber-attacks can have serious consequences, they are often driven by financial gain, espionage, or activism, not ideological terrorism. By separating fact from fiction, policymakers, businesses, and individuals can better address real cyber security challenges.[14]

Motivations for Cyber-Terrorism

One of the main motivations of the cyber-terrorist is obviously to create fear. The other one is to create a spectacular situation so as to inflict as much uncertainty and damage as possible. Unlike other terrorist acts, the perpetrators of cyber-terrorism seldom reveal their intended purpose or identity and mask the launch location of their attack with most sophisticated technological stratagems.[15]

The widespread use of information technology, combined with its ability to provide anonymity and perceived immunity, has allowed even groups without significant military or coercive power to launch impactful attacks on critical infrastructure. These attacks often carry clear political motives. Physical assaults by one country are frequently followed by cyber-attacks on the facilities of the involved parties, creating a new battleground. For example, the conflict between Chinese hackers and the Israeli/Palestinian dispute shows a pattern of escalation. After the 2001 Hainan Incident, where an American plane crashed off China's coast, both countries engaged in cyber-attacks on each other's facilities.

Hunger for Publicity

Like other forms of terrorism, cyber-attacks often target high-profile entities, designed to attract public attention or cause significant damage. Despite limited technical resources, terrorist groups can have a disproportionate impact on public perception through simple cyber activities. Even non-violent actions like defacements and doxing draw media attention, intimidate victims, and boost the attackers' online presence. These low-intensity disruptions show how minimal technical sophistication can still have a major impact. Terrorists are likely to prioritize publicity and disruption, focusing on maximizing the effect of their available cyber capabilities over executing complex attacks.[16]

Targets of cyber terrorism often include vital installations, security infrastructure, assets tied to national identity or history, and critical infrastructure. Attacks also focus on large multinational corporations that represent a specific country. In the past, prominent infrastructure and IT companies have frequently been targeted in such attacks.

Settling Scores: Insider Job?

The growing threat of cyber terrorism highlights the importance of information security. While organizations have implemented defences against external threats, insider risks are equally, if not more, concerning. Trusted personnel, with their knowledge of internal systems, can cause significant damage, leading to administrative paralysis and long-term consequences. This underscores the need for a security approach that addresses both external and internal vulnerabilities.

In organizations tied to national security, internal spies and saboteurs can compromise confidential information, whether intentionally or inadvertently. Identifying abnormal behaviour and potential threats is crucial, achieved through continuous observation and assessment of employees' actions and intentions. Though human observation is fallible and statistical systems can produce false positives, anomaly detection aligns behavioural changes with trustworthiness, ensuring both security and privacy.

Digital Dark Matter: The Hidden Dangers of Cyber-Terrorism

A survey of Fortune 1000 companies revealed a concerning 64% annual increase in cyber-attacks carried out via the Internet. The Internet is becoming a hub for illicit activities, with cybercriminals using anonymizers and 'Onion' networks to carry out a range of cyber assaults. These activities include distributing instructions for making explosives, inciting violence, recruiting for terrorist activities, and soliciting funds to support such endeavours.[17]

Cyberspace is currently home to around 5 billion individuals.[18] While predicting the frequency and duration of cyber activity is challenging, statistics show a significant portion of the global population accesses cyberspace, with billions more expected to join in the coming decades, driving online commerce to over 8 trillion US dollars.[19]

Despite the threats posed by cybercriminals, including terrorists, the expansion of cyberspace seems inevitable, as much of commerce is expected to shift online. Michael O'Connell, Director of Operational Policing Support at Interpol, compares this movement to '2 billion passengers crossing the world.' Cyber travellers navigate the virtual world with remarkable speed, low cost, and near-total anonymity.[20]

Cyber-terrorism Threat Preparedness: Are We Ready?

Historically, the rise of Information and Communication Technologies (ICT) has often prioritized functionality over security. In the push for seamless user experiences and operational efficiency, robust security measures were frequently overlooked. Early internet development, for example, focused more on content delivery than on protecting user data or preventing unauthorized access.

The drive to create intuitive, visually appealing products has often overshadowed security concerns, leaving systems vulnerable to attack. Many companies prioritize rapid user engagement and growth over privacy and security, compromising data protection in favour of usability and market expansion.

Conversely, companies such as Apple have earned praise for strong privacy protections through their tightly controlled ecosystem. Though criticized for limiting innovation and fostering monopoly-like control, Apple's closed approach enhances security by restricting third-party access and software modifications. When properly configured, Apple devices prompt users before allowing apps such as Facebook or Instagram to track their activity, helping safeguard user privacy and limit unauthorized tracking. However, this approach has recently been criticized for limiting consumer choice and stifling innovation.[21]

The 'Apple approach' to privacy and data security underscores the intricate balance between user engagement/experience, innovation, and security in the ICT landscape. While seamless usability and cutting-edge features are crucial for the success of digital products and services, they must not come at the cost of security. A strong security posture is vital to safeguard users, data, and organizations from ever-evolving threats. Achieving the right equilibrium between these three pillars remains a persistent and evolving challenge for the industry.[22]

Users often prioritize convenience and overlook the risks of installing 'free' apps on their phones. A similar trend is emerging with digital TVs, which are increasingly connected to the internet. With millions featuring high-speed video processors, they offer an attractive target for cybercriminals looking to create botnets. As a result, digital TVs may soon become as vulnerable as smartphones.

Digital robots and AI-enabled assistants, including smart vehicles, are expected to become mainstream faster than anticipated. With remote control over home systems like temperature and appliances, hackers could exploit vulnerabilities to access video feeds, manipulate essential services, or even start fires while occupants are away. There have already been cases of insulin pumps and pacemakers being hacked through wireless interfaces, risks their designers underestimated. Improper settings could have fatal outcomes. In the near future, devices that monitor or influence vital body functions may face large-scale cyber threats.[23]

As discussed earlier, the All-India Institute of Medical Sciences (AIIMS) in Delhi experienced a serious denial of service attack, rendering its database inaccessible to millions of outpatients for a substantial period. With the growing trend of health monitoring and medical equipment being interconnected online, there's a looming concern about potential scenarios where hackers, possibly affiliated with terrorist groups, could jeopardize countless lives.[24]

In the present era, even before the integration of AI-driven driving systems, vehicles are equipped with Electronic Control Units (ECUs) containing extensive lines of code. They can aptly be described as 'Computers on Wheels', as they increasingly manage various functionalities, including air conditioning, wiper control, brake actuators, lighting, collision avoidance systems, and the response mechanisms for Automatic Braking Systems and Airbags.

As different manufacturers develop ECUs for vehicles, the need for open and standardized interfaces between them is growing. However, these systems are often designed under the flawed assumption that vehicles operate in a secure, closed environment, much like a pigeon believing it is safe from a cat simply by looking away. With the rise of features such as automatic emergency calls and internet connectivity, these interfaces will increasingly rely on mobile data for two-way communication. While such connectivity brings convenience, it also opens new avenues for cybercriminals and terrorists to exploit vehicle systems, making cyber security an urgent and critical priority.

Cyberterrorism can be as simple as distributing execution videos. Groups like Al-Qaeda and ISIS have used such content to spread fear and prompt international responses. However, the internet also fuels cycles of propaganda, indoctrination, and recruitment. Terrorist organizations exploit the web for influence, taking advantage of Web 2.0's ease of sharing content. This reflects yet another mistaken assumption of a 'harmless' and 'free' digital space. Ultimately, the internet remains the most cost-effective and widely used communication tool, making it simultaneously a powerful asset and a potential threat.

Challenges from 'Going-Dark': Dark Web and Crypto Currencies

Two of the most concerning outcomes of the digital revolution are crypto currencies and the Dark Web. Crypto currencies become especially attractive to terrorist groups when they offer strong anonymity, low traceability, stability to avoid financial loss, and ease of conversion to traditional currency. Terrorists often use them to transfer funds discreetly, alongside informal systems like Hawala.

The Dark Net, originally designed to protect activists under repressive regimes, has also been exploited by terrorist groups. Law enforcement and intelligence agencies have found evidence of its use for transferring information, materials, and crypto currency. With capabilities like hidden web services, encrypted file sharing, anonymous blogs, and chats, the Dark Net allows terrorists to operate beyond the reach of traditional surveillance.[25]

There is no denying that non-state actors, including terrorists, exploit cyberspace for harmful purposes. What is alarming is how cyberspace enables previously insignificant individuals to exert outsized influence. This asymmetry introduces risks that major powers have often underestimated or ignored. A key question remains: can these individuals truly cause the widespread damage that experts warn about? Some may ask why such a catastrophic event has not occurred yet. But consider the fact that airplanes existed for decades before 9/

11. Simply because something has not happened yet, despite the means, does not mean it will not. As Murphy's Law suggests: if it can happen, it probably will.

Challenges in Encountering Threats from Cyber-Terrorism

Challenges from Anonymity Protocols

Identifying attackers during an Internet-based assault remains a major challenge. In cyber-terrorism and information warfare, attacks often involve many hosts, requiring quick and accurate tracking. Yet, the very structure of the internet which is designed to allow anonymity and obscure origins, makes this task extremely difficult and calls for a wide range of tools.

Though several tools exist to trace an attacker's location, their legal reliability is limited. In court, such data must be backed by strong evidence, often including expert testimony, which faces jurisdictional and procedural hurdles. Tracing can involve passive methods (using public data) or active ones (like scanning and pinging), but the latter often struggle to meet the legal standard of proof.

Highly anonymous networks like Onion and Tor are deliberately designed to hide user identities, making tracing through IP addresses nearly impossible. Additional anonymity tools, such as anonymous remailers and peer-to-peer platforms like StealthNet, RetroShare, and AntsP2P, further complicate efforts. Attackers can also hide by accessing the internet from public places like libraries or by infiltrating insecure networks such as public Wi-Fi hotspots.[26]

The Perils of DNS and IP Hijacking

The Internet relies on two foundational systems: the Domain Name System (DNS), which translates human-readable domain names into IP addresses, and the Internet Protocol (IP), which routes data across networks. While both systems are essential for global connectivity, their decentralized governance across numerous organizations introduces serious security vulnerabilities.

DNS hijacking occurs when attackers manipulate DNS records, redirecting users to malicious websites. This can result in stolen personal data, financial losses, and reputational damage. For instance, if a bank's DNS is compromised, users may be unknowingly redirected to a fake login page, where their credentials are harvested.

IP hijacking is another critical threat. It involves altering routing tables to divert or intercept internet traffic. In a worst-case scenario, terrorists could exploit IP hijacking to target critical infrastructure, such as a city's subway control system, potentially disrupting operations, delaying trains, or even causing accidents. The implications range from service outages to public safety crises.

These attacks underscore the internet's fragility and the growing intersection between cyber security and physical safety. Downtime, economic loss, and erosion of public trust are just a few consequences. To mitigate these threats, organizations must adopt proactive security measures: using strong, regularly updated authentication methods, implementing real-time network monitoring, applying security patches promptly, and working closely with reputable DNS and IP service providers.

Ultimately, securing the internet's core systems is not just a technical task, it is a critical safeguard for both digital infrastructure and public well-being.

Bouncing and Onion Routing

Cyber attackers use various evasion techniques, notably 'Bouncing', to hinder tracking efforts. Bouncing refers to methods that obstruct cyber attribution. By leveraging proxy servers, attackers disguise their IP addresses across different global locations. Cyber terrorists typically avoid using their own systems to attack local targets, as modern tools often enable attribution. As a result, bouncing has become a standard tactic. However, detecting and exposing these methods remains legally and technically difficult.[27]

One bouncing variant is the use of remailers, which allow users to send emails under different identities, masking the sender's real address. While recipients cannot identify the sender, the remailer administrator technically can. Some internet services also offer protocol conversion, enabling access to websites, FTP servers, or newsgroups via email. When combined with remailers, protocol converters, and Trojans, cyber attacks can be launched entirely through email. Using public proxies to send these emails adds another anonymity layer.

More recent and effective bouncing relies on 'onion routing,' where individuals permit their systems to serve as bounce points. Based on public proxies designed for anonymity, onion routing encrypts transmissions and sends them through up to 20 proxy nodes. Each proxy only knows the last and next point, not the full route. Like onion layers, each node obscures the source further. While slower, this method offers high anonymity. Tracing an attacker requires that all proxies log traffic' something left to each owner's discretion.

Jurisdictional and Legal Complexities

The jurisdictional and legal complexities are crucial, particularly when identifying a user linked to an IP address at a specific time. In most jurisdictions, this task falls under law enforcement or national security, requiring legal procedures like the Mutual Legal Assistance Treaty or a Letter Rogatory from the overseeing court. However, these processes entail significant delays, which are increasingly out of sync with the fast-paced digital age. Internet service providers, especially those operating across multiple jurisdictions, often cite '*data sovereignty*' as a reason for non-cooperation with foreign governments, despite being open to collaborating with domestic law enforcement.

Despite these challenges, modern law enforcement tools are improving in tracing cyber-attacks. Cyber-terrorists now use specific techniques to hide their identities, sometimes adopting fake personas to mislead investigators. Unfortunately, these methods are becoming more common. However, with the rise of specialized intrusion detection and better cooperation between ISPs and law enforcement, achieving anonymity on the Internet may soon be increasingly difficult. International cooperation, information sharing, and a solid legal framework are essential to combat cyber-terrorism effectively.

Cyber terrorists use clever strategies to evade law enforcement during complex attacks. They breach systems via non-public proxies or by implanting new ones on compromised devices, exploiting firewall weaknesses. They also use 'Bouncing techniques' (see above), deploying multiple IP addresses across various countries, making identification challenging. Additionally, they infiltrate other systems to bounce attacks, using Trojan programs to relay commands through public channels like IRC, Telegram, WhatsApp, or dedicated mailboxes, further enhancing their anonymity.

Telegram and its Abuse by Cyber-terrorists

As discussed earlier, cyber terrorists utilize Telegram, a widely used messaging app, for planning and executing cyber-attacks, taking advantage of its encrypted communication features. Telegram's popularity and security features make it an attractive platform for their activities. Within Telegram, they establish private groups or channels, creating secure spaces to coordinate attacks away from the scrutiny of law enforcement and cyber security experts. These groups serve as central hubs for exchanging malicious tools, tactics, and information on potential targets.[28]

Telegram's anonymity features further facilitate cyber terrorists' operations, allowing them to operate under aliases, shielding their true identities from scrutiny. This anonymity complicates efforts by authorities to trace and apprehend the culprits. Additionally, Telegram's file-sharing functionality enables the distribution of malware, phishing kits, and other harmful software to unsuspecting users. Moreover, it serves as a platform for spreading propaganda and radicalizing individuals, enticing new recruits to join their cause.[29] With its global reach, the platform has been abused by cyber terrorists across different regions, enabling the pooling of resources and expertise for launching coordinated and sophisticated attacks.[30]

Challenges in Cyber Forensics

Another aspect deserving attention is the challenges faced in Cyber-Forensics. With the continuous expansion of storage media, forensic analysis requires copying the entire content to a separate hard drive to protect the original from errors, which can then be used in court to establish facts and prosecute criminals. This often demands hardware upgrades, which may not be feasible for law enforcement agencies due to bureaucratic procurement processes, rendering their forensic assets outdated.

The rapid growth of data, fuelled by the increasing number of devices like laptops, smartphones, smartwatches, digital assistants, and IoT devices, has created a complex digital forensics landscape. Each device type often needs specialized extraction software and hardware, which can be expensive to acquire and maintain. Mobile devices, particularly, present unique challenges due to differences between Apple and Android platforms and frequent software updates that can obsolete forensic tools. This constant technological evolution requires ongoing investments in training and equipment for professionals to effectively extract and analyze data from a wide array of devices. However, budget and capability constraints often hamper investigations.

Future forensic tools must be designed to assist investigators in handling these diverse devices, enabling quick identification of relevant data and relationships among distributed data. This is an area of ongoing research.

Democratization of Secret Communication

In contrast to the past, where encryption was a niche field accessible to only a select few (mostly government agencies), it has now become widely available to the public. As a result, forensic analysts face increasing difficulties in analysing encrypted devices such as hard disks. While many forensic tools incorporate features for password cracking or bypassing (for example, *Encase* offers an optional module for accessing Microsoft's encrypting file system), there are instances where decryption proves exceedingly challenging, particularly when perpetrators employ specialized privacy-enhancing techniques (PETs).

These techniques encompass encryption tools, policy tools, filtering tools, and anonymous tools. While encryption and anonymous tools pose significant hurdles to forensic analysis, the other categories are primarily designed to safeguard the privacy of legitimate users. The array of encryption techniques available not only serve as essential means of data protection but also offer a highly secure method for concealing illicit data, even from forensic investigators.

Increasing abuse of Anonymizers for Cyber-attacks: 'Uncertainty Principle' in Cyber-forensics.

Anonymizing techniques not only conceal communication content but also protect personal information. This is achieved through centralized methods like anonymizing websites, proxies, or insecure Wi-Fi, and decentralized methods like onion routing. When attackers use these tools, forensic analysis typically reveals the Internet address of the central anonymizing computer (proxy) or a node within the onion network. This depends on logging capabilities and the legal feasibility of obtaining the data. As a result, the attacker's chances of evading detection increase. A skilled attacker may prefer these methods over erasing all traces of intrusion, which, though challenging, is possible.

One of the most significant legal challenges in digital forensic analysis is ensuring and demonstrating the integrity of digital evidence, that it has not been altered or tampered with. This challenge mirrors the '*uncertainty principle*' in quantum mechanics, introduced by Werner Heisenberg, which suggests that the act of observing a particle can inherently alter its state. The implication is that the very act of observation disturbs what is being observed.

Similarly, in digital forensics, even the act of accessing or analysing electronic data can unintentionally modify it. For example, forensic tools used to examine a device may inadvertently change file timestamps or metadata, leading to discrepancies in cryptographic hash values, key indicators used to verify data integrity. Such changes, even if unintentional and explainable, can be misinterpreted as evidence of tampering or compromise. This can cast doubt on the authenticity of the evidence and potentially weaken its admissibility in court.

To mitigate this risk, forensic experts are compelled to follow strict protocols, such as creating and working from bit-by-bit copies of original data and maintaining detailed chain-of-custody records. Ultimately, preserving the integrity of digital evidence requires not only technical precision but also legal awareness, as even minor alterations can have major implications for the outcome of a case.

Legal and Policy Aspects in addressing Cyber-terrorism

As cyber-terrorism emerges as the newest form of terrorism, the applicability of existing legal frameworks to cyber threats remains a topic of debate. Traditional laws often struggle to keep up with rapidly evolving cyber tactics, requiring ongoing updates and adaptations. Legal experts and policymakers must address complex issues such as jurisdiction, attribution, and the definition of cyber-terrorism to ensure effective legal responses.

Confronting the ever-changing and dynamic nature of cyberspace presents numerous legal challenges. While cyber threats so far have mainly centred on financial crimes with broader security implications, terrorist use of cyberspace for serious attacks is a growing concern. Though this activity is still in its infancy, complacency is not an option.

A primary consideration for any legal and policy framework is determining the extent to which legal values and principles from the physical world should apply in cyberspace. The cyber world is built on codes and information matrices where cyber-criminals, including terrorists, can remain anonymous and evade detection by security agencies. This raises the issue of whether pre-cyber laws and the values they uphold remain applicable.

The principles guiding legal frameworks are of utmost importance. We must resist the growing trend of blindly adopting protocols from other countries through '*isomorphic mimicry*,' and instead critically examine how those laws align with the values that should inform cyber security policy. This can be also called '*Isolegal Mimicry*'. Isomorphic imitation or mimicry is the tendency of certain jurisdictions to imitate the institutional structures and legal framework of developed countries without actually imbibing the values and understanding inherent in upholding such complex institutions. In other words, blind cut and paste of laws promulgated in foreign jurisdiction without technological knowhow and institutional arrangements would never work.[31]

Before attempting to apply existing legal frameworks to the complex challenges of cyberspace, it is essential to first confront the underlying value conflicts and clarify the ambiguities that shape and justify current legal norms. Cyberspace introduces novel issues, such as cross-border data flows, digital identity, and algorithmic decision-making that often fall outside the scope or intent of traditional law.

A key step in addressing these challenges is resisting the urge to imitate foreign legal institutions or protocols without critically assessing their relevance and effectiveness within one's own legal, cultural, and technological context. Blind mimicry can lead to legal inconsistencies, institutional inefficiencies, or even the erosion of local legal traditions. Instead, jurisdictions must engage in careful, context-specific analysis that balances global best practices with domestic capabilities and priorities. Only by aligning legal responses with the specific realities and values of a jurisdiction can we create a coherent and resilient legal order for the digital age. These may include:

Regard for Privacy while Ensuring Identity Confirmation Upon Investigation
Each country has a unique history regarding privacy concerns. What works in one society may not be applicable in another. Western democracies have evolved through ongoing struggles for rights, often between elite classes and the general public. In contrast, much of the Eastern world has been shaped by prolonged colonization, leading to a different approach to rights. Western societies prioritize individual rights, while many Asian cultures emphasize collectivism, viewing individuals as part of a whole. As a result, the concept of privacy differs between Eastern and Western cultures.

Simply mimicking legal frameworks without considering cultural and historical contexts can lead to long-term inconsistencies. It is crucial for every country to recognize that excessive focus on personal freedom and privacy can undermine international cyber security. The international community should require all Internet service providers to monitor and limit Internet use that threatens the infrastructure or interests of UN member states. Additionally, Know Your Customer (KYC) norms must be consistently enforced in online transactions. While some member states regulate private online activities, others resist, prioritizing individual freedoms and privacy.

Data Sovereignty, Data Localization and Attribution

Simply speaking, *Data Sovereignty* implications involve legal obligation of a service provider (such as a company providing server services or providing social media intermediary services over the Internet) to keep and provide the data created as per the laws of the state where the data has been stored. While *Data Localization* on the other hand refers to laws or regulations requiring data to be stored within a specific geographic location or jurisdiction. This aims to enhance data security, sovereignty, and privacy, often by restricting cross-border data transfers and ensuring local control over sensitive information. In other words, the State can dictate localisation of data created in its legal jurisdiction and compel the service provider to reveal the data as per law.

Data sovereignty, the right of a nation to control data generated within its borders, has become a pressing issue in the digital age. To assert this control, many countries have implemented data localization policies, which restricts the movement of data outside national borders or require data to be stored domestically. For example, China's cyber security law mandates that critical data generated within its borders be stored domestically.

Attribution, the ability to identify the perpetrator of a cybercrime, is another crucial aspect of data governance. Effective law enforcement relies on the ability to trace cyber attacks back to their source. However, the increasing complexity of cybercrime and the use of anonymizing technologies can make attribution challenging.

The interplay between data sovereignty, localization, and attribution is complex and multifaceted. While data sovereignty and localization can help protect national interests, they may also hinder international cooperation in addressing cybercrime. Balancing these competing interests requires careful consideration of the potential benefits and drawbacks of different approaches.

As technology continues to evolve, it is essential to regularly review and update data sovereignty, localization, and attribution laws to ensure they remain relevant and effective. This includes considering the implications of emerging technologies such as artificial intelligence, blockchain, and the Internet of Things. By adopting a flexible and adaptable approach, policymakers can help shape a digital landscape that promotes both national security and international cooperation.

The inherent sovereignty of states leads to jurisdictional fragmentation, implying that a state may not always accept a legal instrument imposed on it, even in the context of the global nature of cyberspace. Jurisdiction entails exclusive responsibility of a sovereign state over its territory and citizens, excluding external involvement beyond its sovereign realm. Despite the UN system's framework, every state is protected by customary international law, preventing any state from claiming absolute sovereignty over cyberspace and implementing regulations unilaterally without the agreement of other states.

To enact legislation is one thing, to assert jurisdiction is quite another, especially when the attackers and computer resources might locate in another's jurisdiction. Cyber-space inherently transcends jurisdictional space and this alone is significant enough to act as an overwhelming obstacle in fastening criminality on an attacker. This necessitates increasing cooperation between law enforcement agencies of different jurisdictions that go beyond time taking legal instruments.

On the other hand, attribution poses a unique challenge as individuals are often hard to identify, and attacks may involve organizations backed by states. Establishing cause-and-effect relationships is particularly challenging, especially when determining whether an attacker acted independently or as a state agent. In such cases, a nation can lawfully respond with force if it demonstrates that a cyber attack constitutes an armed attack under internationally recognized rules of warfare. Otherwise, it may resort solely to criminal proceedings for redress.

In cases where national security is severely compromised, attribution becomes crucial. The affected state must definitively identify the source of the attack, a task complicated by the myriad anonymizing tactics employed by attackers. Rapid advancements in cyberspace leave less room for nations unable to keep pace, placing their law enforcement agencies at a significant disadvantage in tracing responsibility for attacks. The technological complexities of cyberspace, combined with issues of asymmetry and anonymity, greatly amplify the challenges of cross-jurisdictional investigations.

Personal Data and its Commercial Use

Soshana Zuboff in her much-acclaimed work '*The Surveillance Capitalism*' exposed how big tech companies aggregate and sell enormous amount of personal data collected from its users. While there is no denying the fact that the users might have entered into a contract with the service providers to collect data, however the use of their personal information for sale was never expressly authorised by the user, and its assumed authorization by the service provider by implying from a lengthy 'contract' that the user might not have even read should be a subject of notice by policy makers.

In the contemporary digital landscape, personal data has emerged as a lucrative asset, particularly for Big Tech corporations such as Google, Facebook, Instagram, and Twitter. These companies extensively leverage '*behavioural data exhaust*,' the residual traces (metadata) of user activities left across online platforms, to fuel and optimize their commercial strategies. By meticulously analysing this data, they gain profound insights into user behaviours, preferences, and inclinations, enabling them to deliver targeted advertisements, personalized content, and tailored recommendations. While this practice optimizes user engagement and bolsters revenue streams, it raises profound concerns surrounding privacy infringement, consent, and ethical considerations.

The exploitation of personal data by Big Tech not only poses risks to individual privacy but also has broader implications for national security, particularly in the realm of cyber terrorism. The aggregation of vast amounts of sensitive user information creates an enticing target for malicious actors seeking to exploit vulnerabilities in digital infrastructure. Cyber terrorists can weaponize this data to orchestrate sophisticated attacks aimed at disrupting critical systems, destabilizing economies, and compromising public safety. For instance, access to detailed user profiles could facilitate targeted misinformation campaigns, identity theft, or cyber espionage, amplifying the magnitude and severity of cyber threats.

Moreover, the interconnectedness of digital platforms and the extensive sharing of personal data exacerbate the challenge of attribution in cyberterrorism incidents. Identifying the perpetrators behind cyber-attacks becomes increasingly complex amidst the intricate web of data transactions and interactions across various online platforms. This intricate web of data transactions and interactions across various online platforms complicates efforts to trace and hold accountable those responsible for cyber terrorism activities.

The unchecked exploitation of personal data by BigTech companies not only undermines individual privacy rights but also amplifies the risks of cyberterrorism. Addressing these intertwined challenges requires a comprehensive approach encompassing robust data protection regulations that takes into account malpractices involving commercial abuse of behavioural data exhaust, enhanced cyber security measures, and proactive measures to combat cyber threats at both individual and organizational levels.

Adherence to the Principles of Proportionality and Necessity

The penal law requires strict adherence to the principle of proportionality and necessity. A law that disproportionally penalizes criminal infractions is both unjust and gives undue discretion to the prosecution and the judicial officer adjudicating upon the guilt of the accused person. The law must be very clear as to the definition of the crime upon which it fastens criminal liability, and it must incorporate the principle of necessity.

Cyber-terrorism, like its parent concept of terrorism suffers from the deficit of definitional clarity. It becomes increasingly difficult for the legislative bodies, policy makers and those who are tasked with formulating protocols and rules to come up with clearly defined penal provisions while drafting and enacting such provisions. In the legal realm, adherence to the principles of proportionality and necessity is paramount when countering the threat posed by cyber-terrorism. Proportionality mandates that the response to a cyber attack must be proportional to the severity of the threat and must not exceed what is necessary to mitigate the danger. Necessity requires that any action taken must be essential and unavoidable in order to achieve the intended objective of thwarting the cyber threat.

However, applying these principles in the context of cyberterrorism presents unique challenges. The borderless nature of cyberspace, coupled with the difficulty of accurately attributing cyber attacks, complicates the assessment of proportionality and necessity. Moreover, the rapid pace of technological advancements requires continuous adaptation of legal frameworks to effectively address emerging threats while upholding fundamental principles of justice and human rights. Thus, striking a balance between safeguarding national security and preserving individual liberties remains a complex task, requiring ongoing dialogue, collaboration, and adherence to established legal norms and principles.

Cyber-Terrorism and Cyber-Warfare: Legal Complexities

A key question arises: should a cyber-attack linked to state sponsorship be classified as cyber warfare or cyber terrorism? Intent seems crucial in this decision. If the goal is to cause fear and significant harm, and the perpetrators can be clearly identified, the affected state, under international law, can define the threshold for its response. However, covert actions by dominant states, such as the STUXNET attack by the USA, are rarely labelled as terrorism, highlighting inconsistency. Acts of terrorism should be identified based solely on the act, not influenced by political context. The situation is further complicated by state actors using proxy organizations to maintain plausible deniability.

Regional agreements defining the criteria for cyber-terrorism are essential. These would ensure actions by dominant powers, disguised as covert warfare, are recognized as terrorism, regardless of military superiority. Terrorism must be clearly defined as such, without political considerations.[32]

Martens Clause and Legal Challenges to Countering Cyber-Terrorism

The Martens Clause, introduced by Russian diplomat Friedrich Martens in the 1899 Hague Convention II, requires parties in armed conflict to follow the '*laws of humanity*' and '*dictates of public conscience*' when no specific legal provisions exist. This serves as a safeguard, ensuring adherence to fundamental principles of morality and human dignity, even in unforeseen circumstances, such as cyber warfare.

Originally for traditional warfare, the Martens Clause now applies to modern conflict, including cyber warfare. It provides a framework for addressing cyber conflicts, emphasizing human dignity, proportionality, and the prohibition of unnecessary suffering. Given the borderless and evolving nature of cyber terrorism, traditional legal frameworks often struggle to keep pace, making the Martens Clause a vital tool for interpreting legal principles in the absence of specific cyber norms.

Does Cyber-space Requires an Alternative Legal Universe?

While rapid technological advancements demand that legal frameworks evolve, continuously updating laws is seemingly both impractical and counterproductive. This approach has placed an overwhelming strain on law enforcement, the judiciary, and other stakeholders. A more effective solution is to anchor cybercrime investigations and prosecutions in fundamental principles of law and ethics. The Martens Clause offers a crucial foundation, ensuring that justice in the digital age remains rooted in core values such as human dignity and the prohibition of unnecessary harm.

Some legal experts have raised concerns about the growing calls for a new international convention to tackle the challenges posed by computer network attacks and other information operations.[33]

Their objection stems from the belief that despite their perceived novelty, activities in cyberspace do not constitute a fundamentally distinct jurisdiction requiring separate penal provisions from those in traditional legal realms.[34] In essence, there is no separate "Matrix," akin to the fictional world depicted in the famous Hollywood movie, where different laws apply. Terrorists are tangible individuals operating through tangible networks, impacting real assets and causing harm to individuals' lives and welfare. Their actions remain rooted in physical space, involving hardware and networks, including wireless and virtual ones, which rely on physical infrastructure.

It is argued that big tech companies, especially social media intermediaries, should be required to comply with the laws of the jurisdictions where their data originates. The tendency of multinational tech giants to operate outside national laws not only undermines legal sovereignty but also damages public trust in governments. While the unique business model of these companies may require specific accommodations, it is unreasonable to exempt them from the legal jurisdiction of a nation simply because they operate globally. They must recognize that their distinctive business model does not necessarily justify a 'compatible' legal framework.

The information revolution has led to profound changes across multiple domains. As cultural and societal landscapes evolve, so too do the legal concepts that underpin them. For example, traditional views of physical property are increasingly challenged by digital property and its new values. Crypto currencies, despite some resistance, have become a permanent feature due to factors like privacy, ease of exchange, and perceived freedom. Legal constructs are inherently subjective, often shaped by the prevailing moral norms and societal values at the time of their creation.

Cyber-Terrorism and Information Security: The Global Response

Cyber terrorism has emerged as a formidable global threat, transforming the nature of conflict and security in the digital age. Unlike traditional warfare or criminal activity, cyber attacks transcend national boundaries effortlessly, exploiting the internet's inherently borderless infrastructure. This dynamic makes it increasingly difficult for any one country to defend itself in isolation.

Terrorist organizations, state-sponsored actors, and transnational criminal networks leverage cyberspace to disrupt critical infrastructure, spread disinformation, and steal sensitive data—all with relative anonymity and low risk of immediate retaliation.

The complexity and scale of these threats demand a unified and strategic international response. It is no longer sufficient for only technologically advanced nations to bear the burden of cyber defence. Countries across the globe must cooperate by sharing intelligence, establishing common cyber security standards, and building collective capabilities for threat detection and response. Furthermore, global frameworks must be developed to govern cyberspace, promoting responsible behaviour, enforcing accountability, and deterring malicious actors.

Capacity building in less technologically developed nations is also essential. Without adequate security measures in place, these countries can become vulnerable entry points for cyber threats that affect the broader global community. Thus, cyber security must be approached as a shared responsibility, requiring sustained political will, multilateral cooperation, and a commitment to digital trust and resilience.

In confronting the ever-evolving landscape of internet-related security challenges, global unity, proactive diplomacy, and cross-sector partnerships are not just desirable—they are imperative.[35]

Since the early 1980s, discussions on information security have persisted in various international forums, including organizations like the OECD (The Organization for Economic Cooperation and Development). The United Nations General Assembly has similarly engaged in thorough debates and annually passed multiple resolutions regarding "*Development in the field of information and telecommunications in the context of international security.*"[36]

Long Way Ahead?

International forums have largely avoided formulating a comprehensive strategy to assess and counter cyber terrorism threats. The political factors driving this reluctance are beyond the scope of this analysis. However, it can be argued that existing measures lack tangible practical and legal impact.

A case in point is the *Council of Europe's Convention on Cybercrime*, designed to address jurisdictional challenges in the digital age. By harmonizing national laws and establishing cooperation mechanisms, the Convention sought to enable effective cross-border prosecution of cybercriminals. Despite progress, it is unfortunate that the necessary number of states have not ratified it for it to come into force. While many member states face challenges in protecting their critical infrastructure from cyber disruptions, they also express concerns over the potential risks of state-sponsored cyber attacks targeting both government agencies and essential private sector entities.[37]

The UN faces a challenge in establishing consensus on effective legal protocols for cyber security. The debate centres on whether the UN should oversee national activities in cyberspace. Some Member States argue that existing international laws suffice to address cyber threats and express concerns that expanding these laws could infringe on national sovereignty and limit their freedom of action.[38]

In the current landscape of international law, cyberspace is primarily regarded as an extension of existing legal frameworks, where cyber-attacks are considered legally equivalent to physical attacks, as noted in the discussion on the 'Martens Clause' above. This approach largely avoids classifying cyber threats as a distinct category, thus sidestepping the need for specialized treatment. However, there has been some interest within the General Assembly and the Security Council in addressing cyber threats through the establishment of new norms for cyber response and utilization.[39]

Nevertheless, the disparity between international risks and national capabilities in cyberspace undermines the potential for decisive UN action, even in critical situations. Despite this challenge, many Member States argue that the stakes are too high to overlook the growing imperative for the entire UN community to play an active role in responding to the threats posed by cyber-attacks, particularly cyber-terrorism. They advocate for significant efforts to elevate this issue to the forefront of General Assembly debates, where global moral principles are established. The ongoing ambiguity surrounding cyber-attacks perpetuates longstanding questions about their definition, meaning, and repercussions, ultimately benefiting attackers and those with malicious intent on the Internet.[40]

Conclusion: Any Progress is Progress After All

The absence of a centralized coordinating mechanism within the United Nations hinders effective collaboration among various UN agencies with counter-terrorism mandates, limiting their ability to address cyber security challenges comprehensively. Critics argue that the UN system is hindered by the divergent paths taken by its numerous agencies, rather than adopting a unified approach capable of fostering constructive and effective action, including the coordinated formulation of international norms, regulations, or mandates. Additionally, it has also been argued that the calls for more assertive and practically effective measures, beyond mere consensus on principles, seem to have been overlooked.[41]

In the realm of cyberspace, the UN faces a significant obstacle. Member-states hold diverse opinions on whether the UN should oversee national actions in this domain. Powerful nations assert that existing legal principles and treaty laws suffice for addressing cyber-terrorism threats, dismissing the need for UN intervention in international law. Some states fear that expanding international law could limit their national autonomy. While there's a general consensus on treating cyberspace within existing international law, considering cyber-attacks equivalent to physical ones, some advocate for new norms to address cyber threats. Nonetheless, the disparity between global risks and national capabilities weakens the UN's ability to take decisive action in cyberspace when necessary.

4

Protecting the Skies: The Fight against Aviation Terrorism

"Airline travel is hours of boredom interrupted by moments of stark terror."
—Al Boliska

Impact of Aviation Terrorism: From Psychological to Physical

Skyjacked Fear: The Psychological Impact of Aviation Terrorism

Aircraft terrorism, through hijackings, bombings, or attacks on airline facilities, has an outsized effect on public perception compared to other forms of civilian targeting. This is largely due to the *availability heuristic*, a cognitive bias where people overestimate the likelihood of events that are vivid or widely reported. High-profile aviation incidents reinforce this bias, causing many to overrate the risks of air travel despite its strong safety record relative to other transport modes.[1]

Such attacks have consequences that go far beyond physical damage. They trigger political, economic, and psychological ripples, with terrorist groups deliberately targeting aviation to gain publicity and instil fear. The enduring images of 9/11 illustrate how aviation terrorism can leave lasting emotional and symbolic scars.

In recent decades, the aviation sector has seen a rise in sustained terrorist and criminal threats. Everyone onboard—crew, staff, and passengers—is vulnerable. Large aircraft, with minimal crew but many passengers are ideal targets for small, well-organized terrorist groups. These attackers can overpower the crew and control the plane, especially if passengers come largely from one country, increasing pressure on that nation to meet the hijackers' demands.

From Chesterton to 9/11: A Century of Aviation Sabotage

Hijackings by groups such as Khalistani militants, Palestinians, and other Arab terrorists have shown the intense fear and disruption such acts can cause. These incidents also reveal how hijackings can serve as tools of political coercion, putting immense pressure on targeted nations. Even obscure groups can gain global attention through a single hijacking, making aircraft attractive targets. The relative ease of access and potential for high-impact outcomes add to their appeal.

Aircraft hijackings were frequent in the latter half of the 20th century, peaking in 1969 with 85 incidents in one year. A gradual decline followed, driven by stricter security protocols, improved coordination among security agencies, and growing public condemnation of terrorism. In response, terrorists shifted tactics to attacking aircraft and aviation infrastructure through sabotage and bombings.[2]

One of the earliest known acts of air sabotage was the 1933 United Airlines Chesterton crash, where a Boeing 247 was destroyed by a bomb, likely nitroglycerin. Though a gangland motive was suspected, the case remains unsolved and is believed to be the first proven act of commercial aviation sabotage.[3] Numbers vary based on definitions and inclusion criteria for 'sabotage bombings.' Successful mid-air bombings often leave little evidence, making it hard to identify perpetrators.

Terrorists use clever tactics to bypass security and smuggle explosives onto planes. They hide plastic explosives using sophisticated concealment methods and may exploit unaware individuals to transport devices. Semtex, a powerful plastic explosive with low odour and vapour emission, is commonly used. Terrorists mould it into innocent-looking items, such as toiletries or toys, or embed it in luggage to avoid detection.

In a 1990 disclosure, Czechoslovakian President Václav Havel revealed that the former regime had supplied over 1,000 tons of Semtex to Libyan leader Muammar Gaddafi, who likely distributed it to Arab terrorist groups. As only 200 grams can destroy a jumbo jet mid-air, this supply could have served terrorist needs for over 150 years.

The Threat from Above: A Look at Indian Aviation Hijackings

India has experienced numerous hijackings since the mid-20th century, each leaving a lasting mark. A major early case occurred in 1971 when a Pakistan-based militant group diverted an Indian Airlines flight to Lahore. Although passengers and crew were released following intervention by Pakistan's Prime Minister, the aircraft was burned by Kashmiri militants.

On September 10, 1976, six Kashmiri militants hijacked a Boeing 737 at Delhi's Palam Airport. The plane was rerouted to Karachi due to fuel shortage, and after a stop in Lahore, diplomatic coordination led to the safe return of 83 passengers and crew. The hijackers were drugged during breakfast and arrested but later released in Pakistan for "lack of evidence."[4]

This incident led to the suspension of 11 Indian security personnel and a review of aviation security. In 1978, two members of a political party's youth wing tried to hijack a Delhi-Nepal flight but surrendered after political mediation.

On September 29, 1981, Sikh separatists hijacked IC-423 and diverted it to Lahore, where Pakistani commandos rescued all passengers. Later that year, Air India Flight 224 was hijacked during a refuelling stop in Seychelles by 43 mercenaries, ending after prolonged negotiations.[5]

On August 5, 1982, Sikh militant Gurbaksh Singh Majithia hijacked a Delhi-Srinagar flight with a fake bomb to protest a ban on kirpans. Denied landing in Lahore, the plane returned to Amritsar, where he surrendered.[6]

Just two weeks later, on August 20, 1982, another Sikh militant hijacked a Boeing 737 en route from Jodhpur to Delhi. Denied landing in Lahore, the plane returned to Amritsar, where the hijacker was shot dead by commandos.[7]

On July 5, 1984, flight IC 405 was hijacked from Srinagar to Delhi and diverted to Lahore. All 254 passengers were released after 17 hours. On August 24, 1984, seven youth hijacked IC 421 demanding to be flown to the U.S. Instead, they were diverted to Dubai, where UAE officials negotiated the release. One hijacker was extradited.[8]

On September 5, 1986, four Abu Nidal Organization terrorists hijacked Pan Am Flight 73 in Karachi. The attack killed or injured 43 people. Flight attendant Neerja Bhanot heroically helped passengers escape but was killed. She posthumously received India's highest civilian gallantry award, the Ashok Chakra.[9]

In 1993, Indian Airlines Flight 810 was hijacked by a man demanding the release of karsevaks detained after the Babri Masjid demolition. He surrendered after speaking with Atal Bihari Vajpayee, the then leader of BJP; the bomb was fake.[10]

That same year, Hari Singh, a truck driver disturbed by communal riots, hijacked Flight 439. Denied asylum in Pakistan, he surrendered in Amritsar. His "explosives" turned out to be a hairdryer.[11]

On April 10, 1993, four students hijacked a Lucknow-Delhi flight, forcing it to return. Security forces subdued them on landing.[12]

The most notorious hijacking occurred in 1999 when Jaish-e-Mohammed militants took over an Indian Airlines flight from Kathmandu to Delhi. The week-long ordeal ended with the release of three jailed terrorists in exchange for hostages. The crisis exposed major gaps in aviation security.[13]

Though less frequent today, hijackings remain a concern. India has since strengthened aviation security through dedicated agencies like the Bureau of Civil Aviation Security and a special anti-hijack wing of the NSG. Enhanced screening, technology, and international cooperation continue to safeguard Indian skies.

International Legal Regime Governing Aviation Terrorism: Issues and Concerns

Standardization of Protocols Governing Aviation Security

The atrocities of the two world wars and the League of Nations' failures highlighted the urgent need for a unified international body with robust legal mechanisms to ensure global peace. Standardizing protocols for shared interests emerged as a viable solution. The United Nations Charter, while upholding the principle of sovereign equality, recognized the preeminent role of the Big Five nations (the victors of World War II) in maintaining international peace and security. In its landmark 1949 ruling on the '*Reparation for Injuries Case*,' the International Court of Justice affirmed the United Nations' capacity and obligation to assert claims directly against states within the framework of international law, despite not being a state itself.[14]

The '*Reparation for Injuries Suffered in the Service of the United Nations*' case has implications for aviation security and terrorism. It establishes the United Nations' legal capacity to protect its agents, including those working in the aviation sector. This could be particularly relevant in cases where UN personnel are involved in counter-terrorism operations or investigations related to aviation security. By affirming the UN's right to seek reparation for injuries suffered by its agents, the case provides a legal framework for holding states accountable for any harm caused to UN personnel or its agencies in the context of aviation security.

The first international legal instrument governing civil aviation security was the Convention on International Civil Aviation, also known as the '*Chicago Convention*', which was signed in 1944. While the Chicago Convention primarily focused on establishing principles and procedures for international civil aviation, including rules for airspace, aircraft registration, and safety protocols, it laid the groundwork for subsequent agreements and protocols aimed at addressing aviation security threats, including terrorism. Over time, various international treaties and agreements have been established to combat aviation terrorism, building upon the principles outlined in the Chicago Convention.[15]

Since 1963, the international community through the United Nations system has evolved *nineteen* international legal instruments against terrorism out of which about a fourth are focussed towards unlawful interference with civil aviation. A list briefly outlining such conventions that would be most appropriate here.

1. *1963 Convention on Offences and Certain Other Acts Committed on Board Aircraft*
    - Applies to acts affecting in-flight safety;
    - Authorizes the aircraft commander to impose reasonable measures, including restraint, on any person he or she has reason to believe has committed or is about to commit such an act, where necessary to protect the safety of the aircraft; and
    - Requires contracting States to take custody of offenders and to return control of the aircraft to the lawful commander.
2. *1970 Convention for the Suppression of Unlawful Seizure of Aircraft*
    - Makes it an offence for any person on board an aircraft in flight to "unlawfully, by force or threat thereof, or any other form of intimidation, [to] seize or exercise control of that aircraft" or to attempt to do so;
    - Requires parties to the convention to make hijackings punishable by "severe penalties"
    - Requires parties that have custody of offenders to either extradite the offender or submit the case for prosecution; and
    - Requires parties to assist each other in connection with criminal proceedings brought under the Convention.

3. *1971 Convention for the Suppression of Unlawful Acts against the Safety of Civil Aviation. (Montreal Convention)*
   - Makes it an offence for any person unlawfully and intentionally to perform an act of violence against a person on board an aircraft in flight, if that act is likely to endanger the safety of the aircraft; to place an explosive device on an aircraft; to attempt such acts; or to be an accomplice of a person who performs or attempts to perform such acts;
   - Requires parties to the Convention to make offences punishable by "severe penalties"; and
   - Requires parties that have custody of offenders to either extradite the offender or submit the case for prosecution.
4. *1988 Protocol for the Suppression of Unlawful Acts of Violence at Airports Serving International Civil Aviation supplementary to the Convention for the Suppression of Unlawful Acts against the Safety of Civil Aviation*
   - Extends the provisions of the Montreal Convention to encompass terrorist acts at airports serving international civil aviation
5. *2010 Convention on the Suppression of Unlawful Acts Relating to International Civil Aviation*
   - Criminalizes the act of using civil aircraft as a weapon to cause death, injury or damage;
   - Criminalizes the act of using civil aircraft to discharge biological, chemical and nuclear (BCN) weapons or similar substances to cause death, injury or damage, or the act of using such substances to attack civil aircraft;
   - Criminalizes the act of unlawful transport of BCN weapons or certain related material;
   - A cyber-attack on air navigation facilities constitutes an offence;
   - A threat to commit an offence may be an offence by itself, if the threat is credible.
   - Conspiracy to commit an offence, or its equivalence, is punishable.
6. *2010 Protocol Supplementary to the Convention for the Suppression of Unlawful Seizure of Aircraft*
   - Supplements the Convention for the Suppression of Unlawful Seizure of Aircraft by expanding its scope to cover different forms of aircraft hijackings, including through modern technological means;

- Incorporates the provisions of Beijing Convention relating to a threat or conspiracy to commit an offence.

7. *2014 Protocol to Amend the Convention on Offences and Certain Acts Committed on Board Aircraft. (Third Montreal Convention)*

The International Civil Aviation Organization

The International Civil Aviation Organization (ICAO) sets global standards for aviation security. Through Annex 17 of the Chicago Convention, it outlines measures for passenger and baggage screening, cargo checks, and the protection of aircraft and airport facilities. By promoting consistent security practices worldwide, ICAO plays a vital role in safeguarding global air travel.

A core function of ICAO is developing international standards and recommended practices (SARPs) for aviation security. These guidelines help member states implement effective measures and reduce the risk of terrorist attacks.

ICAO also encourages international cooperation to combat aircraft-related terrorism. This includes sharing threat information, conducting joint investigations, and developing counterterrorism best practices. Such collaboration enhances the global aviation system's security and resilience.

'Either Extradite or Prosecute'

The legal framework addressing terrorism involving aircraft is a vital aspect of both international and domestic law, aimed at protecting civil aviation and countering terrorist threats. Incidents such as the September 11, 2001 attacks highlighted the urgent necessity for robust legal instruments to deter and respond to terrorist acts against aircraft and passengers. A foundational principle in this area, as defined by the ICAO, is '*autdedereaut judicare*'.

This principle obligates states to either prosecute individuals reasonably suspected of terrorist activities or extradite them to a requesting state under applicable treaties. It bars states from providing safe haven to hijackers or those committing acts of unlawful interference, and rejects any justification for impunity based on political or ideological grounds.

Despite the comprehensive obligations under international conventions, enforcement remains a challenge. Where a state fails to comply, such as by refusing extradition or declining to prosecute offenders, recourse is generally limited to diplomatic or peaceful sanctions endorsed by the international community. These measures are often inadequate deterrents. Several cases illustrate this shortfall, including the Achille Lauro affair, Egypt's non-compliance with the 1979 Hostages Convention, Italy's failure to execute its 1983 extradition treaty with the USA, and the inaction or complicity of the Taliban regime and Pakistan in the 1999 Air India hijacking from Kathmandu.

Gaps in the Law: The Challenge of Enforcing Aviation Security Conventions

A key deficiency in international civil aviation security instruments is the absence of clear provisions stating that unlawful interference, particularly terrorist acts, does not qualify as a political offense and thus should not be exempt from extradition. This omission is significant, as many aviation-related terrorist acts are politically or ideologically motivated.

Moreover, despite containing standardized civil aviation security protocols, the Annexes to the Chicago Convention, developed by the ICAO, are often treated by contracting parties as non-binding. These Annexes employ mandatory language, stipulating that states *shall* comply, yet their authority is frequently downplayed.

Although the 1944 Chicago Convention granted ICAO jurisdiction over technical aviation matters irrespective of territorial sovereignty, not all member states accept this authority in practice. Civil aviation is inherently technical and requires uniform adherence to global standards, regardless of an aircraft's location. Nevertheless, many states persist in invoking the "sovereignty clause," often unreasonably, thereby obstructing the consistent and effective implementation of ICAO's universal standards.

No Safe Haven: Criminalizing Aircraft Seizure and Related Offences

The definition of hijacking and other forms of unlawful aircraft seizure remains vague and inconsistent. The use of the term *unlawful* itself introduces ambiguity, as a universally accepted legal definition, transcending localized jurisdictions, is necessary for international application. However, national sovereignty over legal jurisdiction has impeded such a unified definition. Still, various international agreements have fostered a common understanding, if not a precise legal standard, of what constitutes unlawful seizure.

Despite a surge in hijackings during the 1960s, the first major international convention addressing aircraft seizure did not emerge until 1970. Hijacking, generally understood as the forcible takeover of an aircraft in flight by someone on board, remained common until 1973, when passenger and baggage screening protocols were introduced. These significantly curtailed hijackings but pushed perpetrators toward more sophisticated methods, such as concealing weapons and explosives.

The peak year for hijackings was 1985, which prompted stringent aviation security reforms and led to a sharp decline by late 1986. Yet, despite a growing consensus on the global threat posed by aviation terrorism, the international community has failed to adopt a universal legal definition. It remains imperative that such acts be treated as criminal offenses, irrespective of national legal frameworks or jurisdictional barriers.

Efforts of the International Community to an Agreed Definition of Aviation Terrorism Offences

A universally accepted definition of aviation terrorism does not seek to impose a single political ideology. While full consensus on every offense is unlikely, states can at least ensure hijacking is consistently criminalized and punished, regardless of political or ideological motives. Consistency and impartiality are essential in addressing this issue. Below is a summary of international efforts to define hijacking and related offences:

1. *Tokyo Convention (1963)*: This convention addresses offenses committed on board aircraft registered in a contracting state while in flight or over international zones. It defines an aircraft as in flight from the start of take-off power until the landing run ends. The convention includes acts of unlawful control or interference, emphasizing hijacking but lacks a detailed definition.
2. *Hague Convention (1970)*: Article 1 defines hijacking as unlawful seizure or control of an aircraft by force, threat, or intimidation while on board. It criminalizes accomplices and attempted hijackings. However, it does not cover remote hijacking or sabotage (e.g., via explosives) and excludes incidents before the aircraft doors are closed, creating definitional gaps.
3. *Montreal Convention (1971)*: Rather than defining hijacking, it covers a broader range of offenses affecting aircraft safety, including remote acts and spreading false information. It applies even when the perpetrator is not on board and does not require the aircraft's doors to be closed.

At the domestic level, states implement legal frameworks aligned with these conventions. These laws typically criminalize aviation terrorism, prescribe penalties, and facilitate international cooperation. They also cover preventive measures like passenger screening, cargo checks, and protection of aviation infrastructure.

Definitional Conundrum: Attempts for a Universal Definition of Hijacking

Despite ongoing efforts, the international community still lacks a clear, universally accepted definition of hijacking. This definitional gap, coupled with the absence of enforcement mechanisms for states that fail to prevent aviation terrorism, weakens global counterterrorism efforts. Repeated hijacking incidents reveal a politically charged and inconsistent legal process, where critical frameworks are often diluted. Without unified standards, consistent protocols, and a rejection of political justifications for violence, effective global action remains out of reach.

A key requirement in countering aviation terrorism is the denial of safe haven to offenders, particularly hijackers. This demands a universally recognized legal framework, aligned with international aviation conventions, that criminalizes aircraft seizure and mandates either prosecution or extradition. Political motives must never shield such crimes. Strengthening global law enforcement cooperation is therefore vital.

Aviation terrorism must be addressed not only as individual criminality but also as a threat to international peace. This includes investigating state complicity, as many attacks are facilitated by rogue regimes. Minimizing hijacking as mere '*unlawful interference*' ignores its reality as a transnational crime that disrupts global security.

Initial steps toward multilateral legal action came with a 1971 US-Canada draft convention proposing ICAO leadership in arbitration. The 1978 Bonn Declaration, endorsed by G7 leaders, urged sanctions against states sheltering hijackers. Though non-binding and hindered by legal ambiguities, it was a major acknowledgment of state accountability in aviation terrorism. The participation of major airlines and manufacturers underscored the economic and moral urgency. Genuine deterrence demands global consensus that harbouring hijackers is both indefensible and damaging.[16]

A United Front: The Global Imperative to Combat Aviation Terrorism

Acts of terrorism targeting international aviation require a firm and coordinated global response. Severe consequences for perpetrators and complicit states are essential to deter such threats. A robust, transnational legal and enforcement framework must ensure that no safe haven exists for aviation terrorists.

1. *Universal Definition:* A standardized, universally accepted definition of aviation terrorism is imperative, as incidents of hijacking or sabotage inevitably affect multiple jurisdictions.
2. *Strengthened ICAO Mandate:* ICAO must be empowered to act decisively, in coordination with Interpol and national intelligence agencies. Developed countries, with their technological capabilities, should lead these efforts. Clear protocols for intelligence sharing and operational cooperation between ICAO, Interpol, and member states would aid both in rapid response and in preventing attacks before they occur.
3. *Clarity over Ideology:* The international community must treat aviation terrorism, including hijacking, as a singular global threat—regardless of political or ideological motives. National sovereignty must not obstruct international action.
4. *Defined Sanctions for Non-Compliance:* States that fail to cooperate, refuse extradition, or obstruct enforcement mechanisms should face predefined, impartial sanctions. Under Article 2(7) of the UN Charter, while domestic jurisdiction is generally respected, the Security Council retains authority to act in response to threats to international peace—aviation terrorism clearly qualifies.
5. *Sovereignty as a Duty, not a Barrier:* In the face of threats to passengers' lives, decisive international action must take precedence. Modern sovereignty entails obligations within international legal frameworks. States today retain only the authority consistent with their responsibilities to the global community.

Beyond Hijacking: The Evolving Threat of Aviation Terrorism

Terrorist organizations have shown alarming ingenuity in targeting civil aviation, exploiting it as a high-impact, low-risk platform for mass casualties and global attention. These attacks often involve detailed planning and resources, ranging from aircraft hijackings to the destruction of aircraft in flight or on the ground, and assaults on aviation infrastructure or ground targets using hijacked planes.

Acts of Sabotage

Sabotage in aviation poses a serious threat to global air travel, creating significant challenges for international security. It involves deliberate disruption of aircraft or infrastructure to cause harm, destruction, or operational failure. Motivations range from political and ideological extremism to criminal intent, but the consequences, loss of life, fear, and economic impact, are universally severe.[17]

In the late 20th century, several major sabotage incidents exposed critical vulnerabilities in aviation security. The most devastating example remains the September 11, 2001 attacks, where four hijacked planes were used to strike iconic U.S. landmarks, killing nearly 3,000 people and transforming global security protocols.

An early case was Turkish Airlines Flight 181 in 1974, hijacked by Palestinian militants and diverted multiple times before German forces intervened. While all hostages were rescued, three hijackers and one passenger died.[18]

The 1985 bombing of Air India Flight 182 by Sikh extremists, which killed all 329 onboard, remains a grim reminder of politically driven sabotage. That same year, the hijacking of Egypt Air Flight 648 by Palestinian militants claimed 58 lives, highlighting the increasing complexity of such attacks and the difficulty of response.

In 1988, Pan Am Flight 103 was bombed over Lockerbie, Scotland, killing 270 people, including 11 on the ground. Libyan involvement led to international outrage and calls for justice. This tragedy spurred the International Civil Aviation Organization (ICAO) to focus more intently on detecting explosives and enhancing preventive security.

Ground Attacks on the Aviation Industry

The history of armed assaults on airports and individuals highlights the persistent threat violent extremists pose to civil aviation. From the early days of commercial air travel, airports and aircraft have been prime targets for terrorist groups seeking to spread fear, cause destruction, and advance ideological or political agendas.

One early and deadly example of international terrorism was the 1972

Lod Airport massacre in Tel Aviv, Israel—now Ben Gurion Airport. On May 30, three members of the Japanese Red Army (JRA), acting in collaboration with the Popular Front for the Liberation of Palestine (PFLP), carried out a brutal assault using Czech-made *Vz. 58* assault rifles and grenades hidden in violin cases. The attack killed 26 people, including 17 Christian pilgrims from Puerto Rico, and injured over 80 others.

In this incident, the JRA, a militant communist group seeking global revolution, demonstrated how terrorist organizations could collaborate across ideological and national lines to carry out violence far from their home countries. This incident highlighted the growing globalization of terrorism and the difficulty of predicting or preventing attacks when traditional security frameworks failed to consider transnational alliances. It underscored the urgent need for international cooperation in intelligence sharing and counterterrorism strategies.[19]

The 1970s and 1980s saw a surge in airport and aircraft attacks by groups such as the Popular Front for the Liberation of Palestine (PFLP), the Abu Nidal Organization, and the Irish Republican Army (IRA). These assaults caused numerous deaths and severely disrupted air travel across Europe, the Middle East, and beyond.

The Liberation Tigers of Tamil Eelam (LTTE) were among the first to integrate sabotage of civil and military aviation into their operations. They created the first terrorist air force and on March 26, 2007, launched an aerial assault on a Sri Lankan military base near Colombo. They later attacked Katunayake and Bandaranaike International Airports, destroying several civilian and military aircraft.

State-sponsored aviation terrorism also became prominent in the 1980s. In 1988, Libyan agents bombed Pan Am Flight 103 over Lockerbie, Scotland, killing 259 on board and 11 on the ground, reportedly in retaliation for U.S. airstrikes on Libya.[20]

The September 11, 2001 attacks, involving the hijacking of four planes and the destruction of the World Trade Centre and damage to the Pentagon, marked a turning point in aviation terrorism. Later attacks, including the 2015 bombing of Metrojet Flight 9268 over Sinai and the 2016 Brussels Airport and Maalbeek metro bombings, further underscore aviation's vulnerability.

Legal consequences have followed many of these attacks. In *Buanocore vs. Trans World Airlines Inc.*, the court ruled the airline was not liable for John

Buanocore's death during the 1985 terrorist attack at Rome's da Vinci Airport, as it had no control over his actions. This case illustrates the legal complexities of assigning liability in aviation terrorism.

Surface-to-air Missile Attacks

Surface-to-air missile (SAM) attacks in the context of aviation terrorism have posed a persistent and alarming threat to civil aviation for decades. The use of SAMs to target aircraft represents an exceptionally lethal form of terrorism capable of inflicting mass casualties and widespread fear.[21]

Some of the earliest documented instances of SAM attacks on civilian aircraft took place during the 1970s and 1980s, particularly in conflict zones like the Middle East and Central America. In late 1978 and early 1979, two *Air Rhodesia* aircraft were destroyed by SAM missiles, resulting in significant casualties. Notably, during the Arab-Israeli conflict in 1973, Israeli civilian airliners were deliberately targeted by surface-to-air missiles fired by Egyptian forces, leading to the destruction of several aircraft and resulting in numerous fatalities.

The 1980s saw a significant increase in SAM attacks, with various militant groups and state actors employing these weapons to target commercial airliners. For instance, in 1983, Korean Air Flight 007 was shot down by a Soviet interceptor aircraft after straying into Soviet airspace, resulting in the deaths of all 269 passengers and crew onboard.[22]

More recently, terrorist organizations and insurgent groups have increasingly utilized SAMs to target aircraft in conflict zones and politically unstable regions. The downing of Malaysia Airlines Flight 17 over eastern Ukraine by a surface-to-air missile in 2014, resulting in the deaths of all 298 passengers and crew onboard, underscored the dangers posed by the proliferation of advanced weaponry and highlighted the need for enhanced aviation security measures.

In the USA, for example, the Aviation and Transportation Security Act (ATSA) of 2001 was enacted in response to the September 11 attacks, enhancing security measures at airports and onboard aircraft. The ATSA established the Transportation Security Administration (TSA) to oversee aviation security and implement screening procedures for passengers and baggage. It also introduced requirements for hardened cockpit doors, air marshal programs, and enhanced security screening protocols.[23]

From Cocaine to Catastrophe: The Link between Drugs and Aviation Terrorism

Aviation terrorism involving narcotics and psychotropic substances presents a serious threat to global security and public health. It enables terrorist groups and criminal networks to exploit the vast aviation system, over 20,000 aircraft operating daily, to traffic drugs across borders, fund terror activities, and undermine the rule of law.[24]

Narco-terrorism primarily involves two activities: airborne drug trafficking and drug handling at airports. These operations are closely linked. In 1987, the UN International Conference on Drug Abuse and Illicit Trafficking highlighted the harmful impact of drug smuggling on civil aviation. This led the ICAO to adopt Resolution A27-12, urging states to implement preventive guidelines.[25]

The UN Office on Drugs and Crime (UNODC) plays a key role in addressing this issue through strategic partnerships and targeted programs. With increased global travel, traffickers use commercial airlines, cargo planes, and private jets—often concealing drugs in luggage, shipments, or human carriers. These acts may involve coercion, violence, and corruption.[26]

The consequences are global and severe: destabilizing regions, eroding governance, fuelling addiction and violence, and providing financial support to terrorist organizations. To counter this, UNODC launched AIRCOP, a joint initiative with INTERPOL and WCO. AIRCOP strengthens law enforcement coordination at international airports, targeting high-risk passengers, cargo, and mail.

AIRCOP helps disrupt drug smuggling, terrorism-related threats, and human trafficking by enhancing inter-agency collaboration between origin, transit, and destination countries. Currently active in 41 airports across Africa, Latin America, the Caribbean, the Middle East, and Asia, it provides training, equipment, and technical support to improve interdiction capacity.[27]

Beyond AIRCOP, UNODC supports governments with legal tools, intelligence-sharing, and border control strategies. It promotes adherence to key frameworks like the UN Convention Against Illicit Traffic in Narcotic Drugs, ICAO security standards, and its own model legislation on drugs and money laundering.

Intelligence Blindspots and Aviation Terrorism: Bojinka Plot, 9/11 failure and more

In 1995, Filipino police and fire fighters accidentally uncovered a terrorist cell manufacturing explosives in a Manila apartment. Investigations revealed that Abdul Basit, the mastermind behind the 1993 World Trade Centre bombing, was involved. Although Basit escaped, his accomplice Hakim Murad was captured. Authorities later discovered their plan, code-named *Bojinka*, to bomb multiple commercial aircraft.[28]

It is a matter of fact that Philippine police shared their findings with the FBI, which chose to ignore them, considering the information unreliable. As a law enforcement agency, the FBI may have hesitated to act on intelligence sourced abroad due to legal and evidentiary concerns. The CIA, however, collected and circulated a report from its Manila contacts, but the FBI withheld this report from American airlines, fearing it would compromise ongoing investigations. Eventually, a diluted version was share which was unfortunately, too late to be of any use. The only solace on the entire fiasco? the Bojinka plot was never executed.[29]

In another case, the FBI's Minnesota office flagged Zaccaria Moussai, who was undergoing flight training but oddly showed no interest in learning to take off or land. Meanwhile, another FBI branch requested permission to investigate foreign Muslims attending U.S. flight schools. Years earlier, Hakim Murad had confessed plans to hijack aircraft and crash them into CIA headquarters. Despite these warnings, inter-agency silos and bureaucracy prevented timely analysis and coordination. Experts argue that such fragmentation contributed directly to the intelligence failure preceding 9/11.[30]

Had ICAO or a related body maintained a central system for gathering and analysing such intelligence, airlines might have received advance warnings. Instead, even within a single country, vital information was lost to bureaucratic infighting. This highlights the urgent need to ensure that any threat to aviation reported by any agency is swiftly conveyed to ICAO and its global network. It would be much better if ICAO had its own network of gathering credible information.

Drones in the Sky: A New Threat to Aviation

We all know that an Unmanned Aerial Vehicle (UAV), commonly referred to as a 'drone,' is a powered aerial vehicle without a human operator onboard.

However, the definition of drone is any unmanned vehicle (whether autonomous or not). There are underwater and terrestrial 'drones' that are not called drones. Drones are commonly employed for numerous purposes such as monitoring, gathering intelligence, research, military missions, and business operations. They are fitted with various technologies, including sensors and cameras, to perform these functions. Their size can range from compact, consumer-level models to large, military-grade devices.

UAVs operate through remote control or autonomously, utilizing onboard AI protocols. UAVs rely on aerodynamic forces for lift and can be designed for both expendable or recoverable missions. These devices can carry various payloads, including lethal and non-lethal options.

UAV technology is advancing rapidly, initially used for targeting human subjects in armed drone operations by US and Israeli security forces. UAVs are now employed in various beneficial sectors such as emergency response, agriculture, fire fighting, pipeline monitoring, and consumer goods delivery. However, criminals and terrorists have also exploited UAVs for illicit purposes, including intelligence gathering, surveillance, and smuggling illicit materials such as narcotics, arms, ammunition, and counterfeit currency.[31]

The misuse of UAVs includes disrupting law enforcement operations, air traffic control, and public gatherings, as well as potential cyber attacks and explosive deliveries, including chemical, biological, and radiological agents.[32]

As early as 1995, the Japanese cult Aum Shinrikyo planned to use remote-controlled helicopters to disperse Sarin gas in the Tokyo subway. Similarly, Osama Bin Laden aimed to use remote-controlled aircraft loaded with explosives to assassinate President George W. Bush and other leaders at the G-8 Summit in Genoa, Italy.[33]

Terrorist groups increasingly use commercially available UAVs to transport arms, explosives, and narcotics across borders. Drones equipped with high-resolution cameras allow terrorists to conduct reconnaissance and surveillance, evading detection and enabling the smooth movement of illicit goods.[34]

Additionally, UAVs facilitate the transport of narcotics, offering stealth and agility, allowing narco-terrorists to bypass traditional border controls. This method enables them to evade detection by authorities, strengthening their operational capabilities.[35]

Modern UAVs are equipped with advanced AI algorithms, self-correction features, improved geo-location, and full autonomy, making their operation increasingly sophisticated. They are commonly equipped with visual recognition, thermal cameras, LiDAR, and multispectral sensors, enhancing their effectiveness in reconnaissance and surveillance.[36]

A significant advancement is the 'Swarm' capability, where multiple drones are coordinated for larger attacks. In 2018, a drone swarm targeted Russian bases in Syria, delivering bombs from over 50 kilometres away.[37] The civilian drone market, valued at $ 43 billion by 2024, indicates rapid growth and accessibility.[38]

Terrorist organizations continue to exploit UAV technology for weapon transport, reconnaissance, and direct attacks on military and civilian targets, using armed drones with improvised explosive devices (IEDs) for attacks on government buildings, military installations, and public gatherings. These operations instil fear and instability, leading to significant casualties and property damage.[39]

The proliferation of UAV technology has democratized aerial capabilities, allowing both state and non-state actors to exploit drones for illicit activities. The affordability and accessibility of UAVs make them an attractive tool for terrorists and criminals.

Although UAVs have been used infrequently in non-combat terrorism, advancements in drone technology—such as high-capacity payloads, extended flight durations, and swarm capabilities—make them an increasingly attractive tool for terrorist activities. As technology advances and drones become more affordable, the potential for misuse grows.

United Against Drone Threats: The Berlin Memorandum

Under the Global Counter Terrorism Forum, member states adopted the Berlin Memorandum on Good Practices for Countering Terrorist Use of Unmanned Aerial Systems, outlining 26 best practices grouped into four key areas:

(i) *Risk Evaluation, Vulnerability Assessment, and Awareness:* States must integrate UAV-related threats into standard risk assessments to identify vulnerabilities and protection gaps. Anticipating evolving terrorist tactics using UAVs is crucial, and each country must evaluate such risks within its national security framework.

(ii) *Clear Regulations and Crisis Protocols:* To deter UAV misuse, enforceable policies must define responsibilities for investigation, prosecution, and sanctioning. Effective counter measures, crisis prevention, and response strategies must be developed, implemented, and widely disseminated.

(iii) *Information Sharing and Stakeholder Collaboration:* Preventing terrorist use of UAVs requires coordinated action among national, regional, and international entities, including non-traditional stakeholders. Common terminology, standard protocols, and unified databases enhance communication and response. Public education, civil aviation coordination, and regulated information sharing—mindful of overload and anxiety—are vital for effective collaboration.

(iv) *Tactical and Technical Counter-measures:* Protective technologies and staff training should be regularly updated. Distinguishing between legitimate and hostile UAVs is critical—using identity chips and enforcing geo-fencing around sensitive sites can aid compliance. Pre-programmed no-fly zones, combined with both kinetic and non-kinetic counter-measures, enhance early threat detection and response.

While nations such as India, Israel, Nigeria, and Ukraine besides the advanced western world, are investing in counter-drone systems, the challenge extends beyond international dialogues. These countries face rising UAV threats from non-state actors, often backed by neighbouring regimes. The involvement of such states cannot be overlooked, and the global community must not tolerate inaction. An effective counter-UAV framework must include punitive measures against countries that fail to prevent UAV attacks originating from their territory.

Drone incursions from Pakistan, mainly for narco-terrorism and related illicit activities, have become an almost daily threat along the Indo-Pak border. Unmanned Aerial Systems (UAS) are increasingly used by criminal and terrorist groups to smuggle narcotics, arms, and surveillance tools into Indian territory. The frequency and sophistication of these incursions suggest a coordinated nexus between drug cartels and extremist elements, often aided by hostile state actors.

This ongoing threat compromises national security and border management. In response, Indian forces, especially the Border Security Force (BSF), have upgraded counter-drone capabilities through radar, anti-drone weapons, and jamming systems. Combating this menace requires not just tactical improvements, but also diplomatic efforts and international cooperation to hold complicit states accountable.[40]

India's recent cross-border strikes under '*Operation Sindoor*' against terror targets in Pakistan reflect mounting frustration over the international community's muted response to Pakistan's continued support for proxy terrorism and the emerging threat of drone warfare. These precision operations mark a significant shift in India's strategic posture, moving beyond diplomatic restraint to proactive defence. By calling Pakistan's long-standing 'nuclear bluff,' India has signalled its growing resolve to dismantle terror infrastructure at its roots, regardless of geography. This assertiveness also underscores a changing security doctrine that prioritizes national security over political caution. Operation Sindoor exemplifies India's commitment to taking decisive action when global mechanisms fail to curb cross-border terrorism and highlights the urgent need for unified international pressure on state-sponsored terror networks.

Use of Unmanned Aerial Vehicles as a Counter-terrorism Tool

Like any other weapon, Unmanned Aerial Vehicles (UAVs) can be leveraged as tools in counter-terrorism. Drone use in combat dates back to the Vietnam War, notably with the AQM-34 Firebee, a jet-powered reconnaissance drone employed by the U.S. military since the 1950s. Initially designed for target practice and surveillance, it was capable of long-range, high-altitude missions.

In the 21st century, the U.S. and allied forces have carried out over 14,000 drone strikes targeting terrorist and military sites, particularly in Afghanistan, Pakistan, Somalia, and Yemen. Countries including China, Russia, Israel, and the USA increasingly use drones for identifying high-value targets, surveillance, signature strikes, and disrupting support systems linked to terrorist activity.[41]

While drones offer benefits such as pilot safety, precision, persistent surveillance, and cost-effectiveness, they also raise concerns over long-term effectiveness. Misidentification of civilian targets, the lowered threshold for lethal force, and collateral damage are significant issues. Moreover, terrorist groups exploit drone strikes for propaganda, weakening counterterrorism efforts. The remote nature of drone operations and cultural misunderstandings may also lead to disproportionate responses.[42]

Drone strikes surged under the Obama administration, focusing on militants linked to Al-Qaeda, ISIS, and Boko Haram. Under Trump, increased autonomy for field commanders led to more targeting errors. In October 2022, the Biden administration reinstated restrictions limiting drone use to active war zones, although commanders can still act with presidential approval for operations beyond those zones.

Drone strikes justified under doctrines of pre-emption face growing legal scrutiny. Debates centre on whether such actions meet standards of necessity and proportionality in international law.[43] Some experts argue that drone strikes by dominant powers violate both international law and the human rights of affected civilians.[44] The legal ambiguity is worsened by the absence of a universal judicial or legislative body capable of resolving such issues definitively. Often, legal justifications are shaped diplomatically or asserted unilaterally, with tacit acceptance inferred from global reactions. This challenge is amplified by the hegemonic tendencies of the P-5 members of the UN Security Council.

Balancing Sovereignty and Global Air Connectivity

Civil aviation is among the most heavily regulated industries worldwide, governed by a dual-tier system of international and national oversight. At the global level, the International Civil Aviation Organization (ICAO) plays a central role, while national agencies, such as India's Bureau of Civil Aviation Security (BCAS), implement and enforce standards domestically. This regulatory "duopoly" spans a wide range of aviation issues.

Headquartered in Montreal and operating under the United Nations, the ICAO is mandated to uphold the five freedoms of aviation, which promote international connectivity and cooperation:

1. The right of an aircraft from one nation to fly over another's airspace.
2. The right to land in another country for non-traffic purposes (e.g., refuelling).
3. The right to unload passengers or cargo in another country.
4. The right to board passengers or cargo in another country.
5. The right to carry passengers or cargo between two foreign countries.

These freedoms reflect shared values on the positive impact of aviation on global society. To enforce them, countries established the ICAO, agreeing to partially yield their sovereignty in exchange for common aviation standards. However, the ICAO respects each state's full sovereignty over its airspace, especially concerning security matters, where national control remains paramount.

The ICAO: A Balancing Act between Global Standards and National

Sovereignty

The ICAO plays a pivotal yet limited role in global aviation. Tasked with setting essential standards and protocols, its authority is bounded by the principle of state sovereignty, requiring nations to implement these rules within their own legal systems. Despite this, ICAO has made notable progress in standardizing the technical aspects of aviation, enabling more seamless global air travel.

However, the fragmented nature of the aviation sector, involving multiple stakeholders with differing priorities, complicates regulation. While effective information sharing is crucial to combat aviation terrorism, ICAO lacks a formal intelligence-sharing framework among member states, an important shortcoming given evolving threat.

Several *core challenges* remain:

- ICAO's technical focus is central to its mandate, yet political dynamics among member states often limit its influence.
- Strengthening cooperation and intelligence-sharing while respecting national sovereignty is essential to improving its counterterrorism role.
- Although ICAO leads in technical and economic aviation matters, it lacks similar authority in security, hindered by states' reluctance to cede control.
- Despite recognizing aviation security as critical, most countries are unwilling to empower a supranational body significantly. While there is some exchange of security technologies and intelligence, a structured framework for joint action remains absent.

To close this gap, ICAO could benefit from a dedicated intelligence and security centre, developed in collaboration with industry bodies like IATA. This would enhance its preventive capacity and better equip it to address future threats to global aviation.

Safeguarding Our Skies: A Blueprint for Preventing Aviation Terrorism

Aviation terrorism—a distinct and high-impact form of violence—poses exceptional challenges due to the symbolic and strategic value of air travel. Its definition remains fluid, shaped by evolving technologies, diverse motivations, and the broader ambiguity surrounding terrorism itself.

This chapter attempted a distillation of the key dimensions of this specialized threat, including its legal, operational, and technological aspects. From the hijackings of the 1970sto today's emerging threats from drones and cyber attacks, the aviation threat landscape is continuously evolving. These developments demand not only tactical vigilance but also systemic and cooperative global responses.

Despite its obvious limitations, the standardization regime under ICAO, has made notable progress. Yet, its effectiveness remains limited by issues of state sovereignty, political inertia, and inconsistent enforcement. Universal criminal provisions for aircraft seizure, sabotage, and unlawful interference must be implemented rigorously to deter and prosecute offenders.

Today's threats extend beyond hijackings to include insider sabotage, aircraft bombings, GPS spoofing, and cyber attacks on air traffic control systems. These evolving challenges demand a comprehensive approach, one that is strengthened by intelligence sharing, standardized airport security protocols, cyber resilience, and capacity-building efforts in less-developed states. Advanced nations must take greater responsibility in supporting the institutional and technical development of these countries, recognizing that the skies have no borders and that terrorists often exploit safe havens in economically disadvantaged regions. International aviation security can only be as strong as its weakest link, making global cooperation not just a moral imperative, but a strategic necessity.

The rapid proliferation of drones and UAVs introduces both risks and opportunities. Their accessibility makes them attractive tools for non-state actors, increasing the potential for airborne attacks on civilian or critical infrastructure. At the same time, these technologies can serve as assets for surveillance and emergency response in aviation security.

Strengthening the ICAO's mandate, ensuring compliance across member states, and fostering real-time intelligence coordination are no longer optional, they are vital. Preventing aviation terrorism requires a global commitment to adaptive strategies, legal consensus, and technological innovation to keep our skies truly safe.

5

Counter-Terrorism Legislation in India: Evolution, Issues, and Trends

"It is the spirit and not the form of law that keeps justice alive."

—**Earl Warren**

Indian Experience with Special Counter-Terrorism Laws: Issues and Challenges

Colonial Legacies

India has a long-standing tradition of enacting robust legal frameworks to combat subversive activities such as terrorism—a legacy shaped by both historical necessity and constitutional evolution. The complexity of anti-terror legislation in India is deeply intertwined with its colonial past, where the British Governor-General wielded extraordinary powers to enact laws without legislative debate. This executive authority, akin to issuing orders in times of urgency, allowed swift responses to threats but often bypassed democratic processes.

Following independence, India's Constitution preserved a similar mechanism: the President's power to promulgate ordinances during exceptional circumstances. This provision serves as a vital tool, enabling the government to address urgent security challenges—such as terrorism—without delay, especially when regular legislation might face prolonged opposition or controversy. However, unlike the unchecked colonial era, India's constitutional safeguards now ensure this power is not misused. Judicial review by the higher courts acts as a vigilant guardian, scrutinizing ordinances to maintain their adherence to constitutional values and human rights.

This dynamic balance between urgency and accountability has been pivotal in shaping India's counter-terrorism laws, allowing the state to respond decisively to emerging threats while upholding the rule of law. It reflects India's ongoing commitment to protect its citizens without compromising democratic principles—a tradition that continues to evolve in the face of modern challenges.

Defence of India Acts

During World War I, the British government introduced the Defence of India Act in 1915, adapting Britain's wartime emergency code for India. This Act allowed the Governor-General in Council to issue strict rules and empowered authorities to detain individuals or restrict personal liberty if they had '*reasonable grounds*' to suspect a person's conduct was '*prejudicial to public safety*.'

A second Defence of India Act was enacted in 1939 at the start of World War II, enabling the government to detain anyone whose actions were deemed harmful to British India's defence, public safety, public order, relations with foreign powers, or tribal areas. Special tribunals were created to enforce wartime regulations, which remained in effect until October 1946.

Interestingly, the British did not limit these emergency powers to declared emergencies. Even in peacetime, they extensively used laws for preventive detention and criminalizing offenses against the state. As early as 1818, a Bengal regulation gave the executive broad authority to detain individuals without sufficient grounds for judicial proceedings, citing reasons like maintaining British alliances or security. In practice, this power was often used to suppress dissent against colonial policies.

Detained individuals had no legal right to know or contest the reasons for their confinement. Detention orders had no time limits and were not subject to judicial review. This regulation was extended throughout British India and, after minor revisions, remained in effect long after independence, eventually being replaced by new laws granting similar powers. The British also created laws criminalizing offenses against the state, including sedition, which was first criminalized in India in 1870.

Rowlatt Act: Targeting Anarchical and Revolutionary Crimes?

The British authorities continued to apply wartime and emergency regulations during periods of relative normalcy, particularly against political dissidents and freedom fighters. This culminated in the Anarchical and Revolutionary Crimes Act of 1919, known as the 'Rowlatt Act,' named after its chairperson.

The Rowlatt Act did not define the 'anarchical and revolutionary movements' it aimed to prosecute. Even after the Defence of India Act expired, the Rowlatt Act preserved detention orders and restrictions on movement, originally authorized during the war. It granted new powers to detain individuals for up to two years, based on suspicion of involvement in such activities. In certain areas, individuals could be detained for suspected ties to specific crimes.

While detainees could appear before an investigating authority, these proceedings lacked procedural safeguards. For example, accused person had no right to legal representation, and the authority could withhold any information that it may adjudge to endanger public safety.

The Rowlatt Act served as a precursor to later counter-terrorism laws, enabling preventive detention and limitations on freedom of movement. It also established procedures for criminal cases, allowing hearings in secret, with no right to appeal. Judicial oversight was minimal, requiring the government to present allegations to the Chief Justice of the High Court, who could then decide whether to establish a special court.

Facing widespread opposition, the Rowlatt Act was eventually repealed in 1922. However, during the 1930s, the colonial government continued to use ordinances to suppress the independence movement. The Government of India Act of 1935 gave provincial legislatures the authority to implement preventive detention laws. Initially, Congress-led governments sought to repeal these powers but began relying on them by 1937 to maintain order and control.

Need for Special Laws to Counter Special Crimes: Continuity

Between 1946 and 1950, similar to the need for the Rowlatt Act, provincial governments enacted 'public safety acts' in response to the upcoming expiration of wartime regulations under the Defence of India Act of 1939. These acts allowed for the preventive detention of individuals, even without a declared state of emergency.

The Government of India Act of 1935 granted sweeping powers to provincial governors, enabling them to issue ordinances in response to perceived threats to the '*peace and tranquillity*' of their provinces. These so-called threats were vaguely defined, often targeting individuals accused of engaging in violence or subversive activity against colonial authority. In practice, the act introduced a veiled form of authoritarian rule, framed under the pretence of preserving governmental stability.

Indian leaders of the national freedom movement were quick to condemn these provisions. Jawaharlal Nehru criticized them as an insult to democratic principles, warning that such arbitrary authority could be weaponized against political dissent. Mahatma Gandhi viewed the ordinance powers as a betrayal of civil liberties, accusing the colonial regime of using 'peace and order' as a cloak for repression. The breadth and vagueness of these powers made them ripe for misuse, targeting not just violent actors, but also peaceful protestors and critics of British rule.

Even Winston Churchill, hardly a critic of imperial authority, famously remarked that such powers would '*arouse envy in Mussolini*,' underscoring the authoritarian spirit behind them. These sweeping emergency powers served as a stark reminder of how colonial legislation often masked coercion as constitutional necessity, a legacy that would shape the cautious evolution of emergency provisions in post-independence India.

Persistence of 'Special Circumstances': Secessionism in Post-Independent India

Between 1947 and 1975, India continued many security and emergency provisions from British colonial rule. While the Indian Constitution protected fundamental rights, its emergency and security clauses mirrored those in the Government of India Act of 1935. These provisions allowed extraordinary powers during emergencies and were supplemented by preventive detention laws, enabling the government to exercise similar powers even without a formal emergency.

India's colonial history saw persistent insurgencies and acts of subversion, often aimed at British colonial rule. These movements sought to end foreign domination, with the British responding through harsh laws and repression against those deemed seditious or critical.

The legislative measures introduced by the British laid a foundation that continued after their departure. Since independence, counter-terrorism and security laws have been periodically enacted, revoked, and reinstated. The British-style criminal justice system in India provided a legal framework that allowed the creation of separate laws to address subversive threats. A key feature of these laws during British rule was the enforcement by paternalistic state officials without involving the public for whom the laws were intended.

After independence, the Constitution's framers acknowledged ongoing secessionist movements, like the Naga insurgency. However, attempts to tackle terrorism often repeated the flaws of India's existing criminal justice system. Despite specialized counter-terrorism laws, Indian institutions—police, prosecution, and judiciary—continued to handle both regular and counter-terrorism cases, risking a continuation of human rights violations in this high-pressure field.[1]

A veteran 'Supercop' (*a moniker used in India for senior Indian Police Service officers who distinguish themselves by their remarkable work)* K.P.S. Gill, in his lecture titled '*The Imperatives of National Security Legislation in India*,' argued that India's struggle against politically motivated violence constitutes a *"chronic crisis of national security,"* deeply woven into the fabric of the nation's identity. Statistics support this claim.[2]

As reported by Arun Venugopal in 'India Worst Hit by Terrorism in 2004,' citing the U.S. government's National Counter-terrorism Centre, India faced a significant portion (293 out of 651) of global terrorist attacks in 2004. Furthermore, internal armed conflicts plague 19 out of India's 28 states. However, a critical tension emerges: how can a democracy balance security needs with the protection of fundamental rights? While some argue that democratic states must avoid enacting regressive laws to prevent a slide into authoritarianism, others emphasize the responsibility of governments to protect their citizens. This dilemma highlights the complex challenges in crafting effective counter-terrorism measures that uphold the rule of law and human rights.

Tackling Terror Through Cyclic Legislation? Compulsions of Governance?

Despite a strong awareness of rights among its citizens, India has a history of enacting apparently harsh temporary anti-terrorism laws. These laws are often repealed due to public opposition, concerns about human rights violations, and fears of misuse, leading to them being called 'draconian.' However, the security issues these laws were meant to address often return with renewed intensity.[3]

Governments often turn to alternative laws, less visible to the public that grant similar powers in a different form. While these laws may initially avoid public scrutiny, human rights organizations remain vigilant, raising concerns about potential violations.

India's approach to counter-terrorism legislation follows a recurring pattern. In response to crises, broad anti-terrorism laws are enacted, raising human rights concerns. These laws are then repealed due to public pressure or reduced threats. However, similar laws are often reintroduced later, sometimes with safeguards but occasionally stricter provisions. This cycle reflects a tendency to '*normalize the exceptional*,' granting emergency powers during normal times, which may be accused later to have the tendency to undermine human rights. India's experience, shaped by its colonial past, is not unique. Other democracies with anti-terror regimes based on Western laws can learn from India's approach in balancing effective counter-terrorism measures with human rights.[4]

India's recent efforts to strengthen anti-terrorism laws have been influenced by several factors that includes lessons learnt from its colonial history, cross-border threats, secessionist tendencies in certain regions and its evolving international legal obligations, including UN Security Council resolutions. While these laws aim to combat terrorism, some provisions have sparked debate and criticism. However, it would be worthwhile to focus on concerns from human rights and civil liberties advocates on several key areas.

1. *Broad Definition of Terrorism:* A major concern is the broad definition of terrorism, which critics argue can be misused to criminalize even lawful government criticism. While these definitions may seem ambiguous, similar broad definitions are found in Western anti-terror laws, reflecting the complex and diverse nature of terrorism.
2. *Special Courts and Procedures:* Critics also raise concerns about special courts and their procedures, including issues with bail, witness protection, confessions, and trials. While these courts are specialized, they still adhere to fundamental safeguards against abuse.
3. *Adverse Inferences:* The ability to draw adverse inferences from certain evidence, such as incriminating materials, is criticized as unfairly presuming guilt. However, when such evidence is substantiated, the inference of complicity is often justified.
4. *Prolonged Pre-trial Detention*: Long periods of pre-trial detention can feel like punishment, even if the accused is later acquitted. Courts have criticized investigative agencies for their resistence to grant bail when trials drag on.
5. *Lack of Oversight:* Critics point to insufficient oversight to prevent abuse by police and security forces. The laws lack mechanisms to prevent arbitrary or discriminatory enforcement and provide broad

immunities to government officials, potentially violating the right to a remedy.

6. *Cyclical Enactment and Human Rights Concerns:* India's counter-terrorism laws have been enacted and repealed in cycles over the past 25 years. Despite some improvements, human rights concerns persist, especially under laws like POTA and UAPA, which are seen by some as misused for preventive detention rather than for prosecuting terrorism.

Counter-terrorism laws are not developed in isolation but are part of a broader legal and institutional framework. Their success depends on the effectiveness of the law enforcement, judiciary, and prosecution systems that also handle other serious crimes.

India's criminal justice system, including its counter-terrorism efforts, has evolved with a focus on human rights and civil liberties, influenced by post-colonial constitutional and international legal frameworks. However, certain colonial-era laws persist, originally designed to maintain imperial control, and these remnants can challenge the modern system's fairness and effectiveness.

Despite a rights-conscious constitution, India's independence did not eliminate separatism and division. Some colonial laws were modified but kept their core elements. Critics argue that India's current administrative challenges stem from a fundamental contradiction in its political system, rooted in a bureaucracy and police force that may conflict with the constitution's principles of democracy, federalism, and development.[5]

The legal and institutional framework inherited from the British, including criminal law, procedure, and policing, shows significant continuity in independent India. The Police Act of 1861, established after the 1857 uprising to reinforce British control, still governs India's police force. Often seen as outdated, this act shaped the police into a paramilitary, hierarchical force. Originally designed to help with revenue collection and maintain colonial rule, it differs greatly from the ideal of policing as a guardian of law and community.[6]

The Indian police force originated during the British Raj as a tool for political control and intelligence gathering, serving as a coercive apparatus for the State. Its main focus was enforcing government authority rather than upholding the rule of law. The British reinforced feudalistic values in Indian society by appointing individuals loyal to their superiors, often disregarding the well-being of the local population.[7] However, the criticism goes unabated even after consistent and periodic assessments of police system in India has largely addressed such colonial anomalies during post-independence era.

The Indian independence movement highlighted the coercive tactics used by the police against those seeking self-rule. During the inter-war period (1917-1939), the police force grew significantly, increasing from about 215,000 in 1932 to over 300,000 by 1943. The armed police grew rapidly during this time, making up 45% of the total force by 1943, up from just 15% in 1932.[8] Such heavy reliance on praetorian-style policing, to an extent, apparently fuelled the continuation of such criticism

The Basic Law-enforcement Structure: A Case Sui-generis

The colonial-era structure of law enforcement in India however, has undergone a significant transformation, evolving into a constitutionally defined federal system. In this arrangement, rather than the Union government, the constituent provincial governments (called 'State Government' in India) now hold substantial authority and assume the primary role in day-to-day affairs. So much so that a famous IPS officer said:

> "*It is a lesson new policeman in India learn early on: they are in charge of everything except perhaps the weather. Their duties range from maintaining law and order and investigating crime to rounding up beggars and disposing of unclaimed bodies.*"

The Constitution grants overarching jurisdiction over the police and public order to the states, not the central government.[9]

However, the central government still retains significant control through various paramilitary forces often deployed to assist civil administration. Additionally, agencies like the Central Bureau of Investigation, the National Investigation Agency, and the Enforcement Directorate have the authority to conduct investigations across state boundaries once a case is under their jurisdiction.

The Indian Constitution promotes a unified approach to governance and law enforcement, exemplified by the All-India Service, including the Indian Police Service, which is centrally managed. This system ensures the central government can maintain uniformity of administration and consistent application of law across the nation, regardless of regional political differences.

However, certain experts allege that post-colonial laws aimed at tackling serious crimes still appear to follow the colonial framework, blurring the lines between exceptional and routine circumstances. Emergency powers, initially meant for crises, have become ingrained in the legal system, with preventive detention laws becoming a permanent feature of India's democratic process.[10]

The Role of Emergency Powers in Counter-Terrorism Legislation

India has invoked emergency powers several times, notably during the 1962 Sino-Indian, and 1965 and 1971 Indo-Pakistani conflicts. While the 1962 war ended quickly, emergency measures lasted until 1968. The 1971 war was brief, but the emergency overlapped with a broader state of emergency declared by Indira Gandhi in 1975, lasting until 1977.

The Indian Constitution retains emergency powers similar to those under British rule, including preventive detention without a declared emergency. The 1950 Preventive Detention Act (PDA) allowed detention without trial for up to a year. Initially a temporary measure, the PDA was renewed until 1969, after which the Maintenance of Internal Security Act (MISA) continued similar provisions. These laws gave the government broad detention powers, bypassing procedural safeguards, which critics argue weakened protections.

Despite reforms, the post-Emergency period did not significantly alter preventive detention powers, and the potential to abuse coercive authority has remained largely unhindered.

Post-1980 Challenges to National Security

In the 1980s, India faced growing security challenges, including the Khalistani insurgency, which led to the assassination of Prime Minister Indira Gandhi. This was followed by a breakdown of law and order in Jammu and Kashmir in 1989, exacerbated by the withdrawal of Soviet forces from Afghanistan and the redeployment of foreign terrorists by Pakistani intelligence (ISI), threatening national security. Local police struggled to manage this growing threat, forcing the central government to intervene in Jammu and Kashmir. The Constitution allows the central government to take control during grave situations, which was also necessary in Punjab due to the Khalistani insurgency.

During the early 1980s, the National Security Act was widely used. In response to the Punjab crisis, the central government dismissed the state government and imposed President's Rule in 1983. In 1984, amendments to the National Security Act extended detention periods and allowed the government to bypass the Advisory Board in certain cases. President's Rule in Punjab lasted until 1992. Human rights groups argue that unless comprehensive reforms are made to the police and justice system, the use of special laws will continue, especially in cases deemed of high importance.[11]

Simultaneously, they also argue that the deployment of these special laws could diminish the political determination to embark on the demanding, long-term endeavour of achieving broader reforms. Such reforms are imperative for enhancing the efficacy of the criminal justice system and elevating the overall level of human rights protection. Furthermore, in most instances, these special laws have replicated or exacerbated the human rights issues inherent in the regular system, thereby jeopardizing the system's credibility.[12]

Beyond the Criticism: Compulsions of a Variegated Society

While arguments against the continued use of special security legislation in India have merit, especially regarding human rights, they often lack a viable alternative. India's security challenges are unique, with diverse and region-specific threats. Unlike nations with more uniform security concerns, India faces localized secessionist movements and enduring insurgencies, requiring a legal framework that can adapt to these issues.

Special laws, though often controversial, are a necessary response to these specific threats. They enable the government to address secessionist and insurgent activities more effectively. However, their use must be accompanied by strong safeguards to prevent abuse of power. Balancing national security with the protection of fundamental rights is critical. Regular reviews and a transparent, accountable legal system are essential to ensure the legitimacy and effectiveness of these laws. With this in mind, let's now examine the implications of special security laws in India.

The Armed Forces (Special Powers) Act, 1958

Background

The Armed Forces (Special Powers) Act, 1958, originated from the 1948 Act, which replaced four emergency ordinances issued in 1947 to address internal security challenges after India's partition. The 1948 Act was based on a British ordinance from 1942 used to suppress the Quit India movement. These laws granted the armed forces significant powers, including the use of lethal force in extreme situations of law-and-order disturbances.

The Naga insurgency in the mid-1950s overwhelmed local authorities, prompting central military intervention. In response, the Armed Forces (Assam and Manipur) Special Powers Ordinance was introduced in 1958 and later became the Armed Forces (Special Powers) Act. This legislation allowed governors to declare areas as 'disturbed,' giving the armed forces extensive powers. However, the role of the central government in this process remained unclear.

Independent India faced significant geopolitical challenges, with partition and internal divisions severely affecting its security. The British departure left behind social, political, and financial turmoil that continued to affect the nation. Additionally, the north-eastern regions of India, which had been geographically connected to Burma, experienced a shift upon independence, with new borders creating tensions with neighbouring regions. Pakistan, with its concerns about India's power, viewed these changes through the lens of regional dominance.

The Precarious Political History of North-Eastern India

The north-eastern region of India was designated as an 'excluded area' under the Government of India Act, 1935. The Governor of Assam, rather than the elected government, held direct administrative power over this region. This arrangement was meant to protect the cultural heritage of the local tribes, but in reality, it allowed the British to avoid the responsibility and cost of administering a vast, economically underdeveloped region which was revenue deficit to the core.

Tensions arose when western-educated youths from local tribes negotiated with the departing British to seek 'independence' for their regions from India. The Indian National Congress strongly opposed these efforts, fearing the division of the country during British withdrawal.

As the British Empire collapsed and departed hastily, a power vacuum emerged in areas like the Northeast and Kashmir. This instability provided an opportunity for insurgent groups to form, one of which was led by A.Z. Phizo[13] declared Nagaland an 'independent' entity on August 14, 1947, marking the beginning of the protracted Naga insurgency in India.

Phizo claimed a plebiscite with 99 per cent Naga support, but the reality was different. The concept of a unified Naga identity was still developing, and tribal unification was far from achieved. The region remained fractured, and educated elites in the Northeast struggled to cope with the power vacuum left by the British.

Pakistani intelligence actively fuelled insurgencies among the Mizo and Naga populations by providing arms and support, aiming to divert Indian security forces into a prolonged conflict.

Rising violence overwhelmed local authorities, highlighting the need for special measures. In response, on May 22, 1958, the President of India issued the Armed Forces (Assam and Manipur) Special Powers Ordinance, granting special powers to armed forces in Assam and Manipur. This led to the passage of the Armed Forces (Special Powers) Act of 1958.[14]

AFSPA: Balancing Security and Civil Liberties: The Rationale

One rationale for enacting such an extraordinary measure was the need to protect military personnel engaged in counterinsurgency operations. The concern that soldiers, without legal safeguards, could face prosecution in civilian courts for possible bona-fide infractions during operations against serious insurgency and additionally to enable the security forces to use all force necessary. In similar situations, imposition of Martial Law, granting the military broad authority, was deemed unacceptable in a newly established democracy. The Armed Forces (Special Powers) Act (AFSPA) emerged as a compromise *via media* between Martial law and imposing emergency, offering limited legal immunity to soldiers while falling short of the extensive powers assumed under Martial Law.

The Legality and Implications of Martial Law in India: The AFSPA Compromise

Contrary to popular beliefs, the Constitution of India explicitly recognizes martial law through Article 34, stating:

> *"34. Restriction on rights conferred by this Part while* martial law *is in force in any area: Notwithstanding anything in the foregoing provisions of this Part, Parliament may by law indemnify any person in the service of the Union or of a State or any other person in respect of any act done by him in connection with the maintenance or restoration of order in any area within the territory of India where martial law was in force or validate any sentence passed, punishment inflicted, forfeiture ordered or other act done under martial law in such area."*

The article has quite a strategic placement in the Constitution. It is an exception to the operation of Fundamental Rights, allowing Parliament to indemnify acts and proceedings carried out under martial law in specific areas. The power to declare martial law is inherent in any state governed by the rule of law. During martial law, civil administration and operation of criminal courts are suspended for the entire duration of Martial law, such that the appointed marshal can issue decrees or orders to enforce law and order without being subject to civil authority in the area.

In India's early democracy, martial law was viewed negatively due to its imposition by the British. To prevent unrestricted military control, India introduced a law granting 'special powers' to the military during domestic insurgencies. This Act primarily allowed armed forces to take decisive action in areas deemed 'disturbed' by the Central Government.

Today, parts of Manipur, Arunachal Pradesh, and Nagaland are periodically declared '*disturbed*' due to ongoing insurgent threats. Unlike martial law, AFSPA grants limited powers to armed forces, considering the specific threats in these areas. Under AFSPA, officers must hand over arrested persons to the nearest police station 'with the least possible delay.' Despite its purpose, AFSPA has faced criticism, mainly for alleged abuses by armed forces personnel.

The Armed Forces (Special Powers) Act, gives the following powers to officers of armed forces only in a 'disturbed area'.

Any armed forces officer in a disturbed area may:

(a) Use force, even lethal, to maintain public order, if necessary, after giving a warning, against anyone violating laws, such as carrying weapons or assembling in groups of five or more.

(b) Destroy any arms depot, fortified position, shelter, or structure used by armed attackers, training camps, or hideouts of wanted criminals.

(c) Arrest, without a warrant, anyone suspected of committing or about to commit a cognizable offence, using necessary force.

(d) Enter and search premises without a warrant to arrest, recover restrained persons, stolen property, or illegal weapons, using necessary force.

AFSPA: Safeguards

The AFSPA does not grant unlimited powers to the armed forces. It is limited to areas declared 'disturbed' and does not replace civil law or local administration. Arrested individuals still have legal remedies, and any arrested person must be handed over to the police as soon as possible. The powers to use force, including deadly force, are restricted to specific conditions, such as the violation of laws prohibiting assemblies or carrying weapons.

AFSPA was enacted in response to severe law and order situations in regions like the northeast and Kashmir, where the local police were insufficient to handle insurgencies supported by external forces. It allowed military forces to act in these regions without imposing martial law, offering them special powers while ensuring accountability.

Special powers are necessary when regular police forces cannot handle the threats posed by insurgents. The military is trained to handle such situations using advanced weapons and real-time intelligence. In the northeast, insurgents were heavily armed and needed military intervention, which AFSPA enabled.

Though AFSPA has been partially lifted in some regions, concerns about insurgent resurgence remain. Human rights groups often overlook the violence inflicted by militants, though any abuse by security forces is unacceptable. The Jeevan Reddy Committee recommended replacing AFSPA with amendments to the UAPA, but the decision remains unresolved due to opposition from security forces.

The law was primarily driven by the inability of civil authorities to handle escalating threats and the need to protect military personnel from unjust prosecution. A similar law was enacted in Punjab during the Khalistan insurgency, expanding the powers of the armed forces in that region.

Kashmir Imbroglio and AFSPA

The security situation in Jammu and Kashmir worsened after the Soviet withdrawal from Afghanistan, with Pakistan's ISI redirecting Mujahideen to the region, further escalating the insurgency. This conflict was driven by internal grievances and foreign support, with Pakistan fostering anti-India sentiment and secessionism through cross-border radicalism.

In September 1990, the central government enacted the Armed Forces (Jammu and Kashmir) Special Powers Act (AFSPA), retroactive to July. Supporters claim AFSPA reduced violent crimes and militant recruitment, citing improved local enlistment in security forces.

Critics, however, highlight concerns over human rights violations and stress the need for alternatives that tackle the insurgency's real causes while safeguarding civil liberties.

AFSPA: Way Forward

While the Armed Forces Special Powers Act grants exceptional authority, it remains unrevised and in force despite mass protests, legal challenges, and review panels. In response to public concerns, the Indian Army enforces a strict internal code of 'Dos and Don'ts' for its personnel.

Significant reforms in handling civil unrest, especially in Jammu and Kashmir, focus on using minimal force and exercising restraint. Operations are often recorded, detainees are promptly handed over to the police, and seized items are properly documented. The military also pursues legal action against personnel accused of rights violations to ensure accountability.

Still, it would be reasonable to conclude here that AFSPA is not an anti-terror law, as it doesn't mention 'terrorism.' Its sole purpose is to provide temporary legal backing and operational freedom to security forces in areas facing serious threats. India's dedicated anti-terror law came later with the Terrorist and Disruptive Activities (Prevention) Act.

Combating Terrorism: The Role of Terrorist and Disruptive Activities (Prevention) Act

The Terrorist and Disruptive Activities (Prevention) Act (TADA), enacted in 1985 and amended in 1987, was a strict anti-terror law primarily aimed at curbing the Punjab insurgency. It granted significant powers to law enforcement nationwide and marked the government's first major effort to legally define and counter terrorism.

TADA emerged due to a perceived failure of existing laws to deal with the growing threat of terrorism. Supporters believed it would simplify judicial procedures and improve counterterrorism efforts. This view was widely endorsed by police forces and a public alarmed by rising violence.

Though initially limited to two years, TADA was repeatedly extended before lapsing in 1995 under growing criticism and claims of misuse. It allowed authorities to detain individuals without substantiating charges for up to a year, admit police confessions as evidence, and conduct secret trials in special courts. Witness identities could be protected, and police could seize property of the accused, although coercive interrogation methods were prohibited.

Section 3 defined terrorism broadly, including actions aimed at intimidating the government, spreading fear, inciting division, or disrupting public services using deadly weapons or harmful substances. Two key conditions had to be met for an act to qualify as a terrorist offence under TADA.

1. *Intent to overawe, strike terror, alienate, adversely affect harmony.*
2. *Use of bombs, dynamite or other explosive substances, inflammable substances, firearms/lethal weapons, chemicals, biological substances, or substances of hazardous nature to cause the above.*

The rest of the cognizable offences were in relation to the terrorist act mentioned above. The Act also made an offence for causing '*disruptive activities.*' Disruptive Activity was defined in the section 4 of the act as:

> *4(2): For the purpose of sub-section (1), 'disruptive activity' means any action taken, whether by act or by speech or through any other media or in any other manner whatsoever;*
>
> *(i) Which questions, disrupts or is intended to disrupt, whether directly or indirectly, the sovereignty and territorial integrity of India; or*
>
> *(ii) Which is intended to bring about or support any claim, whether directly or indirectly, for the cession of any part of India or the secession of any part of India from the Union.*

The Act also defined the meaning of cession, secession and acts which promote killing of a constitutional dignitary or a public servant.

One of the most controversial provisions of this law was Section 15 which made certain confessions made before the investigating police officers *ipso facto* admissible as evidence. This provision was an exception to the general rule stated in Section 25 of the Evidence Act which states:

Section 25 Evidence Act:

> "*Confession to police officer not to be proved: No confession made to a police officer shall be proved as against a person accused of any offence.*"

Section 25 of the Evidence Act is the bedrock of the presumption of innocence of the accused person and dates back to British colonial prejudice implied in India that the local police cannot be trusted to provide justifiable conditions under which an accused person would reveal anything incriminating in his volition. Section 15 of the TADA on the other hand prescribed:

> *"Certain confessions made to police officers to be taken into consideration:*
>
> *(1) Notwithstanding anything in the Code or in the Indian Evidence Act, 1872, but subject to the provisions of this section, a confession made by a*

person before a police officer not lower in rank than a Superintendent of Police and recorded by such police officer either in writing or on any mechanical device like cassettes, tapes or soundtracks from out of which sounds or images can be reproduced, shall be admissible in the trial of such person [or co-accused or conspirator] for an offence under this Act or rules made thereunder."

However, the Act clarified in a proviso to this section that the high officer conducting such an interrogation must inform the accused that they are not required to make a confession and that, if they do, it may be used as evidence against them. Additionally, the officer must ensure that any confession is made voluntarily before recording it. This safeguard is akin to Section 164 of the Criminal Procedure Code, where a magistrate is duty-bound to explain to a person (even a witness) that anything they say can and will be used as evidence. As will be shown subsequently, certain provisions of TADA have been incorporated into the Unlawful Activities (Prevention) Act (UAPA), making it the primary counter-terrorism enactment in India without explicitly terming the law as such. In so many ways therefore UAPA was constantly amended creating a hybrid anti-terror law.

Section 20 of TADA introduced several amendments to the Criminal Procedure Code specifically for cases under TADA. The most significant change was the extension of the maximum investigation period, along with the corresponding provision for default bail, to up to one year.

"Provided further that, if it is not possible to complete the investigation within the said period of one hundred and eighty days, the Designated Court shall extend the said period up to one year, on the report of the Public Prosecutor indicating the progress of the investigation and the specific reasons for the detention of the accused beyond the said period of one hundred and eighty days."

Another important provision of the TADA was the 'statutory presumption of guilt' in certain cases under Section 21.

Presumption as to offences under Section 3(1) In a prosecution for an offence under sub-section (1) of Section 3, if it is proved:

1. That the arms or explosives or any other substances specified in Section 3 were recovered from the possession of the accused and there is reason to believe that such arms or explosives or other substances of similar nature, were used in the commission of such offence; or

2. That by the evidence of an expert the fingerprints of the accused were found at the site of the offence or on anything including arms and vehicles used in connection with the commission of such offence.

It further provided in sub-section (2) of Section 21 that;

"In a prosecution for an offence under sub-section 3 of Section 3, if it is proved that the accused rendered any financial assistance to a person accused of, or reasonably suspected of, an offence under that section, the Designated Court shall presume, unless the contrary is proved, that such person has committed the offence under that sub-section."

Hence, Section 21 provided for a 'statutory presumption of guilt' imposed upon an accused if the prosecution was successful in showing either recovery of incriminating articles/substances, his fingerprint on the site of a terrorist act, or if his involvement in providing/supplying financial assistance to an accused (under prosecution under Section 3 of that Act).

Section 22 of TADA was particularly noteworthy, as it allowed the prosecuting agency to identify a perpetrator through a witness's photographic identification rather than the traditional Test Identification Parade conducted before a Judicial Magistrate with various safeguards. The only safeguard provided in this section was that the accused must have been declared a proclaimed offender.

TADA was a special act and as with any special Act its special provisions had an overriding effect over any other law that was of general nature. In fact, this provision was inserted as Section 25 of the Act:

"***Overriding effect:*** *The provisions of this Act or any rule made thereunder or any order made under any such rule shall have effect notwithstanding anything inconsistent therewith contained in any enactment other than this Act or in any instrument having effect by virtue of any enactment other than this Act.*"

TADA faced substantial criticism on various fronts. A particularly contentious aspect was the stringent provisions regarding bail eligibility in Section 20(8). Although the Supreme Court upheld the constitutionality of this provision in the case of Kartar *Singh vs. State of Punjab*, it did not shy away from acknowledging the severity of TADA. The court noted:

"*We have come across instances where the prosecution invoked the provisions of the TADA Act with an ulterior motive to deny bail to the accused individuals. There were also occasions when, despite ordinary criminal law allowing bail, investigating officers utilized the provisions of the TADA Act to circumvent the authority of the courts. Such misuse of the TADA Act in cases where the facts did not warrant it amounted to a blatant abuse by the police."*

Criticism of TADA

Amnesty International and numerous other human rights organizations raised substantial critiques against TADA. The primary concern centred on its vague definitions of '*terrorism*' and '*disruptive activities.*' According to these groups, the term 'disruptive activities' was so broadly defined that it could encompass even peaceful expressions of political or sincerely held beliefs, effectively penalizing 'political dissent.' They further alleged that the abetment of such activities, as well as the possession of unauthorized arms in areas designated by State Governments, were rendered punishable offenses in such ambiguous and sweeping language that innocent individuals could easily be detained under its provisions.

Amnesty International also expressed concerns about the excessively long permissible detention period without informing the accused of the charges against them. Additionally, the validity and admissibility of confessions made before police officers faced substantial criticism. It is noteworthy, however, that Amnesty International later welcomed the changes introduced in the March 1993 TADA Amendment Act, which reduced the instances where the burden of proof shifted from five to three.[15]

Breaking Free from Colonial Shadows: Confessions and the Police

However, on the whole, Amnesty International's objections to confessions made before police officers seem a bit excessive, especially considering that many Western nations, including the USA , permit such confessions in ordinary criminal proceedings not to speak of terror enactments. For instance, Title 18 of the United States Code, the primary federal criminal code, outlines specific guidelines for confessions under Section 3501.

'18 US Code Section 3501- Admissibility of Confessions:

a) In any criminal prosecution brought by the United States or by the District of Columbia, a confession, as defined in subsection (e) hereof, shall be admissible in evidence if it is voluntarily given. Before such confession is received in evidence, the trial judge shall, out of the presence of the jury, determine any issue as to voluntariness. If the trial judge determines that the confession was voluntarily made it shall be admitted in evidence and the trial judge shall permit the jury to hear relevant evidence on the issue of voluntariness and shall instruct the jury to give such weight to the confession as the jury feels it deserves under all the circumstances.'

The US Code therefore allows confessions as evidence even if made during the custody of the police. The only rider placed is that the trial judge can cause an examination of the 'voluntariness' of the confession made. TADA made a similar safeguard about such confessions.

In the United Kingdom, the Police and Criminal Evidence Act, 1984, allows confessions made before police officers by placing a safeguard in the sub-section (2) and (3) of Section 76; effectively making it plain that if the prosecution wants to use a confession made by the accused in court, but it is claimed that the confession was forced or influenced by pressure or unfair treatment, the court will only allow it if the prosecution proves beyond doubt that the confession was given freely and fairly. Even if no one raises the issue, the court itself can ask the prosecution to prove the confession was not unfairly obtained.

The objections raised by Amnesty International and other human rights groups regarding TADA do not hold up when compared to the laws in two of the world's most liberal democracies. Section 25 of the Indian Evidence Act was instituted due to excessive mistrust of the constabulary due to the perceived oriental mindset of Indian professional classes, leading the British to impose restrictive conditions on police investigations. The colonial constraints due to imagined unprofessionalism of police have persisted even today.

The Parliament intended to address this issue by entrusting higher-ranking police officers with more authority. It is a fundamental principle of law that the abuse of a law ipso-facto does not justify declaring it invalid. Although the Supreme Court, in the Kartar Singh case, upheld the constitutional validity of TADA, it recognized the need for measures to ensure higher scrutiny and appropriate application of the Act. The Court directed the central government to review the implementation and make suitable changes to the Act.

Challenges to the Constitutionality of TADA

It has been rightly argued that TADA addressed many inadequacies in the law and was appropriately stringent for the extraordinary circumstances for which it was enacted. It appears that certain avoidable problems arose when the Act was applied to cases other than terrorist and disruptive activities, and the safeguards provided under the Constitution and other laws were not diligently followed. This led to a strong wave of resentment against the abuse of TADA's provisions.

Nonetheless, the Supreme Court upheld the constitutionality of Section 15, TADA considering;

> '*The gravity of terrorism unleashed by the terrorists and descriptions and the fact that the Legislature was competent to make a law prescribing different rules of proof, even though we at first impression thought of sharing the view of the learned counsel that it would be dangerous to make a statement given to a police officer admissible.*'

Another aspect that attracted significant subsequent criticism was the temporary nature of TADA's enactment. Initially introduced for a two-year period in 1983, it was subsequently extended until 1987 and renewed every three years. As per one estimate, the number of persons arrested under the act was more than 76,000 by June 1994 and twenty-five per cent of such cases were dropped by police without filing any charge sheet, which about 35 per cent of the cases were brought to trial and 95 resulting in acquittal (of which actually only about 2 per cent were convicted).[16] The TADA was allowed to lapse and succeeded by the Prevention of Terrorist Activities Act (hereinafter called POTA) which saw a similar fate.

Prevention of Terrorism Act, 2002 (POTA)

After the TADA lapsed, terrorist incidents continued unabated, and India witnessed several heart-wrenching events. Some of these incidents profoundly shook the conscience of the community as a whole. One of the earliest high-profile incidents was the Lajpat Nagar blast in Delhi in May 1996. This bustling market was rocked by a powerful explosion, killing 13 innocent civilians and injuring dozens more. Investigations linked the attack to Pakistan's Inter-Service Intelligence (ISI). The perpetrators were eventually convicted and sentenced to death in 2012.

The following day, a similar tragedy unfolded in Dausa, Rajasthan, with a bus bombing that claimed 14 lives. The accused, connected to the Jammu and Kashmir Islamic Front, were brought to justice, with the primary culprit receiving a death sentence.

The year 1996 also witnessed the horrific Brahmaputra Mail train bombing in Assam. The explosion caused multiple carriages to derail, leading to the deaths of over 30 people and injuries to more than 150. The Bodo Security Force, a local militant group, was implicated in the attack.

The city of Coimbatore was the target of a series of coordinated bomb blasts in February 1998. These attacks, orchestrated by the Al Ummah terror group, resulted in the deaths of 58 people and injured hundreds. The main conspirator, S.A. Basha, and several associates were convicted and sentenced to imprisonment.

The iconic Red Fort in Delhi was the site of a brazen attack in December 2000. Militants belonging to Lashkar-e-Taiba killed three people in an attempt to disrupt the India-Pakistan peace process. The mastermind of the attack was apprehended only 17 years later.

Just a year later, the Jammu and Kashmir Legislative Assembly was targeted in a suicide attack by Jaish-e-Mohammad militants, resulting in the deaths of 38 civilians.

The most significant and devastating attack was the Indian Parliament attack in December 2001. Carried out by militants affiliated with Lashkar-e-Taiba and Jaish-e-Mohammad, the attack led to the deaths of nine security personnel and brought India and Pakistan to the brink of war.

These attacks, among others, underscore the complex and evolving nature of terrorism in India. They have necessitated a robust counterterrorism apparatus and have had a profound impact on the nation's security policies and public psyche.

In 1999 the Law Commission of India analysed the emerging challenges to national security with a special reference to the need for new counter-terrorism legislation. The Commission proposed a new Prevention of Terrorism Bill based largely on the Criminal Law Amended Bill of 1995.[17]

POTA replaced the Prevention of Terrorism Ordinance (POTO) of 2001 and TADA. It was enacted after intense debate during a joint sitting of both houses of Parliament. Learning from TADA's misuse, the Act included safeguards to prevent abuse of power and protect human rights. Global attitudes toward terrorism had also shifted significantly after the 9/11 attacks on the World Trade Centre.

POTA used the word *"threatened"* instead of "overawe" in defining terrorist acts under Section 3. Section 3(b) made members of an "Unlawful Association" (under the UAPA) liable for terrorist acts if they carried out such acts or possessed dangerous materials while promoting the group's cause. Possession of arms, explosives, or tools leading to death, injury, or property damage was treated as a terror crime.

Section 5 made membership in a terrorist gang or organization a terrorist offence, punishable with up to life imprisonment. Section 7 criminalized the intimidation of witnesses. Section 6 declared holding proceeds of terrorism illegal—a stronger measure than TADA. Section 7 allowed seizure of such proceeds with approval from the state's Director General of Police. Appeals could be made to a high-ranking officer. Section 8 detailed how such property could be forfeited.

Similar to TADA yet Remarkably Different

Though procedurally similar, POTA differed significantly from TADA. It was more comprehensive and aligned with global legislative trends post-9/11. Section 18 allowed the Central Government to update the list of banned organizations. Section 20 made mere membership in such groups a punishable offense. Section 22 criminalized fundraising or aiding terrorist organizations. POTA also introduced provisions for authorized interception of communications, which TADA lacked.[18]

Subsequent amendments to the Unlawful Activities (Prevention) Act continue to permit the interception and admission of such evidence, but these amendments remove the oversight and review mechanism present in POTA since there are special guidelines and standard operating procedures based on the Indian Telegraph Act, 1885 in vogue in central and state governments.

Furthermore, the remand procedure under POTA was notably stringent. After an accused was initially presented before a magistrate, the magistrate could authorize police custody for up to 30 days, an extension from the previous 15-day limit. Subsequently, judicial custody could be ordered for up to 90 days. If the prosecutor requested additional investigation time, the court could extend judicial custody to a maximum of 180 days. This significantly lengthened the period for filing a charge sheet compared to the standard 90-day limit under ordinary law. This provision would later be incorporated into the UAPA.

The bail criteria under POTA were exceptionally stringent, prioritizing societal security over individual liberty. During the initial 180-day investigation period without a charge sheet, courts found it exceptionally difficult to justify bail. Even after a charge sheet was filed, securing bail was challenging unless the police allegations were severely flawed.

In a manner akin to its stance on TADA, the Supreme Court,[19] upheld the constitutional validity of POTA's provisions that allowed confessions made to police officers. POTA itself does not expressly address whether such confessions, obtained under these provisions, can be used to prosecute non-POTA offences, whether they are charged alongside POTA violations or pursued separately. The Supreme Court, however, resolved a similar ambiguity pertaining to TADA in favour of admitting such confessions in non-TADA offences, as evident in the State vs. Nalini case of 1999, where it was established that a properly recorded statement under TADA is admissible for non-TADA offences, even if the accused is acquitted of offences alleged under TADA.

POTA, however, garnered controversy for many of the same reasons that rendered TADA a contentious piece of legislation. The Act faced substantial criticism due to alleged frequent misuse by the state machinery. This legislation swiftly evolved into a significant political concern, ultimately leading to its repeal upon the assumption of power by the new government in 2004. However, the repeal of POTA was not made fully retroactive.[20] Consequently, the provisions of POTA continued to be applied to numerous individuals, despite its formal revocation. Nevertheless, the ruling administration ensured that no court would assume jurisdiction over fresh POTA cases beyond one year following the repeal, stipulating that each case must undergo scrutiny by a central POTA 'review committee' before allowing any pending POTA investigations or prosecutions to proceed. The review committee was also mandated to complete their assessments within one year of the repeal.

Unlawful Activities (Prevention) Act, 1967

India's colonial history is filled with instances of subversive activities by revolutionary societies and their members who challenged the might of the Britishers by their revolutionary methods of selective targeting of British high officials and their properties. This has been one of the most often neglected epics of Indian history. However, the benign part of the revolutionary struggle was over with the partition and birth of India as an independent nation with its own set of issues and challenges. Foremost among these was the challenge from fissiparous and secessionist tendencies propagated by certain disgruntled elements which wanted to short-circuit the egalitarian and democratic structure provided by the Constitution of India.

16th Constitutional Amendment and birth of UAPA

After independence, the National Integration Council recommended placing certain restrictions on fundamental rights to protect the new state's integrity. To implement this, the Sixteenth Amendment and the Unlawful Activities (Prevention) Act (UAPA) were introduced, reviving the Centre's power to ban "unlawful" organizations—a role previously held under the Criminal Law Amendment Act of 1908. Though largely unused for years, the controversies around TADA and POTA led to transferring key provisions into the UAPA, now India's main anti-terror law.

2004: Re-birth of UAPA

UAPA was amended in the year 2004 when POTA was repealed and many provisions of POTA were verbatim added to it. Prior to this, UAPA was not an anti-terror legislation. By enacting the Unlawful Activities (Prevention) Amendment Act, 2004 and by the 2008 and 2019 amendments the UAPA was made a primal counter-terrorism enactment in India. The amended UAPA was entirely different from TADA and POTA in one way. It prominently mentioned that it has been enacted with a focus on counter-terrorism.

The wording of its objective resolution of the Act makes the intent of the legislature crystal clear on two counts.

1. The Act has been made (and amended) with concentration and focus towards taking strict action against the terrorists, their ecosystem, and the organizations.
2. The Act has been enacted to give effect to various international agreements and United Nations Security Council Resolutions. This has been done with an enabling provision in the Constitution. Article 253 of the Constitution which provides that the Parliament can make laws to implement treaties, agreements, or international decisions for any part of India without regards to the strict division of powers in the legislative domains between the centre and the states.

The Unlawful Activities (Prevention) Act has faced criticism for restricting fundamental and human rights. It removed a controversial provision from the now-repealed Prevention of Terrorism Act (POTA) that allowed confessions made to police officers to be used as evidence. Critics, including international human rights organizations, argued this provision violated the right to avoid torture, inhuman treatment, and self-incrimination, and conflicted with the Indian Evidence Act's exclusion of police-recorded confessions.

Confession before Police Officers: Reappearance of Prejudicial Ghost

By eliminating police-recorded confessions as evidence, the UAPA amendment appeared to strengthen protections against torture and uphold fair trial principles. This was hailed as a positive development for Indian law enforcement and the justice system as a whole.

It is sometimes claimed—often repeated by certain human rights activists—that there *are "extensive, long-standing, and widely acknowledged problems in India with police torture and other violations of fundamental rights."* While violation of human rights warrant serious attention, this particular assertion can appear overly generalized and logically inconsistent. It tends to rely on circular reasoning, presuming police misconduct as an established fact rather than presenting it as a conclusion based on objective evidence. In doing so, it risks reinforcing a preconceived narrative rather than encouraging constructive engagement with the complexities of policing and human rights.

While negative perceptions and allegations of police misconduct exist in many countries, including India, it's inaccurate to say such practices are universal, that too specially in India. Abuse of powers by officers of the state is no excuse for denigrating the profession competence of an entire class of professionals. No profession is sacrosanct and there are black sheep everywhere for which institutional vigilance is the right way for correcting anomalies and such abuse of powers.

The prohibition of admitting confessions made before police officers is a distinct issue in India and can be traced back to the colonial-era perspective of viewing the police primarily as a law-and-order enforcement authority rather than as a professional institution capable of conducting modern scientific investigations. Post-independence, there has been a sea change in the training, recruitment, attitudes, and quality of officer as well as cutting-edge cadres in the police organizations in India. The continuance of colonial attitudes against police authorities in India ensures that otherwise professional officers of good conduct and acumen have been denied active participation in scientific investigation which includes recording the statement of witnesses and accused persons which must then be relied upon as evidence.

UAPA: No 'Special Tribunals'

The Unlawful Activities (Prevention) Act (UAPA) serves as a middle path between earlier anti-terror laws like TADA and POTA. Unlike those laws, UAPA ensures terrorism cases go through regular courts, not special tribunals, reinforcing judicial oversight and limiting executive overreach. A recent improvement is the restriction on trials in absentia—enhancing fairness in the process.

Still, challenges persist. Courts can now conduct in-camera hearings to protect prosecution witnesses, but there's no similar shield for defence witnesses. This imbalance could lead to perceptions of bias, echoing earlier criticisms of POTA.

In Bikramjit Singh vs. State of Punjab, the Supreme Court emphasized the need for safeguards in anti-terror laws. It ruled that UAPA cases must be handled exclusively by Special Courts under the NIA Act. Ordinary magistrates may authorize detention only up to 15 days, and only in exceptional cases. Beyond that, jurisdiction rests solely with Special Courts. This decision reinforces the importance of judicial oversight in counter-terrorism cases, ensuring that even stringent laws like the UAPA function within constitutional limits and protect against arbitrary detention.[21]

Summing up India's Counter-Terrorism Legislative Journey

India's approach to counter-terrorism legislation reflects a long and often uneasy balancing act between ensuring national security and upholding democratic freedoms. Since gaining independence, the country has struggled to reconcile these competing imperatives, all while navigating the lingering influence of colonial-era laws and mindsets.

As we have seen much of India's legal architecture for dealing with terrorism has roots in British rule, particularly in repressive laws like the Defence of India Act. In the post-independence era, faced with growing internal threats and insurgencies, India enacted powerful statutes such as the Armed Forces (Special Powers) Act (AFSPA) and the Terrorist and Disruptive Activities (Prevention) Act (TADA). While these laws allowed the state to respond swiftly and decisively, they also drew sharp criticism for enabling human rights violations and weakening institutional checks.

This ongoing tension between state security and civil liberties has been particularly evident in regions like Jammu and Kashmir and the Northeast, where the use of extraordinary powers and military deployment has triggered long-standing debates over accountability, justice, and the rule of law. Preventive detention—a legacy tool of governance—remains controversial, often viewed as an expedient but blunt instrument with a high potential for abuse.

India's counter-terrorism journey has also been shaped by global dynamics. International cooperation, particularly with the United Nations, has added another layer of complexity, with India at times pushing back against what it sees as externally imposed norms that do not always reflect its unique security realities.

Yet amid these challenges, India's democratic institutions have served as a vital counterweight. The judiciary, especially the Supreme Court, has repeatedly stepped in to review and refine the boundaries of state power—asserting that no security imperative can override the Constitution's commitment to fundamental rights.

As India continues to face evolving terror threats, the way forward lies not in choosing between liberty and security, but in crafting a measured response that incorporates both. Counter-terrorism laws must be precise, transparent, and accountable. By reaffirming its democratic values and commitment to the rule of law, India can show that it is possible to confront terrorism firmly—without compromising the freedoms it seeks to protect.

6

Balancing Security and Justice: Procedural Aspects of Anti-Terror Laws

"At his best, man is the noblest of all animals; separated from law and justice, he is the worst."

—Aristotle

There can be hardly any doubt that terrorism is a complex global threat that undermines the safety and stability of nations. Unlike conventional crime, terrorism involves mass casualties, ideological indoctrination, and long-term societal disruption. These unique characteristics necessitate extraordinary counter-measures. The adage *"extraordinary problems require extraordinary solutions"* aptly captures the challenge of addressing terrorism within the confines of traditional legal frameworks.

Terrorism is unlike ordinary crime—it often strikes without warning and is driven not by personal gain, but by ideology. Though it shares traits with organized crime, like tight-knit groups and loyalty, terrorism stands apart due to its political motives. Its aim is to intimidate the public, pressurize governments, or push an agenda, often through tactics like hostage-taking or violent retaliation.

Unlike criminal gangs that seek profit, terrorist groups feed on belief systems that give their actions a sense of moral or ideological legitimacy. This deep-rooted conviction makes counter-terror efforts challenging. In fact, the terrorist mindset can become so entrenched, it mirrors paranoia, making deradicalization a daunting task.[1]

Terrorism stands as a complex and exceptional form of crime due to its distinct characteristics and deep-rooted ideological foundations. Traditional criminal justice approaches are often inadequate in addressing the intricate nature of terrorism. It is therefore important to understand the need for instituting special procedures to tackle terrorists and terror crimes. Recognizing the uniqueness of these special procedures is therefore the first and utmost crucial requirement in developing effective strategies to combat this global threat.

Efficiency over Fairness?

In counter-terrorism, speed often takes precedence over legal safeguards—but at what cost? While quick procedures may seem efficient, they risk undermining fundamental rights and opening doors to abuse. Some experts warn that tailoring justice based on the type of accused sets a dangerous precedent, one that history has seen before, with grim consequences.[2]

Military tribunals, for instance, have often been used not for justice, but for silencing dissent. Political opponents were branded as 'enemies of the state' and condemned without fair trials. Pakistan's extensive use of military trials to stifle dissent against Baluchi insurgents is a grim example.[3] This pattern is a cautionary tale; one where suspicion replaces evidence, and efficiency overrides justice.

The push for deterrence, often in the name of national security, can also skew the system. Nazi Germany, for example, used swift legal executions to rid the state of so-called 'pests'—ordinary criminals labelled threats to public order. It is a chilling reminder that speed must never outweigh fairness, equity, or human rights in any judicial process.[4]

Terrorists as a Sui-generis Class of Criminals: The Question of Presumed Innocence

Terrorists form a unique category of offenders, and applying *Aristotelian equality*—treating unequal differently, seems logical. Some argue that, by attacking the foundations of society, terrorists deserve no leniency. But this view, while instinctively compelling, ignores core principles of fairness in justice. No individual can be legally called a terrorist until convicted; until then, they remain suspects or accused persons.

Natural justice demands that every accused is tried with full rights, both constitutional and human. The seriousness of the crime or desire for deterrence cannot justify stripping away judicial safeguards. A trial's true purpose is to offer both sides an equal footing, ensuring fairness, a cornerstone of any credible legal system.

In a functioning democracy (as opposed to states that merely claim to be democratic), the legal system serves to uphold democratic values, not just enforce order. Creating special courts for certain offenders' risks cultivating narrow, technocratic judicial mindsets. Judges must maintain a broader vision, not become confined to specialized roles.

The National Investigation Agency Act provides a measured example. Special Judges are appointed only in consultation with High Courts and State Governments, and must come from the regular judiciary, not as temporary, special appointees. This maintains balance and legitimacy within the justice system.

In this context we might seek some guidance from the Universal Declaration of Human Rights, 1948 which presupposes that every member state shall ensure in its legal system, principles of equality before the law as well as the right to due legal process. The combination of these two essential rights ensures that the defendant shall get a fair and equitable platform for trial. It would appear that the promise made under the declaration would be void if the law made a distinction between classes of offenders regardless of the severity of the criminal conduct. This approach sees the entire gamut of the need for special procedures from the perspective of the defendant and not from the perspective of other stakeholders.

Shield of Safety: Protecting those who are Against Terrorists

There is, of course, a countervailing consideration of superior magnitude when we consider the fact that terrorist organizations often mirror organized crime syndicates, relying on fear and intimidation and are unlike ordinary criminals. For witnesses against crimes of terror, testifying can be life-threatening. Judges, too, may fear for their safety, and so do police officers, forensic experts, and others within the justice system. Special terror laws aim to protect these actors so they can perform their duties without fear.

Yet, one must remember that the full power of the state stands against the accused. The defendant must challenge every claim and flaw in the evidence. Creating separate judicial forums for terrorists can undermine the very fairness a justice system is meant to uphold. If due process is repeatedly bypassed, even a democracy risks losing its legitimacy.

Emergency legal provisions may be necessary, but only in true emergencies. Critics of legal safeguards for terrorists often argue: why protect those who deny the law itself? But equal protection under law is not a reward for good behaviour; it is the foundation of justice.

Confused?

This discussion is an attempt to explore the reasons and the principles upon which the need to address the menace of terrorism is based. We would try to understand why terrorism warrants extraordinary procedural measures in law, examining the complexities of counterterrorism efforts, the challenges posed by traditional legal frameworks, and the need for a balanced approach that upholds human rights while effectively combating this exceptional crime.

The Nature of Terrorist Crimes and the Need for 'Special' Procedures

Terrorism is a calculated act of violence designed to instil fear and intimidate populations. Unlike traditional crime motivated by personal gain, terrorism is driven by extremist ideologies. Its methods, including bombings, armed attacks, and cyber operations, often result in mass casualties and widespread destruction. The transnational nature of terrorism, coupled with its reliance on advanced technology and recruitment tactics, poses significant challenges for law enforcement and intelligence agencies worldwide.

Another reason why it is exceedingly difficult for ordinary courts to try terrorist crimes is that the trial process itself exposes the court to the exceptional conditions created by terrorism. Terrorism, as a highly violent and organized activity, presents unique challenges that make the task of adjudication particularly daunting. No court is immune to the threat of violence that looms over such cases, and similarly, witnesses are vulnerable to intimidation or influence by the terrorist's associates.

Unlike ordinary criminals, terrorists often have networks of supporters who can exert pressure on existing and prospective witnesses, compromising the integrity of the trial. Just as in organized crime, terrorists may have significant resources at their disposal, and if granted bail, they could wreak havoc on society.

Given these realities, it is crucial to recognize that terrorists must be treated differently from ordinary criminals in significant respects. The first distinctive procedural requirement in such cases is the necessity of special measures to ensure that the trial process is not undermined by the threats posed by terrorism. There are specific parameters that guide the imperative of treating the prosecution of terror crimes differently, reflecting the unique and serious nature of these offences.

1. *Investigative Challenges in Terrorism Cases:* This point encompasses unique procedural complexities arising during the investigation of terrorist crimes.
2. *Search and Seizure in Counter-terrorism:* This focuses on the specialized search and seizure procedures applicable to terrorism investigations.
3. *Arrest, Detention, and Bail in Terrorism Cases:* This highlights the specific legal framework for arrest, detention, and bail in terrorism-related cases.
4. *Special Courts and Trial Procedures:* This covers the establishment of specialized courts, in-camera proceedings, witness protection, evidence admissibility, and other procedural safeguards in terrorism trials.

Investigative Challenges in Terrorism Cases

In India, 'Police' and 'Public Order' are state subjects under the Constitution (7th Schedule, List II, Entries 1 & 2), meaning state police typically handle criminal investigations. However, terrorism is not treated like an ordinary crime.

After the 2008 Mumbai attacks, the need for a specialized central agency became clear. In response, Parliament passed the National Investigation Agency Act, giving the Central Government the power to assign terrorism cases to the NIA when national security is at stake. While states retain primary investigative powers, the NIA has overriding jurisdiction when the situation demands it, especially due to India's international obligations under Article 253 of the Constitution.

The Act clearly defines its mission: to investigate and prosecute offences that affect India's sovereignty, security, and international relations, particularly those linked to global treaties and UN resolutions. As a signatory to international conventions and under growing pressure from resolutions like UN 1267 (1999) and 1822 (2008), India had the compulsion to act decisively.

While some legal scholars argue that the NIA Act challenges India's federal structure, its creation was seen as an urgent step to address terrorism more effectively and fulfil global commitments.[5]

Interestingly, the Indian Constitution does not explicitly describe India as a 'federal' country. This was a conscious decision by its framers. Having just emerged from a fragmented colonial past with regions prone to secession, a precariously nascent India could ill afford encouraging separatist thinking within its legislative institutions. Instead, the term '*Union*' was chosen to stress that states were not sovereign entities coming together, but integral parts of a single nation, with no history of independence.

While the Constitution includes a schedule that divides executive, legislative, and financial powers between the Centre and the states, it also embeds strong unitary features to protect national unity. One such provision is Article 253, which empowers Parliament to make laws on any subject, even those listed under state jurisdiction, if doing so fulfils an international obligation.

Article 253 justifies the legitimacy to the creation of the National Investigation Agency (NIA). Its purpose is to transcend jurisdictional limitations and ensure that terrorism cases involving national and international security are investigated professionally and without jurisdictional squabbles

Before the NIA was created, terrorism cases were often handled by the Central Bureau of Investigation (CBI), either through its Special Crimes Division or at the request of state governments. However, the CBI lacked independent authority to take up such cases and usually required permission from courts or the states. Over time, it became clear that many high-stakes terrorism cases, with serious national security implications, were not being pursued with the urgency and investigative precision they required.

Why? Several key reasons stood out:

1. *Terrorism is a Crime Apart:* Terrorism isn't just another criminal act; it is an assault on the very foundation of the state. While regular crime may threaten public order, terrorism seeks to destabilize or even overthrow lawful governments. It is organized, hierarchical, and often transnational. Modern terror networks, much like hydras, have far-reaching, cross-border operations. With the rise of the Internet, they now recruit, train, and move funds online, relying on donations or ideological supporters rather than illicit gains. Terrorists are not driven by greed; they are driven by ideology, and often willing to sacrifice everything for their cause.
2. *Use of Encrypted Communications by Terrorists and Challenges Emerging*

from Tech: The tools terrorists use such as VoIP, encrypted messaging apps, and secure video chats, create immense challenges for investigators at the state police level who might not have the technological know-how to understand the nuance of investigation involving such technologies. Such sophisticated technologies make it almost impossible for local police to monitor communications effectively without the technical support of central intelligence agencies. Even when local agencies request data from global tech giants, such summons are often ignored or delayed, severely hindering investigations.

3. *Lack of Specialized Capacity at the Local Level:* Terrorism demands a focused and highly skilled response. Local police forces, designed to manage a broad range of public safety issues, often lack the resources, training, and expertise to deal with such specialized, high-stakes crimes, especially when they involve international links and complex digital trails.
4. *Expertise and Knowledge:* Investigating terrorism demands a considerable level of expertise, knowledge, and the involvement of specialist personnel. There was a growing need to establish a central agency with a focus on specialized investigations.[6]
5. *International Cooperation:* Investigating terrorist crimes often necessitates international cooperation through mutual legal assistance treaties (MLATs) and other international instruments. Provincial law enforcement agencies inevitably face limitations, both in terms of territorial jurisdiction and practical operation. Despite the fact that the Criminal Procedure Code does not prohibit provincial police from conducting investigations across state boundaries, it has been observed that it becomes exceedingly challenging for these agencies to operate in jurisdictions different from their own state.
6. *Intelligence Handling:* The analysis, collection, and dissemination of intelligence related to terrorism have evolved into a highly specialized field. Provincial police forces are inherently constrained by their territorial limitations. A national-level agency is better positioned to liaise both nationally and internationally with other intelligence and law enforcement agencies worldwide.

These considerations underscored the need for a specialized central agency such as the National Investigation Agency to address the unique challenges posed by terrorism and ensure a more effective and comprehensive response to these crimes with national security implications.

Regardless, of whether the terror crimes are being investigated by the National Investigation Agency or the local law enforcement agency, the need for special investigation measures remains a high priority due to the very nature and distinctiveness of the terrorist crime. This is the reason that the Parliament enacted the National Investigation Agency Act, and suitably amended the Unlawful Activities (Prevention) Act to enable the investigation agencies to effectively deal with the menace of terrorism.

Special Procedures Related to Seizure of Property

The history of asset confiscation dates back to England's common law, where the term 'felony' combined the Saxon words 'fee' (landholding) and 'lon' (price), signifying a crime serious enough to cost someone their property. Rooted in Saxon and Scandinavian legal traditions, the idea survived even after the Norman invasion of 1066 and helped shape feudal England's legal system. Back then, someone convicted of treason against the King didn't just lose their life—they also lost their land, possessions, and the right to pass them on to their heirs.[7]

The confiscation of ill-gotten gains has deep roots in common law, with governments using it for centuries. For example, if an object caused someone's death, its value could be forfeited to the English Crown as a penalty for negligence. Over time, this evolved into the belief that criminals could be denied property ownership.

The history of civil forfeiture is equally fascinating. Initially, it aimed to effectively prosecute criminals and combat organized crime. Law enforcement soon realized they needed a way to target the proceeds of crime, as criminal syndicates hid funds in various places, and international wire transfers made their operations global. With money laundering on the rise, a global consensus in the 1980s led to the development of civil forfeiture as a key strategy to fight organized crime.[8]

The rationale behind confiscating property obtained through illegal means is twofold. First, it deprives the criminal of any benefit from the property. Second, it prevents anyone else from gaining further advantage from it. English common law identifies four types of seizure: criminal forfeiture, forfeiture linked to convictions, forfeiture of inherently harmful objects (*malem in se)*, and civil forfeiture. The first two require a conviction, making them part of criminal law. In contrast, the latter two are civil in nature, not necessarily tied to a conviction. Proceeds of terrorism, viewed as inherently harmful (*malem in se*), can be confiscated without the need for a criminal conviction.[9]

Civil vs. Criminal Forfeiture

Civil confiscation of property differs from criminal forfeiture. Instead of targeting the person, civil forfeiture targets the 'guilty' property itself (like the proceeds of terrorism). It serves as a pre-emptive measure in counter-terrorism law, aimed at blocking financial resources and assets that could further terrorism. In these cases, the accused person's presumed innocence does not matter. India's Unlawful Activities (Prevention) Act (UAPA) reflects this approach in Section 24A, wherein it maintains that:

1. No person shall hold or possess proceeds of terrorism.
2. Proceeds of terrorism, whether held by a terrorist organization, gang, or individual, are liable to be forfeited to the government, regardless of whether the person is prosecuted or convicted.

There may be situations where it is difficult to act directly against terrorists or their organizations if suspected properties are left untouched. For example, imagine an investigation reveals that a person (X) has invested $1 million, funnelled through hawala channels, into a store that sends funds abroad to a terrorist group. In such a case, allowing the criminal gains to remain with the suspect or be passed on to successors would be reckless. The property's ownership is not as important as the risk it poses for fuelling further terrorist activities. Immediate attachment or confiscation becomes critical to prevent such an eventuality pending final investigation.

Purpose is to Prevent Utilisation of Such Property for Terror

Civil forfeiture provides a legal mechanism for states to reclaim proceeds from unlawful activities, even in the absence of ongoing criminal proceedings. The focus is on the property involved in the crime, not the individual, hence the term '*confiscation in rem.*' This process targets the asset itself rather than the person behind it.

For decades, civil forfeiture has been a powerful tool in the fight against organized crime, terrorism, and other threats to society. Its origins in Europe date back to 1956, when Italian authorities first used it, while in the United

States, it has been in use since 1970. Countries such as Canada, Australia, Malaysia, South Africa, and the UK, all with roots in British common law, have since adopted it as well.

Additionally, civil law countries such as Italy, the Netherlands, Colombia, and the Philippines have embraced civil forfeiture for proceeds related to terrorism and organized crime. These laws enable asset recovery and provide compensation to victims, especially when prosecuting the criminal conduct directly is impractical. To ensure fairness, authorities must establish, based on the preponderance of evidence, that the assets are tied to criminal activity before proceeding with forfeiture.[10]

The RICO Act and Forfeiture in the USA

Civil forfeiture has been most vigorously applied in the USA, particularly in tackling organized crime since the era of Al Capone. The FBI has led efforts against corporate fraud, racketeering, and money laundering. A key legislative tool in these efforts is the Racketeer Influenced and Corrupt Organizations (RICO) Act. This federal law targets organized crime, giving law enforcement a powerful tool to prosecute individuals and groups involved in racketeering, money laundering, and other criminal activities.[11]

The RICO Act not only targets individuals directly involved in criminal activities but also those who indirectly benefit from or support such activities within a criminal enterprise. By applying civil injunctions, treble damages, and civil asset forfeiture, the RICO statute has effectively disrupted various organized crime groups in the USA. However, critics argue that the law has exceeded its original intent and is vulnerable to abuse by both law enforcement and private citizens. As a result, federal and state authorities have taken steps to limit RICO's powers, including shifting the burden of proof to the state and protecting defendants' due process rights.[12]

Accusations Need Evidence

In the context of criminal justice, due process of substantiation remains a critical element. The '*due process of substantiation*' means that prosecution must establish a clear causal chain connecting the property to the act of terrorism or the terrorist entity. In other words, the *corpus delicti* (body of essential facts proving the crime) must first be established, followed by demonstrating the link between the property and the crime. The prosecution must also establish that the act constitutes 'unlawful conduct.' However, this is where civil forfeiture differs significantly from the civil version of illicit enrichment, so the authority cannot simply claim a lack of legitimate income to justify forfeiture.

The Criminal Procedure Code in India grants police and investigators broad powers, including the authority to search premises and arrest individuals for cognizable crimes. These powers are generally sufficient for investigating terrorism, offering significant flexibility. However, terrorist crimes often involve substantial financial angle disclosing organizational reach and concealment of ill-gotten gains. Investigations frequently uncover terrorist groups using fronts like charitable institutions to launder money through donations and extortion.

Terrorists also exploit regular banking channels, such as UPI payments and wire transfers like Western Union, to manage illicit funds. In some cases, crypto currencies have been used to finance their activities.[13]

To empower investigative agencies in untangling such intricate webs of financial transactions, the Unlawful Activities (Prevention) Act was appropriately amended to strike at the very core of such illicit properties. Special procedures for the seizure and forfeiture of these '*proceeds of terrorism*' were subsequently established within the framework of the UAPA.

Forfeiture and Seizure of Proceeds of Terrorism under UAPA

Section 24 of the UAPA defines '*proceeds of terrorism*' as any property '*intended to be used*' for terrorism. The UAPA also prescribes an authority under section 2(e) of the Act to make such a determination. This would be an officer of the rank of Joint Secretary or above who shall give a reasonable opportunity to the person whose property is under seizure and subsequent forfeiture. Section 2(e) of the Act prescribes:

> *2(e) "Designated Authority" means such officer of the Central Government not below the rank of Joint Secretary to that Government, or such officer of the State Government not below the rank of Secretary to that Government, as the case may be, as may be specified by the Central Government or the State Government, by notification published in the Official Gazette;"*

Section 25 of the UAPA also gives powers to the Investigating Officer to seize a property that he believes to be 'proceeds of terrorism'. Section 2(g) of the Act also gives a fairly comprehensive definition of the term '*proceeds of terrorism*':

> *[(g) "proceeds of terrorism" means, —*
>
> *(i) all kinds of properties which have been derived or obtained from*

commission of any terrorist act or have been acquired through funds traceable to a terrorist act, irrespective of person in whose name such proceeds are standing or in whose possession they are found; or

(ii) any property which is being used, or is intended to be used, for a terrorist act or for the purpose of an individual terrorist or a terrorist gang or a terrorist organisation.

Explanation.—For the purposes of this Act, it is hereby declared that the expression

"proceeds of terrorism" includes any property intended to be used for terrorism;]

The expression '*proceeds of terrorism*' is a fairly wide term as per the UAPA. Any property which is determined as *capable* of being used, *intended* to be used, or *suspected* of being used for terrorism is liable to be seized and forfeited on the orders of the court (as per Sections 25 and 26 of the Act).

The Power Differential: Executive Seizures vs. Judicial Forfeiture

Indian law distinguishes between the powers and procedures for seizure and forfeiture of property linked to terrorism. Seizure is specifically granted to the investigating officer, whose actions must be validated by a 'Designated Authority' appointed by the Central Government. Forfeiture, however, falls under judicial authority, handled by the Special Court designated for UAPA-related trials.

This distinction has historical roots. Under the Terrorist and Disruptive Activities Act (TADA), forfeiture was only permitted after the accused was convicted of terrorism-related offences. Prior to conviction, their property could only be attached during the trial. TADA even included provisions allowing for the return of proceeds from forfeited property if the accused, initially absent, later appeared in court and provided a satisfactory explanation for their non-appearance. Section 8 (3)(c) of the TADA clearly prescribed that if a person accused of terror crimes appears within six months of property attachment and proves they didn't abscond or avoid arrest, the property or sale proceeds, minus costs, will be returned to them.

Section 8 of the Prevention of Terrorism Act goes far beyond this liberality against 'proceeds of terrorism' and is prescribed under Section 8:

"8. Forfeiture of proceeds of terrorism:

Where any property is seized or attached on the ground that it constitutes

> *proceeds of terrorism and the Special Court is satisfied in this regard under sub-section (7) of section 7, it may order forfeiture of such property, whether or not the person from whose possession it is seized or attached, is prosecuted in a Special Court for an offence under this Act."*

The legislative approach towards the proceeds of crime has undergone a significant transformation from the days of TADA and POTA to the amended UAPA. The UAPA now provides focused attention on the proceeds of crime, particularly those related to terrorism, and introduces a detailed procedure with safeguards against any property believed to be such proceeds.

One of the key changes is in the definition of 'property.' While TADA and POTA have concise and similar definitions, the UAPA presents a more comprehensive definition. In TADA, the definition of property is outlined in Section 2(1)(gg), which states:

> *[(gg) "property" means property and assets of any description, whether corporeal or incorporeal, movable or immovable, tangible or intangible and deeds and instruments evidencing title to, or interest in, such property or assets, derived or obtained from the terrorist Act and includes proceeds of terrorism;]*

Section 2 (1)(d) of the Prevention of Terrorism Act on the other hand reads:

> *(d) "property" means property and assets of every description, whether corporeal or incorporeal, movable or immovable, tangible or intangible and deeds and instruments evidencing title to, or interest in, such property or assets and includes bank account;*

The definition of property in POTA was evidently made broader (despite the apparent quantitative curtailment of the section) by omitting the words '*derived or obtained from the terrorist Act and includes proceeds of terrorism.*' This change has had the effect of widening the scope of the definition in POTA.

Section 2(1)(h) of the UAPA gave the widest latitude to the definition of property by far. It prescribes:

> *2(1)(h):*
>
> *"property" means property and assets of every description whether corporeal or incorporeal, movable or immovable, tangible or intangible and legal documents, deeds and [instruments in any form including but not limited to] electronic or digital, evidencing title to, or interest in, such property or assets by means of bank credits, travellers' cheques, bank cheques, money*

orders, shares, securities, bonds, drafts, letters of credit, cash and bank account including fund, however acquired;

Note the words '*instruments in any form including but not limited to electronic or digital*', this change was necessitated due to the advent of crypto currencies and like 'instruments' of wire transfer of monetary transactions, which is being done majorly through the internet. This is by far the widest possible definition of property in any law.

The Complexities of Seizing Terrorist Property: Provisions under UAPA

In many countries, asset forfeiture is pursued through a formal criminal justice process. Nations following English common law require evidence beyond a reasonable doubt, which is challenging, especially with white-collar criminals. To tackle this, some governments enact civil forfeiture laws, allowing asset seizure through civil courts or empowering executive officers. In India, civil forfeiture was introduced to address proceeds of terrorism through amendments to the Unlawful Activities (Prevention) Act (UAPA).

Section 25 of the UAPA is a comprehensive tool to deal with 'proceeds of crime'. Simply speaking it enables the investigating officer who, with prior approval from the Director General of Police or of National Investigation Agency (as the case may be), can order the attachment of property suspected to be proceeds of terrorism. If the property cannot be seized immediately, the officer may prohibit its transfer without permission. The 'Designated Authority' under the UAPA must confirm or revoke the order within 60 days, giving the person affected a chance to represent their case. The officer can also seize cash if suspected to be used for terrorism. Any person aggrieved by the order can appeal to the court within 30 days, which may confirm or revoke the order.

This section restricts the use of certain powers during investigations under Chapters IV and VI of the Act, which deal with terrorist offences involving individuals or organizations. It specifically targets proceeds of terrorism and excludes unlawful activities covered under other chapters. Notably, it allows the Investigating Officer to seize or attach property without court involvement, making it an executive function. The officer must record reasons and obtain approval from the relevant Director General (of police or NIA as the case may be) before proceeding.

Unlike Section 102 of the CrPC (now Section 99 of the BNSS), which permits general seizure of property, this provision provides specific authority for actions aimed at forfeiture of terrorist-linked assets. If seizing is impractical, particularly in the case of immovable property, the officer may issue an attachment order prohibiting its use or transfer. This includes serving written orders with details of the property and investigation to affected parties. The officer must also visit and publicly declare the attachment without needing to dispossess or take over the property physically.

The provision requires the Investigating Officer to notify the Designated Authority in writing about any property attachment or seizure under Section 2(1)(e) of the UAPA. The Designated Authority must then confirm or revoke the order within sixty days of such notification. As per the proviso to sub-section 3, the affected person must be given an opportunity to be heard before a final decision is made.

Sub-section 5 empowers the Investigating Officer to seize cash (and equivalent monetary instruments) if there are reasonable grounds to suspect its use for terrorism or as part of a terrorist group's resources. This power complements the general seizure powers. Such cash may be held for up to forty-eight hours unless extended by the Designated Authority.

Section 26 of the UAPA introduces civil forfeiture, which does not require proving an accused person's guilt or establishing ownership of the property if the court finds that the asset is a proceed of terrorism based on investigation evidence. Sub-section 6 mandates that forfeiture can only occur after the Designated Authority confirms the seizure order.

Civil forfeiture under this section empowers a Special Judge to confiscate property suspected of being linked to terrorism. This bypasses the stringent English law standard of proof beyond reasonable doubt and makes it contingent on passing the standard of 'balance of probability' that such property has linkage to terror. The provision ensures that terrorist assets can be removed swiftly, without waiting for lengthy trials, thereby strengthening counter-terrorism efforts.

Balance of Probabilities

Civil forfeiture reduces the burden of proof demanded of the state from 'beyond a reasonable doubt' to a '*balance of probabilities.*' In simpler terms, the anti-terror agency can seize money or assets based on a *"reasonable suspicion"* that funds or assets in question may constitute the proceeds of criminal activities. This reasonable suspicion is codified in the UAPA, as it grants the Investigating

Officer the authority to make an initial determination regarding the proceeds of terrorism. However, this decision necessitates validation from the 'Designated Authority' specified under Section 25 of the Act. In other words, the quasi-judicial subjective satisfaction of the Designated Authority is the only safeguard against arbitrary seizure and forfeiture.

On the other hand, the power to forfeit property is not arbitrary but must adhere to principles of natural justice. The Designated Authority must provide the opposing party (the property owner) a chance to present their case before making a final decision. The burden of proof is now shared between the state and the defendant. Unlike a criminal trial, where the defendant does not have to prove innocence, in civil forfeiture, the defendant often must show that the assets were acquired legally. In other words, the burden of proof is on accused rather than on the investigation agency or the prosecution. Once the court confirms the forfeiture order, as outlined in Section 25(6), the property is forfeited. Section 26 emphasizes the civil nature of this power, stating that it can be ordered even if the property owner is not prosecuted for a related crime. The property does not have to be linked to a specific person or be associated with a conviction.

A fundamental principle underpinning the punitive approach to counterterrorism is the necessity of depriving terrorists and their affiliated entities of financial sustenance if it is determined that their activities have been facilitated, perpetuated, or are currently supported by certain assets. An additional advantage of this enforcement strategy lies in its capacity to dismantle the financial infrastructure that fuels the operations of criminal organizations. Terrorism, much like a parasitic organism, thrives on a consistent influx of money and such other sustenance.

Special Procedures for Arrest, Detention, and Bail

The power to arrest and detain is one of the most significant authorities granted to law enforcement, second only to the power to take a life. This power severely impacts an individual's fundamental right to freedom. While drastic, it is often times necessary to ensure justice. Arresting and detaining a person accused of a serious crime is essential to meet certain requirements for a fair trial. These requirements include:

1. To enable witnesses to come forward and provide their statements without fear or favour.

2. To ensure that the accused does not interfere in the process of the investigation and is detained, at least during the period of the investigation.
3. To prevent the commission of further crimes by the accused.
4. To ensure that the accused stands trial and cooperates with the investigation.

Law on Preventive Detention

To ensure a fair trial for individuals accused of terror crimes while accounting for potential threats to public safety, it is often imperative to detain the accused until the court assesses whether compelling grounds exist for bail. In such cases, the balance between national security and individual liberty takes precedence, and proceedings related to terror offences are not to be equated with conventional criminal processes.

A just investigation and trial necessitate active pursuit, arrest, and detention of the accused until judicial determination of their culpability. In certain situations, pre-emptive arrests are made when individuals are suspected of intending to incite violence or commit acts of terrorism—this form of detention, rooted in prevention rather than punishment, is known as *preventive detention*.

India's preventive detention framework has its origins in the colonial era and was codified post-Independence through the Preventive Detention Act, 1950. This Act permitted detention of individuals deemed threats to national security, foreign affairs, or public order, and applied to both citizens and foreigners. Though safeguards existed to check arbitrariness, the power remained exceptional.

The Supreme Court in *Sasthi Chaudhary vs. State of West Bengal* clarified that preventive detention entails confinement without trial, where authorities lack sufficient evidence for a formal charge or conviction, yet hold reasonable suspicion of future threats.

Unlike punitive detention, which addresses past conduct, preventive detention aims to avert future actions falling under Entries 9 of List I and 3 of List III in the Seventh Schedule of the Constitution. No offense is proven, no charges framed; instead, confinement is justified on the basis of probability and suspicion, not judicially established guilt.

The various Preventive Detention enactments faced criticism for stifling democracy in India under the guise of protecting the nascent republic. The state of Jammu and Kashmir had its own preventive detention statute, named the Public Safety Act, which provided the executive with the power to order the detention of individuals on grounds of public safety and maintaining order. These acts enabled authorities to detain individuals suspected of inciting violence or engaging in acts prejudicial to the state's tranquillity. Preventive detention in ordinary times is indeed rare in developed countries; however, India experienced serious disturbances, necessitating such powers to enable the executives to maintain public order.

Preventive detention laws were rigorously challenged in constitutional courts. Despite the challenges, most preventive detention acts survived and were utilized. In *A.K. Gopalan vs. State of Madras*, the Supreme Court upheld the validity of the Preventive Detention Act, 1950. However, the courts frequently criticized the high-handedness of the executives, ensuring that authorities adhered to the safeguards enshrined in the Act and that the arrest and detention process did not violate the safeguards in Article 22 of the Constitution.[14]

India saw the enactment of several laws with provisions for preventive detention. Here is a list detailing such acts:

1. Preventive Detention Act, 1950.
2. Maintenance of Internal Security Act, 1971.
3. Conservation of Foreign Exchange and Prevention of Smuggling Activities Act, 1974.
4. National Security Act, 1980.
5. Prevention of Illicit Traffic in Narcotic Drugs and Psychotropic Substances Act, 1998.

Preventive Detention: Constitutional Safeguards

Article 22, situated within the fundamental rights chapter, exempts preventive detention from direct judicial scrutiny by establishing a distinct administrative (quasi-judicial) review mechanism. It prohibits preventive detention beyond three months unless an advisory board—comprising persons who are, have been, or are qualified to be High Court judges—affirms sufficient cause. However, the government retains effective discretion over the appointment of these board members. Furthermore, legislation can override the requirement for advisory board review altogether, thereby granting wide latitude to the executive in matters of preventive detention.[15]

While the 44th Amendment retained preventive detention, it significantly altered its constitutional structure. The Chief Justice of the High Court, rather than the government, was empowered to appoint advisory board members. The board's chair had to be a sitting High Court judge, and the other members sitting or retired judges. Previously, Parliament could permit preventive detention without advisory board oversight; the amendment revoked this, mandating judicial review for detentions exceeding two months.

The 1978 amendment revised Clauses (4) and (7) of Article 22 to strengthen procedural safeguards. Key changes included:

i. Reducing the maximum detention period without advisory board confirmation from three to two months.
ii. Requiring the board to consist of three High Court judges—appointed upon the Chief Justice's recommendation—with the chair being an incumbent judge.
iii. Adding an explanation to identify the 'appropriate High Court' for appointments.

However, these changes have never been enforced. Despite adverse observations by the Supreme Court in *A.K. Roy vs. Union of India* (paras 52 and 113), the original Article 22 remains operative, rendering the 1978 amendments inoperative in practice.[16]

The existence of an ongoing prosecution does not bar the issuance of a preventive detention order, nor does such an order preclude future prosecution (*Hardan Saha vs. State of West Bengal*). Preventive detention may be imposed in anticipation of, during, or after a criminal prosecution, including after discharge or acquittal. The detention order may even be based on the same facts underlying a prosecution, whether pending or merely contemplated.

Additionally, a detention order may be issued even after a criminal case is withdrawn for lack of evidence. In such cases, it lies within the subjective satisfaction of the detaining authority to determine whether sufficient grounds exist to detain the individual in order to prevent future conduct prejudicial to public order or related interests.

Pre-Trial Detention and Procedural Safeguards

The Supreme Court, in its renowned pronouncement during the *Anuj Garg vs. Hotel Association of India* case in 2008, emphasized that *"Personal freedom is a fundamental tenet which cannot be compromised in the name of expediency unless there is a compelling State purpose.*" Preventing terrorist acts is a compelling state interest, necessitating specific legal provisions that permit extended pre-trial detention for those accused of such crimes. Investigating terrorism typically demands more time, resources, and poses heightened risks, requiring that officers be granted sufficient time to gather evidence.

However, inordinate delays in framing charges during pre-trial detention raise crucial questions about how long a terrorism suspect can be held without formal accusation. Balancing individual rights with national security, many legal systems incorporate safeguards, such as judicial review, legal representation, and clear detention limits, to prevent unjustified prolonged incarceration.

Extended Period of Detention for Terror Offences: Compulsion or Imperative?

Terrorism and national security cases often require extended detention periods due to complex investigations involving international networks, intelligence, and the need to prevent imminent threats. While such detentions are necessary for thorough investigations, concerns about potential civil liberties violations remain. These powers aim to provide authorities enough time to gather evidence and prevent societal harm. However, the length of detention without formal charges continues to be debated.

To address these concerns, legislative frameworks such as the Unlawful Activities (Prevention) Act (UAPA) set clear limits for pre-trial detention. Section 43D of the UAPA specifies a maximum detention period of 90 days, extendable by another 90 days (up to 180 days), during which the prosecuting agency must present evidence. Additionally, Section 167 of the Criminal Procedure Code (CrPC) (now Section 187 of the BNSS) governs pre-trial detention, with Section 43D offering modifications to allow for charge sheets within 180 days from arrest. Non-filing of charge sheet by the investigation agency within this period gives an automatic right to bail in favour of the accused. In fact, the extension of 90 days (after first 90 days) is also not automatic. The prosecution needs to provide detailed reasons as to why it requires an additional 90 days to complete the investigation.

The Legal Framework for Bail in Terrorism Cases

The right to bail and the strict application of bail provisions in terrorism cases are key components of the Indian legal system. The Supreme Court has emphasized the right to bail as a fundamental element of justice. In *Francis*

Coralie Mullin vs. Union Territory Delhi, the Court held that any procedure to deprive an individual of life or liberty must be reasonable, fair, and just.

In *Maneka Gandhi*, the Supreme Court stated that arbitrary, oppressive, or fanciful procedures are unconstitutional, as they violate the reasonableness principle in Article 14. For a procedure to be valid, it must be enacted by a competent legislative body and not infringe upon other constitutional rights, such as Articles 14, 22, or 19. Furthermore, a procedure may be unreasonable even if it does not violate natural justice principles. The validity of laws under Article 21 must also be assessed through Articles 14 and 19, with the Court scrutinizing challenges based on arbitrariness or unreasonableness.[17]

The Supreme Court has stressed time and again that the right to life and personal liberty must not be deprived by unjust or unreasonable procedures. Laws must be inherently just, reasonable, and fair, and failure to meet these criteria could render the law unconstitutional.

In light of these legal principles, while the necessity to keep individuals accused of terrorism behind bars is clear to ensure the investigation is not hindered, the ongoing incarceration during trial has been a subject of consistent scrutiny by the higher courts.

Najeeb's Case: A Balancing Act between Speedy Trial and Anti-Terror Laws

The case *Union of India vs. K.A. Najeeb* represents a shift in how courts in India handle bail applications in terrorism cases. The Kerala High Court granted bail to Najeeb, arrested by the National Investigation Agency (NIA) for alleged involvement in a terror conspiracy. This marked a departure from the usual strict bail standards under the Unlawful Activities (Prevention) Act (UAPA).

Najeeb, associated with the Popular Front of India, was accused of attacking a Malayalam professor over a perceived blasphemous exam paper. Despite repeated bail denials between 2016 and 2021, the High Court eventually granted bail after Najeeb's prolonged pre-trial detention, citing the failure to meet the speedy trial mandate under the National Investigative Agency Act (NIA Act) of 2008.

The State contested the decision, arguing that granting bail violated Section 43D of the UAPA, supported by prima facie evidence. However, Najeeb's defence highlighted the acquittals or short sentences for most co-accused and emphasized his right to a speedy trial. The Supreme Court examined whether the High Court erred in granting bail, acknowledging its limited power to overturn such decisions.

Citing the *Shaheen Welfare* Case, the Court recognized that excessive delays in trial violated the right to life and liberty under Article 21, justifying bail even in UAPA cases. The Court emphasized the need for efficient trials to ensure guilt is determined within a reasonable timeframe. After that period, despite UAPA's stringent bail provisions, bail should be granted.

This case highlights that, while national security concerns are important, the core principle of criminal proceedings is to establish guilt through fair and efficient trials, ensuring justice and maintaining public confidence in the legal system.

Balancing Justice and Efficiency

While a strong legal system deters crime and terrorism, these benefits should not overshadow the pursuit of justice itself. Legal proceedings should be timely, but their effectiveness is not solely measured by speed. Every trial requires upholding fundamental principles, even if it extends the process, albeit reasonably.

In any criminal case, particularly those involving terrorism, preventing wrongful convictions must remain the foremost priority, even in the face of apparent national security concerns. The seriousness of the alleged offence or the gravity of the potential punishment should not overshadow this principle. Convicting an innocent person not only results in a grave miscarriage of justice but also undermines public trust in the entire criminal justice system. The presumption of innocence is especially critical in cases where the accused has been subjected to prolonged incarceration, and even more so when the trial is unreasonably delayed. Safeguarding this principle ensures that justice is not compromised in the pursuit of expediency or security.

Bail functions as a vital safeguard of an accused person's constitutional rights, reflecting the foundational principle that individuals are presumed innocent until proven guilty. It allows for conditional release in recognition that liberty should not be unduly curtailed, especially in the absence of a conviction. However, special legislations such as the Unlawful Activities (Prevention) Act (UAPA) introduce stringent departures from general criminal procedure, and these must be critically examined for consistency with constitutional guarantees.

As a special provision, Section 43D of the UAPA imposes significant restrictions on the grant of bail, creating a framework that heavily favours continued detention once a charge sheet supported by relevant and admissible evidence is filed. A closer reading of Sections 43D(5), (6), and (7) reveals a multi-layered prohibition.

Section 43D(5) bars bail for individuals accused under Chapters IV and VI, relating to terrorist activities and associations, unless the Public Prosecutor is given an opportunity to be heard and the court is satisfied, based on the case diary or police report, that the accusation lacks prima facie credibility. Section 43D(6) clarifies that this bar operates in addition to the regular provisions governing bail under the Code of Criminal Procedure and other laws. Further, Section 43D(7) categorically excludes from bail consideration any non-citizen who has entered India illegally, permitting exceptions only in rare circumstances and requiring the court to record specific reasons in writing.

Together, these provisions erect a high threshold for bail under the UAPA, which, while intended to address grave threats to national security, must still operate within the framework of constitutional protections and the overarching need to prevent the miscarriage of justice.

In the 2019 case of *National Investigation Agency vs. Zahoor Ahmad Shah Watali*, the Supreme Court reversed the Delhi High Court's bail grant to Watali. The Court noted:

1. The admissibility of evidence is a matter for trial (Para 34).
2. The High Court misapplied the law, disregarding admissibility and failing to assess the material on broad probabilities (Para 35).[18]

Thus, it has been ordinarily observed that UAPA's Chapters IV and VI create significant hurdles for granting bail in terrorism and unlawful activity cases. Courts are reluctant to grant bail unless compelling reasons are presented. Prolonged detention may influence bail decisions, but the Supreme Court's post-Najeeb rulings do not show a consistent trend.

Special Courts and Trial Process in Terrorism Cases

In terrorism trials, protecting the identities of intelligence sources is vital. Confidentiality can be so crucial that closed-door proceedings (called '*in-camera* 'in legalese) are the only option. This is necessary to safeguard witnesses testifying against terror suspects. Revealing sensitive information could endanger lives and violate the rights of others.

In-Camera Trials

Terrorism cases frequently involve sensitive information concerning national security, intelligence, and counter-terrorism operations. Given these extraordinary circumstances, in-camera trials are essential to prevent the inadvertent disclosure of classified information. Such exposure could endanger investigations, compromise intelligence sources, and obstruct future security efforts.

The rationale for in-camera proceedings includes:

1. *Protection of Witnesses:* Terrorism trials pose serious risks to witnesses, who may fear retaliation from terror networks. In-camera hearings protect their identities and testimony, encouraging cooperation.
2. *Avoiding Public Spectacle:* High-profile terrorism trials often draw media attention, inadvertently glorifying terrorists and inciting further violence. Closed hearings reduce this risk.
3. *Securing Sensitive Information:* Details related to terror investigations are often highly sensitive; public disclosure may endanger lives and security operations.
4. *Upholding Fairness:* While protecting national security is vital, so is ensuring a fair trial. In-camera proceedings strike a balance, enabling justice without external pressure or intimidation.
5. *Preservation of Evidence:* Public hearings may unintentionally reveal confidential investigative techniques. In-camera settings maintain the integrity of such evidence.
6. *Curtailing Propaganda:* Terrorists may exploit open trials to spread ideology. Closed sessions limit their ability to do so.

Expediency in Conducting a Trial: Experience with Special Courts and Special Procedures

A fair and prompt criminal trial is essential to justice, ensuring the accused person's right to proper treatment. Yet, even with special procedures and courts, prolonged trials hinder justice, frustrate the public, and weaken trust in the legal system. Delays affect all: the accused in custody, victims and their families, and the broader community seeking closure. The Supreme Court's ruling in *Union of India v. Najeeb* underscored the burden of extended incarceration and highlighted the urgent need for a more efficient judicial process.[19]

Special Courts were meant to fast-track justice, especially in sensitive cases such as terrorism. Yet, critics argue that they often fall short of this promise.

One major reason cited is the use of non-continuous trials—a practice that, in effect, makes them no different from regular courts. Hearings get scattered over months, sometimes years, and even basic steps like framing charges under Section 240 CrPC (now Section 251 BNSS) take time, as judges must be fully satisfied before proceeding.

Although resource constraints are often blamed, the reality is that such drawn-out trials might hurt everyone involved. Victims wait for closure, accused individuals remain in limbo, and the public loses faith in the system. Adding to the problem, higher courts sometimes fault investigation agencies for these delays, damaging their credibility. But finger-pointing rarely solves the issue. What many critics miss is the complex, high-stakes nature of terrorism investigations, and the intense pressure under which these agencies operate.[20]

The ramifications of this approach to case disposal are manifold. Protracted trials undermine the fundamental principle of expeditious adjudication, a cornerstone of fair justice. The imposition of multiple court appearances on witnesses, particularly those without professional obligations, can lead to conflicts and reduced cooperation. Lengthy proceedings increase the risk of witness intimidation or obstruction, eroding public confidence in the justice system and discouraging witness collaboration. Under the Unlawful Activities (Prevention) Act, prolonged trials result in extended pre-trial incarceration, inflicting undue hardship on accused persons irrespective of guilt.[21]

Central Investigation Agencies and Institution of 'Special' Courts.

In India, it is a common practice to appoint a single 'Special Judge', normally an additional Sessions-level judge, to handle sensitive cases investigated by agencies such as the CBI, NIA, and ED. The National Investigation Agency Act, empowers the Central Government to set up Special Courts for trying 'Scheduled Offences' listed in Schedule I to the NIA Act.

This Act draws its constitutional authority from Parliament's control over intelligence and criminal law (Union List Entry 8, and Concurrent List Entries 1 & 2). Its goal? To create a national body with concurrent jurisdiction for probing offences that threaten India's sovereignty and internal security.

The NIA Act lays out a distinct process for investigating such 'Scheduled Offences' under Section 6 and allows both Central and State Governments to establish Special Courts. While both tiers of government have exercised this power extensively, the discretion granted to States under Section 22 has sparked judicial debate. Appellate courts have often struggled with the vague language of the statute, leading to differing interpretations across jurisdictions.[22]

Special Courts designated by the Central Government are explicitly defined in Section 11, which simply states that the Central Government, after consulting the Chief Justice of the High Court, can notify one or more Sessions Courts as Special Courts for specific areas or cases.

Section 22 allows the Centre and States to set up Special Courts for NIA or State-investigated Scheduled Offences. These courts exclusively handle UAPA cases in their area. Under Section 16, they can directly take cognizance of such offences based on a complaint or police report, without the accused being committed to trial.

Special Procedures for the Protection of Witnesses

Traditional procedural safeguards, designed to uphold due process and public perceptions of fairness, may prove inadequate in terrorism cases where witnesses apprehend grave personal harm, or that to their family or associates, from disclosure of their identity to the defendant, the defendant's associates, or the public. While primary responsibility for witness protection rests with investigative and prosecutorial authorities, the court plays an indispensable role in safeguarding witness and victim rights, thereby fostering continued participation in the judicial process.

Section 44 of the Unlawful Activities (Prevention) Act criminalizes the disclosure of such identity, whether intentional or inadvertent, with imprisonment as a penalty. In effect, this empowers courts to protect witnesses in sensitive cases. Proceedings can be held in-camera if the court believes it is necessary, and if a witness's life is at risk, the court may take steps to conceal their identity and address. These measures can include holding hearings at undisclosed locations, omitting the witness's details from public records or judgments, and banning media coverage. Anyone violating such protective orders may face up to three years in prison and a fine.

In short, in such cases, Special Courts can implement protective measures for witnesses to ensure a secure trial, without compromising fair trial rights. These measures, if requested by the prosecution, may include redacting identifying details of the witness, holding in-camera proceedings, using pseudonyms, voice distortion, or video link testimony, or any other measure to protect the identity of the witness.

Section 17 of the NIA Act and Section 44 of the UAPA further provide legal authority to protect witness identity, ensuring their safety while maintaining justice. Violating these protections can lead to severe penalties, underscoring the importance of safeguarding witnesses in terrorism-related cases.

Conclusion

The prosecution of terrorism cases presents unique challenges due to the very structure and complexity of terror crimes that has far reaching consequences both for the society as a whole and those individuals who are accused for perpetrating terror. The very threat environment that terrorists create poses unique prosecution challenges, a requirement that necessitates a distinct procedural framework. Unlike conventional crimes, terrorism often involves intricate networks, clandestine operations, and transnational dimensions. To effectively combat this threat, special procedures are indispensable.

Whether it is safeguarding the lives of witnesses, judges, police officers or others who are concerned from the prosecution side, the State has an obligation to ensure that the environment of threat and intimidation does not affect prosecution of such crimes adversely. Protection of the innocent and victim must be paramount in terrorism cases. Given the high-risk nature of these crimes, witnesses are often susceptible to intimidation, coercion, or even threats to their lives. Robust witness protection programs are essential to ensure their safety and to guarantee the integrity of the judicial process.

While establishment of special tribunals and courts has been a common response to the challenges posed by terrorism, the effectiveness and judicial efficacy of these bodies requires a re-look, as mere re-constitution of a particular court without adequate reforms in the judiciary does hamper effective prosecution of such cases. While there is no denying the fact that specialized forums can possess the expertise, resources, and security measures required for efficient and effective prosecution. However, it is imperative to balance the need for expeditious trials with the fundamental rights of the accused. The dual requirement of efficiency with due regard for fairness is something that every prosecution system will find hard to balance.

7

Counter-Terrorism and Human Rights Law

'Remember that hope is a powerful weapon even when all else is lost'

—Nelson Mandela

Let us start this chapter with certain basic questions:

1. What are human rights?
2. Are humans born with certain rights that are universally valid, inalienable, and naturally inherent?
3. Are these entitlements subject to restrictions or are determined by changing circumstances, political or otherwise?
4. Do culture, politics, or other considerations have a bearing on how a person needs to be treated?
5. Is the law the same for everyone until one is accused of committing a terrible act, such as terrorism?

These are some questions we may consider as law students or practitioners when determining our stance on counter-terrorism strategies. Human rights, by definition, are fundamental entitlements inherent to all individuals simply by being human. They are not necessarily contingent on the laws under which one may currently be answerable. Human rights are universal, inalienable, and indivisible; they apply to everyone, cannot be taken away, and are interconnected. These rights form the foundation of a just society, ensuring dignity, equality, and freedom for all. Human rights are intrinsic and not granted by any state or authority, transcending nationality, gender, ethnicity, religion, or other characteristics. They cover a wide range, from the right to life to the rights to nourishment, education, employment, health, and freedom.

As the United Nations website describes:

> *"Human rights are rights inherent to all human beings, regardless of race, sex, nationality, ethnicity, language, religion, or any other status. Human rights include the right to life and liberty, freedom from slavery and torture, freedom of opinion and expression, the right to work and education, and many more. Everyone is entitled to these rights, without discrimination."*[1]

Dr. Durga Das Basu delineates the definition of human rights succinctly,

> *"Human rights are those minimal rights, which every individual must have against the State, or other public authority, by virtue of his being a member of human family' irrespective of any consideration."*[2]

Universal Declaration of Human Rights 1948

UN's Universal Declaration of Human Rights is a comprehensive document that is declarative of human rights but does not *per se* define what they are. It declares and codifies a total of 27 such rights (the first three articles are declarative and the rest of the 27 articles actually define what these rights are) that it declares as per Article 2:

> "*Everyone is entitled to all the rights and freedoms set forth in this Declaration, without distinction of any kind, such as race, colour, sex, language, religion, political or other opinion, national or social origin, property, birth, or other status. Furthermore, no distinction shall be made on the basis of the political, jurisdictional, or international status of the country or territory to which a person belongs, whether it be independent, trust, non-self-governing or under any other limitation of sovereignty.*"

(The Declaration was adopted by the UN General Assembly in Paris on 10 December 1948 during its 183rd plenary meeting).

As implied in this declaration, human rights are fundamental entitlements that no authority or ideology can take away, regardless of its power or structure. These rights are universal, granted to all simply by being human. They cannot be denied, even by law, and apply universally, extending beyond state actions to include individual actions.

This chapter will focus and restrict itself on human rights solely in the context of counter-terrorism.

National Security, Torture and Human Rights Imperatives

One of the most inhumane applications of counter-terrorism strategies is the use of torture, often called '*enhanced interrogation techniques*,' ostensibly justified on the pretext of national security imperatives. These tactics, while presented as exceptional, clearly violate civil, political, economic, and cultural rights, undermining the core principles of human rights laws.[3]

There exists an unmistakable legal prohibition against the use of any form of physical coercion on individuals under investigation or trial, whether they are ordinary criminals or individuals accused of terrorist acts. However, the torture of one human being by another has a long history, and state-sanctioned torture is not a recent phenomenon, as evidenced by the political histories of various regions.[4]

Imperialistic colonial policies have left their mark on countries such as India, Algeria, most of the Arab world, Australia, China, and around the globe, with a plethora of gruesome acts of torture committed in the name of imposing one's concept of justice upon another. Torture was once a sanctioned method for extracting confessions, particularly during the pre-modern era when it was justified due to its perceived effectiveness and sometimes served as the only available method when other evidence was lacking. In his *magnum opus*, '*Arthashastra*,' the ancient Indian political strategist Kautilya prescribes numerous torture techniques for extracting confessions from captives.[5]

During medieval times, several Muslim rulers employed terrifying measures and public displays in which supposed enemies of the state were tortured to death.[6] The Britishers were no exception when it came to human rights violations, subjecting countless prisoners to the most inhumane and degrading treatment in their designated concentration camp on Port Blair in the Andaman Islands.[7]

Torture, though long condemned under international law, witnessed a troubling resurgence in the aftermath of 9/11, this time in a more covert and institutionalised form. Efforts were made to rebrand and legally justify coercive methods under the guise of 'enhanced interrogation techniques,' aimed at extracting so-called 'actionable intelligence' from detainees. What emerged was a distinct post-9/11 framework of torture, marked not by its brutality alone, but by its bureaucratic sanction.

U.S. authorities, including the Department of Justice, issued classified legal memoranda, later infamously known as the 'Torture Memos', providing detailed guidance to military and CIA personnel. These documents effectively legitimised acts that would otherwise constitute torture, redefining legal thresholds for pain and suffering to permit a wide range of abusive practices. These methods continued largely unchecked until global condemnation erupted following the exposure of systemic detainee abuse at Abu Ghraib prison in Iraq.

In response to the backlash, the U.S. President ultimately moved to disavow and roll back these practices, but not before the episode had significantly undermined the global human rights framework and eroded moral leadership. The post-9/11 era thus stands as a stark reminder of how legal frameworks can be manipulated to justify inhumane treatment—raising enduring questions about accountability, ethics, and the rule of law in the context of national security.[8]

It is striking how national security concerns led even fair-minded, liberal political figures and government lawyers to support legal instruments permitting torture. Despite applying innocuous euphemism, those executing such measures often imposed their own limits, leading to fatalities or severe injuries. These incidents were sometimes dismissed as the actions of 'bad apples,' with internal inquiries that rarely changed the outcome.[9]

Surveillance Capitalism and Human Right Concerns: The Right to Privacy and to Live with Dignity

Another human rights concern revolves around the extensive and all-encompassing nature of surveillance, characterized by the wholesale collection of bulk data directly at the source, enabling real-time monitoring of individuals without due legal process (or expedient and swift processing of 'legal requests' in the garb of judicial proceedings under the United States Foreign Intelligence Surveillance Act, and Clarifying Lawful Overseas Use of Data Act or CLOUD Act. In her book, '*The Age of Surveillance Capitalism*,' Shoshana Zuboff offers a comprehensive examination of the practices of the major five information technology giants (such as Google, Meta, etc.). She illuminates their seemingly covert, unwritten agreement with the American state and its allies, wherein profit is seamlessly interwoven with the gathering of intelligence in violation of every known law enacted for protecting privacy.

Zuboff posits that this emerging form of capitalism poses a significant threat to individual privacy, autonomy, and democratic ideals. She contends that surveillance capitalism has given rise to a system in which people themselves become the commodity, with their personal data serving as the raw material for an entirely new form of marketing strategy dominated by the Big Tech companies and certain social media giants. Additionally, Zuboff delves into the consequences of surveillance capitalism on society, politics, and the economy, asserting that it holds the potential to undermine personal freedoms, exacerbate social inequalities, and erode the very foundations of democracy.[10]

Other writers have argued that technology has enabled western state agencies to conduct mass surveillance reminiscent of totalitarian regimes in many ways. Information technology has facilitated the construction of communication networks that allow clandestine state agencies to collect individuals' private data with a mere click of a button, all without judicial oversight. It is somewhat naïve to assume that, in a surveillance-dominated communication environment, privacy invasion would be limited to data collection alone.[11]

The information gathered through such invasive procedures can easily be misused to coerce targeted individuals into actions they would never be compelled to undertake otherwise. Nowadays, clandestine agencies in the west can conduct prolonged surveillance operations on journalists, intellectuals, and others perceived to hold dissenting views towards the state's interests. Information gathered through these surveillance programs can then be used to fabricate criminal proceedings to stifle dissent and suppress uncomfortable opinions. Such surveillance is often justified under the pretext of protecting national security, but the reality appears to be quite different. These alarming trends have been observed even in nations that claim to champion democratic values.

The Obligation of the State to 'Know': Eminent Domain of State Surveillance

Terrorism poses an extraordinary challenge to modern states, compelling them to adopt proactive measures, including surveillance, to prevent acts of terror. It is undeniable that the state bears a fundamental and urgent duty to protect its citizens from such threats. Equally, however, the state carries an enduring obligation to uphold and safeguard the human rights of all individuals, including the right to privacy and due process, principles that lie at the heart of democratic governance.

These dual responsibilities are not mutually exclusive but interdependent. The effective use of surveillance technologies to prevent terrorist acts must be anchored in legal frameworks that respect human dignity and civil liberties.

At the same time, the state must ensure that victims of terrorism receive justice, support, and redress. All these obligations, preventing attacks, preserving rights, and delivering remedies, ultimately serve the same goal: ensuring public safety while maintaining public trust.

To prioritize one obligation at the expense of the other is to weaken both. Surveillance without safeguards erodes freedoms; rights without security leave populations vulnerable. A balanced approach, where counter-terrorism surveillance is precise, accountable, and legally bounded, is essential to preserving both national security and democratic legitimacy. Only then can the state meet its full responsibility in a manner that is both effective and just.

The International Human Rights Law and its Implications for Countering Terrorism

What is International Human Rights Law?

International Human Rights Law (IHRL) is essential in shaping counter-terrorism strategies, aligning with various branches of international law, such as humanitarian law, refugee law, and criminal law. It provides a legal framework for assessing the lawfulness of counter-terrorism measures. While terrorists may violate human rights, the responsibility for ensuring human rights protection during such measures lies with state authorities, especially those bound by human rights treaties. IHRL promotes and safeguards fundamental rights through treaties and customary international law, recognizing the inherent freedoms of every individual.[12]

IHRL forms a foundational pillar of international law, designed to protect the inherent dignity and equality of all individuals. It draws from treaties, conventions, customary practices, and judicial interpretations, creating a comprehensive framework that binds states and guides global governance. IHRL not only defines the rights individuals are entitled to, such as life, liberty, and freedom from torture, but also imposes obligations on states to respect, protect, and fulfil these rights. In an increasingly interconnected world, IHRL serves as a moral and legal compass, ensuring that power is exercised with accountability and justice across borders.

IHRL: The Core Concepts

IHRL affirms the inherent dignity and worth of all humans, regardless of nationality, race, gender, or religion, and enshrines universal and inalienable rights. These rights include civil, political, economic, social, and cultural freedoms. Key treaties, like the *International Covenant on Civil and Political Rights* (ICCPR) and *International Covenant on Economic, Social, and Cultural Rights* (ICESCR), lay the foundation of IHRL. The ICCPR safeguards civil and political rights such as life and freedom from torture, while the ICESCR protects economic and social rights like work, education, and health.

Additional instruments such as the *Universal Declaration of Human Rights* and the *Convention against Torture* provide further guidance on human rights. IHRL holds governments accountable for human rights violations and plays a key role in promoting global justice through courts, mechanisms, and civil society. The UN Security Council has shaped IHRL, balancing security and human rights in counter-terrorism efforts.

Enforcement of IHRL and its Challenges

Enforcing IHRL is a collaborative effort involving international bodies like the UN Human Rights Council and treaty-specific committees, as well as the ICJ and ICC, which provide judicial mechanisms for disputes and prosecutions. Domestic courts also contribute by incorporating international standards into their decisions.

Despite its global significance, the implementation of international human rights law (IHRL) faces persistent challenges, particularly the tension between cultural relativism and universalism. Cultural relativism emphasizes that values and norms differ across societies, questioning the applicability of a single global standard. In contrast, universalists argue that certain rights, such as freedom from torture, equality before the law, and the right to life, are fundamental to human dignity and must apply everywhere, regardless of cultural context. This tension complicates consensus, enforcement, and legitimacy, raising difficult questions about how to respect cultural diversity while ensuring that core human rights are upheld universally and consistently.

Despite the development of IHRL, violations continue due to weak institutions, political instability, and over assertion of state sovereignty. In some cases, governments prioritize national security or economic interests over human rights, allowing abuses to go unpunished. The lack of a global police force or a universal international court further limits enforcement. While institutions such as the ICC hold individuals accountable for serious crimes, their jurisdiction is limited, and their effectiveness relies on states' willingness to cooperate.

The rise of non-state actors, transnational corporations, and technological advancements adds complexity to IHRL enforcement. These actors often operate beyond state legal systems, making accountability difficult. Emerging issues, such as technology's impact, refugee rights, climate change, and discrimination, also require attention. Legal experts agree that states bear primary responsibility to prevent terrorism and ensure effective remedies for victims, making human rights protection a collective global effort.

Counter Terrorism and International Human Rights Law

While terrorist groups apparently are not bound by international treaties such as the ICCPR, they are still subject to the principles in the Universal Declaration of Human Rights (UDHR). The UDHR affirms the inherent dignity and worth of all individuals, regardless of their affiliation or status, making it clear that even non-state actors must respect basic human rights.

While terrorist groups may function outside traditional legal frameworks, they remain morally accountable for their actions. Regardless of their political or ideological motivations, they must respect fundamental human rights, including the rights to life, liberty, and protection from torture. Violations of these rights cannot be justified under any cause. Although human rights treaties are primarily binding on states, international law increasingly recognizes that non-state actors, especially those exerting territorial control, must not act with impunity. States, meanwhile, bear legal responsibility if they exercise effective control over such groups or allow them to operate with tacit approval. When terrorist activities originate from a state's territory or occur with its knowledge or support, that state may be held internationally accountable. Under international law, all states are obliged to prevent and suppress terrorism and ensure accountability for human rights abuses by non-state actors.

These legal nuances highlight the tensions between how human rights abuses by non-state actors and violations by states are treated. Recently, the UN has acknowledged that certain human rights obligations may apply to non-state actors, especially when they govern territories and populations, blurring the line between state responsibility and non-state actions.[13] Since the 1990s, a multitude of United Nations bodies have urged non-State groups to adhere to human rights laws and have established specialized mechanisms to address instances of abuse.[14]

The responsibility for safeguarding human rights is a collective concern, clearly articulated in the preamble of the Universal Declaration of Human Rights. The preamble states that *"every individual... shall strive... to promote respect for these rights and freedoms... to secure their universal recognition and observance."* This principle is reinforced in various United Nations resolutions. Additionally, Article 29(1) of the Universal Declaration of Human Rights acknowledges that *"everyone has duties to the community."*

Similar points are reiterated in the preambles of the International Covenant on Civil and Political Rights (ICCPR) and the International Covenant on Economic, Social and Cultural Rights (ICESCR). Furthermore, common Article 5(1) of ICCPR and ICESCR emphasizes that no 'State, group, or person' possesses the right to undermine or curtail the rights of others unless permitted by human rights law.

Institutional Approach to Human Rights Obligations of States

In 2005, an institutional mechanism was established to strengthen human rights enforcement: the Special Rapporteur on Human Rights and Terrorism. This independent expert identifies human rights trends in counter-terrorism efforts, fosters dialogue, and helps develop international standards. Their work is crucial in ensuring that human rights remain a key focus in the fight against terrorism.[15]

The Counter-Terrorism Committee (CTC) of the Security Council has become more proactive in countering terrorism while increasingly emphasizing human rights. This shift is evident as the CTC works to ensure counter-terrorism measures respect fundamental freedoms. To improve coordination across the UN system, the Counter-Terrorism Implementation Task Force (CTITF) was created to align counter-terrorism policies and initiatives among various UN agencies.

At the international scale, the implementation of effective counter-terrorism strategies is scrutinized by supra-international judicial oversight through non-human-rights specific courts and bodies, such as the International Court of Justice, the European Court of Justice (ECJ), or sub-regional African Courts. The African Court on Human and Peoples' Rights (ACHPR) serves as a vital complement to the sub-regional human rights courts in Africa. Established by African states, the ACHPR is dedicated to safeguarding human and peoples' rights across the continent.[16]

Although limited by territorial and jurisdictional constraints, judicial bodies, particularly the International Court of Justice, mandate adherence to international human rights law and related instruments. Despite these limitations, it can be argued that international courts have positively impacted the implementation of human rights obligations under various United Nations legal frameworks.[17]

Counter-Terrorism: Human Rights vs. National Security Considerations

The tension between national security imperatives and human rights obligations has grown increasingly pronounced, challenging the principle of universal human rights. This conflict is exemplified by cases like Uruguay, where accountability was demanded for actions by its security forces on Argentine soil, highlighting the complexities of extra-territorial jurisdiction. Balancing state sovereignty with global human rights standards requires nuanced approaches, as security measures often encroach upon individual liberties.

The scrutiny of universality underscores the need for consistent application of rights across borders, yet differing national priorities complicate enforcement. Strengthening international cooperation and transparent legal frameworks is essential to reconcile these competing demands, ensuring that security efforts do not undermine fundamental freedoms while fostering accountability for violations, regardless of where they occur,[18] and Germany being prompted to take measures to prevent violations by its companies abroad.[19] A recent development includes the recognition of obligations extending to activities occurring within a nation's territory and other places under its jurisdiction, with a direct and reasonably foreseeable impact on the right to life beyond its borders.

The Extraterritorial Application of Human Rights Law: Implications for Counter-Terror Strategy

The traditional view that human rights obligations only apply within state borders has been increasingly challenged. International courts and human rights bodies now recognize that states can be held accountable for human rights violations outside their territory.

Two main exceptions to the territoriality principle have emerged. First, states can be held responsible for actions in territories they control, even without formal sovereignty. This includes situations like military occupations or indirect governance. Courts in Europe, the Americas, and Africa have affirmed this principle. Second, states are accountable for actions by their agents or organs outside their borders.

Despite these principles, the practical application is controversial. The USA, for example, argues that its human rights obligations do not extend to places like Guantanamo Bay or certain war zones, a stance criticized by international human rights bodies.[20]

The case of *Al-Skeini vs. UK* emphasized 'effective control' as key in determining state responsibility. The European Court of Human Rights held that the UK was liable for the deaths of Iraqi civilians at the hands of British forces. This decision highlights that states cannot avoid accountability for human rights abuses by their forces, even abroad, when they have effective control (*Al-Skeini v. UK*).

Unilateral counter-terrorism actions have complicated the application of extraterritorial human rights law. UN Security Council Resolution 1373, which mandates states to fight terrorism, has been criticized for potentially eroding human rights protections. The tension between security and human rights remains a challenge.[21]

While international human rights law (IHRL) has increasingly extraterritorial reach, significant challenges persist. States continue to debate their obligations, and implementing IHRL in contexts like military occupations and counter-terrorism operations requires continuous effort. Nevertheless, IHRL's enforcement through forums like the International Court of Justice and regional courts offers a degree of accountability, even if their effectiveness is debated.

The Imbalance of Security and Human Rights in Counter-Terrorism: A Positive Paradigm

Resolution 1373 is concerning because it doesn't ensure a balance between fighting terrorism and protecting human rights. The Special Rapporteur on Countering Terrorism has highlighted these issues, but in practice, states use vague definitions of terrorism. This can lead to broad measures that violate many human rights, going against the principle of legal certainty.[22]

Resolution 1373's issues have been partly addressed, but some have worsened over time. After 9/11, many resolutions focused heavily on national security, often at the expense of human rights. However, more recent Security

Council resolutions now include clauses that highlight states' obligations to international laws, including human rights, refugee, and humanitarian laws. (see UN Security Council Resolution 1456).

A positive shift is the recognition that human rights are not just an add-on, but an integral part of counter-terrorism efforts. The Global Counter-Terrorism Strategy now acknowledges that human rights violations can contribute to conditions that fuel terrorism. It highlights that states benefit in the long run by incorporating human rights obligations into their counter-terrorism strategies and laws. The UN General Assembly's Comprehensive Counter-Terrorism Strategy emphasizes that protecting human rights and ensuring effective counter-terrorism measures are not opposing goals, but complementary and mutually reinforcing. The Strategy's preamble notes the interconnectedness of development, peace, security, and human rights.

The Impact of International Human Rights Regime on Counter-Terrorism Measures

The growing trend of conducting special terrorism trials in recent years has raised concerns about how rights violations can disrupt the criminal process. These concerns can complicate efforts to apprehend suspects, share evidence, provide legal assistance, or rely on certain evidence. Post-9/11 counter-terrorism activities have shown that ignoring human rights and the rule of law can hinder both preventing terrorism and enforcing laws.

Additionally, the lack of clear definitions in Resolution 1373 has worsened legal challenges. The Security Council has increased state obligations, but with diminishing clarity. Resolutions 2178 and 2396 require strict measures against "foreign terrorist fighting," while Resolution 1624 calls for the prohibition of terrorism incitement, yet none offer clear definitions. These vague provisions in these resolutions have led to measures that infringe upon human rights, including political dissent suppression, press restrictions, and interference with humanitarian workers.[23]

As expected, states have argued that their human rights obligations are secondary to their commitments under Chapter VII of the UN Charter, especially regarding terrorist blacklists. Courts and human rights bodies have ruled that while states must fulfil these obligations, they must also respect human rights, including allowing individuals to challenge measures against them. Despite complex issues, courts have affirmed that human rights, particularly due process, cannot be ignored and must be considered alongside Security Council obligations.[24]

Derogation of Human Rights in Emergencies

States have some flexibility to adjust domestic laws in exceptional situations, as long as they comply with international norms. Derogation, or temporarily suspending certain rights during public emergencies that threaten the nation's life, is allowed under international law but comes with strict limitations.

To justify derogation, states must prove a severe public emergency that affects the whole population and demands extraordinary measures. Any restrictions must be necessary, proportionate, and limited in scope and time. Certain rights, such as the right to life, freedom from torture, and the right to a fair trial, remain protected at all times.

India's Constitution permits reasonable restrictions on fundamental rights, particularly in the interest of national security, public order, and sovereignty. These restrictions are subject to judicial review to ensure they are proportionate and in alignment with international human rights standards. However, under counter-terrorism frameworks, these limits often expand broadly and risk undermining civil liberties. The *Bhartiya Nagarik Suraksha Samhita* (BNSS), which replaces the Criminal Procedure Code, reflects this tension. While it seeks to modernize procedural law, concerns remain that certain provisions may enable extended detention or surveillance in the name of national security without adequate safeguards. A parallel can be drawn with the now-repealed Section 124A of the Indian Penal Code, which criminalized sedition and was often criticized for suppressing freedom of expression under the guise of protecting national integrity. Thus, the implementation of BNSS must be closely scrutinized to ensure that security measures do not disproportionately infringe upon constitutional rights.[25]

While international human rights law (IHRL) is meant to apply universally, the implementation of counter-terrorism practices has varied, even though the universality is generally acknowledged. Over time, the IHRL framework has adapted to meet the challenges posed by terrorism and counter-terrorism efforts. Despite these challenges, the legal system is now better equipped to address these issues.[26]

The Erosion of Legal Certainty in Counter-Terrorism Measures: Overkill?

The IHRL framework has faced ongoing challenges, weakening its effectiveness.

The long-term impact depends on whether the international community shifts towards a rule of law approach, as outlined in agreements. A key issue is the challenge to the rule of law, where vague and broad definitions of terrorism have undermined legal certainty in prosecuting alleged terrorist acts.

The broad definitions, leading to more prosecutions, conflict with the need for clarity and precision in criminal law. This has serious implications for freedom of expression, political dissent, democracy, and human rights. The rise in prosecutions is evident in statements from political leaders like former US President Obama, who urged for more stringent laws, beyond ordinary criminal statutes. This led to the cessation of investigations into torture and extrajudicial killings during CIA detention, which was criticized as a 'whitewash' of the 'War on Terror' crimes.[27]

Incitement, Glorification and Support to Terrorist Activities: Human Rights Concerns

The effectiveness of counter-terrorism strategies depends on public perception and acceptance. Regardless of how these measures are presented by the state, their evaluation is based on democratic values and human rights frameworks agreed upon by nations.

The United Nations, through its Security Council, has the authority to address human rights violations, not only by state parties but also by individuals and organizations, including those labelled as terrorist groups. The focus of anti-terrorism laws has shifted from simply labelling acts as criminal to targeting any support, whether material, financial, ideological, or otherwise, that contributes to terrorism.

Ideological support plays a crucial role in fuelling terrorism, alongside finance, weapons, and materials. The global fight against terrorism has moved from criminalization and prevention to addressing the societal processes that lead to terrorism.

Moreover, glorifying or supporting terrorism has been criminalized in international laws, including those under UN Security Council Resolution 1624 (2005) and the Council of Europe's Convention for the Prevention of Terrorism. While the European Convention is regionally binding, it has influenced global interpretations of anti-terrorism measures.

UN Resolution 1624 was adopted in the wake of 7/7 London bombings (2005). It condemns the glorification and justification of terrorist acts and reaffirms that incitement to terrorist acts is contrary to the letter and spirit of the principles of the United Nations. The resolution strongly condemns the incitement and glorification of terrorism, which threatens human rights and global stability, urging urgent action by states under international law—while reaffirming that freedom of expression must be protected, with lawful and necessary restrictions only.

The resolution suggests that within the phrase '*to take all necessary and appropriate measures*,' the contracting parties (states) are obliged to legally prohibit incitement to commit terrorist acts. It highlights the importance of freedom of expression as articulated in both the Universal Declaration of Human Rights and the International Covenant on Civil and Political Rights (ICCPR). Additionally, it emphasizes that states must ensure that their counter-terrorism measures align with the responsibilities outlined in international law.

Incitement to Terrorism and Indian Laws

Incitement to terrorist acts has been duly criminalized in Indian law in the Unlawful Activities (Prevention) Act, 1967 (UAPA) in Section 18 of the Act which prescribes:

> *"18. Punishment for conspiracy, etc.—Whoever conspires or attempts to commit, or advocates, abets, advises or [**incites**, directly or knowingly facilitates] the commission of, a terrorist act or any act preparatory to the commission of a terrorist act, shall be punishable with imprisonment for a term which shall not be less than five years but which may extend to imprisonment for life, and shall also be liable to fine."*

The section outlines stringent criminal penalties for advocating, advising, inciting, or maliciously facilitating a terrorist act or any act leading to its commission. Notably, the Act does not expressly reference UNSC Resolution 1264 in its objective resolution. However, when interpreted alongside the Objective Resolution of the National Investigation Agency (in conjunction with Schedule I of the Act), it appears to effectively meet the criteria outlined in Resolution 1264. The prohibition against inciting terrorist acts and the mandate to criminalize such activities existed prior to the adoption of Resolution 1264.

In international law also, there is a specific prohibition on propaganda activities aimed at inciting armed conflict, which inherently encompasses terrorist acts. Article 20(1) of the ICCPR extends this prohibition to non-state actors, compelling states to criminalize individual-led war propaganda. Moreover, international law prohibits propaganda intended for subversion or internal armed conflict by prohibiting intervention in the domestic affairs of states.[28]

The Incitement Dilemma: Addressing Limitations in Counter-Terrorism Legislation

Both the ICCPR and CERD are limited in addressing terrorism, as they only prohibit incitement linked to national, racial, or religious hatred and focus on specific crimes like war or genocide, not terrorism. They also function more as guiding frameworks than enforceable criminal laws. In contrast, UNSC Resolution 1624 and the Council of Europe Convention directly target terrorism, requiring states to adopt criminal measures against incitement—though only the latter clearly mandates a distinct offence.

Modern terrorism, sometimes driven by violence itself rather than political goals, has evolved, especially through social media. Groups such as ISIS use online platforms to glorify horrific acts, demanding legal responses that treat incitement as a separate crime. Post-9/11 developments reflect the need to distinguish support for terrorism from actual attacks, but this requires laws with clear definitions to avoid ambiguity and protect human rights.

However, both UNSC Resolution 1624 and the Council of Europe Convention lack precise definitions of incitement. Terms like 'provocation' or 'prohibition of incitement' are vague and don't fully capture the wider range of terrorist-related conduct, which includes both violent acts and supporting actions.

Defining Incitement to Terrorism in International Law: Implications for Counter-terror Policies

Resolution 1264 calls on states to 'prohibit...incitement' but does not define it precisely. It distinguishes incitement from the 'justification or glorification (apologia)' of terrorism, which states are not required, and may even be discouraged, from criminalizing, according to the Secretary-General's Guidelines. These interpret incitement as direct encouragement to commit terrorist acts. In contrast, the UN Human Rights Committee takes a broader view, emphasizing that terms like 'praising' or 'justifying' terrorism must be clearly defined to avoid disproportionate limits on free expression.

The Council of Europe Convention provides the widest scope to criminalize 'incitement to terrorism,' requiring states to outlaw 'public provocation to commit a terrorist offense. This includes any public message meant to incite terrorism, even without explicitly promoting violence, if it risks leading to terrorist acts. Such provisions allow bans on speech that praises attackers, insults victims, seeks terrorist funding, or portrays terrorism as necessary.

Balancing Freedom of Speech and Incitement to Terrorism in International Law

The European Parliament's 2008 resolution introduced a 'threshold probability' standard, requiring that incitement to terrorism show a real likelihood of leading to violence—not just advocacy. This flexible approach, influenced by the European Court of Human Rights (ECtHR), evaluates the context, speaker, and audience instead of applying a strict probability test. Critics argue it restricts free speech excessively. Some propose that incitement should only be criminalized when it poses an immediate and likely risk. However, proving a direct causal link between incitement and terrorist acts is often unrealistic, as incitement tends to shape broader violent environments rather than trigger specific acts.

The UN Secretary-General's Guidelines suggest restricting speech only when it clearly increases the risk of terrorism or leads to criminal conduct, requiring a high threshold. Since many national laws lack ECtHR-style oversight, this stricter standard might be more appropriate. Still, the UN Special Rapporteur supports the ECtHR's contextual approach as a global best practice in balancing risk and intent.

Resolution 1624 (2005) stresses the danger of extremist ideologies and calls for preventive action. Yet, the Secretary-General's narrow reading of 'incitement', limited to direct, high-risk calls to violence—may reduce the Resolution's effectiveness. By contrast, the Council of Europe Convention defines incitement more broadly, allowing action against indirect or lower-risk provocations.

Ultimately, a balanced approach is needed—one that tackles dangerous ideologies before they incite violence, while also protecting fundamental rights and freedoms.

Big Brother is Watching: The Implications of Mass Surveillance on Human Rights

The Impact of International and Extraterritorial Surveillance on Human Rights
Laurent Richard and Sandrine Rigaud, in *Pegasus: How a Spy in Your Pocket Threatens the End of Privacy, Dignity, and Democracy*, expose how covert agencies use cyber tools to infect phones and spy on individuals, violating their privacy, dignity, and democratic rights. Their work highlights a growing threat to freedoms due to unchecked surveillance.[29]

Technological progress over the last two decades has transformed surveillance. Traditional wiretapping has been replaced by mass data collection, allowing agencies and BigTech to use algorithms to extract personal details without consent. Privacy advocates argue such surveillance is only justifiable in emergencies like war or imminent terrorist threats.

After 9/11, intelligence agencies realized that gathering data alone was not enough; connecting disparate intelligence became essential. As a result, efforts intensified to integrate and analyze vast amounts of information. For example, in 2006, the US National Security Agency created the largest database of call logs, and the New York Times revealed the US had gained access to financial data from SWIFT.[30]

Privacy experts warn of the dangers of using aggregated data to falsely suggest criminal behaviour. This concern was central to the 1989 US Supreme Court case *United States Department of Justice vs. Reporters Committee for Freedom of the Press*, where the Court noted the risks of compiling publicly available criminal records to imply ongoing criminality.

The expansion of surveillance powers calls for stronger oversight to protect privacy and rights. Without checks, national security efforts risk undermining democracy and eroding fundamental freedoms.

The Surveillance Dilemma: Protecting Public Safety While Preserving Privacy
However, there is no denying the fact that data can lead to interpretations that were not apparent when the data set was is discreet units and analysis of such data units threw patterns hitherto invisible. This is precisely what is intended to be achieved by combining large data sets. The suggestive value of analysis and interpretations done by algorithms and further refined by human analysts is the backbone of crime prediction by data analytics.

It is further argued by security expert whether the allegation that the privacy rights of individuals are affected by the predictive behavioural analysis from data mining is actually true. Considering the fact that during the later part of the first decade of 21st century customers of online platforms have voluntarily agreed to share their 'behavioural data exhaust'[31] it can be reasonably argued that any subsequent data analytics for suggesting pattern can therefore reliably be used by the security agencies to predict patterns suggesting criminality. The agencies have been maintaining database including that on chemicals, criminal patterns, modus operandi, gangsters, criminal profiling, fingerprints etc. Such databases are regularly subjected to intelligent algorithms to understand patterns and predictions to not only investigate but also to prevent future crimes. One may reasonably ask how is that different from getting some insights from the behavioural data exhaust?

The Digital Transformation of Intelligence: Privacy Implications and Human Rights Concerns

The rise of the Internet ushered in the era of Information Technology Enabled Services (ITES), transforming communication and reshaping intelligence gathering. While offering new opportunities, it also introduced challenges in monitoring individuals and assets.

Computational intelligence began during World War II with military code-breaking and the development of ENIAC—the first general-purpose electronic digital computer. Built for calculating artillery trajectories, ENIAC automated complex, time-consuming tasks, enhancing accuracy and speed in tactical planning. Weighing 30 tons and spanning 1,800 square feet, ENIAC laid the groundwork for modern intelligence computing.

Intelligence has long informed policy and enabled proactive responses to threats. Law enforcement later adopted predictive tools to anticipate riots, gang activities, and terrorism. While intelligence focuses on forecasting and advising policymakers, law enforcement operates post-event, building criminal cases through fact analysis and legal procedures.

Big Tech and the New Era of Intelligence Gathering: Privacy Crusaders or Informational Hegemon?

Social media platforms like Facebook and Twitter often present themselves as privacy champions, especially amid growing regulatory scrutiny. However, compliance can be expensive, and many private companies hesitate to bear these costs. In India, law enforcement faces more resistance from US-based platforms than their counterparts in Western countries, where cooperation is often smoother.

Recently, India has become more assertive, requiring offshore internet intermediaries to comply with local directives. While privacy concerns raised by these platforms are valid, the transfer of Indian users' behavioural data to foreign servers poses national security risks, including potential misuse to target individuals or influence domestic affairs—without offering reciprocal benefits to Indian users.

Surveillance Powers and Privacy Concerns in India

In India, security agencies have broad powers to intercept communications under the Telegraph Act and Information Technology Act. While safeguards exist, concerns remain about the potential for abuse. Unlike in the USA, warrants are not always required for surveillance, and *authorized officers* can initiate interception based on reasonable suspicion. This raises questions about the balance between security and privacy in India.

The surveillance landscape in India is relatively limited compared to the Big-Five countries (UK, USA, Canada, Australia, and New Zealand), which are at the forefront of the Internet revolution and host many major tech giants. However, Indian laws grant significant latitude to '*authorized officers*' of security agencies to initiate surveillance without obtaining a formal warrant from a judicial forum. Section 91 of the Code of Criminal Procedure (CrPC) (now same section of BNSS) empowers a court or police station officer to issue a summons or written order for the production of documents or other things required in connection with the investigation of a criminal offence.

Unlike in the USA and other Western jurisdictions, India does not have a strict separation between foreign and domestic intelligence. Indian intelligence agencies are authorized to place surveillance requests based on a reasonable apprehension of danger to the sovereignty and integrity of India or other similar grounds. Despite the broad powers granted to security agencies, there are inherent safeguards built into the process. The highest officers of the state authorize such interceptions, and these orders are reviewed by special executive committees constituted for this purpose.

In conclusion, while India's surveillance laws provide significant powers to security agencies, rules governing their operation also include mechanisms designed to prevent abuse. However, the lack of a requirement for judicial warrants and the broad scope of surveillance powers continue to raise concerns about the potential for privacy violations and the need for stronger oversight to protect individual rights.

Built-in Safeguards in India against Arbitrary Surveillance

The misuse of electronic intelligence and surveillance capabilities can lead to serious consequences both for the individuals affected and body politic in general. The political fallout from the 'Pegasus' snoopgate highlights how allegations of unauthorized surveillance can harm national politics and mislead the public. However, India's legal surveillance framework includes safeguards to protect individual privacy.

The legal regime addresses the three privacy pillars: acquisition, retention, and dissemination. Surveillance is authorized only by designated officers with approval from the head of the relevant Home Department, and further interception requires continued sanction.[32]

Surveillance on specific identifiers (e.g., phone or email) is time-bound. Recordings must be destroyed unless required for court or official use. Dissemination follows strict procedures, and penalties apply for non-compliance or misconduct. Whistleblowers play a key role in exposing abuse, and mechanisms exist to address such concerns through formal channels.[33]

Balancing Privacy and Security: The Need for Transparency in Surveillance

Upholding the human right to privacy necessitates that the surveillance regime prioritizes transparency. This can be accomplished by disclosing non-sensitive information such as the nature and purpose of surveillance, the methods and rationale behind data analysis, and the intended use of the gathered information. Furthermore, surveillance mechanisms should be institutionalized through the establishment of an IT-enabled paperless system, enabling prompt backtracking and accountability in the event of power abuse, and facilitating thorough investigations into allegations. Alongside clearly delineated internal authority frameworks, legislative scrutiny fosters a measure of accountability through the regular release of appropriately redacted public reports.

The State, nevertheless, possesses the inherent authority to safeguard society from the threats posed by terrorists and organized criminal syndicates, without necessarily being held hostage to its obligations towards human rights protection. National security, in emergent instances, must take precedence over concerns regarding an individual's need for privacy. From this unequivocally statist perspective, the State holds an eminent domain to intercept communications that it deems worthy of consideration.

The adage '*Every man's home is his castle*' underscores the inviolability of an individual's personal domain, akin to a temple. However, it is equally apt to assert that while every man's home is a castle, no man can fortify his castle against the sovereign's authority. This legal maxim, originating from English common law, emphasizes the principle that the sovereign power of the State can supersede individual rights. In the context of privacy protection, this maxim is sometimes invoked to justify the government's intrusion into an individual's privacy in the pursuit of national security or other legitimate interests.

The delicate balance between individual privacy rights and national security imperatives has been a subject of ongoing debate, particularly in the face of advancements in technology that have empowered governments to amass vast troves of data about their citizens. The overarching question remains: does the adage '*Every man's home is his castle*' still hold sway in the context of contemporary privacy protection? The answer hinges on the ability of each society to strike a harmonious equilibrium between these competing interests.

Striking this balance requires continuous evaluation and adaptation of safeguards to prevent misuse and protect fundamental freedoms. While the State's authority to ensure security is paramount, it must be exercised with transparency and accountability to maintain public trust and uphold the principles of democracy.

Much of the criticism of the surveillance regimes instituted by democratic societies revolves around privacy, its meaning and value, and how it is affected by surveillance. Privacy advocates have warned of the proliferation of virtual private networks and encryption algorithms that would make it increasingly difficult for unscrupulous individuals and governments alike to intercept and read private communications. This is notwithstanding the fact that such communication technologies can and are used by terrorists.[34]

There is growing concern due to communication protocols used by terrorists *going dark*, as is increasingly evident from counter-terrorism investigations conducted by the National Investigation Agency against modules in India created by overseas handlers affiliated with the Islamic State (ISIS).[35]

Modern security agencies rely on technology-enabled and less intrusive methods of collecting information. Monitoring of public spaces by intricate webs of CCTV cameras, the automatic interception and retention of internet and telecommunication traffic, and the use of artificial intelligence to make sense of behavioural data churned by social media intermediaries are just some of the ways in which collective information of millions of individuals can be analysed for desired filtration. The modern surveillance regime is unique in that there is an increasing redundancy of the need to put a human observer in the loop for capturing, retaining, and preliminarily analysing such data. Algorithms perform these tasks instead of human agents. Human intervention is expected to decrease further with the advent of advanced artificial intelligence.

In a true democracy, the power to challenge authoritarian overreach and uphold civil liberties lies with the people. When civil society freely demands transparency and accountability, especially in cases of privacy violations, it compels the security apparatus to evolve. Surveillance practices must align with the principle of proportionality, ensuring that any intrusion into private life is justified by a compelling need to protect public safety. This dynamic balance between security and freedom strengthens democratic resilience, reminding us that in an open society, oversight is not an obstacle to safety but a vital part of safeguarding both rights and national security.

In essence, while surveillance is crucial for national security, it must be balanced with the protection of individual privacy. The evolving technology landscape demands that surveillance practices be continuously scrutinized and regulated to ensure they remain proportional and respectful of human rights.

Changing Contours of Privacy Concerns: Artificial Intelligence and Surveillance

The field of Artificial Intelligence traces its origins back to 1943 when Alan Turing, the British mathematician and creator of the first electronic computer system, proposed that a computer system could exhibit 'intelligence' when its responses could not be distinguished from those of a human. Initially limited to specific tasks like driving, operating machinery, or playing chess, AI systems have made remarkable progress. Today, AI appears to surpass human abilities (at least in speed) in translating natural language, drafting stories, improving written drafts, recognizing patterns and faces, and mimicking speech. If we are to believe technology optimists, AI-driven vehicles are expected to be commonplace by 2030, particularly in developed nations.[36]

AI systems continuously evolve through learning algorithms, adapting, and improving based on data sets and interactions with humans. Innovations such as perplexity, Chat GPT, Grow AI, DeepSeek, etc., are astounding to even the most sceptical AI pessimists, challenging the notion that true machine intelligence is purely science fiction. However, the proliferation of AI raises concerns about privacy in an increasingly transformed cyber landscape.

Looking ahead, the adaptation of laws to match the dynamic realities of the cyber world remains critical. The scope of surveillance obligations beyond national borders poses a challenge that human rights courts will likely need to address. Until November 2022, many experts in cyber technologies doubted the feasibility of AI. Yet, within months, these doubts were shattered with the launch of Chat GPT, an AI language model displaying human-like speech and knowledge assimilation. AI's potential to revolutionize cyberspace is undeniable, though it presents numerous privacy challenges for individuals.

Artificial Intelligence (AI) harbours significant potential for positive strides across various domains. Nevertheless, there is an escalating apprehension regarding its potential exploitation by security agencies both private and public to surveil unsuspecting individuals. The amalgamation of AI and surveillance technologies has facilitated unparalleled capabilities, empowering governments, and security agencies to engage in widespread surveillance, thereby carrying profound implications for privacy and civil liberties.[37]

A principal avenue for the misuse of AI in surveillance lies in the deployment of advanced facial recognition systems. These systems leverage sophisticated algorithms to scrutinise facial features and compare them against extensive databases. Although initially crafted for legitimate objectives such as criminal identification and heightened security, the technology is susceptible to exploitation. Security agencies can utilise AI-powered facial recognition to surveil public spaces, trail individuals, and assemble comprehensive profiles without their awareness or consent.[38]

Another disconcerting aspect of AI misuse in surveillance pertains to predictive policing. AI algorithms, when supplied with historical crime data, can ostensibly forecast the probable locations and times of future crimes. Nevertheless, this method gives rise to ethical concerns, as it may perpetuate biases inherent in historical data, unfairly singling out specific communities. If wielded improperly, predictive policing could serve as a tool for unjust profiling and unwarranted surveillance of innocent individuals.[39]

Social media monitoring represents another sphere where AI may be utilised for surveillance purposes. Security agencies can employ AI algorithms to sift through extensive data on social media platforms, analysing user behaviour, sentiments, and connections. This not only elicits privacy concerns but also poses the risk of chilling effects on free speech and expression, as individuals may engage in self-censorship due to apprehensions about government scrutiny.[40]

AI-fuelled data analysis has the potential to be manipulated for conducting intrusive surveillance on individuals' online activities. Western security agencies are already harnessing machine learning algorithms to oversee emails, chat conversations, and browsing history. The substantial amount of data that AI can process facilitates a level of scrutiny that was previously inconceivable, prompting significant inquiries into the erosion of digital privacy.[41]

The incorporation of AI into drone technology significantly enhances the surveillance capabilities. Autonomous drones, fitted with AI-powered cameras, possess the capability to track and trail individuals, delivering real-time footage of their movements. This not only prompts concerns about continuous aerial surveillance but also the potential for misidentification or unfounded accusations stemming from algorithmic misinterpretations. The integration of AI with biometric technologies, such as voice recognition and gait analysis, adds an additional layer to the surveillance landscape. Security agencies can utilise AI algorithms to identify and monitor individuals based on distinctive biometric markers. This, too, raises substantial privacy concerns, particularly when deployed lacking proper safeguards and oversight.[42]

Furthermore, the surreptitious deployment of AI-powered malware for digital surveillance poses a severe threat. Unscrupulous actors can release sophisticated malware embedded with AI capabilities to infiltrate devices, oversee communications, and extract sensitive information. Such tactics not only jeopardise individual privacy but also undermine the security of personal and corporate data.

To counter the potential misuse of AI in surveillance, there is an urgent requirement for robust legal frameworks and ethical guidelines.[43] Striking a balance between national security interests and individual rights is imperative. Governments must formulate clear regulations dictating the permissible use of AI in surveillance, ensuring transparency, accountability, and adherence to human rights principles. While the United Nation's approach has hitherto has been to influence law making (in the member states) by issuing model law codes or essentially by issuing non-binding guidelines, the approach surely has its limitations.

While AI offers transformative opportunities, its possible abuse by unscrupulous security agencies for mass surveillance raises substantial ethical, legal, and societal concerns. Safeguarding against these abuses demands a united effort to establish ethical guidelines, legal frameworks, and public awareness campaigns that underscore the significance of preserving individual privacy and civil liberties amidst the ever-evolving landscape of technological capabilities.

Conclusion

While international human rights law is clear on what constitutes human rights, the age of artificial intelligence and the possibility of 'Orwellian' mechanisms in surveillance have cast a sombre shadow on individuals' ability to protect their privacy. Despite the frequent *pious homilies* parroted by Big Tech about their quest to ensure privacy, the reality is that their voracious hunger for exponentially increasing 'user engagement', '*behavioural data exhaust*' and their use as oil has created an unprecedented possibility of an 'Big-Tech Super-State.'

In the same breath, we shall emphasise that any incitement or support for terrorism online shall not be tolerated. Protection of privacy cannot be used as a shield to disable law enforcement agencies in their mission to protect lives by preventing terror crimes. Surveillance by state authorities has seen a paradigm shift as Big Tech capabilities in mass surveillance have become a reality due to the accumulation of massive amounts of data from their customers' online activities. This data exhaust is a treasure trove for predictive analysis, a subject that has bewildered advocates of privacy and the state's obligation to protect their citizens from terrorist acts. The delicate balance between national security concerns and an individual's right to see, hear, and say anything that they sincerely believe in sometimes becomes shaky.

8

Preparatory Acts of Terrorism, Prevention and Counter-Radicalisation

"*Terrorism is an enemy of humanity and there can be no ifs and buts in dealing with it. We must overcome all such forces sponsoring and exporting terror*".

—**Narendra Modi**

Prevention seeks to anticipate and thwart terrorism by analysing risks and intelligence that signal potential threats. Its goal is to influence behaviour and events early, minimizing the likelihood of harm. Traditionally, preventive measures are categorized into primary, secondary, and tertiary levels, ranging from corrective efforts like education and de-radicalization to punitive responses.

Primary prevention targets the underlying socio-economic drivers and perceived injustices that fuel extremism. Secondary prevention engages at-risk communities through state-led interventions aimed at reducing vulnerability to radicalization.

This chapter focuses on tertiary prevention, where criminal intent manifests in planning and conspiracies. The shift from post-crime response to pre-emptive action reflects the adaptive nature of modern terrorist strategies.

Criminalisation of Preparatory Acts of Terrorism: Principle of Pre-emption, Precaution and Preventative Paradigm

The criminalization of preparatory acts of terrorism refers to the legal measures taken by jurisdictions to prosecute and penalize individuals involved in activities that precede or support the planning and execution of terrorist acts, even if the actual attack has not been carried out. These acts, also called *"Precursor Acts,"* and these include planning, gathering resources, training, recruiting, and any other actions intended to facilitate or prepare for a terrorist act.

The objective is to act before it's late. Instead of waiting for a potential conspiracy to be executed, it is crucial to arrest the progression of such conspiracies by stopping acts that may seem inchoate and innocuous separately but are geared towards the future commission of a terrorist act or acts.

The Shift Towards Preventive Measures

The 9/11 attacks marked a turning point in global counterterrorism, prompting a shift toward preventive measures. Criminalizing preparatory acts of terrorism became a focus, with legal frameworks strengthened through international conventions and resolutions.

The USA and its allies moved from localized, law enforcement-based strategies to global, military-focused interventions. Under the Bush administration, terrorism was redefined as a global threat, with groups using advanced technology and recruiting educated individuals for sophisticated attacks.

The Role of the Information Technology Revolution

The criminalization of preparatory terrorist acts was significantly shaped by the information technology revolution. This allowed security agencies to predict terrorist planning through surveillance of actions that initially appeared innocuous. Examples include intelligence inputs of foreigners getting trained for becoming pilots while not bothering to learn landing procedures, monitoring orders for bomb-making chemicals, overseas wire transfers to suspects, online radicalization, and chat groups endorsing extremist ideas. Such analyses helped identify patterns suggesting a higher probability of future attacks.[1]

Western agencies were shaken by the realization that terrorism had reached their own societies, orchestrated remotely by groups in the middle east and Pakistan. Attacks targeted Western civilians and military forces abroad, underscoring the need to criminalize preparatory acts to prevent escalation into mass violence.

The early 21st century introduced a 'preventative shift' and 'pre-emptive' strategy in counter-terrorism. Post-9/11, the USA used overwhelming military power in Afghanistan to eliminate perceived threats. The focus shifted from isolated terrorist incidents to dismantling the broader capabilities of groups labelled as 'enemies.'

However, history shows that these large-scale military interventions resulted in asymmetrical warfare, leading to massive casualties without neutralizing the Taliban. With the withdrawal of allied forces, it became clear that the Taliban's strength had been underestimated. The Kabul administration, backed by the USA, proved fragile, with control largely limited to the capital.

The Rise of ISIS

ISIS, the Islamic State of Iraq and Syria, emerged from the remnants of al-Qaeda in Iraq following the US-led invasion in 2003. Initially part of the insurgency against US forces and the Iraqi government, ISIS capitalized on instability caused by the Syrian civil war, sectarian tensions, and power vacuums to expand its control over territory. By 2014, ISIS had enforced brutal rule and proclaimed a caliphate.

US policy faced challenges in recognizing the growing threat posed by ISIS early on. Initially, the focus was on addressing other elements in the region, leading to an underestimation of ISIS's potential and the consequences of the power vacuum in Iraq and Syria. The rapid rise of ISIS took many by surprise, as did its ability to recruit foreign fighters and utilize social media for propaganda and recruitment.

Intelligence Gaps and Geopolitical Shifts: Role of Foreign Fighters

The failure to recognize ISIS's emergence and rapid ascension was partly due to intelligence gaps, shifts in the geopolitical landscape, and the complex nature of regional conflicts. It took time for a concerted global effort to form, involving various nations, to combat ISIS and push back against its territorial control.

Between 2013 and 2019, an estimated 300 Americans joined ISIS, and in total, more than 53,000 people from roughly 80 countries joined the group. The rise of ISIS was significantly bolstered by its adept utilization of technology across various domains, enabling recruitment, propaganda dissemination, and financial operations. ISIS exploited social media platforms, producing slickly crafted videos and engaging in online campaigns to attract fighters globally. Their propaganda skilfully manipulated narratives, presenting a distorted image of heroism and religious duty, making recruitment accessible to individuals worldwide.[2]

Technological Exploitation: Online Radicalisation

The ISIS's use of online platforms transformed how extremist groups communicate and recruit. Beyond Twitter, Facebook, and Telegram, they tapped into encrypted apps, dark web forums, and online magazines like *Dabiq* and *Rumiyah*. These digital spaces became tools for spreading propaganda, recruiting members, and planning attacks.

ISIS propaganda targeted vulnerable individuals seeking belonging and purpose. Blending religious zeal with graphic violence, ISIS created emotionally charged content. Social media's visual nature amplified their shocking imagery, such as beheadings and executions, designed to provoke fear and fascination.

They also used religious symbolism to justify their actions, branding themselves as defenders of Islam and promoters of a global caliphate. Their radical interpretation of Islamic law appealed to disillusioned individuals and those alienated from mainstream religious or social systems.

Financial Operations

Technology also facilitated ISIS's financial operations, allowing them to generate income through illicit means, including online fundraising, crypto currency transactions, and the exploitation of digital payment systems. They exploited loopholes within financial networks to clandestinely move funds across borders.[3]

The rapid evolution of technology also presented challenges for authorities attempting to counter ISIS. It provided the group with the ability to adapt rapidly, exploiting encryption, anonymous communication channels, and the dark web to evade detection and surveillance by law enforcement agencies.[4]

The challenges presented by ISIS transformed the law-enforcement mindset in the USA and European countries and the axiom of '*countering violent extremism*' saw a paradigm shift towards '*preventing violent extremism*' while clearly emphasising the value of long-term vision in the prevention of terrorist crimes by employing measures that would highlight patterns and network of individuals and organizations preparing and planning strikes.

The Evolution of Counter-terrorism: Criminalizing Preparatory Acts of Terrorism

The criminalization of preparatory acts of terrorism reflects a significant shift in legal thinking, driven by the demand for preventive counter-terrorism strategies. This evolution acknowledges that waiting for an attack to occur is no longer viable in the face of rapidly evolving threats such as jihadi terrorism and the rise of ISIS. In response, many countries have expanded legal frameworks to criminalize early-stage preparatory acts such as radicalization, propaganda dissemination, and online recruitment. Notably, several jurisdictions now prosecute returnees who have served as foreign fighters abroad.

India, despite having the world's second-largest Muslim population, has seen minimal participation of its citizens in ISIS-related activities. This is often credited to its use of preventive legal measures, particularly the Unlawful Activities (Prevention) Act (UAPA) and the powers vested in the National Investigation Agency (NIA). These tools enable authorities to intervene early, even before concrete acts of terrorism are carried out. This shift embodies the precautionary principle in criminal law, focusing on identifying and mitigating risks before they escalate. This form of governance emphasizes anticipation over reaction.[5]

All said and done, the reliance on preventive logic raises critical legal and ethical concerns. Critics caution that such frameworks may erode legal certainty and weaken fundamental rights by prioritizing risk management over due process. In India, where no dedicated anti-terror law exists, the UAPA's expanding scope illustrates the complex challenge of adapting laws to emerging threats while upholding constitutional safeguards.[6]

The Criminalization of Preparatory Acts: A Risk Management Approach to Counter-Terrorism

The criminalization of preparatory acts in counter-terrorism raises significant legal and ethical questions. While proponents argue it is necessary to prevent attacks, critics contend it infringes on individual rights. The precautionary principle advocates for preventative measures to avoid harm, even with incomplete scientific evidence. In counter-terrorism, it suggests criminalizing preparatory acts to avoid the risk of a terrorist attack.

However, the relationship between risk and law in counter-terrorism is more complex than the precautionary principle suggests. It provides a framework for decision-making but does not offer a definitive solution. The challenge is balancing harm prevention with protecting individual rights, as human rights should always be preserved.

Risk management in counter-terrorism involves making future terrorist acts more predictable by analyzing behaviours of individuals or groups nearing terrorist actions. The precautionary principle focuses on pre-emptive measures, aiming to address perceived risks proactively. It assumes that risks can be mitigated by predicting behaviours that lead to terrorist acts, even under uncertainty.[7]

Although measuring exact risks in terrorism is impossible, precautionary decisions consider future scenarios based on scientific principles. These include methods like pattern recognition, legal surveillance, and data mining based on empirical evidence, not assumptions or fear (Baker & Simon). The state security apparatus has a responsibility to detect and pre-empt risks. Failure leads to security failures, as seen in the Kargil War, the 2001 Indian Parliament attack, and 9/11.

The precautionary principle suggests that lack of conclusive evidence should not stop preventative measures. The state must protect citizens from harm even when substantive proof may not be sufficient to launch a formal prosecution. Arguments supporting this include:

- (i) *Cost-Benefit of Inaction:* The risks of inaction often outweigh those of preventative measures. A terrorist attack's consequences can be severe, justifying a proactive approach.
- (ii) *Evolving Threats:* Terrorists continually adapt. Relying on reactive measures leaves states vulnerable to new threats.
- (iii) *Importance from intelligence point of view:* Intelligence gathering can provide insights into potential threats even without definitive proof.
- (iv) *Risk Assessment:* Risk frameworks help prioritize counter-terrorism efforts and resources.
- (v) *International Cooperation:* Sharing information and coordinating efforts enhances states' ability to prevent threats.

In conclusion, the *precautionary principle* supports a proactive counter-terrorism approach. By investing in intelligence, risk assessment, and international cooperation, states can better protect citizens while upholding democracy and human rights.[8]

The Shift to Future Temporality in Counter-Terrorism Law

The concept of 'future temporality' in legal frameworks marks a shift from focusing on past and present crimes to a preventative approach aimed at future potential crimes. This evolution in legal systems emphasizes risk prevention, marking a significant change in modern criminal justice practice.

Traditionally, judges base judgments on conclusive evidence of a crime already committed, rather than on precursor acts that could lead to terrorism if not prevented. The conditionality of 'would have' depends on the prosecution's ability to show that such acts, if left unchecked, *would have* led to a terrorist attack due to their predictable connection to such events.

Preparatory acts of terrorism are offences that don't require specific concrete acts. These can include mere membership in or allegiance to a terrorist group.[9] There is no condition of invariable concomitance, meaning thereby that it is not necessary to prove that the act would have definitely happened if not prevented. Preparation and its indicative acts itself are a sufficient condition. Preparatory acts are criminalized under the assumption they lead to attacks unless stopped. The criminalization of such acts is not new; one can be convicted for conspiracy to commit an offence even without physical participation. For example, Section 61 of the Bhartiya Nyaya Samhita holds individuals liable for *agreeing* to commit an offence, even if only one party takes an action toward it.

For instance, if four individuals (A, B, C, D) plan an armed robbery to fund a bomb plot and are arrested after 'A' buys firearms, the overt offence is purchasing illegal firearms. However, the entire conspiracy is demonstrated through seized mobile devices, which shows the group's communication with an ISIS handler. The devices reveal their allegiance to ISIS and videos on how to kill police officers. This case exemplifies how modern counter-terrorism law criminalizes preparatory acts, shifting from reactive to proactive counter-measures against terrorism.

In the above hypothetical case each member of the group would be liable for preparatory acts under sections 61, 147, 148, and 150 of the Bhartiya Nyaya Samhita, alongside relevant sections of the Unlawful Activities (Prevention) Act (sections 18 and 20). Law enforcement authorities in India can proceed against such individuals based on conspiracy evidence, emphasizing the preventative nature of current counter-terrorism law.

Preventative Measures in Counter-Terrorism Legislation: The Unlawful Activities (Prevention) Act

The Unlawful Activities (Prevention) Act (UAPA) includes several provisions designed to prosecute preparatory acts of terrorism. These provisions underscore the shift towards a preventative focus in counter-terrorism strategy, emphasizing the need to address potential threats before they materialize into actual terrorist acts.

For example, sections 17 to 22 of the law deal with various offences related to terrorism. Section 17 criminalizes fund-raising for terrorist activities, with penalties of five years to life imprisonment. Section 18 targets conspiracy, attempts, and facilitation of terrorism, also punishable by five years to life imprisonment. Section 18A penalizes organizing terrorist training camps, while Section 18B targets recruiting individuals for terrorism. Section 19 criminalizes harbouring or concealing terrorists, with penalties of up to life imprisonment. Section 20 punishes membership in terrorist groups, and Section 21 addresses holding terrorist-derived property. Section 22 penalizes threats against witnesses, with imprisonment and fines.

The UAPA's Chapter IV includes a total of 14 sections on punishments for terrorism, with eight focusing on preparatory and auxiliary acts, highlighting the emphasis on preventative counter-terrorism measures. Chapter V addresses the forfeiture of terrorist proceeds, and Chapter VI penalizes membership and support for terrorist groups. The precautionary principle continues to shape prosecutorial efforts in counter-terrorism, despite concerns about its impact on criminal law. The UAPA's focus on future temporality shifts criminal law from being a last resort to a proactive tool for preventing terrorism, making it more instrumental in safeguarding society against terrorist threats.

Navigating the Legal Terrain of Terrorism Prevention in India

Terrorism can plunge a nation into chaos, creating massive security challenges. In India, events such as the 2001 Parliament attack, the 2008 Mumbai Taj Hotel assault, and ongoing threats in Kashmir highlight the urgent need for strong action. In such high-stakes situations, the state must act decisively to prevent terrorist activities, even at the planning or conspiracy stage, to avoid accusations of inaction. The state's primary role is to protect its people, and criminalizing the planning and conspiracy of terrorism helps thwart violent plots before they materialize. However, this approach requires a careful balance between security and individual rights, along with a professional legal system to handle such sensitive cases effectively.

The Challenges of Substantiating Terrorist Conspiracies in the Criminal Justice System

Proving a conspiracy in the criminal justice system is incredibly tough. A conspiracy often exists only in the minds of the conspirators, with evidence generally inferred from their actions. While confessions or reliable witness testimony can serve as evidence, courts often require more than just statements to prove a conspiracy. The line between planning and carrying out terrorist acts is wide, as seen in ISIS's method of recruiting sleeper cells through online radicalization. Given the global spread of terrorist networks, the law must address everything from planning to execution, including online recruitment. While early intervention and anticipatory prosecution are crucial, overreliance on surveillance can lead to false positives and miscarriages of justice. Defining the threshold for a conspiracy is critical, as rushing prosecutions without clear evidence risks higher acquittals and civil liberties concerns.

An Illustration

Imagine a senior law enforcement officer, 'X', in an Anti-Terrorism cell receives a tip about a group chatting online, discussing the need for their minority community to unite against perceived historical injustices. Further investigation reveals that they are using secret chats to talk about using violence to teach the majority community a lesson. However, months of surveillance reveal no concrete evidence of terrorist activity like bomb-making or reconnaissance. Their conversations remain vague, without any specifics on methods, targets, or plans. In this case, it's premature to call it a conspiracy. In the US, federal law (18 U.S.C. § 2339B) defines a conspiracy as an agreement to commit a crime, even without specifics on execution, and criminalizes providing material support for such activities.[10]

In India however, the scenario described above would not necessarily reveal a cognizable offense. While preventive detention laws like the National Security Act could be used to detain individuals, it would not be appropriate to act under the Unlawful Activities (Prevention) Act at this stage, as there is insufficient evidence of a terrorist conspiracy. Both the Bhartiya Nyaya Samhita (BNS) and the Unlawful Activities (Prevention) Act give law enforcement broad power to act swiftly when there is material suggesting a conspiracy, even before a terrorist act occurs. The real challenge lies in substantiating this conspiracy in court. Public opinion and political costs are at stake if major cases lead to acquittals.

The key question is when to intervene, which would require law enforcement to gather enough evidence during preliminary investigations and surveillance to support prosecution. Decisions on when to arrest and prosecute should be made on a case-by-case basis by experienced professionals, mindful that their methods and evidence will be scrutinized in court. While preventive action is a valuable tool, it must balance security with fundamental rights, supported by strong legal frameworks, oversight, and commitment to the rule of law.

Need for a Proactive Criminal Justice Counter-terrorism Strategy?

Countering terrorism is a major challenge for criminal justice systems. Prevention is vital, but existing frameworks often struggle against advanced threats and limited resources. A strong strategy needs clear laws, effective investigation tools, flexible evidence rules, and global cooperation. While this aims to reduce violence and uphold the rule of law, many countries lack the capacity to implement such frameworks without straining their systems or risking human rights violations.

Modern terrorism uses technology not only for weapons but also to spread fear globally. The 26/11 Mumbai attacks were a turning point, televised live, they gave terrorists worldwide publicity. Evidence showed handlers deliberately created a gruesome spectacle. In response, India set up the National Investigation Agency (NIA) to investigate terror cases centrally.

The shift toward prevention means new laws now criminalize actions like promoting terror ideologies, spreading violent content, or funding terror under cover of charity. Still, securing convictions is tough, prosecutors must prove guilt beyond reasonable doubt. Under Section 18 of UAPA, even seemingly harmless acts can be punished if they help in preparing for terrorism, reinforcing the law's preventative focus.

High Policing?

Contemporary policing has evolved far beyond Lord Robert Peel's idea of a vigilant constabulary. Today's model, known as 'High Policing,' emphasizes covert, intelligence-led operations using cutting-edge surveillance technologies to disrupt terrorism at the planning stage.[11] While concerns about secretive and coercive practices may evoke Orwellian fears, modern democracies rely on legal procedures and are guided by legislative and judicial oversight to ensure lawful action.

In democratic frameworks, terrorism is treated primarily as a criminal offence rather than just political violence. India, however, faces a unique combination of threats, from insurgencies and Left-Wing Extremism (Central India) in Jammu and Kashmir, and the North-East, which demand a hybrid model. This means blending strategies from both war-based and criminal justice approaches to address these diverse risks effectively.

This convergence has seen real success in recent years. Agencies like the National Investigation Agency (NIA), state police, and central armed forces now work in tandem, intervening early in conspiracies, often while terrorists are still planning or sourcing funds. By acting before threats fully materialize, this coordinated approach has disrupted potential attacks while they were still forming.[12]

Preventing Radicalisation: Promoting Counter-radicalization

Radicalization is the process where individuals adopt extreme beliefs that justify violence as a means to bring about social or political change. While not all who radicalize become terrorists, this shift in mindset often lays the groundwork for recruitment into terrorist activities. Recruitment occurs when someone is actively persuaded to take unlawful action under the banner of terrorism.

In most cases, radicalization precedes recruitment, acting as the trigger that makes a person open to joining or supporting terrorist operations—whether by carrying out attacks or helping behind the scenes as an Over Ground Worker (OGW). Still, it's crucial to remember that only a small fraction of radicalized individuals go on to commit acts of terror. Their journey can often be interrupted through early interventions by families, peers, or authorities.[13]

Counter-terrorism: A Balance Between Law Enforcement and Prevention

Modern terrorism thrives not just on weapons and tactics, but on the spread of extremist ideologies. Radicalization—the process of adopting beliefs that justify violence—threatens the core of democratic life. A heavy-handed military or purely punitive response often deepens social divides and breeds resentment, undermining long-term stability. To truly counter extremism, criminal justice systems must go beyond force and invest in de-radicalization as a vital preventative strategy.

In India, after the 26/11 attacks, laws like the National Investigation Agency Act (2008) and updated provisions under the Unlawful Activities (Prevention) Act (UAPA) expanded the state's capacity to respond to terrorism. These legal tools support pre-emptive action, helping to target fringe elements and support systems that fuel terrorism before violence occurs.

By contrast, the U.S. response post-9/11 leaned heavily on militarized tactics—pre-emptive strikes, detention without trial, and even torture at places like Guantanamo Bay and Abu Ghraib. The PATRIOT Act gave sweeping powers to security agencies, triggering global concern over human rights abuses. While initially aggressive, the USA later pivoted to a more integrated model—coordinating military, intelligence, and law enforcement efforts to address terror threats while restoring some balance between security and civil liberties.

Prevention through Counter-radicalisation

Over the past two decades, one lesson stands out clearly: countering radicalization requires more than just surveillance—it needs proactive engagement. Experts, law enforcement, community leaders, and even victims of terrorism must work together. A key part of this strategy is dismantling the ideological pull of global jihadist narratives. Muslim voices working in communities and prisons have repeatedly emphasized that these narratives have no basis in Islamic teachings.[14]

Jihadist groups often claim their violence is rooted in traditional Sunni jurisprudence. However, research has thoroughly discredited these claims, showing they twist religious texts to serve political aims.[15]

That said, being proactive does not mean being paranoid. Overreaching, by viewing entire communities as suspect, can backfire. Counter-radicalization must be precise, focusing only on those showing signs of violent intent or being actively recruited. A collaborative approach involving local police, intelligence, responsible NGOs, and community influencers is more effective than taking action on the basis of blanket suspicion.[16]

Importantly, programmes should not be disguised as counter-terrorism efforts. When initiatives are law enforcement-led or feel intrusive, they risk alienating the very people they aim to protect. Suspicion, profiling, and fear can tear communities apart, undermining social cohesion and actually aiding extremist recruitment.[17]

Political will is essential for effective counter-radicalization. It requires sustained bipartisan commitment, not opportunistic rhetoric during election cycles. Leaders must rise above partisan divides, recognizing that safeguarding national security demands unity, consistency, and foresight. Prioritizing long-term stability over short-term political advantage is not just responsible governance, it is a moral imperative in the fight against extremism and for the safety and cohesion of our society.

Not all radical views are violent, but they still need to be addressed, calmly and logically. Social media platforms must step up too. Instead of waiting for harmful content to go viral, tech companies should work daily with authorities to stop it early.[18]

Automated moderation and delayed government action falls awfully short. Social media platforms, often governed by foreign laws, limit local enforcement capabilities. Unlike nations with robust intelligence frameworks such as the U.S. and other Five-Eye countries, most other countries lack the authority or tools to act swiftly, leaving dangerous content online and undermining national security efforts.

Open debate remains the strongest defence against radical ideologies. When extreme views are exposed to reason and public scrutiny, they often lose their appeal and credibility. Suppressing ideas can inadvertently amplify them; instead, we must confront them with dialogue. Coercive measures should be reserved for those who incite violence, suppress others' voices, or pose a clear threat to democratic values—not merely for holding controversial or non-violent beliefs.

Counter-Radicalisation: What is the Way-Forward?

An effective strategy to counter radicalism must focus on empowering communities. Active, engaged citizens are best positioned to strengthen social cohesion and address the real causes of violent extremism. Community-led efforts leverage local knowledge, trust, and networks to prevent individuals from being drawn into radical ideologies. This grassroots approach is more effective than top-down interventions, as it fosters inclusion and responds to specific cultural and social dynamics.

Such initiatives should be led by political leaders and socially conscious individuals, not law enforcement, to avoid perceptions of coercion or surveillance. Excessive state involvement risks the programmes being dismissed as 'state-sponsored,' which can alienate communities and expose participants to accusations of betrayal by extremists. Trusted local figures—religious leaders, educators, and civil society actors—can better challenge extremist narratives and offer meaningful alternatives.[19]

In some minority communities, loyalty is often linked to a conservative identity that values strict adherence to religious practices, sometimes based on misinterpretation. Community engagement helps address these misconceptions from within, reducing the appeal of radical ideologies. By fostering dialogue, building trust, and promoting shared values, community-based counter-radicalization can offer a sustainable, inclusive response to extremism.[20]

Individual Centred Counter-radicalisation Approach

We must move beyond the simplistic view that eliminating terrorist leaders is enough to curb radicalism. A more targeted approach is needed, one that addresses the individual drivers behind radicalization. Once an at-risk individual is identified, families should be discreetly informed and engaged in de-radicalization efforts. However, revealing the person's identity to the wider community should be avoided due to potential risks.

Counter-radicalization should prioritize human security over narrow national security goals. Identifying vulnerable individuals can be enhanced through cooperation with Internet-based social media platforms (called 'intermediaries' in India). Those exhibiting patterns of engaging with extremist content can be flagged using advanced AI algorithms, which these platforms already possess.

Rather than relying on coercion, regulators should assure intermediaries that their cooperation will remain confidential and legally protected unless due process requires disclosure. While these platforms claim to offer 'free' and 'secure' communication, they must also uphold their legal responsibility to help identify users at risk of radicalization, firmly but without heavy-handed tactics.

Counter-Radicalisation: Effectiveness

Counter-radicalization programmes are more effective when vulnerable groups see them as supportive rather than punitive. This requires an empathetic, stigma-free approach that avoids exposure and punishment. In some minority communities, strong social bonds can lead to shielding wrongdoers, as fear of ostracism or being labelled a traitor discourages cooperation with authorities. Therefore, creating a safe, protective environment is key to encouraging community support.[21]

Police, local authorities, and civil society must actively engage minority communities at all levels, men, women, elders, youth, and businesses, while avoiding profiling or stereotyping. Broad, inclusive strategies that address grievances and reduce marginalization are essential. Supporting civil society organizations that represent minority voices can build trust, bridge gaps with the government, and foster long-term resilience—provided these organizations are empowered and adequately resourced.[22]

Countering Support and Promotion of Terrorism and Violent Ideologies

Evolution of Online Radicalisation

Terrorist groups have continually adapted to evolving technologies, using them to amplify their reach, obscure their identities, and evade detection. The digital age has provided extremist networks with powerful tools to radicalize, recruit, and coordinate across borders. Encrypted messaging apps such as WhatsApp, Telegram, and Signal allow for secure, anonymous communication, shielding operatives from surveillance and complicating efforts by law enforcement to intercept threats. The Dark Web, largely outside the scope of regulation, offers additional safe havens for distributing extremist content and illicit materials.

Online radicalization, however, predates today's platforms. Early efforts relied on chat rooms, blogs, and password-protected forums, where ideological indoctrination was slower but still effective. The landscape shifted dramatically with the rise of social media. Al-Qaeda was an early adopter of online propaganda, but ISIS transformed digital outreach into a global recruitment strategy. Under Abu Bakr al-Baghdadi, ISIS used platforms like Twitter with unprecedented intensity and sophistication. In 2014 alone, an estimated 46,000 ISIS-affiliated Twitter accounts were active, many newly created, indicating a strategic push to swell its ranks.

What made ISIS's approach particularly potent was its use of multilingual propaganda. Sympathizers fluent in English, Arabic, and other regional languages localized extremist messaging, embedding it within online communities and making it resonate with disaffected youth. This shift from static forums to dynamic, algorithm-driven platforms has enabled extremist narratives to spread faster and deeper, presenting an ongoing challenge for counterterrorism efforts in the digital realm.[23]

ISIS online activists initially used Telegram as a kind of control room to coordinate public propaganda. Telegram was considered more secure (with end-to-end encryption); it allowed users to form large groups (the maximum group size has gone up from 200 in 2014 to 10,000 in 2017) and to share and download a large volume of videos, audio, texts, and images directly on the app. However, after a crackdown on extremist accounts in the later part of 2014, the core of ISIS propaganda operation was more systematically relocated to Telegram. Telegram remained a relatively reliable platform for ISIS supporters until the Paris attack in November 2015.[24]

Following revelations that the Paris attackers had communicated on Telegram, the company stated that it was 'disturbed' to learn that Telegram's public channels were being used by ISIS-related channels. Despite the crackdown, the ISIS operatives employed various alternatives, including the use of proxy and Tor browsers to trying out new messaging application such as Threema, but it did not work in most cases since it was paid service and restricted its group members to a limited 50 accounts. ISIS handlers and other supporters in most cases stuck to Telegram by using it through Virtual Private Networks (VPNs) or other anonymizers that could conceal location and IP address.[25]

More specifically, violent extremist groups, including ISIS supporters, have adopted sophisticated tactics to evade detection and countermeasures. These include:

- *Masquerading*: Replacing inflammatory account names with innocuous ones to blend in and bypass blocking protocols.
- *Redundancy*: Deploying multiple backup channels, akin to mirror websites, to anticipate and circumvent platform suspensions.
- *Data Compression*: Condensing key content from crucial channels or websites into single files or e-books, readily disseminated across various platforms like data storage services and online communities.

Furthermore, ISIS sympathisers prioritise fostering ideological cohesion within their networks. They employ manipulative tactics to accelerate the radicalisation of individuals, subtly drawing them closer to their ideology and objectives.

Terrorist's Modus Operandi: How they do it?

To avoid compromising operational secrecy and potential intelligence infiltration, extremists typically refrain from explicit discussions about plotting and targets. Instead, they rely on nuanced assessments of recruitment candidates based on various factors, including:

- *Age:* Younger individuals are often considered more susceptible to radicalisation.
- *Educational background:* Higher levels of education might indicate greater potential for strategic roles. Contrary to popular belief, high level of secular education might not create adequate resistance to dogmatic-radicalisation material as evidenced from numerous cases of engineers, doctors and other professionals joining the ranks of terrorists.[26]
- *Religious knowledge:* Familiarity with Islamic law can enhance an individual's perceived value within the group.
- *Engagement patterns:* Consistent and prolonged engagement with extremist content, particularly within closed-circuit chat groups, signifies a deepening commitment to the cause.

Once identified as promising candidates, individuals are often invited to migrate to more secure one-on-one communication platforms for further indoctrination and potential recruitment. Interestingly, group administrators actively discourage overt discussions about operations and targets within the broader group, instead advocating for in-person meetings or conversing on end-to-end encryption applications.

The rise of the Islamic State (ISIS) posed a significant threat to global security, with India witnessing sporadic but concerning attempts by individuals to join the group. In this context, the National Investigation Agency (NIA) emerged as a much-valued and professional investigation agency, spearheading India's counter-ISIS initiatives. NIA's mandate encompassed investigating and prosecuting terror-related offences, including those with international ramifications.[27] This made it uniquely equipped to tackle the ISIS threat. The agency adopted a multi-pronged approach:

- *Proactive Intelligence Gathering:* Building on existing networks and partnerships, the NIA actively received intelligence in conjunction with relevant intelligence agencies on potential ISIS recruits and sympathizers. This included monitoring online activity, analysing travel patterns, and collaborating with local law enforcement agencies and security agencies abroad.[28]

- *Swift and Decisive Action:* Upon identifying targets, the NIA moved swiftly to neutralize potential threats. Raids conducted by NIA teams on suspected hideouts disrupted recruitment plans and prevented travel to conflict zones. These operations served as a strong deterrent, discouraging individuals from considering affiliating with ISIS.
- *Forensic Analysis and Legal Proceedings:* The NIA's expertise scientifically oriented investigation accords highest reliance on evidentiary validation by forensic analysis proved consistently effective in building strong cases against suspected ISIS sympathizers. Seized digital devices, financial records, and communication logs formed the basis for watertight legal proceedings, ensuring that those brought to justice faced due process.
- *Public Awareness and De-radicalization:* Recognizing the role of ideology in driving radicalization, the NIA also focused on raising public awareness about the dangers of extremist ideologies through its consistent proactive disclosures about investigations in the media.

Content Moderation and De-platforming: Is it Successful in Counter-radicalization?

Content moderation is a crucial responsibility of social media platforms, involving the review and regulation of user-generated content to ensure compliance with platform policies and community standards. This process includes identifying and removing harmful, misleading, or offensive material that may incite violence, spread hate, or promote extremism. A particularly contentious aspect of content moderation is the practice of '*deplatforming*', the removal or banning of individuals or groups whose views are considered dangerous, offensive, or contrary to public safety and democratic norms.

Deplatforming involves restricting access to digital spaces for users who violate platform rules, especially those promoting extremist ideologies. This practice has sparked significant debate. Proponents argue that it disrupts the visibility and reach of harmful actors, limiting their ability to recruit, organize, or influence vulnerable audiences. Critics, however, question its effectiveness and raise concerns about censorship, arguing that it may drive radical content further underground, making it more difficult to monitor.

Scholars and policymakers are increasingly exploring whether deplatforming is an effective tool in the fight against terrorism and radicalization. While it may not eliminate extremist ideologies, deplatforming can significantly reduce the audience and influence of radical figures, slowing the spread of harmful content. However, it must be applied judiciously, balancing security needs with freedom of expression. Effective deplatforming strategies require transparency, due process, and cooperation between governments, platforms, and civil society to ensure they are part of a broader, rights-respecting counter-extremism framework.[29]

Deplatforming has proven to be an effective strategy as it has been shown to have significantly diminished audiences, disrupting extremist communities, and impeding their ability to benefit from search engines, indexing, and algorithmic recommendations on prominent platforms. Research confirms that while deplatforming seems effective in undermining online extremist communities and reducing their audience, it does not necessarily result in an overall decrease in extremist online activity, as these groups often migrate to platforms like Telegram, which offer secure communication services.[30]

Some communities adopt a victimhood narrative, viewing themselves as under attack by authorities and tech companies. While deplatforming can reduce extremist visibility and shrink their audience, it has limits. Banned groups often move to encrypted apps or the Dark Web, making detection far harder for intelligence agencies.

Despite these challenges, deplatforming appears to help isolate extremists and disrupt their reach. However, scholars note that a strong sense of belonging and community remains a key factor in the depth of radicalization, something that cannot be addressed through technology alone.[31]

Content moderation plays a crucial role in countering terrorism and extremist misuse of the internet. Though largely self-regulated, the Indian government is increasingly setting clear guidelines and enforcement mechanisms to tackle radical content and hate speech. This marks a shift toward a regulatory model where platforms manage content, but the government retains authority to ensure compliance with anti-extremism standards.[32]

Moreover, the growing automation (algorithm-based AI-enabled) in content moderation accentuates the significance of determining factors in keyword lists and databases. The presence of opaque algorithms and a lack of transparency pose significant risks to fundamental rights and accountability. Nonetheless, inconsistencies persist in enforcement protocols, including issues such as a lack of transparency, limited understanding of algorithm capabilities in content moderation, and a lack of cooperation from social media intermediaries.[33]

First Line of Defence Against Preparation: Target Recruitment and Training

Studies have revealed that terrorist groups deliberately target vulnerable individuals, especially youth, by identifying behavioural patterns linked to disconnection and low self-worth. While terrorism is often tied to socio-economic and political factors, understanding why certain individuals are more susceptible to extremist ideologies still lacks solid research.

Schmid and Jongman's *Political Terrorism* (1988) noted a surprising lack of reliable evidence in social science literature, a concern that remains relevant post-9/11 despite a surge in studies and conferences on radicalization and deradicalization. This academic boom has produced thousands of papers but often without concrete conclusions, leading to generalizations.

Studies note with concern that recruiters exploit online anonymity to offer at-risk youth a false sense of belonging and purpose, using secretive digital spaces where individuals seek validation without fear of judgment.[34]

The capacity to cultivate close-knit, anonymous communities online serves as a potent catalyst for sustained engagement, both positive and negative. While these communities can foster a sense of belonging and shared values among activists, they also provide fertile ground for the radicalization of like-minded individuals.

Terrorist groups manipulate ideological or religious beliefs to recruit vulnerable individuals, promising a higher calling or a sense of adventure, power, and rebellion. This recruitment strategy mirrors challenges faced by law enforcement in managing organized crime, where recruitment continues despite increased pressure, as seen with the Mumbai mafia in the 1990s.

Terrorism recruitment is driven by factors like ideological leadership, access to weapons, financial resources, and local socio-economic conditions. While grievances are often cited as causes, they are insufficient to explain terrorism, especially in regions like Jammu & Kashmir or in jihadist contexts. Recruitment remains a critical issue in managing both terrorism and organized crime.

Closing the Gaps: Legal Framework against Preparatory Acts of Terror

The Unlawful Activities (Prevention) Act (UAPA) in India targets terrorism-related recruitment and training under Sections 18A and 18B. Section 18A criminalizes the organization or facilitation of terrorist training camps, with penalties ranging from five years to life imprisonment and a fine. Section 18B focuses on the recruitment of individuals for terrorist acts, imposing similar penalties. These provisions extend beyond physical camps, as online platforms like Telegram and WhatsApp used for radicalization and recruitment are also covered. Administrators of such platforms can be prosecuted under these sections for promoting terrorism.

The UAPA provides a comprehensive legal framework for tackling terrorism, enabling law enforcement agencies to take action against terrorist activities, financing, and the establishment of terrorist camps. While the law empowers decisive action, effective implementation requires close coordination among law enforcement, intelligence agencies, and international partners. Additionally, addressing causes such as developmental vacuum/disparities and religious extremism is essential for preventing radicalization. However, it is crucial to ensure that the provisions of the UAPA are consistently applied while respecting human rights and civil liberties, balancing counter-terrorism measures with the protection of fundamental freedoms.

Strategies to Deal with Terrorist Recruitment and Training

Early detection and prosecution of terrorist trainers and recruiters depend heavily on human intelligence. The UN Convention against Transnational Organized Crime (UNTOC) highlights the importance of incentivizing individuals to provide information about organized criminal groups, including terrorists. Offering leniency or reduced punishment for cooperation, as outlined in Article 26(1)(a) of the UNTOC, encourages members to come forward[35] India's NIA Act, 2008, supports this by providing witness protection under Section 17, allowing witnesses to testify without fear of retaliation.

Balancing prosecution with human rights is challenging. While incentivizing cooperation is essential for counterterrorism, granting immunity or reduced sentences to serious offenders raises concerns about justice and victim rights. The use of informants can also impact the fairness of trials, especially given the limitations of witness protection and the potential for provocation. To maintain impartiality, the credibility of prosecution witnesses must be carefully assessed. Given the violence in terrorism cases, additional security measures, such as police escorts and secure safe houses, are vital for witness protection and preventing retaliation or obstruction of justice.

Legal Limitations: Tackling Modern Terrorism

The digital age has revolutionized the tactics of violent extremists, enabling them to radicalize, recruit, and inspire attacks online, bypassing traditional power structures. This 'democratization of terror' allows individuals to act as influential agents, disrupting leader-based dynamics. The rapid spread of disinformation and declining trust in media further complicate counterterrorism efforts. Governments face the challenge of countering these threats while protecting civil liberties. Effective measures require digital forensics, international collaboration, and partnerships with civil society to challenge extremist narratives and build community resilience.[36]

Terrorist networks now employ dynamic, hybrid warfare strategies, blending conventional and unconventional tactics with criminal activities. This approach challenges traditional law enforcement, especially in countering online propaganda. By manipulating narratives, these groups exploit the digital landscape to fuel radicalization. The digital world offers access to vast information but also creates an environment of uncertainty, allowing extremist ideologies to thrive. Unlike state actors, terrorists operate without constraints, using hybrid tactics that disregard societal norms and legal boundaries, posing significant global security challenges.

'Network Effect' and Terrorist Recruitment

The 'network effect,' as discussed by Iansiti and Lakhani in *Competing in the Age of AI*, describes how a product or service gains value as more users engage with it, creating more connections and interactions. For terrorist networks, this effect is both powerful and dangerous.[37]

Terrorist groups have skilfully exploited this effect in the digital age to expand their reach and capabilities. By leveraging distrust of mainstream media, these groups present themselves as alternative sources of truth, attracting individuals who feel alienated. The Internet and social media amplify this, allowing terrorist networks to recruit, radicalize, and coordinate globally, transcending geographic limits and reaching marginalized communities. This decentralized network makes it harder to disrupt their operations. Essentially, terrorists exploit the same principles that businesses use to grow customer bases, using digital connectivity to spread violence. Social media further amplifies this effect, creating echo chambers that facilitate radicalization. Terrorists use platforms to recruit and spread propaganda, often masking their digital footprints with tools like VPNs, complicating traditional surveillance methods. Despite efforts by alliances like 'Five Eyes' (Five Eyes: Australia, Canada, New Zealand, UK, US intelligence alliance), social media's focus on user privacy remains a significant obstacle, highlighting the tension between security and individual rights.

Digital Age: A Double-Edged Sword for Counter-terrorism

It is an irony of digital landscape that it appears to significantly favour insidious groups such as terrorists, providing them with tools that reduce their visibility. Encrypted platforms and the Digital Age enable recruiters to reach potential recruits worldwide, all without detection by their families or communities. Social media's time delay also allows recruiters to carefully craft appealing identities for recruits, offering a more controlled and deceptive environment than face-to-face recruitment.

Recruiters infiltrate target communities with greater freedom than in the physical world, and once tasks are assigned via social media, terrorists require minimal resources to carry out attacks. The internet is used to research targets, acquire weapons, or even conduct cyber-attacks, where the weapon itself could be a computer. This ease and speed of communication enable hybrid warfare, particularly by non-state actors, allowing terrorists to expand their reach with less cost, effort, and risk compared to traditional military tactics.

Role of Internet Intermediaries: Mere Moderators or Proactive Stake-holders?

While internet service providers, particularly those offering social media services, seem proactive in combating hate speech and violent extremism online, their approach often leans heavily on automated detection of objectionable content through machine learning algorithms. Yet, this strategy overlooks the essential need for deeper analytical deductions centred on the real causes and mechanisms driving the spread of extremist ideologies.

The way technology works and how social media platforms are built strongly impact how companies handle harmful content. While algorithmic detection and machine learning have greatly enhanced the ability to automatically identify such content, human review remains indispensable for defining and assessing borderline cases.

However, the reliance on human content moderators itself raises ethical concerns due to the psychological toll associated with reviewing harmful material. Consequently, social media companies' policies on terrorist content appear to be constrained by both technological limitations and moral considerations. Consider the case of Twitter (now 'X'), which typically addresses extremist behaviour by deactivating accounts (de-platforming). However, this tactic frequently devolves into a futile cycle as new accounts quickly emerge, rendering the entire process ineffective. Consequently, terrorists resort to operating in encrypted spaces like high-security platforms, torrent browsers, and onion-based websites, masking their identities and activities.

The Admissibility Paradox: Are Our Legal Rules Equipped for 21st-Century Terrorism?

To improve the criminal justice response, there's a necessity to re-evaluate the 'admissibility' paradox surrounding digital evidence sourced from social media profiles and other online footprints. The traditional insistence on corroborating digital evidence with testimonial validation contradicts the fundamental validation process. Courts demand testimonial validation from social media company representatives for the admissibility of digital evidence obtained through internet service providers. However, the information provided by these platforms is system-generated and lacks human mediation, negating the necessity for validation by an active employee.

In this context reference is frequently made of the 'Best Evidence Rule',[38] which would be akin to a legal dogmatism rather than adhering to the changing dynamics of electronic evidence. One of the reasons why Internet intermediaries show reluctance is due to apprehensions that such disclosure would invariably lead to call for appearance of their company employees escalating costs. Requiring physical presence during every hearing for cross-examination burdens global companies whose employees may not feasibly attend due to their limited knowledge of individual cases. This places undue strain on these companies without adding substantial value to legal proceedings.

Conclusion

The adage '*prevention is better than cure*' holds particular weight in the realm of counterterrorism. Proactive measures, from deterring individuals from joining extremist groups to inhibiting the acquisition of weapons, are paramount in mitigating the devastating consequences of terrorism. The rapid dissemination of radicalizing propaganda through digital platforms underscores the need for a comprehensive approach that extends beyond traditional law enforcement. Every member of society has a stake in preventing terrorism and a role to play in countering its insidious influence.

Contrary to harmful stereotypes, terrorists are seldom inherently evil but often vulnerable individuals manipulated through sophisticated indoctrination. Exploiting grievances, fears, and social isolation, extremist ideologies are cunningly packaged and delivered through online platforms. These virtual spaces serve as fertile ground for radicalization, where potential recruits are groomed and prepared for acts of violence.

Counter-terrorism today faces serious challenges, as terrorist groups continually evolve with sophisticated recruitment strategies and psychological manipulation. Traditional enforcement and intelligence methods, though essential, are insufficient on their own. Efforts rooted solely in surveillance and policing risk alienating communities and missing dynamism of radicalisation.

Sustainable counter-radicalisation must involve society at every level, fostering trust and active collaboration. Engaging local communities, especially by empowering respected local leaders, is critical in building resilience against extremist ideologies. These leaders hold the cultural insight and moral authority to identify early signs of radicalisation and offer credible alternatives.

Genuine partnerships between security agencies and communities promote mutual understanding and shared responsibility. Only by combining strategic intelligence with grassroots engagement can we address both the symptoms and causes of radicalisation. A holistic, community-driven approach transforms counterterrorism from reactive containment into proactive prevention, safeguarding both security and the social fabric.

9

The Poppy Fields of Terror: The Narco-Terrorism Threat

"*It is even better to act quickly and err than to hesitate until the time of action is past.*"

—**Carl von Clausewitz, 'On War'**

Narco-terrorism: Emotive Undertones

In security policy discourse, both foreign and domestic, *narco-terrorism* is frequently used as a catch-all term, lacking a universally agreed definition. Historically, the term was first coined in 1983 by Peruvian President Belaunde Terry to describe violent assaults by drug cartels targeting law enforcement agencies.[1] These cartels, such as those led by Colombian drug lord Pablo Escobar, used brutal tactics, assassinations, massacres of police personnel, and silencing of dissent, to secure and expand their narcotics empires.

These criminal syndicates, primarily concerned with profit and trade protection, employed violence strategically to influence government actions and deter enforcement. Terror, in this context, was a tool, not the objective, making their ideology transactional rather than political or religious.

In recent years, however, the concept of narco-terrorism has shifted. It now often refers to the use of drug trafficking as a means to finance or facilitate terrorism. This evolution aligns with the United States Drug Enforcement Administration (DEA)'s interpretation, which emphasizes narcotics as a funding source and operational enabler for terrorist groups.

'*Narco-terrorism may be characterised by the participation of groups or associated individuals in taxing, providing security for, or otherwise aiding or betting drug trafficking endeavours in an effort to further, or fund, terrorist activities.*

This definition brings terrorist groups and organization at the epicentre highlighting the fact that recently some terrorist organizations have been using narcotics trade to sustain and further their terrorist activities.[2]

It is a stark reality that every gram of illegal narcotics (coming from cartels associated with terrorist organizations) use by a hapless drug-addict ultimately promotes terrorism and organized criminal syndicates. A common drug peddler might be completely oblivious of his contribution in promoting terrorism as an accessory. The connection is more sinister than you might imagine. It is no longer a question whether the drug trade is apparently making someone rich (the peddler), the question is 'how the terrorists are able to finance their operations from the money of their future victims?'

The greatest threat to our national security in coming decades would be posed from narco-terrorism as is being evident from promotion of mistaken perceptions that tend to normalize drug-abuse as 'everyone is doing it, so it must be ok'. The forces inimical to our national interest (in fact, to our very existence) are persistent in their designs which are being evidenced by their efforts of sending exceptionally huge shipments of thousands of kilograms of narcotics into their target country.[3]

Following list (incidents of drug seizure in the recent past) might suffice to make an assessment of overwhelming risks that India is facing today:

1. *Massive Drug Load seized off Gujarat coast:* During the last week of February, 2024, ATS Gujarat, along with Indian Coast Guards intercepted a Pakistani ship carrying more than 2,500 kilograms of hashish (a resin like derivative of cannabis) and other assorted narcotics off the coast of Gujarat. Initial investigation revealed that the ship loaded the shipment in Afghanistan.[4]
2. *Large-scale Drug Seizure in Gujarat:* In December 2023, Indian authorities intercepted a shipment of over 2,000 kilograms of heroin and methamphetamine concealed in a cargo container at the Mundra Port in Gujarat. The narcotics, originating from Afghanistan, were believed to be destined for distribution across India.[5]
3. *Massive Heroin Bust in Punjab:* In September 2023, Punjab Police uncovered a major drug trafficking operation, seizing approximately 500 kilograms of heroin smuggled from Pakistan. The drugs were

concealed in a shipment of goods intended to cross the Indo-Pak border illegally.[6]

4. *Interception of Narcotics at Tuticorin:* In August 2023, Customs officials at the Tuticorin Port in Tamil Nadu intercepted a consignment of nearly 300 kilograms of cocaine in a container which was declared to be containing wooden logs. As per the initial investigation conducted by the Directorate of Revenue Intelligence the suspected container originated from Panama, and was transited through the ports of Antwerp and Colombo.[7]
5. *Narcotics Seizure in Mumbai:* In June 2023, Mumbai Police seized a significant quantity (133 kilograms) of MDMA (Ecstasy) tablets concealed in a consignment of electronic goods imported from Europe. The interception highlighted the increasing use of international routes by narco-terrorists to smuggle drugs into India.[8]

The swift interception of large drug consignments is a testament to the relentless efforts and growing capabilities of India's law enforcement agencies. However, these repeated attempts also highlight the enduring and serious threat that narco-terrorism poses to national security.

In the Indian context, this threat is further exacerbated by the active sponsorship of narco-terror operations by hostile neighbouring states, particularly Pakistan. Drug abuse and narco-terrorism are inextricably connected, forming a dangerous nexus that challenges not only law enforcement but also the broader frameworks of criminal justice, internal security, and national resilience. It is imperative to recognise this linkage as part of a broader continuum that undermines the country's social fabric, economic stability, and strategic interests.[9]

Drugs, Guns, and Fear: The Menace of Narco-Terrorism

Narco-terrorism, as a hybrid form of terrorism involving organized crime, presents unique features that distinguish it from more conventional forms of violent extremism. It thrives on the synergy between street-level traffickers and white-collar enablers, blending criminal enterprise with ideological motives. Some terrorist organizations, such as al-Qaeda and several Pakistan-based groups, exploit political fractures in both host and target nations to build drug networks that finance their activities and, over time, establish quasi-state structures.[10]

Unlike purely ideological terror groups, narco-terrorism entities primarily seek financial gain through the drug trade to sustain operations. Their transnational scope allows them to traffic narcotics and launder money across borders, often in collaboration with or in support of terror organizations. Their hybrid nature also makes them highly adaptable, exploiting law enforcement gaps and ungoverned regions to avoid detection.

Their tactics range from bribery and intimidation to assassinations and bombings, all aimed at securing drug routes and weakening state authority. This convergence of criminal and terrorist methods poses a significant challenge for traditional counterterrorism, which tends to focus on ideological drivers. Addressing narco- terrorism demands a more integrated strategy targeting both the criminal infrastructure and its terrorist alliances—some of which involve seemingly legitimate actors within society.

Let us now examine some of these distinctions more closely:

Self-Financing

As noted earlier, the term *narco-terrorism* was first used by regimes seeking international attention, portraying drug cartels as terrorist organizations to justify border-containment policies.[11] Drug cartels were long viewed as organized criminal syndicates, despite using terror tactics. Before this, ideologically driven terrorist groups (hereafter 'archetypical' terrorists) primarily financed their activities through civilian contributions, sympathetic groups, or covert state support to harm adversarial interests.[12]

Over time, these 'archetypical' terrorists recognized the financial potential of drug cartels. A key example is the partnership between Colombia's FARC (Revolutionary Armed Forces of Colombia) and the Cali drug cartel, which provided substantial funding to FARC. By the 1980s and 1990s, illegal cocaine trade generated billions of dollars, with FARC taxing 10% of all cocaine trade in their regions, contributing several hundred million dollars annually to their finances.[13]

The alliance between Transnational Criminal Syndicates (TCS) and terrorist groups became increasingly profitable, offering not just financial support, but weapons, human trafficking, money laundering, and political influence. While shared goals may sometimes unite them, mutual benefit remains the primary motivator.[14]

Another example is the collaboration between Hezbollah, a Lebanese terrorist organization, and the Mexican drug cartel 'Los Zetas.' Originally formed by ex-Mexican special forces, Los Zetas controls trafficking routes and engages in extortion, kidnapping, and human trafficking. Hezbollah's operations in Mexico and the USA used Lebanese and US businesses to launder billions, further expanding its financing network. Middle Eastern terrorist groups have increasingly relied on Mexican cartels for money laundering.[15]

Los Zetas, one of the most powerful drug cartels, has infiltrated the USA, operating largely in the southern states, utilizing illegal immigrants and secret tunnels along the US-Mexico border. US investigations have uncovered Hezbollah's revenue from illegal cigarette smuggling in the USA, financing its operations in Lebanon.[16] Similar collaborations between Pakistan-based terrorist organizations and international drug cartels have also emerged.[17] This chapter will explore these connections further.

Distinctive Operational Architecture

Narco-terrorism operations are unique, with complex layers of assets, financial transactions, supply-chain operatives, and over-ground workers (OGWs), many of whom are unaware they are supporting terrorism. Narco-terrorists often disguise their activities through charitable work, especially in areas where the state has failed to provide basic services and corruption is widespread. Drug cartels in Latin America, the Middle East, and Pakistan typically operate through a vast network that includes industries, real estate, financial services, and politics to launder money.[18]

Terrorist organizations and drug traffickers increasingly use distributive cell structures to achieve their goals. While there may be centralized leadership, day-to-day activities are delegated to compartmentalized cells, with legitimate businesses used for money laundering alongside drug dealing. This organizational setup enhances security by separating leadership from operatives. Both groups also employ similar methods to conceal profits and raise funds.[19]

They use informal transfer systems like 'hawala,' bulk cash smuggling, multiple accounts, and front organizations. Fraudulent documents and networks of trusted couriers facilitate smuggling and secure communications.[20]

Unlike traditional money laundering, terrorist groups and drug cartels often rely on their networks of supporters to independently launder funds, presenting them as legitimate income. Records of transactions help funnel money through seemingly legitimate businesses while maintaining cartel control. Terrorist groups, such as Hezbollah and others in Lebanon and Pakistan, may even engage in narco-smuggling to generate funds.[21]

In 2008, US and Colombian law enforcement uncovered an international cocaine-smuggling ring linked to Hezbollah through Operation 'Titan.'[22] In 2010, US authorities prosecuted Ayman Joumaa for trafficking Colombian cocaine to Los Zetas and laundering profits to Hezbollah. Hezbollah and Los Zetas also used legitimate-seeming investments, such as racehorse sales, to launder millions of dollars.[23]

Terrorist organizations involved in narcotics often maintain specialized wings for drug trade, collaborating with cartels, immigrants, and politicians to create a layered network. While drug cartels use terror tactics to expand their businesses, terrorist groups rely on cartels' money-laundering expertise to fund their operations.

Operatives are not required to have any ideological commitment

Unlike hardcore terrorists, many OGWs and operatives in a narco-terrorist's supply chain may be unaware of their contribution to terrorist activities. For instance, those arrested trafficking illicit drugs from Pakistan may not realize the drugs are being smuggled by Pakistani terrorist organizations. These individuals are motivated by financial gain, oblivious to the larger agenda they support. Terrorist organizations in Pakistan, Latin America, and the Middle East often collaborate despite ideological differences. Notable examples include alliances between Hezbollah and Los Zetas, and between Sikh militants and Pakistani terrorist groups. These groups form strategic partnerships driven by mutual interests, such as financial gain or inflicting harm on shared enemies. The logic follows: 'Your enemy's enemy is your friend.'

Ordinary drug peddlers, white-collar criminals laundering money for narco-terrorists, corrupt government officials, and legal counsel for arrested operatives may not share ideological motives but still significantly aid narco-terrorists' objectives.[24]

Counter-measures against Narco Terrorists Invariably Require International Cooperation

The convergence of organized crime, terrorism, and international drug cartels presents a growing global threat. This dangerous alliance, with deeply interconnected networks, requires enhanced cooperation among intelligence and law enforcement agencies worldwide. Narco-terrorists exploit jurisdictional fragmentation and the difficulties of international cooperation, expanding their influence and illicit activities.[25]

Law enforcement faces immense challenges as narco-terrorists have global reach and complex money-laundering networks. These groups often exchange services: criminal organizations use trafficking routes, while terrorist groups contribute military training and tactics designed to instil fear.

Prosecuting narco-terrorist operatives requires a clear evidence chain linking them to illicit activities, necessitating global collaboration with social media, telecom operators, financial institutions, and law enforcement. Money launderers often use financial experts and accountants to conceal profits in businesses and offshore havens, requiring specialized financial expertise to unravel complex trails.

Combating narco-terrorism is one of the most difficult challenges for law enforcement. The covert nature of these networks involves individuals motivated by financial gain, not ideology, making it difficult to link them directly to terrorist organizations.

Long term damage to the vitality of the nation

Unlike traditional terrorist operations that rely on fear and sabotage, narco-terrorist activities aim for long-term, sustained damage to a nation's core. By targeting its most promising demographic, youth, narco-terrorists seek to undermine the economic, social, and political integrity of a country. They aim to destroy a nation's pride by corrupting its systems and poisoning its younger generation. In broader terms, organized narcotics networks operated by terrorists inject a slow poison into a nation's fabric, weakening its vital structures.

Narco-terrorists often begin by infiltrating border and fringe areas, exploiting existing rifts between these regions and the political elite. They establish networks among criminal gangs drawn to the lucrative, illicit opportunities they offer.

They also use innovative methods to infiltrate media circles, employing subliminal tactics to lure younger generations into drug dependence. By funding movies that glorify drug abuse, capitalism, and the pursuit of easy money through crime, they normalize and glamorize drug use.[26] As a result, the younger generation increasingly sees drug abuse as a normal part of life.[27] This phenomenon contributes to the growing support for drug legalization, despite significant medical opposition.[28] Bollywood movies like *Satya* (1998), *Udta Punjab* (2016), *Gangs of Wasseypur* (2012), and *Company* (2002) often glorify gangsterism and the drug trade.[29] Recently, films like *Sadda Haq* (2013), *The Mastermind Jinda Sukkha* (2015), *Gaddar* (2015), and *Quom De Heere* (2014) have further romanticized terrorists, portraying them as martyrs and heroes.

The Silent Enemy: India's Battle Against Narco-Terrorism

Transnational crimes pose a significant threat to regional and national development. India, located at the crossroads of dynamic yet volatile socio-political landscapes and bordering two of the world's largest narcotics production hubs, is especially vulnerable to these challenges.

The Golden Crescent, spanning Afghanistan, Iran, and Pakistan, borders India's western frontier and is notorious for its extensive opium poppy cultivation. As the primary source of heroin, this crescent-shaped region is a global epicentre of opium production. The cultivation of opium in the Golden Crescent is deeply tied to a complex web of challenges, including drug trafficking, narco-terrorism, organized crime, corruption, and regional instability.[30]

To the east, the Golden Triangle, spanning Myanmar, Laos, and Thailand, is another major opium-producing region. Historically, this area has been a key hub for heroin manufacturing and distribution, supplying a significant portion of the global market.[31]

Internet, Globalization and Narco-terrorism

While globalization has fostered social integration, economic growth, the rise of social media, and global communication, it has also intensified threats from organized crime syndicates, such as the collaboration between Latin American drug cartels and Middle Eastern terrorist groups. The internet and the spread of advanced technologies have allowed terrorist organizations to expand globally. Despite sanctions on countries like Iran and Libya for allegedly supporting groups like Hezbollah, these organizations have evolved into international narco-terrorist entities, generating more funds than they previously received from their host countries.

Similarly, terrorist groups in Pakistan and Afghanistan have engaged in narco-terrorism, with tactical support from the Pakistani security establishment,[32] becoming profitable and self-reliant. These groups can bribe high-ranking officers in the security establishment to maintain operational freedom.[33]

The rise of ISIS and the Taliban further fuelled narco-terrorism, as these groups became states with defined political units. Narcotics trade provided a steady revenue stream, enabling large-scale narco-terrorism operations. The Taliban controlled over 85% of the global illicit opium trade. A United Nations Security Council report on narcotics states that the illicit drug trade is the Taliban's primary revenue source. Since the Taliban's re-establishment, there has been an increase in heroin seizures from Afghanistan into India and other regions.[34]

Organizational Uniqueness of Narco-terrorism

Is narco-terrorism merely a variant of organized crime? What distinguishes it from traditional drug cartels, and why is the entry of terrorist organizations into the drug trade especially alarming when law enforcement already targets drug trafficking? These are important questions. Organized crime involves conspiratorial acts aimed at profit, typically coordinated through a hierarchical structure of closely linked operatives who use illegal means or laundered funds for unlawful or seemingly legitimate goals.[35]

Narco-terrorism is a distinct criminal model, not just a subset of terrorism. It involves terrorist groups using the narcotics trade both for self-financing and to inflict long-term harm on adversaries. Its complexity lies in its covert operations, often disguised beneath layers of criminal and legitimate fronts. Sometimes, even law enforcement may mistakenly treat narcotics control and counter-terrorism as unrelated domains.

Pakistani terrorist organizations have deeply penetrated state structures, often seen associating openly with senior military and political figures. This reflects the emergence of a 'state within a state.' In Pakistan, the drug trade fuels a parallel economy benefitting corrupt elites, including politicians, civil servants, and military officers. The complicity of state institutions is evident in the impunity enjoyed by leaders designated as 'Global Terrorists,' who continue operations without interference. Pakistan routinely disregards international calls for legal action, rejecting requests for prosecution despite substantial evidence.[36] This persistent defiance of global norms highlights Pakistan's deliberate circumvention of international law.

Pakistan and its Institutional Linkages with Narco-terrorists

Narco-terrorism poses a grave threat to India's national security, undermining its efforts to realize global power ambitions by destabilizing its social, economic, and political foundations. Pakistan's persistent use of its security establishment and affiliated terror networks to inject drugs and weapons into India reflects a calculated strategy. These groups leverage advanced technologies like drones to smuggle arms and narcotics, often using international cargo routes. Large quantities of heroin and opium derivatives—sourced from Taliban-controlled areas—are trafficked into India.[37]

As early as in 1994 a *Washington Post* report revealed that former Pakistani Prime Minister Nawaz Sharif accused Army Chief Gen. Aslam Beg and ISI Chief Gen. Asad Durrani of proposing, in 1991, a heroin-financing scheme to fund covert military operations. CIA reports cited during US congressional hearings confirmed widespread drug-related corruption and close ties between Pakistan's political and military elite and drug kingpins.[38] The ISI, Pakistan's powerful intelligence agency, continues to pursue its own agenda, often beyond civilian oversight.

Pakistan's military has long been accused of operating independently, often supporting insurgents and illicit programs without civilian consent. Over decades, the ISI has facilitated the drug trade in areas with heavy poppy cultivation, especially in Khyber-Pakhtunkhwa (KP), formerly the North West Frontier Province. Towns such as Landi Kotal, Jamrud, and Darra Adam Khel became hubs for trafficking drugs and weapons, often with little interference from state forces.[39]

These tribal regions have resisted central authority, operating under their own customs and laws. Pakistani agencies have selectively enforced laws, and ISI reportedly helped establish heroin refineries, even employing Chinese chemists to process opium for international markets.[40]

Given the Taliban-ISI nexus behind narco-terrorism targeting India, it is crucial for India to mount a robust, self-reliant counter-strategy. While global pressure, such as FATF downgrades or international censure, is useful, India cannot depend solely on international responses, which have historically been ineffective.

Since the late 1970s, India has endured state-sponsored terrorism from Pakistan. There is ample evidence that Pakistan's government, through the ISI, funds terrorism in India using money from drug trafficking and illegal arms sales. Despite this, the global community has been slow to act decisively, enabling Pakistan to persist in its destabilizing agenda.[41]

Pakistan's long-standing strategy includes exploiting ethnic and religious divisions, especially in states like Jammu and Kashmir, Punjab, Rajasthan, Assam, and the Northeast. The ISI deliberately fosters disaffection among vulnerable youth by capitalizing on perceived economic disparities and religious sentiments, pushing them toward the drug trade. The US withdrawal from Afghanistan also dried up funds for Pakistan's supposed counter-terror operations, further incentivizing its reliance on narcotics revenue.[42]

Terror operations are expensive, and Pakistan's economic woes have limited state funding. As a result, the army has grown increasingly reliant on drug-funded terror networks. These groups now even channel bribes to senior military officials.[43]

Multiple eyewitness accounts from terrorists arrested in Jammu and Kashmir, Punjab, and other regions confirm Pakistan's systematic use of terror operatives to achieve foreign policy objectives, particularly in Jammu and Kashmir.

Money-Laundering and Narco-Terrorism

Money laundering is the process of concealing the origins of illegally obtained funds, masking the identities involved, and converting the proceeds into assets that appear legitimate. The vast profits from the narcotics trade have deeply infiltrated the global financial system, influencing corporate sectors and monetary markets. These illicit funds are used to buy political influence, finance election campaigns, undermine governments, acquire businesses, and destabilize socio-economic systems.[44]

The drug trade generates enormous cash flows in short periods, creating logistical challenges in storing and transporting money. Latin American cartels, drawing from American organized crime practices, adopted complex techniques such as layering, moving funds through numerous transactions and offshore shell companies, to obscure ownership.[45]

White-collar criminals in tax havens like Switzerland, Cyprus, Liechtenstein, and Monaco further developed mechanisms to repatriate laundered money after routing it through layered financial networks. Indian terrorists such as Dawood Ibrahim have used similar strategies to invest illicit funds in real estate across multiple countries, including India, to avoid detection by law enforcement.

The following are some of the methods through which ill-gotten funds from narcotics trade are laundered:

1. *Hawala Transactions:* An informal system of money transfer that operates outside of traditional banking channels, often used for illicit purposes.
2. *Investment in Real Estate:* Using illegally obtained money to purchase property, which can be difficult to trace back to its source.
3. *Investment in Foreign Business:* Investing illicit funds into businesses abroad to conceal their origin.
4. *Travel and currency exchange agencies:* Laundering money through the purchase and sale of foreign currency or travel-related services.
5. *Bank Deposits and Loans or 'Smurfing':* Breaking down large sums of money into smaller, less suspicious transactions spread across multiple accounts or loans.
6. *Gambling Joints:* Laundering money through casinos or other gambling establishments, where large cash transactions are common and can be easily concealed.
7. *Double Invoicing:* Issuing two invoices for the same transaction, allowing one to show inflated prices and the other to appear legitimate. Narco terrorists use double invoicing by creating fake or inflated invoices for goods. This disguises illicit funds as legitimate business transactions, helping them launder money and evade financial scrutiny.
8. *'Parking' of funds in tax havens:* Using jurisdictions with lax tax laws and banking secrecy to hide illicit funds and avoid paying taxes. This is often achieved by establishing complex corporate structures (shell companies) in tax havens. By routing payments through these entities, narco terrorists and other TCS can obscure financial transactions and evade taxes.
9. *Currency Smuggling:* Illegally moving cash across borders to evade detection and scrutiny.
10. *Conversion of Cash in Kind:* Exchanging physical assets, such as jewellery or art, for cash to legitimize illegal gains.

Pakistan's regional strategy increasingly relies on terrorism, with narco-terrorism fitting seamlessly into this model due to its ability to fund operations. The

Pakistani military, constrained by limited state resources, cannot alone support terrorism. However, it operates one of the world's most extensive military-run business empires, often managed by recently retired senior officers.[46] These ventures offer a convenient front for funnelling illicit drug money into ostensibly legitimate enterprises.[47]

Favourable climatic conditions and rugged terrain in western Pakistan support both poppy cultivation and terrorist operations. While the army has occasionally acted against the tribes of Khyber-Pakhtunkhwa, it has more often exploited their martial skills to advance its anti-India agenda. The operational freedom granted to narco-terrorists aligns with this approach.[48]

Estimates suggest Pakistan's security forces earn over $ 2 billion annually through illegal narcotics.[49] A major portion of this revenue funds efforts to destabilize India. Pakistan's toolkit has included everything from tribal invasions of Jammu & Kashmir in 1948 to exploiting Sikh and Kashmiri militants, inciting rebellion in the Northeast, and using drones to smuggle arms.[50]

After the Pulwama and recent attack on innocent tourists in Pahalgam in Jammu and Kashmir, Pakistan realized that any major act of terrorism could provoke severe Indian retaliation.[51] As a result, it shifted tactics, placing greater emphasis on narco-terrorism, evident in the scale of drug seizures in India. With conventional terrorism proving costly, narcotics will become Pakistan's preferred weapon.

Narco-terrorism now represents a major and growing threat to India's national security. Pakistan's strategy focuses on flooding India with narcotics, eroding its social fabric and destabilizing its economy by introducing illicit cash. This shift highlights the centrality of narcotics in funding Pakistan's broader security objectives. India's growing economy, especially the real estate sector, offers lucrative channels for laundering drug money.[52]

India's Options

India must respond decisively to Pakistan's evolving security strategy, where narco-terrorism is emerging as a key tool of asymmetric warfare. Drawing on lessons from the USA post-9/11 counter-terrorism model, adapted for the Indian subcontinent, India needs innovative, coordinated, and resource-efficient strategies to tackle this hybrid threat.

At the core of this response must be a revamp of India's security-intelligence apparatus. Despite post-Kargil reforms, intelligence and enforcement agencies still operate in silos. The Narcotics Control Bureau (NCB), though professional, has only about 1000 personnel, mostly on deputation, limiting its capacity for coordination across states and central bodies. Expecting the NCB to lead the national counter-narcotics effort alone would be unrealistic.

To address this, both the NCB and the National Investigation Agency (NIA) must be expanded and staffed with professionals experienced in anti-narcotics operations. A Joint Action Group, headed by a dedicated director and comprising officers from the NIA, CBI, ED, IB, and state police from Punjab, Jammu & Kashmir, Rajasthan, and the North-East, should be created to ensure integrated counter-narcotics operations.

The Ministry of External Affairs must also take a proactive role by consistently presenting credible evidence of Pakistan's involvement in narco-terrorism at global forums. While Pakistan's complicity is widely suspected, sustained diplomatic pressure backed by documentation can compel international accountability.[53]

Domestically, law enforcement agencies must adopt advanced technologies and infrastructure to disrupt narcotics trafficking networks. This requires bringing in domain experts, such as forensic accountants, money trail analysts, and cyber and interception specialists, from the open market on a contract basis. The outdated model of relying solely on deputation is proving insufficient; on the other hand, permanent staff often lack the ability and updated skills necessary to counter sophisticated narco-terror operations.

Narco-terrorism, as a hybrid crime, has evolved through three phases: drug cartels using terror for self-preservation; terrorist groups entering the drug trade for funding; and now, narcotics being used strategically to destabilize target countries. This weaponized form of narco-terrorism is now central to Pakistan's proxy war tactics against India.

Given its composite nature, narco-terrorism spans multiple offences, money laundering, terror financing, corporate fraud, organized crime, and violations under narcotics and penal laws. Effective investigations demand multi-agency coordination and specialized knowledge in intelligence, finance, and law enforcement. An inter-agency, interdisciplinary task force is essential for coordinated action, particularly involving the NIA, ED, NCB, CBI, and relevant state police forces.

Within this framework, the Enforcement Directorate (ED) must create a dedicated wing to investigate money laundering linked to narco-terrorism. These cases often involve complex financial transactions and heightened risks due to the involvement of terrorist actors. Attaching experienced officers from the NCB and state police on a case-by-case basis will bolster investigative capabilities. Closer coordination among the NIA, ED, CBI, and NCB is vital to dismantling these criminal-terrorist networks and safeguarding national security.[54]

Investigative Complexity in Narco-terrorism Cases

Narco-terrorism is a distinct and insidious form of terrorism, marked by covert operations and deep infiltration into target societies. Unlike conventional terrorism, which often uses overt violence, narco-terrorists exploit systemic vulnerabilities through clandestine means. Pakistan's state-backed terrorism infrastructure embodies this strategy, using narco-trafficking both to fund operations and destabilize neighbouring countries.

India faces a serious challenge in countering this multifaceted threat, which endangers national security and erodes societal stability. Given its complexity, narco-terrorism requires a thorough and focused causality analysis.

The Complexity of the Crime

Investigating the link between drug trafficking and terrorism is among the most complex tasks, due to the tangled causal chain and involvement of multiple actors. The nexus often includes white-collar professionals, financial advisors, legal consultants, and public officials, some of whom may be unaware their actions contribute to narco-terrorism.

Proving *mens rea* (guilty knowledge) in such cases is especially difficult. Indirect evidence like money trails and call data may not suffice to establish guilt beyond a reasonable doubt. Prosecution becomes more complicated when accused individuals offer to become protected witnesses. While the Indian Evidence Act and the updated Bhartiya Nyaya Samhita (BNS) provide for witness protection, narco-terrorism cases demand stronger safeguards, ensuring not just anonymity but protection of life and livelihood as well.

Protection of Witness Identity

The NIA Act and UAPA include provisions to protect the anonymity of witnesses who provide incriminating statements. Section 17 of the NIA Act mandates that courts, upon request from the witness or the prosecution, take measures to shield the witness's identity. These measures may include concealing the witness's identity in recorded statements and imposing a ban on revealing details that could identify them.

The UAPA also criminalizes such disclosures, even by the prosecution. Unlike Witness Protection Programs under the CrPC or BNS, these measures focus on protecting the identity of the witness rather than providing physical security. This approach ensures witnesses testify without fear, bypassing the defence's right to identify those providing testimony.

Similar provisions for 'Protected Witnesses' should be added to the NDPS Act and the Prevention of Money Laundering Act, given the use of terror tactics by narco-terrorists against potential threats to their operations.

Jurisdictional Issues in Prosecution of Narco-Terrorism Cases

Prosecution of narco-terrorists faces jurisdictional challenges due to the transnational nature of their activities. Narco-terrorists often employ sophisticated money-laundering techniques, moving large sums through offshore shell companies and tax havens such as Cyprus, the Cayman Islands, and the British Virgin Islands, which are known for their lack of cooperation with international law enforcement agencies.[55]

These jurisdictions' non-cooperation complicates prosecutions, especially when Internet Service Providers (ISPs) also refuse to assist due to privacy laws or data sovereignty legislation. Investigating narco-terrorism requires expertise in documenting money trails and preparing Mutual Legal Assistance Treaty (MLAT) applications, which state police often lack at the regional level.[56]

The convergence of drug trafficking and terrorism across multiple jurisdictions makes international cooperation crucial. Effective prosecution of narco-terrorists is often limited to central-level agencies.[57] Another issue arises from the territorial limits of national laws, which may not extend beyond a country's borders, hindering efforts to prosecute criminals operating internationally. Differences in legal frameworks further complicate the process, with varying extradition procedures and mutual legal assistance treaties.[58]

Narco-terrorists exploit jurisdictional gaps, weak borders, and limited law enforcement resources to evade capture. This highlights the need for enhanced international cooperation, intelligence sharing, and capacity building.[59] Combating narco-terrorism requires a comprehensive approach involving strengthened legal frameworks, harmonized extradition procedures, and greater collaboration among nations.

Inter-agency Coordination

The prosecution of narco-terrorism cases is often hindered by poor inter-agency coordination, largely due to the distinct mandate of each agency. As a hybrid crime, narco-terrorism requires the involvement of multiple agencies, which often fragments investigations. In India, for instance, the Enforcement Directorate (ED) handles money laundering, the National Investigation Agency (NIA) probes terrorist links, and the Central Bureau of Investigation (CBI) investigates bribery and corruption. Ideally, the Narcotics Control Bureau (NCB) or NIA should lead, but the involvement of state police often complicates coordination. Investigation of hybrid crimes such as narco terrorism requires interdisciplinary and interagency cooperation.

A key remedy is to amend the Schedule of the NIA Act, 2008, empowering the NIA as the sole lead agency once it assumes charge of a case involving narco terrorism. This amendment should explicitly include the Narcotic Drugs and Psychotropic Substances (NDPS) Act and allow the NIA to investigate related financial crimes under the Prevention of Money Laundering Act (PMLA), rather than deferring to the ED. Although Section 8 of the Act permits investigation of connected offenses, the Schedule focuses primarily on conventional terrorism, not narco-terrorism's hybrid character. Including the NDPS Act would address this legislative gap.

Section 9 of the NIA Act should also be amended to mandate cooperation from all central and state agencies. While central bodies under the Ministry of Home Affairs already coordinate with the NIA, there is no legal compulsion for central autonomous or externally governed agencies such as armed forces (under the Ministry of Defence), CBI, ED, and Directorate of Revenue Intelligence. A clear statutory obligation would ensure seamless collaboration across agencies, strengthening the investigation of complex, cross-cutting offenses.

Evidence Collection, Admissibility and Validity

Narco-terrorists operate through intricate networks of individuals, transactions, and activities that may appear benign when seen in isolation. For convictions, investigators must establish a clear link between the accused and the conspiracy, using both oral and documentary evidence. Any break in the chain of causation or ambiguity in the accused's role can weaken the case.

Consider a scenario where a Chartered Accountant (CA) is secretly hired by a drug peddler who receives heroin from an operative linked to the 'X' terrorist group in Pakistan. The CA launders the drug proceeds by routing them into cash-heavy businesses like petrol pumps, restaurants, retail stores, and cinemas. These businesses help reintegrate the illicit funds into the formal banking system. The CA and businesses earn commissions, while the CA also collaborates with offshore launderers who funnel funds into tax havens via shell companies. Ultimately, this money is invested in real estate across India and abroad.

To secure convictions, prosecutors must establish the role of each entity in this laundering chain. While some business owners may be unaware of the terror links, complicating the establishment of *mens rea*—the CA, peddler, and those with demonstrable complicity should still be prosecuted.

Investigators would employ call log analysis and contact chaining. Contact chaining is a method of analyzing communication data, open source, financial transactions etc. to identify connections between individuals. It involves starting with a specific person or 'seed' and mapping out their contacts. This process can be extended to include contacts of those contacts, creating a network of connections to trace relationships between suspects. Where international links exist, authorities must navigate legal instruments like the Mutual Legal Assistance Treaty (MLAT) and coordinate with bodies like FATF, FIU-India, INTERPOL, and UNODC.

The prosecution must establish consistent, corroborated connections, causal or strongly correlative, between communications and financial flows, leading back to the CA and peddler. If these links are proven, conspiracy charges under various laws can be firmly applied.

It is important to note that the example provided represents a relatively straightforward case. Real-world investigations are far more complex, often involving actors unaware of the illicit nature of the funds they process.

Resource Crunch

Investigating narco-terrorism cases demands substantial resources, including multidisciplinary teams comprising financial and technical experts, forensic scientists, law enforcement personnel, and tactical units. Such operations require significant funding, which many provincial agencies lack. The transnational nature of narco-terrorism further complicates matters, especially when wealthy white-collar criminals are involved, who can afford top-tier legal defence, making prosecution and conviction even more challenging.

These investigations also require international cooperation, often involving overseas missions by investigation teams, placing considerable financial strain on agencies. Only national-level agencies with adequate resources and central government support are equipped to manage such complex operations effectively.

While some provincial agencies possess the necessary expertise, they often lack the capacity to handle inter-state or cross-border dimensions. To address this, a coordination centre under the Ministry of Home Affairs could be institutionalized to support and guide state-level enforcement in tackling such intricate cases.

Corruption and Complicity

It is naive to assume that government officials are immune to the covert tactics of narco-terrorists, who often exploit and co-opt unscrupulous individuals within the system. Corruption within law enforcement, the judiciary, and other institutions poses a significant threat to the effective prosecution of narco-terrorism. This hybrid crime, combining drug trafficking and terrorism, demands impartial and rigorous investigation. However, when corrupt elements infiltrate the very agencies meant to combat it, the effort is severely undermined.[60]

Corruption in law enforcement can compromise investigations. Officers may be bribed, coerced, or even willingly collaborate with drug syndicates.[61] These individuals may leak confidential information, ignore criminal activity, or obstruct cases to protect themselves or their accomplices.[62] This not only weakens enforcement but erodes public trust. Agencies must monitor their personnel closely and act decisively against internal collusion. Severe punishment of insiders, as has occurred in past cases, is essential.[63]

The judiciary, too, can be compromised. Judges, prosecutors, or court staff may accept bribes or yield to political pressure, resulting in lenient sentences or wrongful acquittals. Cases from Latin America reveal collusion between judges and drug cartels, with some facing prosecution.[64] Manipulated proceedings, altered evidence, or biased rulings enable narco-terrorists to evade justice.[65]

Corruption within government also creates systemic vulnerabilities. Politically connected individuals may misuse their power to facilitate trafficking, launder money, or offer logistical support to terrorists. This includes exploiting regulatory gaps, diverting public resources, or weakening anti-money laundering and counter terrorism frameworks.[66]

Narco-terrorists routinely use intimidation, bribery, and violence to sway investigations. In Latin America, such tactics are well-documented. With access to immense funds, drug cartels across the Middle East, Pakistan, and the Americas bribe officials to shield their operations.[67]

Conclusion

Narco-terrorism, a hybrid and hydra-headed crime, fuses the violence of terrorism with the illicit profits of organized crime, posing a grave challenge to global security. Unlike traditional organized crime focused solely on profit, narco-terrorism adds political destabilization and violence to its arsenal. The symbiotic relationship between drug trafficking and terrorism magnifies their destructive reach, making them uniquely dangerous.

Investigating these crimes is highly complex due to the transnational operations and layered networks involved. Narco-terrorist groups use sophisticated methods and are often shielded by corruption and intimidation, which obstruct investigations and weaken law enforcement institutions.

The damage narco-terrorism inflicts on a nation's core cannot be overstated. Apart from enriching criminal syndicates, the drug trade fuels corruption, social unrest, and violent crime. In India, it now stands as one of the most serious national security threats, undermining economic growth, social cohesion, and political stability.

Corruption and coercion are central tools in the narco-terrorist playbook. Bribery, threats, and legal manipulation foster a climate of fear and impunity, eroding public confidence in justice institutions and weakening investigative agencies.

To counter this threat, stronger synergy among India's security and law enforcement bodies is critical. Coordinated operations, information-sharing, and institutionalized Joint Action Groups can significantly improve their effectiveness. Moreover, deeper engagement with global bodies like INTERPOL and the UNODC is essential to tackling the cross-border dimensions of this menace.

In conclusion, narco-terrorism is a dynamic and deeply rooted threat that demands a comprehensive, unified response. Through better inter-agency cooperation, international partnerships, and targeted strategies, India can effectively confront and neutralize this evolving danger.

10

Cashing in on Chaos: The Business of Terror-Funding

> "*We put the world's financial institutions on notice: if you do business with terrorists, if you support them or sponsor them, you will not do business with the United States of America.*"
>
> **—President George W. Bush**

Like many overused terms, '*terrorist financing*' often evokes images of dangerous criminals amassing funds through intimidation and violence. However, the actual financial structures behind terrorism are far more complex and elusive. For most people, and even for many seasoned counter-terrorism professionals, this remains an opaque and highly technical domain. The intricacies of terror finance regularly perplex even experienced investigators who have spent years tracing suspicious transactions.[1]

This chapter offers a modest attempt to present a consolidated yet insightful overview of Counter Terror Financing and Money Laundering (CTF-ML), along with its many complexities. It aims to give readers a foundational understanding of how terror financing has evolved, particularly during the twentieth century, while acknowledging that a full grasp of this arcane subject requires deeper exploration of specialized literature.

What is Terrorist Financing?

At its core, Terrorist Financing (TF) refers to any act, direct or indirect, that provides financial support to terrorism, carried out knowingly and intentionally, whether through action or omission. A more formal understanding comes from legal definitions that assign penal liability to such conduct.[2]

Functionally, TF is the illicit provision of funds or resources to terrorist individuals, organizations, or affiliates to enable activities such as attacks, recruitment, training, and weapons procurement. This support may be explicit or implicit, for instance, when an otherwise legitimate organization knowingly aids terrorist actors.

TF includes a wide array of criminal activities: money laundering, fraud, extortion, drug trafficking, and illicit trade. It typically functions through complex, transnational networks that exploit gaps in the global financial system.

The fundamental aim of TF is to strengthen terrorist groups so they can carry out violence, spread fear, and pursue ideological or political goals. While definitions differ by jurisdiction, TF generally involves offering tangible support, monetary or material, that aids terrorist operations in measurable ways.

International community through *United Nation's International Convention for the Suppression of the Financing of Terrorism* in the Article 2 of the convention defines Terrorist Financing making it legally binding it through Article 2 which states that a person commits a terrorist financing offence if they knowingly provide or collect funds, directly or indirectly, to support acts of terrorism. This includes funding acts listed in specific international treaties or any violent act meant to kill or seriously harm civilians not involved in conflict. The purpose must be to intimidate the public or force a government or international organization to act, or refrain from acting, through fear, coercion, or violence.

The article clearly states that an offence is constituted even if the funds were not actually used to commit a terrorist act; mere attempts are penalized as if the act were completed. However, the Convention primarily offers a definitional framework for terror financing to guide national legislation, limiting its scope to activities with an international dimension. If the funds, fundraiser, and intended recipient are all within a single state's borders, the treaty does not apply. Specifically, the Convention is inapplicable when the offence occurs entirely within one member state, the offender resides there, and no other state has jurisdiction—unless otherwise covered under Articles 12 to 18.[3]

A major challenge in countering terror financing lies in the flawed belief, often held by Western democracies, that current regulatory systems are built upon a full understanding of terrorist financial operations hence they must be universally applied. This oversimplifies the issue, which in reality involves complex economic and logistical networks requiring a multifaceted strategy to address effectively.

This analogy is comparable to treating an illness with a diverse combination of potent chemicals, hoping that their collective potency will lead to a cure without first understanding the causative factors underlying the disease. As with the human body, counter-terrorism strategies cannot be effectively operated on the basis of trial and error since instead of one, several human lives are involved. Instead of combating terror with errors, the approach required should be fundamentally distinct from addressing traditional terror offenses, which exhibit clearly identifiable characteristics.

Hybrid Nature of the Offence

Terrorist financing presents complex challenges for research and investigation, largely due to the difficulty in corroborating and legally substantiating such activities. Apparent links between routine financial transactions and terrorism are often speculative or at least extremely hard to unravel and substantiate.

There are additional complexities involved such as the fact that many individuals involved may be unaware of their role in enabling such financing (innocent conduits). This makes it imperative to adopt a systematic, evidence-based approach to identify what qualifies as terrorist financing, determine thresholds of complicity, trace links to illicit activities, and distinguish between masterminds and unwitting participants.

Unravelling the Mysteries of CTF-ML: Beyond the Western Notions

Understanding terrorist financing (TF) requires a nuanced approach that takes into account the socio-economic context in which such activities occur. One useful method is to analyse testimonies from accused individuals. These accounts help uncover how terrorist groups mobilize resources and evade scrutiny. For instance, arrests often reveal connections to hawala networks or cash handlers, who may disclose information under pressure. Despite popular belief, TF is not limited to money, anything of value can serve the same purpose. Even small acts, like a shopkeeper regularly supplying food to known terrorists, can constitute terror financing if done with knowledge of the group's identity.

However, focusing solely on monetary transactions creates blind spots in financial monitoring systems. Terrorists often rely on value-based exchanges, not cash, especially in smaller, self-financed operations like 'lone wolf' attacks.

A narrow definition centred on money encourages excessive reliance on asset freezes, blacklists, and financial service regulation, strategies that may be inadequate.[4]

Recent investigations show cash and deposits often play a secondary role in terrorist economies. Individuals posing as volunteers for charities may funnel donations to extremist causes. Al-Qaeda has financed operations through commodity trading, while narco-terrorists depend on drug profits. Pakistani groups like Falah-e-Insaniyat (FIF) channel charity funds to terror groups. In India, Naxalites extract value through tendu leaf trade, illegal mining, and construction contracts.[5]

TF, therefore, extends far beyond money, it encompasses all forms of value transfer. In India's northeast, insurgents routinely extort money from local businesses and even government departments. Investigations by the National Investigation Agency (NIA) revealed that senior officials were being extorted and such activities continue unabated.[6]

Groups such as Falah-e-Insaniyat (FIF) in Pakistan, a front for Jamaat-ut-Dawah (a rebranded Lashkar-e-Taiyyba), raise donations under the guise of charitable work. Their ambulance services and other social projects have earned them goodwill, helping to launder terror funds. Recently, Indian authorities uncovered FIF cells within India working to secretly fund terror operations.[7]

Beyond the Money-Trail: Intricacies of Terrorist Financing

An over-reliance on tracking the 'money trail' in current regulatory frameworks for terror financing seems mismatched with how terrorists actually fund their operations. This method is most effective in regions where formal financial systems are dominant, but terrorist groups often operate in areas with weak or absent formal financial infrastructures, such as Burkina Faso, Myanmar, and South Sudan.[8]

In these regions, shadow financial systems like hawala and cash-based trade sustain terrorist activities. Around 70% of terrorist groups operate in areas where formal financial services are minimal, and financial regulations have little impact on nearly a third of globally designated terrorist organizations.[9] Western analyses often overlook how non-Western financial systems function, leading to gaps in understanding.

Terror-finance research, therefore, is not just about tracing money but also about examining the value chains terrorists build to support their operations. This includes donations, goods, medical care, and charitable acts used to build goodwill. Investigations by the FBI and Israeli Defence Forces have shown that terrorist groups such as al-Qaeda and ISIS have used platforms on the dark web, accepting donations in crypto currencies to fund weapons purchases.[10]

Thus, understanding terror finance requires moving beyond Western-centric frameworks. Effective counter-terrorism strategies must adopt an open-minded approach, consistently updating to address new methods of financing. Terrorists will continue to adapt, so investigators must stay vigilant and informed.

How do Terrorists Finance Themselves? A Case Study of Aum Shinrikyo

Aum Shinrikyo, founded by Shoko Asahara in 1984, was a secret cult that gained significant following in the 1990s. Initially named 'Aum Shinsen Association,' it was registered with Tokyo's Metropolitan body in 1989. By the 1990s, it had thousands of members in Japan and Russia, with offices in Moscow, Vladivostok, Frankfurt, and New York.[11]

The cult raised funds through membership fees, sales of religious items, and unrelated businesses like computer shops and noodle factories. It also relied on covert donations from wealthy supporters, including properties bequeathed by loyal members. Despite Asahara's limited education, Aum attracted highly educated members, often recruited through yoga classes.[12]

The group's following included young intellectuals, including medical professionals, biochemists, and engineers, who sought an alternative to mainstream society. While many were from privileged backgrounds, some were from working-class families. Asahara resorted to torture and murder to seize followers' assets.[13]

Aum amassed over 100 billion yen ($ 1 billion) in assets, including 16 properties across Japan, a helicopter, boats, gold bars, and cash. Authorities recovered 700 million yen ($ 7 million) and 10 kilograms of gold from a single building during raids.[14]

The cult's wealth stemmed from brainwashing followers into surrendering all their assets and running businesses like noodle shops. It also engaged in extortion, selling Asahara's blood and bathwater, and may have been involved in illegal drug manufacturing.[15]

Aum's teachings centred on survival through adherence to their ideology, which included renouncing worldly possessions. Members gave up assets, including homes and credit cards, and the cult sold religious training and paraphernalia while operating legal businesses globally. They may also have supplied drugs to criminal groups.[16]

Distinguishing Features of Terror Finance

Terrorist financiers face a significant challenge that sets them apart from traditional criminals: the need to conceal both the source and destination of their funds. This secrecy is crucial for individuals and organizations involved in terror financing. Unlike regular criminals, terrorists have little concern for taxes or typical financial regulations. Their motivations and financial considerations are shaped by very different factors. Below are some key characteristics that distinguish terrorist financing:

Secrecy and Illegitimacy

The need for secrecy in terrorist financing arises from its illicit nature, requiring concealment to avoid detection and prosecution. Unlike legal financial transactions, terrorist financing operates in the shadows, presenting unique challenges to global security. Illegitimate sources, such as extortion, drug trafficking, and organized crime, are the main funding sources for terrorist activities, and they function outside legal oversight, necessitating secrecy to evade law enforcement.[17]

Terrorist groups use covert financial networks, employing methods like shell companies, front organizations, and informal transfer systems to obscure the origin and destination of funds. This secrecy enables them to avoid exposure and disruption, sustaining operations and extremist ideologies.[18]

Secrecy in terrorist financing extends to modern technologies like crypto currencies, which provide new channels for raising and transferring funds. The anonymity of digital currencies and the use of blockchain technology allow terrorists to conduct transactions beyond the reach of authorities, complicating efforts to track and prevent their activities.[19]

Organizational Necessity

Like any other organization, terrorist groups need to compensate their operatives and ensure that the value they create, including money, remains under their control. Financing their operations through strategic use of financial networks is essential for their survival. Without this, their organizations cannot sustain themselves. For this reason, any counter-terrorism strategy focusing solely on neutralizing terrorists has limited chances of success.

Terrorists use financial channels to evade detection through money laundering, front organizations, digital currencies, and by obscuring the origins and destinations of funds. Secrecy also protects them from internal and external threats, including intelligence infiltration and member betrayal. For terrorist organizations, managing financial resources through covert networks is not just a strategy but a fundamental necessity. Therefore, combating terrorist financing requires strong international cooperation, improved regulatory measures, and technological innovations to dismantle these networks, disrupt funding flows, and weaken terrorist structures.[20]

Clever Use of Legitimate Channels

Terrorist organizations strategically exploit legitimate financial channels to fund their operations. They often create front organizations or charities that appear to operate legally but act as conduits for laundering illicit funds. By using these seemingly legitimate entities, terrorists conceal the true nature of their financial transactions, making it difficult for authorities to detect and disrupt their activities.

Additionally, terrorists take advantage of regulatory loopholes to evade scrutiny. This clever use of legitimate channels not only provides a cover of legitimacy but also enables terrorists to access resources and support from unsuspecting individuals and institutions.[21]

Ideological Motivations

Unlike typical corporate or legitimate organizations, terrorist financing is not driven by profit or economic gain. For terrorist groups, violence is a tool to achieve political or ideological objectives. The primary motivator is ideology, whether political or religious, rather than financial gain. Funds obtained through illicit means are used to recruit, spread propaganda, and cover operational costs in pursuit of their agenda.

This distinction highlights the complexity of countering terrorist financing, as traditional financial deterrents may be ineffective against individuals driven by deep ideological convictions. Addressing the ideological roots of terror financing is essential for developing comprehensive strategies to disrupt and dismantle terrorist networks.

Adaptability and Flexibility

Terrorist financing methods are highly adaptive, evolving swiftly in response to countermeasures by authorities. This continual shift poses a significant challenge for law enforcement and regulatory bodies, which often struggle to match the pace of innovation. Terrorist groups exploit emerging technologies, such as crypto currencies, encrypted messaging apps, and Dark Net marketplaces, to obscure their financial trails and avoid detection.

For example, certain terrorist organizations have tried and successfully operated crowd-funding campaign disguised as a medical relief fund for war-affected children. Promoted through anonymous social media pages and backed by fake testimonials, the campaign received substantial amount of donations in crypto currency from sympathizers worldwide. The funds were then funnelled through a chain of digital wallets and converted into prepaid debit cards, which operatives used across borders to purchase drone components and communication equipment without drawing attention.[22]

Such imaginative and evasive tactics demonstrate the cleverness of terrorist financiers, who continually probe regulatory cracks and leverage new tools to stay ahead. This evolving landscape underscores the urgent need for continuous innovation, global cooperation, and intelligence sharing among governments, financial institutions, and security agencies. Only by remaining equally agile and forward-looking can authorities effectively disrupt terrorist financing networks and safeguard global security.

'Lying Low'

Unlike the corporate sector, terrorist organizations do not promote or publicize their activities before striking. They operate in secrecy, keeping their financial signatures discreet and below detection thresholds. Their financing networks are often lean, relying on minimal resources and low-cost methods to sustain operations. Rather than building elaborate financial infrastructures, terrorists prioritize efficiency and adaptability, using informal mechanisms like *Hawala*, crypto currency, unregulated remittance services, and cash smuggling to move money quietly and efficiently.

For example, a small terror cell might transfer funds through a local grocery store that doubles as an informal money transfer hub, disguising operational expenses as supply payments. By routing small amounts through multiple intermediaries, they avoid attracting attention, while still financing propaganda, weapons, and recruitment.

These decentralized and inexpensive systems allow terrorist groups to function effectively on modest budgets while remaining elusive. Their use of inexpensive technologies and informal networks complicates traditional counter-financing strategies, which are often geared toward detecting large-scale or centralized financial flows. Addressing these challenges requires more agile, intelligence-led strategies that target the unique structure of low-cost terror financing models.

Vital Breath of Terrorist Ecosystem

The need for terrorist organizations to secure funding is central to their existence. Without steady resources, these groups cannot function, making the disruption of their financial ecosystems a key element in any effective counter-terrorism strategy. A focused approach targeting the nodes that support terrorism, its funding streams, logistical channels, and enabling networks, offers a sustainable path to dismantling such entities.[23]

In contrast, strategies that ignore the socio-political and economic drivers of terror financing often miss the deeper causes, addressing symptoms rather than motivations. Combating terrorist funding effectively requires understanding *why* these organizations persist, not just *how* they do. Long-term success lies in addressing the root conditions that allow terror finances to flourish.[24]

Terrorist groups often use psychological manipulation and propaganda to justify their activities and attract support. Organizations like ISIS, al-Qaeda, and Hamas portray themselves as protectors of Islam and the oppressed, branding dissenters as '*Takfir*' (infidels) to be punished. They selectively reinterpret religious teachings to guilt and coerce vulnerable community members into contributing. Using peer-to-peer networks, they exploit teenagers, housewives, and the poor to donate under the guise of supporting a 'Global Jihad'. Any counter-terror financing effort that fails to challenge these ideological narrative risks being ineffective.[25]

Stages of Terror Financing

Quite akin to money laundering, terror financing involves concealing both the origin and destination of funds to avoid detection by surveillance systems. However, unlike drug cartels or criminal syndicates driven primarily by profit, terrorist organizations operate with ideological or political motives, using financial secrecy as a strategic tool rather than a means of personal enrichment.

While both practices rely heavily on evasion and deception, terror financing is distinct in its ultimate aim, advancing extremist agendas rather than accumulating wealth. This distinction, despite surface-level similarities, underscores the need to treat terror financing as a uniquely complex threat.

The Myth of Clean Terrorist Funds

Unlike conventional money laundering, which often involves the proceeds of crime, especially in organized criminal syndicates, terror financing does not always rely on illicitly obtained funds. In fact, a considerable portion of the money funnelled into terrorist networks can originate from entirely legal sources.

Terrorist groups may indeed profit from criminal activities like narcotics trafficking, but they also receive substantial funding through lawful donations made via charities, non-profit entities, and religious or cultural organizations. For example, Pakistani terrorist groups have long benefited from public contributions made under the guise of supporting 'Jihad' in Kashmir. This legality at the point of origin marks a distinctive and challenging feature of terror financing.

Low Denominations and Volume of Funds

Unlike traditional criminal organizations focused on profit maximization, terrorist groups prioritize operational security and ideological goals. As a result, they often avoid large-scale transactions and instead rely on low-profile, informal financial networks. These discreet practices make tracing their financial flows significantly more difficult, posing a major challenge for law enforcement agencies attempting to disrupt their funding and dismantle their operations.[26]

Ostensible 'Charitable-Humanitarian' Façade

Terrorist financing often emphasizes the legitimate appearance of funds received through charities and other lawful-looking sources. This is why terrorist organizations frequently portray themselves as defenders of their community, claiming to fight oppression or support victims. Small sums allocated for specific terrorist acts are easier to hide and often escape scrutiny. In some cases, organizations may ostensibly engage in charitable activities while simultaneously diverting significant funds to support terrorism through concealed cash outflows.[27]

'Ideological Commitment'

A key distinction lies in ideological commitment. While money launderers are typically motivated by profit, terrorist financiers often act out of ideological allegiance to the groups they support. This ideological drive reinforces their secrecy and makes their operations harder to detect. Understanding this distinction is essential for differentiating between conventional money laundering and laundering done for terrorist purposes. Terrorist organizations may finance themselves both strategically, over the long term to sustain their infrastructure, and tactically, for specific operations or attacks.

Strategic versus Tactical Terror Financing

Whether strategic or tactical, financing for terrorism involves processes akin to money laundering with differentials as discussed above. Let us understand how terrorists might finance for tactical and strategic purpose delineating the differences as follows.

Strategic Financing

Terrorist financing operations often employ deceptive fundraising strategies to mobilize support and generate funds. The 'Sikh for Justice Referendum 2020' campaign, for example, exploited the Sikh Diaspora's grievances to incite rebellion against the Indian government while raising substantial funds through religious and community gatherings.[28]

Insurgent groups in India's northeast and Naxal-affected regions frequently rely on extortion rackets and levies to finance their activities. These groups may also extort ethnic diaspora members, threatening to report them to immigration authorities. While such *contributions* may appear voluntary, individuals within these diaspora communities often face pressure from influential leaders to donate. Terrorist groups may establish small-scale businesses, such as retail shops and shell companies, to generate a steady stream of income.

Tactical Terrorist Financing

Terrorist groups frequently use sophisticated tactics to conceal their financial operations and avoid detection. One common method is *structuring*, sending multiple wire transfers below the reporting threshold to different accounts held by willing associates. These individuals then withdraw the cash and deliver it to the intended recipient, leaving minimal trace.

Another widely used technique is reliance on *hawala* networks, informal money transfer systems that operate outside formal banking structures. These systems allow cross-border fund movement without a paper trail, making detection difficult for law enforcement agencies.

Terrorists also transport physical cash or traveller's checks while travelling to target zones. Though less efficient than electronic transfers, this method offers anonymity and avoids digital monitoring. Additionally, digital payment platforms such as Google Pay or Paytm are used to send numerous small transfers that accumulate into significant sums. These amounts are then withdrawn in cash by intermediaries and passed along, masking the origin of the funds.

A wide range of legitimate financial mechanisms are also exploited, charities, front companies, street vendors, import-export businesses, and informal lenders all serve as vehicles. The disguises used include investments, donations, salary payments, reimbursements, or loan repayments—any seemingly lawful transaction can be a cover.

Terrorist groups have also used commercial enterprises as dual-purpose operations. The LTTE, for example, maintained a tanker fleet in the 1980s, conducting both legal cargo transport and covert arms smuggling. Hamas has used business ventures to bankroll its militant infrastructure while enriching leadership. The Provisional Irish Republican Army operated a network of profitable taxi firms even as it carried out violent attacks, sometimes targeting competitors under the guise of political resistance.

Understanding these tactics sets the stage for analyzing the *stages of terrorist financing*, which closely mirror those of money laundering.

Stages in Terror Financing

Stage One: Acquisition and Consolidation

Much like other money launderers, terrorist organization might acquire funds meant for strategic and tactical terrorist activities through donations or other means. Once such funds are acquired these are transported or relayed to the intended targets through middlemen dedicated to the objectives of the organization.

For example, terrorists can use small shopkeepers to launder funds for hiding in their bank accounts that can be supplied to other people in the chain whenever required. Funds are also siphoned through charitable organization by showing charity works and other such activities in which small of amounts of cash are spread over multiple purchases (such as food items, medical supplies, regular payments made to the families 'victims' of police action, 'scholarships' given to wards of terrorists who died in action, etc.).

Stage Two: Dematerialization and Placement

This is a critical step in terrorist money laundering, which involves funnelling of significant funds through multiple transactions to obscure their origin. Dematerialization converts illicit funds into untraceable forms such as crypto currencies or precious metals, while *Placement* integrates these funds into the legitimate financial system via complex transactions and shell companies.

This process makes detection and disruption difficult for authorities. Terrorists adeptly exploit modern financial tools and regulatory gaps for laundering, with one method known as '*smurfing*.' In this technique, cash is distributed to individuals ('Smurfs'), who then deposit small sums into multiple bank accounts to evade detection.

Once deposited, the *Placement* stage is accomplished, enabling the financing of terrorist activities while eluding law enforcement scrutiny. Another method involves the use of front companies, where terrorists select businesses and bank accounts owned by seemingly innocuous individuals with significant wealth and reputable social standing. These individuals receive large cash sums, which are subsequently deposited into their accounts, completing the Placement process.

Layering

Layering is a technique employed by money launderers to obscure the origins of illicit funds. For instance, terrorists may invest in financial assets with high liquidity and fungibility, such as unlisted stocks, gold, vehicles, and quality trade goods. They may also invest in real estate, apartments, houses, and commercial properties. By transferring money between business accounts under the guise of investments and loans, they create a complex web of transactions.

These funds can then be funnelled overseas through seemingly legitimate business transactions. Terrorists often utilize complicit financial institutions with insiders who launder substantial amounts while providing financial advice to terrorist organizations.

Third Stage: Integration and Stabilization

After the laundered funds have been channelled, consolidated, placed, and layered, they are eventually given the appearance of legitimacy and integrated into the legal economy. This can be achieved through investments in businesses yielding legally earned dividends or in assets like artwork, which can be enjoyed or sold for intrinsic value. Income from investments or proceeds from sales can then be repatriated to the country where the crimes occurred, ensuring availability to the ultimate criminal beneficial owner.

Terrorist Financing: Web of Ideology and Operations

Terrorist organizations demonstrate notable ingenuity in laundering money, using sophisticated methods to conceal the origins of illicit funds. Unlike typical money laundering schemes, those linked to terrorism involve unique challenges. While both aim to obscure the source and use of money, terrorist financing also reflects the organization's strategic and tactical priorities.

This financing goes beyond transactions, functioning within complex ethnic and cultural networks. These communities not only support terrorist groups logistically and financially but also serve as recruitment grounds. Shared ideological beliefs often lead to voluntary contributions, embedding terror financing within the social and cultural structures of the communities involved.[29]

Financing terrorist activities requires detailed planning to balance immediate tactical demands with long-term goals. Funds are directed to key areas such as recruitment, propaganda, and acquiring weapons, all while minimizing detection. This strategic use of resources differentiates terrorist financing from conventional money laundering, which typically benefits individuals or criminal enterprises. In contrast, terrorist financing poses a far greater threat to international security and stability.

Combating Terror Finance: International Institutional and Legal Framework

The rigorous implementation of international Counter-Terrorism Financing (CTF) strategies largely began after 9/11. However, several key pre-9/11 international legal frameworks laid the foundation for global responses to terror financing, particularly its narcotics-related aspects. These include:

- *UN Single Convention on Narcotic Drugs (1961)*

- *UN Convention on Psychotropic Substances (1971)*
- *UN Convention against Illicit Traffic in Narcotic Drugs and Psychotropic Substances (1988), also known as the Vienna Convention*

Together, these conventions created a global legal structure for the '*war on drugs*,' regulating substances such as opium, heroin, cocaine, cannabis, ecstasy, and LSD. The 1988 Vienna Convention expanded this framework by requiring countries to cooperate in seizing and confiscating proceeds from drug trafficking. It promoted mutual legal assistance in extradition, search and seizure, document service, and cross-border legal processes. Importantly, it also challenged bank secrecy laws that obstruct information sharing and called for the criminalization of drug-related money laundering, laying the groundwork for the international anti-money laundering (AML) regime.

Before the late 1990s, the UN imposed sanctions on states like Libya and Iran for supporting terrorism, but non-state actors remained outside the legal scope. This changed in 1999 with the UN Convention for the Suppression of the Financing of Terrorism, which required member-states to criminalize the funding of terrorist activities. Recognizing the central role of finance in terrorism, the convention stressed international cooperation among law enforcement, financial institutions, and governments.

The 1999 Convention obliges signatory states (State Parties) to identify, freeze, or confiscate assets linked to terrorism. Financial institutions must monitor and report suspicious transactions. States are also required to prosecute or extradite individuals involved in terror financing and support international investigations. Notably, banking secrecy cannot be used to deny mutual legal assistance, reinforcing a global commitment to cutting off financial lifelines to terrorism and promoting cross-border cooperation to protect international security.

Paradigm Shift in CTF Policies post 9/11

In response to the September 11, 2001 attacks, the United Nations Security Council adopted UNSC Resolution 1373, introducing comprehensive and unprecedented measures to curb terrorist financing. This resolution became a cornerstone in the global effort to combat terrorism funding, expanding upon earlier UN sanctions frameworks, such as UNSC Resolution 1267, which targeted al-Qaeda and the Taliban after their 1998 attacks on U.S. embassies in Kenya and Tanzania.

Resolution 1373 significantly broadened the scope of counter-terrorism measures by urging states to *create their own lists of designated terrorist organizations*, moving beyond the centralized UN sanctions approach. Its core provisions include:

- Mandating all nations to prevent and suppress terrorist financing, criminalize the provision of funds for terrorist activities, and freeze terrorist assets without delay.
- Elevating terrorist financing to a serious criminal offence, with countries expected to offer full legal cooperation in investigations and prosecutions, including sharing evidence.
- Calling for strengthened border controls, stricter management of identity papers and travel documents, and improved measures to block terrorist movement.
- Stressing the importance of international information sharing, recognizing the link between terrorism and organized crime.
- Reinforcing the need to strengthen legal frameworks against 'rogue states' while expanding focus to "non-state actors" such as terrorist and criminal groups. This effort contributed to the development of an international blacklist of suspected terrorists.
- Establishing the Counter-Terrorism Committee (CTC) to monitor implementation and assist states requiring technical or legal support.

In addition to UN efforts, the European Union (EU) also took significant steps toward institutionalizing effective legal responses to terrorist financing. Key EU initiatives include:

The European Convention on Laundering, Search, Seizure, and Confiscation of the Proceeds from Crime 1990

The Strasbourg Convention, formally known as the Convention on Laundering, Search, Seizure and Confiscation of the Proceeds from Crime, came into force in September 1993. It marked a significant step in combating money laundering by targeting proceeds from a broad range of criminal activities, not just drug trafficking. The convention aimed to strengthen international cooperation among Council of Europe member-states and other nations globally. It introduced comprehensive measures for defining laundering offences, enabling the confiscation of criminal proceeds, and requiring the disclosure of bank, financial, and commercial records to aid in the tracing and identification of illicit assets.

The European Convention on the Laundering, Search, Seizure, and Confiscation of the Proceeds from Crime, and on the Financing of Terrorism 2005

This convention builds upon the Strasbourg Convention by extending its scope beyond laundering and confiscation of criminal proceeds. It addresses the interception of '*clean*' *money*, funds derived from legitimate sources but intended for criminal purposes, a critical concern in the fight against terrorism financing. The convention emphasizes the need for *rapid access to financial information* and details about assets held by criminal and terrorist organizations, recognizing this as vital for the effective implementation of both preventive and enforcement measures.

EU Money Laundering Directives

These efforts are reflected in a series of four directives. The First Directive (1991) established the foundational framework, requiring EU member-states to align their laws with the Financial Action Task Force's 40 Recommendations (FATF 40). It focused primarily on a limited group of financial institutions and proceeds from narcotics-related crimes. The Second Directive (2001) broadened both the scope of predicate offenses and the range of institutions covered, extending obligations beyond banks to include key '*gatekeepers*' such as lawyers, notaries, accountants, auditors, tax advisers, real estate agents, casinos, auctioneers, and dealers in high-value goods. The Third Directive (2007) further strengthened the regime by explicitly targeting terrorist financing in addition to money laundering, and introduced more robust requirements for customer due diligence than its predecessors.

EU Council Common Position

The EU maintains a unified and regularly updated list of individuals, groups, and entities involved in terrorism, enabling the freezing of their assets. This list includes organizations such as Babbar Khalsa, Al-Aqsa Martyrs Brigade, Aum Shinrikyo, Hamas, Khalistan Zindabad Force, Liberation Tigers of Tamil Eelam (LTTE), and Palestinian Islamic Jihad, among others. This mechanism serves as the EU's implementation of UN Security Council Resolution 1373, broadening the scope of sanctions and asset freezes to cover those suspected of terrorist involvement.

USA PATRIOT Act

Though the Patriot Act is a U.S.-specific law, its significance lies in catalyzing a global shift in counter-terrorist financing (CTF) efforts after 9/11. Enacted shortly after the attacks, the Act introduced sweeping provisions affecting all financial institutions with direct or indirect ties to the United States. While domestic in scope, its influence has extended internationally, shaping CTF norms and practices adopted worldwide.

The legislation established a range of robust measures to combat terrorist financing, many of which are now considered global best practices. As such, the Patriot Act remains essential in discussions on international CTF efforts due to its far-reaching impact. It significantly strengthened global efforts against narco-terrorism by enhancing financial surveillance, expanding intelligence-sharing, and empowering law enforcement to track illicit drug-trafficking networks funding terrorism. Its provisions allowed for aggressive monitoring of suspicious financial transactions, aiding in the disruption of money laundering schemes linked to drug cartels. By targeting the financial lifelines of narco-terror groups, it bolstered international cooperation and reduced the operational scope of these threats.[30]

Title III of International Money Laundering Abatement and Financial Anti-Terrorism Act of 2001

The Act explicitly prohibits covered financial institutions, primarily U.S. banks and U.S. branches of foreign banks, from establishing correspondent accounts with foreign shell banks, which lack a physical presence in their country of incorporation and are not affiliated with any regulated financial group. Such banks are also barred from transacting with other institutions.

The legislation further imposes enhanced due diligence requirements on correspondent and private banking relationships involving foreign banks, applicable to both U.S. institutions and U.S. branches of non-U.S. banks. Notably, the Act asserts 'long-arm' jurisdiction, enabling U.S. authorities to target the assets, accounts, and transactions of foreign money launderers with any U.S. nexus.[31]

The Financial Action Task Force (FATF)

Originally established as the Groupe d'Action Financière (GAFI), the Financial Action Task Force (FATF) is an inter-governmental body formed at the 1989 G-7 Summit in Paris to address the growing threat of international money laundering. By the end of 2011, it included 34 member-countries and two regional organizations. Its initial aim was to analyze money laundering methods, develop countermeasures, and assess the effectiveness of national and global efforts.

Operating independently, FATF formulates and promotes policies to protect the global financial system from money laundering, terrorist financing, and the funding of weapons proliferation. Its recommendations are widely recognized as the global standard for *anti-money laundering (AML)* and *counter-terrorist financing (CFT)* frameworks (AML-CFT).

As terrorist financing became a greater concern globally, FATF's role expanded to include CFT, and more recently, to combat the financing of weapons of mass destruction (WMDs). FATF works in close coordination with bodies such as the IMF, World Bank, and United Nations, playing a key role in advancing international cooperation against financial crime.[32]

FATF: A Standard-Setter, not a Lone Watchdog

The Financial Action Task Force (FATF) is often mistakenly seen as a global financial watchdog. While it plays a key role in combating money laundering, terrorist financing, and proliferation financing, its functions go beyond mere oversight. The FATF's primary role is to set international standards and guidelines to prevent these illicit activities and monitor member-countries' compliance.

Operating within a broader financial regulatory ecosystem, the FATF works closely with other international organizations and national authorities to build a strong anti-money laundering and counter-terrorist financing (AML-CTF) framework. Thus, while influential, the FATF is not the sole protector of the global financial system. Numerous organizations, including the IMF, World Bank, and national regulators, share responsibility for financial oversight.

Understanding the FATF's role within this wider landscape helps us appreciate its contributions to global financial integrity.

Monitoring Function

FATF tracks countries' progress in implementing AML-CFT measures through self-assessments and mutual evaluations. Governments labelled 'non-cooperative' face significant moral, political, and economic pressure. For example, Austria banned anonymous savings accounts due to FATF pressure, while Eastern European and former Soviet states, including Russia, swiftly enacted reforms when placed on the 'Non-Cooperative Countries and Territories' List.

Standardization of AML and CFT Regimes

FATF sets global standards for combating money laundering, terrorist financing, and WMD proliferation. Its core focus is the FATF Recommendations, which were updated in February 2012 to address proliferation, particularly regarding states like Iran seeking WMD capabilities. FATF also issued a 'Typologies Report on Proliferation Financing' in June 2008, detailing trends and methods in financing WMD programs, reflecting its commitment to evolving threats.

Advice, Research, and Analysis of Latest Trends

FATF plays a critical advisory role in combating money laundering and terrorist financing. By monitoring emerging trends and techniques, it provides valuable insights to member states and international organizations. Its reports highlight non-compliance with CFT-AML protocols, drawing international attention to violations. This pressure can prompt corrective measures, especially when non-compliant states risk downgraded ratings from global financial institutions.

FATF's *typology reports* offer in-depth analyses of criminal techniques, serving as valuable resources for law enforcement, financial institutions, and policymakers. As a leader in CFT-AML research, FATF helps countries enforce laws effectively, strengthening defences against illicit financial flows. Through its advisory role, FATF plays a vital part in promoting global financial integrity and security.

FATF's 40 Recommendations: Standard Protocols to Combat Money Laundering and Terrorist Financing

The '*Forty Recommendations,*' first published in 1990 and revised in 1996, 2003, and 2012, provide global standards to combat money laundering, terrorist financing, and proliferation financing. These guidelines aim to protect the integrity of the financial system through effective legal frameworks, preventive measures, and international cooperation.

- *Regulatory Framework:* The initial recommendations focus on establishing a legal and institutional framework. Countries are urged to criminalize money laundering and terrorist financing, create competent authorities for law enforcement, and ensure the availability of necessary legal powers and resources for investigations. Among others, these recommend that Adequate regulatory and supervisory systems should also be in place for financial institutions and designated non-financial businesses and professions (DNFBPs) to prevent financial misuse.

- *Prevention:* The second set of recommendations addresses preventive measures. Financial institutions and DNFBPs must conduct customer due diligence (CDD), which includes identifying and verifying customer identities, understanding business relationships, and monitoring transactions for suspicious activities. Enhanced due diligence is required for higher-risk transactions and customers. Countries should also implement mechanisms for reporting suspicious transactions and for freezing and confiscating assets linked to illicit financial activities.
- The third set emphasizes transparency and beneficial ownership. Countries should ensure that legal entities maintain accurate, up-to-date records of beneficial ownership and prevent misuse of corporate structures for illegal purposes.
- The fourth set underscores international cooperation, urging countries to establish information-sharing mechanisms, including mutual legal assistance and cooperation with foreign financial intelligence units (FIUs).

Overall, FATF's 40 recommendations create a comprehensive framework for countries to combat financial crimes and safeguard the global financial system's integrity. Adhering to these standards is crucial for ensuring transparency and security worldwide. Other international bodies also contribute to these efforts in combating money laundering and terrorist financing.

The International Monetary Fund (IMF)

As a cornerstone of the post-World War II economic order, the IMF promotes international monetary cooperation and stability. Its near-universal membership enables countries to collaborate on strategies to combat money laundering and terrorist financing. While the IMF has long been involved in anti-money laundering efforts, the 9/11 attacks intensified its focus on counter-terrorism financing (CTF).

The IMF plays a key role in assessing financial sectors and offering technical assistance to strengthen them. Through the Financial Sector Assessment Program (FSAP), developed with the World Bank, the IMF evaluates entire financial systems, identifying vulnerabilities and helping national authorities implement corrective measures. This strengthens financial resilience and supports the global effort to combat financial crimes.

Additionally, the IMF, in partnership with the World Bank, contributes to policy development and produces guides, handbooks, and papers on subjects like Financial Intelligence Units, legislative drafting, and the impact of terrorism on financial markets. Through these efforts, the IMF helps member countries improve their capacity to fight financial crimes and protect the global financial system.

Questions on IMF's Role in Countering Terror Financing

In May 2025, the IMF approved a $ 1 billion loan to Pakistan under its Extended Fund Facility, sparking sharp criticism from India, which abstained from the vote. India cited serious concerns that the funds could be misused to support state-sponsored terrorism, especially in light of the Pahalgam attack in April 2025, which claimed numerous lives. India argued that Pakistan's long-standing record of using proxy militant groups for cross-border destabilization makes it a high-risk recipient of international aid.

This decision has renewed global debate over the accountability of multilateral financial institutions and their responsibility to ensure that funding does not indirectly fuel terrorism. It also highlights the urgent need for stronger financial safeguards, similar to those outlined in the U.S. PATRIOT Act. Enacted in the aftermath of 9/11, the PATRIOT Act empowered U.S. authorities to monitor and intercept financial flows linked to terrorism, tightened anti-money laundering controls, and promoted international intelligence cooperation. Applying similar principles to global lending—such as thorough vetting of recipients, conditionality tied to counter-terrorism compliance, and transparency in fund allocation, could help prevent misuse.

In the absence of such mechanisms, repeated IMF bailouts risk legitimizing and subsidizing behaviour that undermines regional and global security, particularly when recipient states such as Pakistan are financing terror directly or through narco-terrorism channels.

The Basel Committee on Banking Supervision (BCBS)

Formed in 1974, the Basel Committee on Banking Supervision (BCBS) includes representatives from central banks and banking supervisory authorities from 27 countries, including the USA, Japan, and several EU states. The committee develops supervisory standards, guidelines, and best practices. While the BCBS provides overarching recommendations, it allows individual authorities to adapt them to national systems through statutory measures or other approaches. Key areas in its guidance include transparency in payment messaging, account opening and customer identification procedures, customer due diligence, and promoting international cooperation.

The Egmont Group

Established in 1995, the Egmont Group fosters international cooperation among Financial Intelligence Units (FIUs) created by various countries, particularly after the September 11 attacks. Its main goal is to enhance national anti-money laundering (AML) efforts by providing a collaborative platform for FIUs. Membership is open to any FIU meeting the criteria, including those acting as central, national agencies responsible for receiving and, when allowed, requesting financial information. Member FIUs also analyse and share this data with relevant authorities. Through its inclusive approach and shared standards, the Egmont Group plays a key role in strengthening global financial crime combat efforts.

The Wolfsberg Group

The Wolfsberg Group, founded in 2000 by 11 global banks, aims to set industry standards for Know-Your-Customer (KYC) practices and counter-financing of terrorism and anti-money laundering (CFT-AML). Established in response to major money laundering scandals, the group works to combat these issues within the private banking sector. It has created comprehensive guidelines on customer due diligence, correspondent banking, and risk-based approaches, regularly updating them to address emerging threats. Beyond banking, organizations like the International Association of Insurance Supervisors (IAIS) and the International Organization of Securities Commissions (IOSCO) also issue directives on best practices for combating financial crimes.

Shifting Sands of Terrorist Financing: New Challenges, New Opportunities

As noted earlier, the global AML-CFT regime underwent a paradigm shift following the September 11 attacks. The U.S. government and its allies played a crucial role in driving this focus. While the Financial Action Task Force (FATF) and the Egmont Group have been effective in setting common standards for AML and CFT, they still lack real enforcement powers, relying primarily on a 'name and shame' strategy.

However, significantly, FATF's 'Call of Action' blacklisting approach has proven successful, especially targeting non-cooperative states. Originally aimed at tax havens, it now includes jurisdictions with significant AML-CTF-PF deficiencies. As of February 2024, only North Korea, Iran, and Myanmar remain on the FATF blacklist.[33]

FATF also employs a 'Grey List' for jurisdictions under increased monitoring. This gives countries an opportunity to address deficiencies and avoid escalation to the blacklist. This approach has led to improvements in countries such as Egypt, Lebanon, Indonesia, and the Philippines. As of 2024, 21 countries, including the Philippines, Monaco, South Africa, Vietnam, and Syria, are on the Grey List.[34]

US Counter-Terrorism Financing: A Contentious Approach

Despite efforts by the FATF, IMF, and UN agencies, gaps in CTF-AML persist. The U.S. strategy of unilaterally seizing assets and imposing sanctions on Islamic terrorist groups, their affiliates, and individuals has faced criticism for its often hasty and inaccurate targeting. This approach has fostered scepticism, particularly in Middle Eastern countries, and made some U.S. allies reluctant to share information or coordinate responses. Critics argue that the U.S. strategy depends heavily on 'actionable intelligence' rather than transparent, legally robust investigations.

Global Dissonance in Counter-Terrorist Financing Policies

A significant discord exists between American and European views on CTF-AML implementation. Brazil, for example, disputes claims that its Tri-Border region is a hub for terrorist financiers, citing economic concerns. Similarly, Malaysia denies allegations of allowing front companies to operate within its borders. The U.S. often prioritizes immediate threats of terrorism, while European nations focus more on broader financial stability. Countries such as Indonesia, the Philippines, and Kenya, despite facing terrorist attacks, have been slow to act on terrorism financing due to concerns over political financing. Even nations like Paraguay, which collaborate with the USA, show reluctance to pursue CTF-AML measures due to similar fears. In Pakistan and Bangladesh, influential political figures hesitate to align with the USA due to concerns over voter base alienation.

Divergent Perspectives on Counter-Terrorist Financing: A Global Challenge
Disparities in capacity hinder the global implementation of CTF-AML measures. Countries like Burkina Faso, Cameroon, and Haiti, despite having the political will, lack the necessary resources to effectively combat terrorism financing. Additionally, political elites often prioritize social welfare over investments in CTF/AML initiatives, exacerbating the challenge.

Terrorists Evolving Tactics in the Face of Counter-Terrorist Financing Measures
While the international CTF-AML framework initially succeeded in using asset seizures and surveillance, critics argue that terrorists have adapted by shifting operations to less regulated areas. These criticisms highlight the framework's effectiveness, as terrorist groups remain resilient in their financial strategies. Assessing the true 'ineffectiveness' of CTF-AML policies is difficult without comprehensive data on the full scope of terrorist financing.[35]

Harnessing Technology for Enhanced AML/CFT: A Path Forward
Emerging technologies such as Artificial Intelligence (AI) offer potential for improving CTF-AML measures, streamlining processes, and reducing costs. AI can help implement global AML/CFT standards, foster financial inclusion, and reduce unintended exclusion. Although some countries face capacity limitations, the international community can assist resource-constrained nations in integrating necessary CFT/AML technologies. AI can enhance real-time monitoring, improve risk assessments, and streamline compliance operations, creating a more resilient defence against terrorist financing.[36]

The Talent Gap in AML/CFT: Recruitment and Retention Challenges
Securing skilled personnel for CTF-AML initiatives remains a challenge, especially in regions with limited technological resources. Recruitment difficulties are compounded by high turnover rates, requiring ongoing training and recruitment efforts. Moreover, keeping staff up to date with evolving regulations adds further strain, especially in sectors with specialized requirements.

Overcoming Operational Challenges in CFT-AML Implementation
Implementing effective CFT-AML strategies requires navigating complex systems, such as integrating KYC data. Standardizing data quality for centralized fraud and crime analysis is essential but complicated by varying data formats.

Collaboration between financial institutions and regulatory bodies is crucial for enhancing information sharing and developing innovative technologies to improve the detection and prevention of financial crimes.

Strengthening the Global Fight Against Terrorist Financing: Preventing Terror Financing

Preventing crime before it occurs is crucial, and this holds true for terrorist financing. Just as with any crime, addressing the financial support behind terrorist activities is key to maintaining a healthy society. Resources such as funds are vital for terrorist organizations, and preventing their access is half the battle. For CFT-AML preventive measures to succeed, several prerequisites must be met:

- *Tailor strategies to local conditions:* Effective prevention requires understanding the unique political, social, and economic context of each jurisdiction. Rigid protocols without this understanding can backfire.
- *Raise awareness* of risks and mitigation strategies among all stakeholders.
- *Early intervention:* Act before it's too late.
- Strengthen *financial intelligence*, analysis, and regulatory frameworks.
- *Foster international cooperation*, especially in real-time information sharing.
- Ensure *universal and consistent implementation* of Know Your Customer and due diligence practices.

As discussed earlier, understanding the socio-economic and political conditions that allow terrorists to bypass formal financing channels is crucial. Terrorists often employ innovative methods, such as exploiting charities and religious institutions to mask their activities. Law enforcement must actively collect reliable information on such abuses.

Enhancing Regulatory Adequacy

Regulatory adequacy refers to the sufficiency and comprehensiveness of laws and regulations designed to prevent terrorist financing. Despite progress, significant challenges persist, mainly due to non-cooperative states and inconsistent adherence to standards set by international organizations like the Financial Action Task Force (FATF).

The FATF has been successful in setting standards and integrating them into CTF-AML policies worldwide. This success is largely due to the financial sector's technical expertise, similar to the aviation industry. The global financial system is increasingly interconnected through technology, facilitating effective CFT/AML regulation.

Countries that fail to comply with these standards risk isolation from the global financial system. As such, regulatory adequacy has been achieved to a reliable degree. However, early intervention requires due diligence and knowing the identities of entities involved in transactions. As discussed earlier, technologies enabled by Artificial Intelligence (AI) offer great promise for detecting vulnerabilities before terrorist financing occurs.[37]

The FATF is also advocating for new technologies such as *Distributed Ledger Technology (DLT)* to improve cross-border transaction traceability and identity verification. With proper regulation, DLT could enable shared ledgers across institutions, enhancing monitoring and potentially reducing *Customer Due Diligence (CDD)* costs.

DLT, particularly blockchain, holds transformative potential in strengthening the global banking system's ability to combat money laundering and terror financing. By providing a decentralized, secure, and tamper-resistant record of transactions, blockchain enables real-time verification and end-to-end traceability, making it far more difficult for illicit financial flows to be hidden within opaque, multi-jurisdictional networks. The transparency it offers disrupts traditional avenues for concealing funds, such as layering and shell entities. Smart contracts can further automate compliance protocols, enforce regulatory rules, and instantly flag high-risk transactions, thereby reducing human error and enforcement gaps.

Cross-border payments, often exploited for laundering and terror financing—can be subjected to unified oversight through interoperable blockchain platforms, enhancing coordination among financial institutions and regulatory bodies. Immutable audit trails strengthen accountability and deter manipulation of records. When integrated with AI-driven analytics, DLT can detect complex financial crime patterns. For maximum impact, global implementation must be underpinned by robust legal standards, data-sharing agreements, and multilateral cooperation to ensure consistency and effectiveness.[38]

Enhancing Regulatory Efficiency and Effectiveness

Regulatory adequacy alone isn't enough to prevent terrorist financing. Regulatory efficiency—achieving objectives in a timely and cost-effective manner, remains a challenge. Over-regulation and complex requirements can hinder compliance, creating gaps in oversight and enforcement.

This issue requires a tailored approach. Every jurisdiction must calibrate its CFT-AML policies to ensure that legitimate financial transactions are not burdened by redundancies. Financial institutions often find CDD and monitoring processes challenging, resulting in poor data quality, difficulties in updating information, and customer dissatisfaction.

The collection and verification of CDD data can be cumbersome, involving numerous document requests and in-person submissions. Experts also note that risk analysis driven by CDD often relies too heavily on rigid rules rather than context, excluding disadvantaged individuals who struggle to meet requirements. Inflexible CTF-AML policies can hinder financial inclusion, particularly for marginalized groups.[39]

A Ticking Time Bomb: Emerging Trends in Terrorist Financing

Dark Net

A notable gap exists between how terrorists finance their activities and how law enforcement perceives these methods. Despite ongoing investigations, terrorist networks continually innovate their funding strategies, often exploiting emerging technologies. A recent surge in crypto currency-based crowd funding by groups such as ISIS and al-Qaeda, through the dark web, highlights their ability to raise substantial funds.[40]

The Dark Net, often linked to crime, fraud, and now terrorist financing, is a hidden segment of the internet accessed through specialized browsers like Tor. While the Surface Web, visible to most users, is just the tip of the iceberg, the Deep Web lies beneath, comprising the majority of the internet and remaining unsearchable. The Dark Net, within the Deep Web, harbours illicit activities such as pornography, drug trade, and terrorist communications.

The Silk Road, a notorious Dark Net marketplace for drugs, was shut down by the FBI in 2013. Despite its closure, similar platforms quickly emerged, demonstrating the resilience of the Dark Net. Figures like WikiLeaks and the use of Bitcoin have also been linked to this hidden realm. While activists and journalists in oppressive regimes sometimes rely on the Dark Net for secure communication, terrorists increasingly exploit its anonymity for operations.

Terrorist use of the Dark Net became evident in 2013 when intercepted communications between al-Qaeda leaders were traced to the platform. This highlights the appeal of the Dark Net to terrorist organizations seeking secure communication channels. However, it also complicates counterterrorism efforts, as monitoring activities on the Dark Net is inherently difficult. Counteracting its role involves improving cyber security, international cooperation, and intelligence sharing among law enforcement agencies. Collaborating with tech companies to develop tools for detecting illicit activities is also critical.

Despite its criminal associations, the Dark Net is not entirely negative. It serves as a platform for dissidents and whistleblowers to communicate safely, and holds potential for legitimate uses. However, the prevalence of illegal activities necessitates proactive measures to mitigate its impact on global security.

Lone Wolf and Self-Funding: Challenges for Effective CFT-AML Strategies

The term 'Lone Wolf' traces back to Louis Beam, the self-described Ambassador-at-Large for the white supremacist group 'Aryan Nations'. He popularized the concept of 'Leaderless Resistance' in the 1990s. This approach involves decentralized, autonomous individuals or small groups advancing political or ideological agendas independently, often without external support, driven by radicalized beliefs. Such individuals, referred to as 'Lone Wolves', may align with extremist ideologies, drawing inspiration from groups like ISIS.[41]

'Lone Wolf' terrorists are a unique challenge for counterterrorism financing due to their independent nature. Operating without a structured organization, they enjoy greater operational security and flexibility, making them hard to track and disrupt. The Dark Net and crypto currencies are essential tools for evading detection, providing platforms for anonymous communication, recruitment, and the acquisition of illicit goods. Crypto currencies allow 'lone wolves' to finance their activities and coordinate attacks while minimizing detection risks. Additionally, the Dark Net enables them to access extremist ideologies and propaganda, fuelling radicalization.

A notable case is Victoria Jacobs (aka 'Bakhrom Talipov'), convicted in

2024 for using crypto currency to fund Syrian-based terrorist groups. Her case highlights the growing threat of crypto currency in terrorism financing and the need for robust law enforcement measures.[42] This conviction sets a precedent for prosecuting 'lone wolves' in crypto currency-based financing, emphasizing the necessity of continuous adaptation in counter-terrorism strategies.

Some terrorists, particularly those not affiliated with organizations or working independently as 'lone wolves', use legitimate sources such as employment income or bank loans to finance their activities. Foreign Terrorist Fighters (FTFs), who travel to conflict zones like Syria to join groups like ISIS, often establish businesses to generate revenue for their travel. Investigations have uncovered cases of asset sales and credit purchases just before planned travel.[43]

The ISIS and al-Qaeda developed sophisticated strategies to exploit foreign fighters for financing, using religious rhetoric to justify activities like theft and robbery under the guise of '*Maal-e-Ghanima*' (*Maal-e-Ghanima* is an Islamic legal term for war booty, including captured property and prisoners). These funds were then used to purchase weapons and explosives, enabling violent attacks. Such practices highlight the dangerous combination of religious manipulation and criminal enterprise in modern terrorism financing.

Social Media and Crowd-funding

Social media has facilitated networking among individuals with extremist views, blurring the lines between radicalization and terrorism. It enables individuals to reinforce their beliefs, often leading to violent actions. Platforms such as WhatsApp, Telegram, Facebook, Twitter, and Instagram allow terrorists to connect globally, recruit followers, and raise funds.

One disturbing trend is '*digital swarming*', where geographically dispersed individuals rapidly mobilize toward a target through encrypted platforms. This phenomenon is particularly evident in places like Kashmir, where separatists have used social media to incite and coordinate violent protests.[44]

Crowd-funding platforms have also become a tool for terrorist financing. These platforms, typically used for legitimate purposes, can be exploited by individuals or entities supporting terrorism to raise funds under the guise of charitable causes.[45] As crowd-funding continues to grow, so does the risk of terrorist groups misusing it.

Challenges in Investigating Terrorist Financing via Social Media

Countering terrorism financing through social media presents numerous challenges. Law enforcement often struggles to differentiate between sympathizers and actual terrorists. Tracing funds transferred through the internet can be difficult, especially when intermediaries are based abroad. Additionally, the bureaucratic hurdles posed by social media companies, which require compliance with foreign laws, delay investigations.

Tracking terrorist financing on social media platforms remains a daunting task. Collaboration between authorities and the private sector is vital to access data and enhance the efficiency of counter terrorism efforts. However, there is a need to adapt legislation and ensure better reporting from social media platforms and crowd funding sites to combat these threats effectively.

Conclusion

Terrorist financing is a persistent global security challenge, as every operation requires money, and terrorists are no exception. However, unlike legitimate businesses, terrorists use their resources to cause harm and spread fear. Their methods of money laundering and financing have grown more sophisticated and harder to track. They constantly explore new ways to bypass traditional banking systems and financial networks.

Investigating terrorist financing presents significant challenges for law enforcement agencies. The complex nature of financial transactions, often involving intricate networks and advanced techniques, demands specialized skills and expertise. Effective counter-terrorism efforts require cooperation between financial intelligence units at both national and international levels, as well as coordination with local law enforcement agencies.

Siloed investigative structures face inherent weaknesses, making real-time collaboration in information sharing, analysis, and dissemination essential for tackling terrorist financing. Investigative agencies can greatly benefit from corporate structures, particularly through data visualization and analytics, with the support of artificial intelligence and machine learning tools. These technologies can help identify red flags and track suspicious financial transactions in real time.

The rise of technologies like the dark web and crypto currencies has given terrorists new ways to fund their activities. These technologies allow them to raise funds anonymously and quickly, making it harder for authorities to detect and block their financial flows. Additionally, the use of social media platforms has facilitated the recruitment of new members and the spread of extremist propaganda.

An effective counter-terrorism strategy must be tailored to the socio-political context of each region. Understanding local dynamics is crucial for identifying vulnerabilities and developing appropriate countermeasures. A one-size-fits-all approach will likely fail, as the factors driving terrorism vary significantly across regions.

While counter-terrorism financing and counter-money laundering (CTF-ML) measures are vital, it is important to avoid unintended consequences. Over-strict adherence to customer due diligence (CDD) protocols can lead to financial exclusion, particularly for marginalized or vulnerable groups. Striking a balance between security and financial inclusion requires careful consideration.

NOTES

11

The Silent Arsenal: The Menace of CBRN Terror

"The value of a thing sometimes lies not in what one attains with it, but in what one pays for it—What it costs us."

—**Nietzsche**

A Toxic Timeline: CBRN Attacks Through History

The silver screen has often foreshadowed real-world threats, particularly in the realm of terrorism. Long before chemical, biological, radiological, and nuclear (CBRN) weapons became a global concern, Hollywood was already portraying their terrifying potential in terrorist hands. Films like *Die Hard with a Vengeance* (1995), *The Rock* (1996), *Mission: Impossible* (1996), and *The Sum of All Fears* (2002) vividly imagined the chaos such weapons could unleash.

Take *The Rock*, for example. This action-packed thriller turned Alcatraz Island into ground zero for a potential CBRN disaster. A rogue group of U.S. Marines, led by a grim Brigadier General, armed themselves with VX nerve gas—an incredibly lethal substance, deadly even in microscopic amounts. With major cities under threat, the film starkly illustrated how devastating even a single missile armed with VX could be.

More than just a blockbuster, *The Rock* delivered a powerful warning. It confronted audiences with the possibility of a real-world CBRN attack, a threat many had only considered science fiction. With gripping tension and strong performances from Sean Connery and Nicolas Cage, the film's message was clear: these dangers are not just cinematic fantasies but potential realities. It thrilled audiences while leaving them with a lingering sense of unease, and awareness.

From Fiction to Fact

Although only a small fraction of terrorist plots involves chemical, biological, radiological, or nuclear (CBRN) weapons, the mere possibility has alarmed policymakers and the public. Between 1990 and 2020, non-state actors were responsible for 565 CBRN-related incidents globally, with the United States, Russia, and Iraq accounting for the highest numbers—118, 49, and 43 respectively.[1]

CBRN attacks remain rare compared to other terror tactics, yet technological advances raise the risk of their use in hybrid warfare, threatening public health systems. Most such attacks have not involved genuine weapons of mass destruction (WMD), as creating effective delivery mechanisms is complex. Aum Shinrikyo's 1995 Tokyo subway attack, using homemade Sarin gas, killed 13 and injured thousands, showing how extremist groups can inflict mass harm even without state-level resources.

Understanding the motives and preventing access to CBRN capabilities is critical. Though acquisition remains difficult, the fear of international backlash may deter use. Still, some groups could obtain such weapons amid unstable political environments. While state sponsorship or theft are possibilities, most capabilities stem from attacks on nuclear, chemical, or biological facilities. Over 200 such incidents have been recorded, with chemical events being most frequent.[2]

Though most incidents caused limited casualties, some resulted in large-scale harm.[3] Terrorists have used varied ideologies and methods, and while past trends may not forecast future threats, advances in technology and cases like the Islamic State suggest the potential for a true WMD event remains. Authorities must remain vigilant without exaggerating the threat.

A Short History of CBRN Terrorism

During the Cold War, bioterrorism was not a major concern. A key early incident occurred in 1984, when followers of 'Osho' Rajneesh, a cult in Oregon, USA, sought to influence local elections by contaminating food with *Salmonella typhimurium*. The resulting outbreak caused 751 cases of salmonellosis in a county that normally saw fewer than five. Though bioterrorism was initially ruled out, an FBI probe uncovered vials of the bacterium at the cult's lab. Cult members later admitted to contaminating salad bars and a water tank.[4]

Aum Shinrikyo's Bioterror Horror and Beyond

Aum Shinrikyo, a Japanese cult, pursued multiple CBRN programs. They attempted to produce botulinum toxin and *Bacillus anthracis* but failed to acquire lethal strains. Their most notorious attack used Sarin gas in the Tokyo subway, killing 13. Credible evidence suggests they may have also detonated a nuclear device on May 28, 1993, near Banjawarn Station, Australia. Witnesses reported flashes and explosions; seismic activity recorded was 170 times stronger than known mining blasts. Investigations linked the cult to uranium mining and a sophisticated lab operated by former Soviet nuclear scientists. If true, this would have been the only case of a non-state actor successfully detonating a nuclear device ever.[5]

Other Major Bioterrorism Incidents

In the late 1990s, al Qaeda began a biological weapons program, likely influenced by U.S. concerns. However, it remained in its infancy by 2001, and the U.S. invasion of Afghanistan disrupted it. Jihadi groups have shown interest in biological weapons but tend to prefer simpler, more accessible tools.[6]

The 2001 anthrax letter attacks targeted news outlets and U.S. senators with highly refined airborne spores. The FBI identified Bruce Ivins, an anthrax expert, though doubts persist.[7]

In 2002, Chechen terrorists took over a Moscow theatre with 800 hostages, threatening to use chemical agents. Russian forces used a knockout gas to end the siege, but over 100 hostages died due to its strength and inadequate medical support.[8] Though not a direct CBRN attack, it showed the potential for chemical threats and highlighted the challenges in response and ethical considerations during rescue operations.

In 2013, Ricin-laced letters were sent to U.S. political figures, including President Obama. The toxin, derived from castor beans, is lethal even in small doses. The FBI arrested Shannon Richardson, who admitted to sending the letters to frame her estranged husband. She was sentenced to 18 years.[9]

The growing threat of bio-terrorism underscores the urgent need for advanced systems to secure biological materials and medical protocols. Cases discussed above reveal the potential for real threats and the catastrophic consequences of bio-terrorism. These cases highlight the critical role of forensic science in identifying perpetrators, tracing sources of infection, and securing convictions.

CBRN Ambition: What Drives Terrorists to the Brink?

Understanding Terrorist Motivations Behind CBRN Pursuits

This seemingly simple issue conceals intense complexity. Assuming terrorists are solely driven by a disregard for civilian life is an oversimplification. The real question is: why would a terrorist group pursue CBRN methods, knowing such actions would likely provoke overwhelming reprisals from the state and international community?

To grasp their motivations, we must view it from the strategic calculus of terrorist organizations. CBRN interest manifests in three ways: declared intent without capability; acquisition of capability without use; and actual deployment. This can be illustrated through al-Qaeda (intent without confirmed capability), ISIS (intent, capability, and use), Rajneesh's group (use without ideological intent), and Aum Shinrikyo (intent, capability, and use).

Al-Qaeda's Pursuit of CBRN

Following the 9/11 attacks, al-Qaeda intensified efforts to acquire CBRN capabilities. Evidence includes intercepted literature and public statements by its leaders. Since the mid-1990s, reports have surfaced of attempts to procure chemical agents (e.g., Sarin, VX), biological toxins (e.g., Anthrax, Ricin), and radiological or nuclear materials.[10] However, most reports remain speculative.

Al-Qaeda's '*Encyclopaedia of Jihad*' detailed acquiring and deploying biological and chemical weapons. Osama bin Laden once claimed al-Qaeda had chemical and nuclear weapons for deterrence, and a US court heard testimony of efforts to use aircraft to spread bio-agents.[11]

While substantial intent to acquire nuclear materials existed, no evidence confirms success. UK intelligence once claimed documents pointed to dirty bomb development in Afghanistan, though these were unverified.[12] Bin Laden urged Muslims to match Western military power, calling WMD acquisition a religious duty.[13]

Al-Qaeda saw CBRN weapons not only as tools of terror but also as symbolic weapons to instil fear and elevate their credibility and deterrent posture.

ISIS: Weaponizing Religious Extremism

ISIS's CBRN adventures likely evolved from Zarqawi's teachings, which included training cells in chemical and biological warfare.[14] It pursued a radical Salafist ideology that justified extreme violence for achieving its caliphate ambitions. Part of its terror campaign included publicized mass executions and mutilations.

Jihadi cleric Nasir al-Fahd's 2003 *fatwa* endorsed WMD use against non-believers. Since such weapons didn't exist during the genesis of Abrahamic religions, extremist clerics used interpretation to justify their deployment. Salafi ideology treats violence as a tool for political dominance.

ISIS became the first non-state actor to develop and weaponize a banned chemical agent with a delivery system. After losing Mosul in 2017, production ceased—suggesting no alternative sites then—but intelligence later indicated possible relocation to the Euphrates River valley.[15]

In July 2015, ISIS used mustard gas-laced mortars against Kurdish YPG forces in Hasakah, Syria. It marked a new level of chemical warfare by non-state actors. *IHS Conflict Monitor* reported ISIS carried out chemical attacks at least 76 times.[16]

ISIS's actions reflected a willingness to use any means available, spiritual, political, or technological, to further its ideological goals.

The Rajneesh Bioterror Incident: A Rare Exception

In 1984, followers of '*Bhagwan*' Rajneesh contaminated salad bars in The Dalles, Oregon, with Salmonella to incapacitate voters ahead of local elections. Their aim was to suppress turnout among non-Rajneesh residents and boost their candidates' chances. This resulted in widespread illness and federal investigations that eventually exposed the plot.

Unlike ideological terrorist groups, Rajneesh's cult had no long-term strategy involving CBRN agents. Their use of biological agents stemmed from an internal power struggle and tactical desperation, not doctrinal belief.

This incident remains one of the few globally where biological weapons were used without an overarching ideological or military purpose, making it unique in bio terror history.

Aum Shinrikyo: Doomsday and Devotion to WMDs

Founded on a distorted version of Vajrayana Buddhism, Aum Shinrikyo's leader, Shoko Asahara, taught that killing 'impure' people was a spiritual act. He gained loyal followers through charisma, enforcing obedience even among doubters.

Aum's interest extended beyond chemicals. They pursued laser weapons and sent emissaries to consult Russian scientists, including Nobel laureate Dr. Nikolay Basov. Members attempted to steal laser technology from NEC and Mitsubishi.[17]

Aum Shinrikyo's founder Asahara admired dictators such as Hitler and viewed impending conflict with the US as justification for acquiring CBRN capabilities. He intended to trigger a crisis to validate his apocalyptic prophecies and justify government overthrow.

The Tokyo subway Sarin gas attack in 1995 was the culmination of this belief system, resulting in multiple deaths and thousands of injuries. Aum's example demonstrates how millenarian ideology and cultic control can drive actual WMD use.

Simplistic views of terrorism fail to account for the wide spectrum of motivations and methods behind CBRN interest. From symbolic intent (al-Qaeda) to strategic use (ISIS), accidental application (Rajneesh), or apocalyptic belief (Aum), each group's use—or avoidance—of CBRN agents reflects its unique ideology and goals.

Understanding these nuances is crucial for assessing future threats and shaping counterterrorism strategies.

The Role of State-Sponsored Terrorism in the Acquisition of CBRN Capabilities by Terrorist Organisations

Terrorism is commonly understood as the use of violence by individuals or groups, primarily non-state actors, to achieve political objectives. Most definitions emphasize violence and political motives, typically involving actors operating independently of state systems, though they may enjoy varying degrees of state support.

In recent decades, the strategic use of non-state actors by states to pursue political goals has become a central concern in international security. Many global conflicts originate from terrorist activities backed by or tolerated within state borders. State sponsorship of terrorism can take many forms, ranging from overt support, such as Iran's backing of Hezbollah or the Taliban's sheltering of Osama bin Laden, to more covert arrangements with plausible deniability, such as those involving Pakistan.

Such support enables weaker states to engage in asymmetric warfare. By using terrorist groups as proxies, these states can project power and influence far beyond their conventional capabilities, avoiding the risks of direct military confrontation. State sponsorship is thus a calculated strategy—one that allows states to advance ideological, political, or strategic objectives while minimizing direct exposure.

A particularly alarming dimension of state-sponsored terrorism is its potential to accelerate the proliferation of CBRN weapons. States can provide financial aid, logistical support, or technical expertise, facilitating access to CBRN materials, illicit procurement networks, and even clandestine training programs. These capabilities significantly enhance the operational scope of terrorist organizations, increasing the threat of catastrophic attacks.

This relationship between state sponsors and terrorist groups reflects the complex interplay between state and non-state actors in global politics. States may deliberately support CBRN ambitions to sow instability, deter adversaries, or gain leverage through intimidation—all while maintaining deniability. The covert nature of such partnerships complicates attribution and makes response efforts more difficult.

The risk is further compounded when rogue elements within state security or intelligence agencies act independently, supplying CBRN materials without the knowledge or approval of political leadership. In countries such as Pakistan, Iraq, Libya, and certain other Middle Eastern states, powerful security establishments often operate autonomously. These actors may facilitate CBRN proliferation outside formal state policy, bypassing oversight mechanisms and diplomatic accountability.

History provides several clear examples of how state sponsorship can transform terrorist groups. Iran's support helped Hezbollah evolve into a sophisticated guerrilla and terrorist force. Libya's arms shipments sustained the Provisional Irish Republican Army's campaign against Britain during times when regular supply lines were disrupted. Pakistan, meanwhile, has long employed terrorist proxies in its asymmetric strategy against India.

The costs of such sponsorship are not confined to the targeted states. The United States, for example, spent an estimated $ 2 trillion on its war in Afghanistan, including the hunt for Osama bin Laden.[18] That bin Laden was eventually found and killed near a major Pakistani military academy highlighted the extent of Pakistan's duplicity in supporting terrorism. Since then, Pakistan has shifted tactics, moving from overt support to enabling groups in Kashmir through financial self-reliance and narco-terrorism.

State-supported terrorist groups are also more resilient against counter-measures. Backing from a state provides access to safe havens, consistent funding, and logistical support—making it harder for target regimes to dismantle such organizations or achieve strategic victory.

Despite these risks, including potential global condemnation, many state sponsors take care to prevent their proxies from accessing CBRN capabilities. However, the threat remains real, especially when political leadership is weak or when security institutions act beyond civilian control.

The intersection of state sponsorship and CBRN proliferation presents one of the gravest threats to global security today. Understanding and addressing this nexus is essential for effective counter terrorism and non-proliferation efforts.

World's Most Dangerous Gamble: Pakistan's Nuclear Weapons

Pakistan asserts that its nuclear assets are protected by robust and comprehensive institutional measures, reportedly modelled on U.S. security protocols. These include concentric physical security layers around nuclear stockpiles, rigorous personnel vetting, advanced surveillance systems, and strict secrecy protocols.[19] The physical security reportedly includes armed guards, barriers, and underground storage facilities.

Personnel involved in the nuclear program are said to undergo intensive screening to exclude individuals with extremist affiliations. While Pakistan's political leadership nominally oversees the nuclear arsenal, operational command resides with the Pakistani Army, which uses identification codes and a 'two-man rule' for launch authorization.

Despite these advertised safeguards, there are serious concerns about the effectiveness of these measures during crises. Extremist ideologies have deeply penetrated the Pakistan Army since the Zia-ul-Haq era, raising doubts about the institutional reliability of these protocols. The army has a well-documented policy of using extremist proxies against India and Afghanistan, further complicating its nuclear posture.

Many of Pakistan's nuclear facilities are located near regions with significant terrorist activity. Attacks on military sites, such as the one on Wah Cantonment, have exposed the risk of radiological incidents and the potential for unauthorized seizure of nuclear material. The collaboration between extremist sympathizers within the military and terrorist groups adds a critical layer of risk, as does the possibility of nuclear technology being transferred to such organizations.[20]

The most alarming scenario, though considered improbable, is the deliberate transfer of nuclear weapons by the Pakistan Army under external influence or coercion. Nevertheless, this underscores the need for continuous vigilance and international cooperation to strengthen Pakistan's nuclear safeguards. Addressing the presence and activities of terrorist groups in Pakistan's tribal and frontier regions remains essential to risk mitigation.

Pakistan remains a global focal point for jihadist ideology. The 2012 attack on the Minhas Air Force Base near Islamabad, suspected of storing part of Pakistan's nuclear arsenal, illustrates the audacity and capability of terrorist groups to strike high-value targets despite military operations.[21]

In the past 17 years, at least seven other nuclear-related facilities have been targeted. In 2007, a suicide bomber struck a bus en route to the Sargodha Air Base, which houses a large stockpile of nuclear warheads. Kamra Air Base was similarly attacked in 2008. On November 4, 2023, terrorists assaulted the Mianwali Air Force Base, another suspected nuclear storage site.[22]

Despite Pakistan's insistence on secrecy, satellite imagery has identified roughly fifteen nuclear-related sites across the country, all of which could become potential targets if jihadists gain adequate motivation and support.

The threat of Pakistan's nuclear weapons falling into terrorist hands is a serious, well-documented concern.[23]

Several interlinked factors compound this risk. Pakistan's volatile political environment, the presence of numerous militant groups, and a relatively young nuclear weapons program lacking deep-rooted institutional safeguards all contribute to vulnerabilities. Moreover, the Pakistani military's historical ties with extremist organizations cast doubt on its ability to reliably secure nuclear materials.

A nuclear weapon in terrorist hands would have catastrophic consequences. A detonation in a major city could cause hundreds of thousands, or even millions of casualties, with fallout spreading far beyond Pakistan's borders and creating long-term environmental and health disasters.

Although recent counter-terrorism operations by Pakistani forces show progress, the threat of nuclear terrorism remains pressing and complex. The history of duplicity within the Pakistani security establishment, especially its concealment of Osama bin Laden, underscores the urgent need for transparency, accountability, and international engagement.

CBRN Catastrophe: Preventing Weaponization by Terrorists

Detecting and preventing terrorist acquisition of CBRN capabilities remains one of the most formidable challenges to global security. The threat posed by terrorist groups and other non-state actors spans a wide array of weapons capable of causing mass casualties and catastrophic disruption. As discussed earlier, the potential for such actors to obtain and deploy CBRN weapons introduces a unique set of hurdles, due both to their destructive power and the significant difficulties involved in detection and interdiction prior to use.

One particularly concerning development is the potential use of drones capable of carrying heavy payloads (50 kg or more) to disperse chemical or biological agents over targeted populations. Similarly, the possibility of deploying a radiological dispersal device, or 'dirty bomb,' using materials sourced from discarded x-ray machines or medical radiological equipment, presents a serious risk. Drones may serve as ideal delivery platforms for such unconventional weapons.[24]

A major obstacle lies in the clandestine methods employed by terrorist groups to acquire CBRN materials. Unlike conventional arms—which often leave traceable trails through global trafficking routes, CBRN components can be sourced through black markets, smuggling networks, or even facilitated by rogue state actors. While obtaining these materials is already a major hurdle, the challenge is compounded by the expertise required to weaponize them. The development of viable CBRN weapons demands access to technical knowledge, specialized equipment, and secure laboratory environments.

The Aum Shinrikyo case remains a chilling example of this convergence of resources and intent. It has already been discussed how the highly educated followers of cult leader Asahara successfully weaponized Sarin gas and other toxic agents. Operating out of advanced laboratories in locations such as Kamikuishiki, Japan, and Banjawarn Station, Australia, they evaded detection for years. Remarkably, they even acquired a Russian Mi-17 military helicopter, which was kept at their compound in Kamikuishiki. Despite these suspicious undertakings, the group managed to obtain critical raw materials without attracting sufficient scrutiny. For instance, in Australia, they paid large sums to acquire harmful chemicals, and when an initial shipment was confiscated, they simply procured another through intermediaries.[25]

Another layer of complexity is introduced by the dual-use nature of many CBRN substances. Numerous agents used in industry, agriculture, and healthcare have legitimate applications but can also be weaponized by malicious actors. This duality complicates law enforcement efforts to distinguish between lawful and illicit activities. Additionally, the proliferation of online resources and open-access scientific databases has made it easier for terrorists to gain the necessary technical know-how.

Effective prevention is further hindered by the lack of consistent international cooperation. Given the cross-border nature of both terrorist networks and the CBRN materials supply chain, robust global collaboration is essential. However, geopolitical rivalries, mutual distrust, and concerns over sovereignty often impede coordinated efforts. Intelligence-sharing, joint training, and multilateral enforcement frameworks are critical but underutilized tools in this context.

Another widespread misconception is that only large, well-funded terrorist organizations are capable of developing or acquiring CBRN weapons. In reality, smaller cells or even lone-wolf actors may pose a more immediate and unpredictable threat. These individuals often display heightened suicidal tendencies and ideological extremism, which makes them more likely to pursue weapons of disproportionate impact, such as CBRN agents. Ironically, the complexity and technical challenge of CBRN weapon development may appeal to tech-savvy extremists with the resources to acquire relevant materials online or commercially.[26] Walter Laqueur presciently noted that individuals or small autonomous groups were the most likely candidates to resort to '*weapons of super violence*.'[27]

Securing critical infrastructure from potential CBRN attacks also poses immense logistical and operational challenges. Sites such as nuclear power stations, biotech research labs, and transportation hubs are attractive targets. Protecting them requires not only physical security and surveillance but also inter-agency coordination and integration with private-sector operators and international bodies.

Technological innovation adds further urgency to these efforts. Emerging fields such as synthetic biology and nanotechnology may eventually allow terrorist actors to develop more sophisticated CBRN weapons. Staying ahead of this curve demands ongoing investment in both R&D and the development of advanced detection, containment, and response mechanisms.

Interestingly, no state has yet been known to deliberately outsource its weapons of mass destruction capabilities to a terrorist organization for use against another country. This restraint likely stems from the understanding that any such attack would invite devastating retaliation. The 9/11 attacks, though not involving CBRN weapons, demonstrated the catastrophic consequences of asymmetric warfare. The psychological and political impact of those attacks, amplified by real-time global media coverage, prompted massive and prolonged military responses, notably the U.S.-led invasions of Afghanistan and Iraq.

Axis of Evil: Nations Fuelling the CBRN Threat

There is considerable variation in the degree of control that states exercise over terrorist organizations they support. Some states are unable to fully manage these groups, raising the risk that such organizations might one day target their sponsors. This control ranges from tight oversight via intelligence and military agencies to mere influence by political elites. *Plausible deniability* plays a crucial role here, as CBRN terrorism enables states to disavow involvement more easily than in conventional attacks. Biological and chemical strikes, in particular, can be misattributed or misidentified.

States most likely to back CBRN terrorism often share key features: covert sponsorship of terrorism, pursuit of WMD programs, and repression of dissent. These states often maintain a *principal-agent* relationship with terrorist groups, offering shelter and support while maintaining distance from their operations.[28] Addressing this nexus of politics and terrorism requires sustained international pressure, including sanctions and diplomatic isolation.

International condemnation, economic sanctions, and digital democratization often force sponsoring states to publicly restrain their proxies. However, this is rarely more than a temporary halt. Iran's backing of Hezbollah and Pakistan's support for jihadist groups demonstrate how operations continue under the radar despite international scrutiny. Temporary pauses in activity should not be mistaken for long-term disengagement from efforts to acquire CBRN capabilities.

Time is critical. Non-state actors often operate under the guise of charities or NGOs, with reliable funding streams and long-term planning strategies aimed at acquiring such weapons. Many sponsoring states are governed by corrupt or unstable regimes lacking effective WMD command and control systems. As more states reach or surpass the nuclear threshold, the quantitative and qualitative risk of state-enabled CBRN terrorism increases.

Such states often exploit delay tactics in international forums, using diplomatic cover provided by allies to evade accountability. The structure of the international system, coupled with U.S. dominance, encourages adversarial states to adopt asymmetric approaches, including WMD terrorism, to counterbalance American power.

The development of the U.S. National Missile Defence system is seen by some as heightening this threat. Nations such as North Korea, Iran, and Iraq have devoted significant resources to developing deterrents against perceived U.S. hegemony. Missile defence systems may push adversaries toward low-cost, high-impact WMD terrorism as an alternative means of retaliation.

Ideology is another powerful driver of state support for terrorism. Iran exemplifies this trend, accused by the USA and its allies of being a major sponsor of radical groups like Hezbollah. Since the 1980s, Iran has sought to export its revolutionary ideology through these non-state actors. Similarly, under President Zia-ul-Haq, Pakistan saw a rise in extremist indoctrination, using proxy terrorist groups to pursue strategic goals against India.

Despite clear evidence of Pakistan's role, it has often avoided criticism due to imagined 'geostrategic considerations', a leniency that contrasts with how Iran is treated. This double standard undermines global efforts to combat terrorism. It was only after 9/11 that U.S. policy shifted to seriously address Pakistan's role, showing that strong condemnation usually follows attacks on Western interests, not on regional rivals.

Military interventions have also failed to eliminate state sponsorship, as seen in Afghanistan, Iraq, and Libya. The ideological affinity between states and terror groups like Hamas or Hezbollah is deeply embedded, sometimes enabling these groups to integrate into political structures. Such relationships cannot be dismantled overnight.

Therefore, counter-terrorism strategies aimed at denying CBRN capabilities must go beyond coercion and address the specific political and psychosocial contexts that sustain these groups.[29] Without understanding these dynamics, coercive strategies risk backfiring, potentially driving groups to seek WMD capabilities.

The Financial Action Task Force (FATF) measures against Pakistan have had limited success. Groups like Jaish-e-Muhammad and Falah-e-Insaniyat retain public support through their social welfare work, allowing them to survive despite pressure. Without addressing these local inter-linkages, coercion alone will not yield sustainable results.

On June 16, 2025, the FATF issued a strong condemnation of the heinous terrorist attack on innocent civilians in Pahalgam on April 22, 2025. The global watchdog expressed grave concern over the massacre, underlining its intent to intensify scrutiny of countries' efforts to combat terror financing.

> *"Terrorist attacks kill, maim and sow fear across borders. The FATF condemns in the strongest terms the barbaric attack in Pahalgam on April 22. Such atrocities are not possible without financial networks and the complicity of systems that enable the flow of funds to terrorist actors,"*

The FATF's condemnation comes as India intensifies its campaign to expose the Pakistani establishment's deep-rooted complicity in cross-border terrorism. India has taken credible and targeted actions against terror infrastructure operating from within Pakistan, backed by incontrovertible evidence linking the perpetrators of atrocities against Indian civilians in Kashmir to Pakistan-based terror organizations. These militant groups, sustained by a covert nexus with state institutions in Pakistan, reflect a disturbing pattern of state-sponsored terrorism. This includes the systematic diversion of international financial aid towards arms procurement and the expansion of extremist networks.

While punitive measures and diplomatic pressure remain necessary, a deeper understanding of the internal motivations driving such state sponsorship is critical for crafting a long-term counter-terrorism strategy. Some regimes might be persuaded to recalibrate their policies if credible political or economic alternatives are offered to address the factors they exploit to justify such support.

Terrorism, ultimately, is a tactic—not an independent enemy. A mature and strategic response must focus on dismantling the financial and ideological ecosystems that sustain it. This includes exposing the true intentions of the sponsoring state, engaging in direct diplomatic and strategic efforts to contain it, and taking firm, demonstrable action against terror operatives and their networks.

As its actions in Balakot and the recent 'Sindoor' operation has demonstrated, India has moved beyond the earlier approach of relying primarily on international appeals in the aftermath of terrorist attacks. With a renewed internal resolve and a sharper strategic focus, New Delhi is now actively combining diplomatic engagement with decisive, independent action. This shift strengthens, rather than dilutes, the urgency and credibility of India's counterterrorism posture, demonstrating that it is prepared to act resolutely to protect its sovereignty, even as it continues to build international consensus against state-sponsored terrorism.

Defending Against Doom: Global Cooperation on CBRN Terrorism

In his acclaimed work *Nuclear Terrorism: The Ultimate Preventable Catastrophe* (2004), Graham Allison delivers a stark warning: the most devastating act of terror in human history is both imaginable and, crucially, preventable. He argues forcefully for stringent global control over fissile materials and the urgent need to prevent nuclear weapons from falling into the hands of states outside the Non-Proliferation Treaty (NPT). Although no terrorist group has yet successfully acquired nuclear materials (the curious case of Aum Shinrikyo remains inconclusive) the threat is far from hypothetical. Al-Qaeda has openly declared its intention to use nuclear weapons if ever the opportunities present itself.

The allure of CBRN terrorism lies in its potential for mass disruption and casualties. For extremist groups targeting hegemonic powers like the USA and its allies, CBRN weapons represent a force multiplier, capable of transforming asymmetric warfare into global catastrophe. The pattern of early 21st-century attacks, from 9/11 onward, reflects a growing appetite for high-impact, symbolic violence. In this context, CBRN terrorism is not a distant nightmare but a strategic ambition, demanding urgent international cooperation and robust counter-proliferation measures.

Revelations about Pakistani scientist A. Q. Khan's proliferation activities exposed a global black market in nuclear technology, where components and materials could potentially reach non-state actors. If terrorist groups secure enough funding and technical expertise, developing a nuclear device becomes a dangerous possibility. Groups like al-Qaeda and Aum Shinrikyo, driven by revenge, could also build crude radiological weapons to generate chaos and psychological trauma.

The threat of non-nuclear WMDs remains credible. Aum Shinrikyo and ISIS have already used chemical agents, showing that such capabilities are within reach for determined actors. The pressing question is not whether terrorists would use CBRN weapons, but *when* and *where*. Dismissing the threat due to limited evidence is risky. Ignoring early signs under the belief that 'ignorance is bliss' invites disaster when dealing with CBRN threats from non-state actors.

Bush Doctrine Blunder: The Limits of Pre-emption and Unilateralism

The Bush Doctrine of pre-emption, particularly its application in Iraq, revealed significant limitations. Its strategy to prevent Iraq from acquiring WMDs was undermined by intelligence failures and a lack of credible evidence. Acting without verifiable proof led to immense suffering in the region and long-term damage to U.S. goodwill in the Middle East. The doctrine also blurred the line between *pre-emption*, responding to imminent threats, and preventive war, which targets hypothetical risks. This ambiguity strained alliances and raised doubts about the legitimacy of unilateral U.S. actions.

Moreover, bypassing international institutions bred resentment and risked alienating key partners, weakening global counter-terrorism cooperation. The doctrine also rested on the flawed assumption that eliminating potential WMD programs would cripple terrorist threats. In reality, most terrorist groups focus on acquiring simpler, more accessible weapons, rendering the doctrine's emphasis on high-tech WMDs potentially misguided.

The Limits of Criminal Law: Countering CBRN Terrorism

Criminalizing the acquisition of CBRN weapons by non-state actors, while symbolically important, does little in practice, most states already possess legal mechanisms to address such threats. Since enforcement remains a national prerogative, the international community has limited influence beyond offering guidelines or support. After 9/11, however, the world witnessed a dramatic shift in attitudes toward terrorism. Support for international institutions like the United Nations surged, and both the UN General Assembly and Security Council quickly adopted a series of counter-terrorism measures. This marked a significant turn toward multilateral cooperation, particularly in addressing the looming threat of CBRN terrorism. Regional bodies and specialized agencies also began to play a key role in this global effort.

Increased focus on terrorist access to weapons of mass destruction led to a renewal support for counter-proliferation frameworks, including treaties such as the NPT and CTBT. But more targeted efforts emerged to prevent CBRN materials from falling into the hands of terrorists. For example, UN Security Council Resolution 1540 (2004) stands out as a pivotal measure, requiring all UN members to adopt legal and institutional safeguards against WMD proliferation to non-state actors. Similarly, the International Convention for the Suppression of Acts of Nuclear Terrorism (2005) criminalizes the use, theft, or possession of nuclear material with malicious intent and promotes legal cooperation. The broader biological weapons regime, anchored by the BWC and reinforced by UNSCR 1540, focuses on disarmament and non-proliferation obligations. Together, these instruments form a vital, yet still evolving—framework aimed at curbing the gravest threats of our time.

United Nations Security Council Resolution 1540

The 21st century has seen a troubling rise in mass-casualty terrorist attacks, highlighting the devastating potential of such groups acquiring advanced capabilities. The prospect of terrorists obtaining nuclear weapons poses a severe threat to global security. While alarmist predictions are best avoided, the international community acknowledges the gravity of this risk. The adoption of UN Security Council Resolution 1540 in 2004 was a pivotal move, requiring all member states to implement strong counter-proliferation measures and block non-state actors from accessing weapons of mass destruction (WMDs).

UNSCR 1540 compels states to enact and enforce domestic laws prohibiting non-state actors from developing, acquiring, or using nuclear, chemical, or biological weapons. It complements existing treaties, especially the Chemical Weapons Convention (CWC), by urging universal ratification and reinforcing the importance of strict national controls. Unlike the CWC, which focuses on state actors, UNSCR 1540 directly targets threats from non-state groups, setting a broader framework for counter-proliferation. It mandates accounting, securing, and regulating WMD-related materials across their entire lifecycle.

Despite these advances, challenges remain. Treaty adherence is uneven, and enforcement and verification mechanisms still require improvement. Addressing threats emanating from terror-sponsoring states such as Pakistan along with network of terror organizations, is key to long-term prevention. Stronger international cooperation, better information sharing, and increased capacity building are essential. While UNSCR 1540 has enhanced compliance and standardized export controls, the evolving threat landscape demands regular updates to its mandate and mechanisms to ensure its continued relevance and effectiveness.

Chemical Weapons Convention

The CWC, in force since 1997, imposes strict regulations on its 184+ member-states. It bans the development, production, stockpiling, and use of chemical weapons, requiring states to declare and destroy existing stockpiles. Facilities involved in chemical weapons production since 1946 must be reported and either dismantled or converted for peaceful use under international oversight. To prevent misuse, the CWC also mandates disclosure of commercial and military sites producing highly toxic chemicals or their precursors.

Enforcement is led by the Organization for the Prohibition of Chemical Weapons (OPCW), which oversees a robust inspection regime. Thousands of on-site inspections, of both civilian and military facilities, have demonstrated the OPCW's effectiveness in ensuring compliance. By May 2024, 193 nations had declared and destroyed 72,304 metric tons of chemical weapons. However, the absence of key states like Egypt, Iraq, Israel, North Korea, and Syria remains a challenge. Persistent diplomacy seeks to bring them on board.

While the CWC has significantly reduced state-held chemical weapons, its focus on declared state activities limits its reach. Inspectors are authorized only at official sites, leaving a gap in monitoring non-state actors. As the risk of diversion into illicit hands persists, especially with dual-use chemicals, the CWC's continued vigilance over precursors remains essential.[30]

Convention on the Physical Protection of Nuclear Material

The Convention on the Physical Protection of Nuclear Material (CPPNM) is a cornerstone of global counter-terrorism efforts and one of twelve key legal instruments endorsed by the UN. Alongside the 2005 Convention against Nuclear Terrorism, it remains the only binding international agreement focused specifically on securing nuclear material from illicit acquisition and misuse.

CPPNM obligates member states to protect nuclear material within their territories, including during domestic and international transport, whether by land, sea, or air. It requires robust measures for prevention, detection, and prosecution of offences related to nuclear material, with such crimes classified as extraditable under applicable bilateral treaties.

The International Atomic Energy Agency (IAEA) supports implementation through its Nuclear Security Plan of Activities. This includes advisory support, technical assistance, capacity building, and guidance for enhancing physical protection of nuclear materials and facilities. The IAEA also aids in detecting illicit nuclear activities and assists countries in developing strong legal frameworks to safeguard nuclear security.

Safeguarding Radioactive Sources: IAEA's Code of Conduct

The IAEA developed the *Code of Conduct on the Safety and Security of Radioactive Sources* as a non-binding yet essential tool to guide national policies, laws, and regulations on radioactive source management. Initially drafted in 1998 with a focus on sealed sources, the code was officially published in 2004. Following the 9/11 attacks, its scope was expanded to include source security.

The code applies to all radioactive sources that pose serious risks to human health and the environment. It provides a foundational framework for managing such materials and encourages states to incorporate key safety and security standards into their national legislation. It also sets threshold quantities for 26 radionuclides, 16 of which are frequently used at levels that could cause harm if mismanaged.

To support implementation, the IAEA runs outreach programs promoting safeguard agreements and additional protocols. It also deploys legal and technical experts to help states align with international instruments designed to strengthen defences against nuclear terrorism.

Biological Weapons Convention: Absolute Prohibition on Offensive Use

The Biological Weapons Convention (BWC) strictly prohibits the development of delivery systems for biological agents intended as weapons, allowing only defensive measures like vaccines, protective gear, and detection technologies. It also implicitly bans the transfer of biological weapons, materials, or technologies to non-state actors, forbidding their provision to any state, group of states, or international body. Operative paragraph 8 obligates states to refrain from supporting non-state actors in developing, producing, transferring, or using biological weapons and delivery systems. Additionally, under operative paragraph 2, states must prevent such actors from engaging in or assisting others in these activities.[31]

Despite its prohibitions, the BWC lacks robust compliance and verification mechanisms. Article 5 permits bilateral or multilateral consultations through a formal consultative meeting (FCM), relying solely on data submitted by concerned states—without independent verification. Article 6 allows parties to report violations to the UN Security Council with 'all possible evidence,' yet no such referral has occurred, even in the presence of compelling proof.

To reinforce these norms, UN Security Council Resolution 1540 mandates states to adopt national laws preventing non-state actors from acquiring biological weapons or related capabilities, including supportive activities. It complements existing treaties and customary international law by emphasizing proactive domestic implementation.

Proliferation Security Initiative

Since the 9/11 attacks, global efforts to prevent terrorists from acquiring chemical, biological, radiological, and nuclear (CBRN) capabilities have intensified. A key priority has been stopping the trafficking of delivery systems, materials, and technologies linked to such weapons. This focus led to the creation of several initiatives, notably the Proliferation Security Initiative (PSI).

Launched in 2003 by the U.S. President, the PSI is a global, voluntary effort to prevent the spread of weapons of mass destruction (WMDs), their delivery systems, and related materials. Open to all committed states, it had 112 participants by June 2022, including Australia, France, Germany, and Italy.[32]

Distinct from traditional international organizations, the PSI has no treaty or permanent bureaucracy, enabling quick and adaptable action. Its focus on interdiction and its *Statement of Interdiction Principles* have disrupted key trafficking networks. The PSI fosters tight cooperation among intelligence, law enforcement, and government agencies, allowing agile responses to proliferators who often operate through front companies, exemplified by the A.Q. Khan network.

Beyond interdiction, the PSI helped spur the adoption of UN Security Council Resolution 1540, reinforcing its role in shaping international counter-proliferation norms. Through practical collaboration and intelligence sharing, it remains a crucial tool in the global effort to block WMD proliferation.

Future Trends and Emerging Technologies in CBRN Terrorism

Current discourse around the threat of CBRN terrorism is largely shaped by two polarized viewpoints. One emphasizes the growing danger posed by non-state actors acquiring CBRN capabilities, particularly through dual-use technologies that were once the exclusive domain of state-sponsored scientists. The other, more dismissive stance, downplays the likelihood and potential impact of such threats, arguing that terrorist groups lack the capacity to cause large-scale disruption with these weapons. Both perspectives often appear to suffer from emotional bias, relying more on speculative assertions than verifiable evidence.

What is urgently needed is a balanced, evidence-driven approach that neither sensationalizes the threat nor underestimates its evolving nature. The proliferation of emerging technologies, largely due to their rapid development and adoption in civilian sectors, has significantly lowered the barrier for misuse. Tools once confined to advanced research labs are now increasingly accessible in the public domain, often with limited regulation.

Artificial Intelligence-enabled systems (such as autonomous drones and robotic platforms), the Dark Web, the Internet of Things (IoT), crypto currency, nanotechnology, synthetic biology (including gene editing), 3D printing, and sophisticated malware all present new avenues for exploitation by non-state actors. These technologies can be repurposed to develop improvised CBRN capabilities, enhance delivery systems, or obfuscate planning and communication. As access expands and the line between civilian and military applications blurs, the threat landscape becomes more complex, and more urgent to address with informed, strategic vigilance rather than reactive rhetoric. To gain a clearer understanding, let us examine the implications of select emerging technologies in the context of CBRN terrorism:

Artificial Intelligence Enabled Hardware Systems

Artificial Intelligence Enabled Hardware Systems (AIEHS), commonly known as drones, have the potential to transform both warfare and civilian applications. However, their autonomous operation and ability to function in hazardous environments raise serious concerns in the context of CBRN terrorism. These systems could be weaponized to deliver, disperse, or detonate chemical, biological, radiological, or nuclear materials with precision, far surpassing human capabilities. For instance, UAVs equipped with AI could deliver chemical or biological agents with surgical accuracy, increasing casualties. Similarly, autonomous underwater vehicles could deploy explosives or release harmful substances in marine environments. The potential for misuse underscores the need for robust counter measures and international cooperation.

Cyber Technology: A Digital Arsenal for Terrorists

Cyber technology, encompassing software and computer programming, has emerged as a potent tool for harm, posing a significant threat when exploited by terrorist groups. This digital arsenal includes malware, exploitation of Internet of Things (IoT) devices, and the misuse of digital currencies for terror financing. Cyber capabilities enable terrorists to disrupt critical infrastructure, steal sensitive data, and spread propaganda. These technologies also facilitate the execution of physical attacks, including those involving CBRN materials, by compromising industrial control systems or medical facilities.

The convergence of cyber and physical domains intensifies the challenge of preventing CBRN terrorism. With the proliferation of IoT devices expanding attack surfaces, adversaries gain avenues for remote exploitation, from disrupting power grids to compromising nuclear facilities. The rise of AI and machine learning introduces new complexities, enabling automated attacks that evade conventional security measures. As the line between physical and digital worlds blurs, "cyber-physical" attacks become a real and significant threat. For example, exploiting vulnerabilities in chemical plants or nuclear reactors could release hazardous materials or cause radiological incidents. Safeguarding against these hybrid threats requires comprehensive strategies linking cyber and physical security.

Biotech-Weaponization

Emerging technologies present terrorists with unprecedented opportunities to inflict mass harm while evading detection. The growing accessibility of biotechnology, fuelled by the rise of citizen science and DIY bio-labs, has lowered the barriers to entry for individuals outside traditional institutions. Skilled bio-hackers, often operating independently of academic or corporate oversight, can now manipulate genetic material and potentially engineer harmful biological agents. This democratization of biotech raises serious security concerns, as it enables the development of bio-weapons without the need for state-level resources. As these capabilities become more widespread, the risk of their misuse by malicious actors increases significantly.[33]

The integration of crowd sourcing and high-end computing in biotechnology research exemplifies how these advances could be misused by terrorists. Current research on gene editing techniques such as CRISPR-Cas9 (CRISPR-Cas9 stands for 'Clustered Regularly Interspaced Short Palindromic Repeats and CRISPR-associated protein 9'). This gene-editing technology allows precise, low-cost DNA modification. In the context of bioterrorism, it could be misused to create more virulent or drug-resistant pathogens, significantly increasing the threat of engineered biological attacks on civilian populations*)* reveals how innovations in synthetic biology lower the barriers for creating biological agents with catastrophic potential. Synthetic biology enables the creation of novel pathogens and enhances existing ones, increasing virulence and evading detection. The rise of biotech research facilities globally raises concerns over dual-use technologies falling into the wrong hands.

Advancements in nanotechnology also present both beneficial and dangerous possibilities. While nano materials are useful for targeted drug delivery in medicine, they can be weaponized for surreptitious distribution of chemical or biological agents. Nano-scale sensors and detection systems, although valuable for early detection of CBRN threats, also present challenges in adapting to stealthy delivery methods.[34]

Addressing the evolving threat of CBRN terrorism demands a proactive and interdisciplinary approach that combines technological innovation, strategic foresight, and robust international cooperation. Investments in advanced detection systems, resilient critical infrastructure, and cutting-edge cyber-defence capabilities are no longer optional, they are essential. Terrorist actors have long since outgrown outdated tactics; once known for using pagers and bulky cell phones to send coded messages, they now actively exploit emerging technologies for nefarious purposes. From encrypted communications to autonomous systems and synthetic biology, these groups continuously adapt to the digital age. Combating this complex threat requires more than just scientific knowledge or policy frameworks, it calls for the seamless integration of ethical governance, security planning, and real-time intelligence sharing. As we face increasingly sophisticated threats, only a coordinated global response grounded in vigilance, innovation, and shared responsibility will be sufficient to safeguard humanity from the catastrophic potential of CBRN terrorism in the 21st century.

From Backyard to Battlefield: The Risks of DIY Technology

The fusion of key features in emerging technologies allows amateurs to engage in global 'Do-It-Yourself' (DIY) movements. Platforms such as YouTube and Instructables have opened opportunities for autodidacts to explore technological advancements from the comfort of their homes. The DIY movement leverages open-source platforms to foster virtual communities focused on innovating new technologies, which has revolutionized biology and fuelled the growth of community labs and groups in North America, Europe, and Asia.

DIY Drones, with over 80,000 members worldwide, exemplifies this trend.[35] While these groups emphasize responsible use, they often operate outside conventional safety regulations, creating challenges for law enforcement and intelligence agencies. Concerns arise regarding these groups inadvertently contributing to malicious activities through knowledge or technology sharing.

However, it would be unwise to give in to apocalyptic fears simply because technological breakthroughs are accelerating. Historically, there is no clear correlation between scientific advancements and the destructive power of terrorism. In other words, scientific progress and technological innovation are not the sole factors driving terrorist groups to acquire and deploy CBRN weapons. Several intervening factors may motivate a lone actor or non-state group to pursue such a path, outweighing the limited rewards from terror tactics. The repercussions of deploying CBRN weapons would be catastrophic, with severe collateral damage affecting the general population. A terrorist group might recognize that such an attack would backfire not only on itself but also on the innocent public on its safe heaven. That being said, the case of Aum Shinrikyo, while unique, cannot be used to stoke unnecessary alarm.

Despite possessing the technical and financial means, only a few terrorist groups have pursued CBRN weapons, with most opting for conventional weapons like firearms and explosives. Only Aum Shinrikyo and the Islamic State have utilized chemical weapons, highlighting the potential threat posed by groups with both the intent and means to deploy CBRN weapons. However, this on its own does not imply that other groups would not at least try.

The feasibility of converting CBRN materials into weapons depends on intangible factors, such as tacit knowledge and interdisciplinary collaboration. A bio-hacker, for example, would face enormous challenges in developing and deploying a new pathogen alone, requiring skilled collaborators and facing complexities in weaponization. While scientific breakthroughs such as synthetic biology may aid pathogen creation, they do not necessarily address the challenges of delivery and dissemination.

It is also important to assess the practical contributions of specific technologies to the CBRN threat. For example, while 3D printing may struggle with toxic or radioactive metals, micro-reactors face operational hurdles in producing chemical agents. However, advancements in technology also provide opportunities to mitigate CBRN threats. Unmanned aerial and ground vehicles enhance border security and CBRN detection, while biometrics and RFID chips improve security and inventory control. Advanced sensor technologies and forensic methods help detect and attribute CBRN incidents, strengthening overall security efforts.

While emerging technologies and their use by terrorists would require further exploration, it is evident that their increasing democratization is cause for concern. The Fourth Industrial Revolution, marked by rapid advancements in AI, has lowered the barriers to complex applied sciences. Fields such as data analysis, design, and research, once exclusive to highly skilled experts, are now accessible to individuals with minimal expertise.

The proficiency needed to effectively use these technologies has decreased, a phenomenon known as 'de-skilling,' making them accessible to a broader audience. AI-driven avionics and intuitive flight controls have simplified drone operations in complex airspaces. Similarly, automated 3D printing has reduced the expertise required to produce sophisticated components.

However, the proliferation of these technologies, especially given their dual-use capabilities, presents significant risks from non-state actors. These technologies have already disrupted scientific and industrial sectors, and their intersection with the ongoing digital revolution presents challenges for law enforcement and policymakers. As these technologies become more democratized and decentralized, regulating and distinguishing between legitimate and malicious uses will become increasingly difficult.

12

The Digital Caliphate: Emerging Tech and the Terrorist Nexus

"*Only years of practice will teach you the mysteries and bold certainty of a real gardener, who treads at random, and yet tramples on nothing.*"

—**Karel, Capek** (on the limitations of robots)

The Ethics of Innovation: Technology and Terrorism

Before exploring the contours of 'new' terrorism, it would be worth pausing to ask: what exactly was 'old' about terrorism? One useful lens is to examine not just ideology, but the operational methods, tactics, and local contexts that shaped earlier movements. Traditionally, terrorist groups were primarily driven by rigid ideological or nationalist goals, whether seeking regime change, independence, or revolution. Their operations were largely confined to specific geographic areas, with attacks often directed at clearly defined state targets. Tactics were relatively limited, relying on small arms, improvised explosives, and low-tech sabotage. In essence, the 'old' terrorism was more localized, predictable, and constrained by both technology and the political landscape. Understanding these past patterns is crucial to grasping how dramatically the threat has evolved in the modern era.

The nature of terrorism has shifted significantly. Modern non-state actors are becoming global. Unlike old terrorism, which was rooted in ideology and traditional weaponry, the new terrorism transcends ideology and embraces new weapon systems. It is rapidly becoming international, if not entirely global. Technologies such as the Dark Web, Artificial Intelligence, and CBRN capabilities have given rise to a new breed of internet-savvy terrorists, whose political goals may or may not stem from addressing grievances. In fact, they might not have any real grievances to speak of.

Importantly, many of the technologies that terrorists exploit have dual-uses. While they also serve counter-terrorism purposes, the democratization of high technology has transformed the landscape. These technologies, combined with the widespread use of the internet, open up unprecedented possibilities for individuals to influence events in both positive and harmful ways.

Consider a software engineer working for a multinational company who could develop a remotely controlled robot to alter critical chemicals at a sensitive site. If this engineer turns rogue, he could wreak havoc by modifying the software code and embedding a 'switch' that, when activated on a specific date, transforms the mixture into a lethal gas. Imagine a terrorist organization recruiting brilliant students, sending them to top technical universities in the West to study high technology. Once employed in top companies, these students could implant secret software codes into sensitive systems, enabling future attacks orchestrated by the same terrorist group. While hypothetical, these scenarios are increasingly possible due to the versatility of emerging technologies.

The Rise of Big Tech and the Erosion of State Control

The widespread democratization of technology has significantly altered the global power structure, shifting influence away from traditional state actors and toward individuals and corporations. Today, with relatively easy access to powerful digital tools, small groups and even lone individuals can execute complex tasks that were once the exclusive domain of governments or major institutions. This transformation has rendered many conventional mechanisms of oversight and regulation less effective, challenging established notions of state control, security, and governance.

Yet, there is a paradox in this so-called '*democratization of technology*.' As Justice Louis Brandeis once observed, *"We may have democracy, or we may have wealth concentrated in the hands of a few, but we can't have both."* His warning, originally aimed at monopolistic corporations undermining democratic capitalism, resonates today in the age of Big Tech. While technology has become more accessible, a handful of companies now wield enormous economic and political power. The concentration of influence among tech giants has not only disrupted traditional markets but also raised serious concerns about their role in shaping public policy. When corporate leaders hold sway over democratic institutions, it becomes increasingly difficult to impose meaningful checks and balances on their actions.

In a way, the rise of Big Tech companies as data giants has further complicated matters. These companies collect vast amounts of data, surpassing the capabilities of most governments. While states have the legal authority to collect and analyze data (and to regulate how it is done), the sheer volume of information generated by digital interactions makes it a daunting task. The resource-heavy nature of surveillance, coupled with privacy concerns and democratic norms, limits the ability of most countries to implement surveillance models like China's. This disparity gives Big Tech an edge in identifying and mitigating threats, while governments struggle to keep up.

Though Big Tech companies appear to have invested heavily in detecting threats and anomalous behaviour, they often resist strict regulatory oversight. Their preference for complying with U.S. laws, where many are based, creates challenges for law enforcement in other jurisdictions. Real-time access to content-related data, crucial for investigations, is frequently hindered by jurisdictional disputes and legal complexities. This regulatory gap weakens efforts to combat terrorism and cybercrime.

We would avoid speculative narratives on the catastrophic potential of emerging technologies in the hands of terrorists. While recognizing the gap between technological advancement and counter-terrorism capabilities, the focus remains on understanding the challenges and opportunities of this evolving landscape.

The Evolving Landscape of Cyber Terrorism

While the term '*cyber terrorism*' is often bandied about, concrete examples remain relatively scarce. Nevertheless, the increasing adoption of emerging technologies by both terrorist groups and counter-terrorism agencies is transforming the operational landscape. Terrorist organizations have leveraged drones for attacks, exploited social media for propaganda and recruitment, utilized the Dark Net for financial transactions, and employed encryption to evade detection.

In response, counter-terrorism agencies have adapted by harnessing machine learning and advanced data analytics to identify suspicious patterns. Offensive cyber operations, including preventive hacking, have been employed to access encrypted data, while the collection of vast datasets underpins intelligence-driven counterterrorism efforts. This dynamic interplay between technological innovation and its application by both sides underscores the complexities of the modern security environment.

The Ethical Labyrinth of Emerging Technology: Balancing Security and Liberty

Emerging technologies often trigger intense debate, particularly regarding their use by security agencies in counter-terrorism. The deployment of drones, widespread surveillance, and regulation of encryption raise ethical concerns—especially around privacy and internet security. These issues demand thoughtful, informed deliberation.

Addressing them requires ethical reflection. In a world where technology is increasingly democratized, quick judgments on government actions or individual use can be misleading. Many innovations shaping today's landscape stem from individuals unconnected to terrorism. Understanding the motivations behind terrorist adoption of technology—rather than reacting with fear—can improve counter-terrorism strategies.

Technologies such as AI-enabled hardware systems (AIEHS), Big Data, machine learning, Tor routers, and the Dark Net hold immense potential for both good and harm. Like fire, they can build or destroy. However, many ethical concerns arise less from inherent risks and more from inflated fears and media sensationalism.

The emerging field of Techno-Ethics plays a critical role in navigating the complex intersection between technology and human values. It brings to light five major ethical dilemmas associated with emerging technologies: (a) the risks posed by artificial intelligence, (b) data privacy concerns, (c) sustainability challenges, (d) health and psychological impacts, and (e) the misuse of data and disinformation.[1] Techno-ethicists emphasize that decisions made around these technologies are not abstract—they can influence millions of lives. Errors in judgment, policy, or deployment can result in irreversible harm, amplifying inequality, misinformation, and even geopolitical instability.

We would open our discussion with a fundamental ethical question: Do fears—sometimes exaggerated—about the misuse of emerging technologies justify restrictive laws that may suppress democratic expression and innovation? Conversely, are these powerful tools prematurely dismissed as mere novelties, or worse, monopolized to disproportionately expand state surveillance and control? These are not theoretical concerns but urgent, real-world dilemmas. As emerging technologies increasingly shape our societies, it is essential to question who controls them, how they are regulated, and whether their development genuinely serves the public good or merely entrenches existing power structures.

Skies under Threat: The Drone Terrorism Challenge

Imagine a beautiful, fine afternoon in the heart of London. An international convention of diplomats from all over the world is just concluding with a top diplomat giving his final remarks. Suddenly, a swarm of about 100 weaponized mini-drones enters the venue and kills every diplomat of importance. Each weaponized drone is equipped with a modified small firearm with five armour-piercing bullets. Each drone has a predefined facial recognition algorithm trained to recognize a target human face out of thousands of different faces. The bullets are fired automatically upon detection of the target face. No group takes responsibility for the attack. The convention was meant to address '*Emerging Threats to National Security.*' Forty diplomats and other high-ranking security officials died immediately. Precision strike par excellence!

Everything described in the scenario above is possible today with the state of existing 'emerging' technologies. The future is already here. Facial recognition protocols and algorithms, along with the software that performs the recognition, can be compacted into a tiny area within the drone, requiring less than a terabyte of space. Every drone can be trained if it is equipped with AI-enabled machine learning software. Swarming drones have already been developed in China and other countries, achieving almost the status of a sport. Imagination can become reality quite easily.

Early drones, developed primarily for military use, were exorbitantly expensive to operate and maintain. Israel was the first country to use drones for attacking its targets, primarily individual Arab terrorists. Modern drones have become affordable due to advancements in miniaturized motors and batteries, enabling quadcopters to lift payloads of hundreds of kilograms and achieve airworthiness for more than an hour. Beyond visual range capabilities of drones became possible due to high-bandwidth (2.4 GHz) transmitters that provide high-resolution real-time imagery and excellent control by ground-based pilots. Drone speeds have sometimes exceeded 100 km/h, giving rise to a new sport, drone racing.

The Spectre of Future Warfare: Insights from "Ghost Fleet"

P.W. Singer and August Cole's '*Ghost Fleet: A Novel of the Next World War*' offers a chilling glimpse into a future dominated by technological warfare. While the narrative primarily unfolds within the context of a great power conflict, its portrayal of emerging technologies and their potential misuse is equally relevant to the realm of terrorism. The novel serves as a cautionary tale, demonstrating how innovations designed for peaceful purposes can be weaponized by non-state actors with devastating consequences.

By imagining a future where drones, cyber attacks, and artificial intelligence reshape the battlefield, the authors highlight the potential vulnerabilities of traditional security paradigms. While the scale of conflict depicted in 'Ghost Fleet' may seem far-fetched, the underlying trends and technological advancements it explores are already reshaping the global security landscape.

From Gatwick to Punjab: The Drone Threat Comes Home

In 2018, Gatwick Airport in the United Kingdom experienced a shutdown prompted by widespread apprehension over sightings of UAVs. Subsequently, in September 2019, terrorists employed drones to launch attacks on Saudi oil facilities, sparking global alarm regarding security measures against the potential weaponization of UAVs by extremist groups.

Concurrently, law enforcement in the Indian state of Punjab intercepted several drones near the India-Pakistan border, laden with significant amounts of weaponry, ammunition, and other materials intended for use by militants. Subsequent investigations conducted by the National Investigation Agency (NIA) and local police revealed that Pakistan based Khalistan terrorist organizations were instrumental in arranging considerable quantities of arms, ammunition, and high-quality counterfeit Indian currency delivered via drones across the Pakistani border into India. The larger conspiracy revealed that such materials were to be used by Indian terrorists to commit acts of terrorism in the Indian state of Punjab.[2]

Drone Swarms: The Next Evolution of Terror

The capabilities of drones have seen phenomenal growth in both hardware and software. Improvements include increased range, speed, payload capacity, AI-assisted control and coordination methods, and advanced locomotion techniques. In the current armed conflicts between Israel and Hamas and between Ukraine and Russia, drones have been used with devastating effects.

As with most dual-use technologies, terrorists have adopted drones for standoff attacks against various targets. Efforts to counter drones are evolving, but they face challenges such as minimizing unintended impacts, navigating diverse physical environments, and keeping up with rapid technological advancements.

Countering and neutralizing terrorist drones is already challenging and will become increasingly difficult as the legal use and capabilities of drones expand. Additionally, drone miniaturization and swarming present new challenges. It is entirely possible to arm a swarm of drones with deadly chemicals and deliver the payload to a specific target or over a wide area. Countering such a swarm would be a nightmare for any existing anti-drone technology.

Swarm drones' attacks have actually happened. In 2018, a drone swarm attacked two Russian bases in Syria, where 13 fixed-wing drones attempted to deliver aerial bombs from over 31 miles (50 km) away. These homemade drones were relatively low-tech compared to commercial off-the-shelf systems. However, even homemade drones are likely to see technological improvements, thanks to forums and websites dedicated to the sale of drone parts, enabling individuals to build custom drones.[3]

Another technology that could enhance the efficiency of drone swarms is ad-hoc Bluetooth networks. These networks are low-power, local systems that self-organize and share information in real-time. As computing power continues to improve, so will the ability of drone swarms to self-organize and self-coordinate, significantly enhancing their autopilot capabilities. Another challenging development is the increased battery energy density that has led to the creation of micro drones, which are small enough to fit in the palm of a hand.

Such mini drones can carry optical cameras, range hundreds of metres, reach speeds up to 15 mph, and cost under $ 200. In 2020, the United States FAA approved the commercial use of drones beyond the pilot's line of sight, complicating efforts to counter weaponized drones. Many countries, especially in the developing world, lack comprehensive counter-drone mechanisms; simply instituting guidelines and regulations (remember '*isolegal mimicry*'?) is insufficient. This lack of effective regulation makes these regions attractive markets for illegal drones and increases the risk of their use by malicious actors such as terrorists.[4] In other words nothing would be achieved by issuing guidelines and regulation unless there is a technologically sufficient capability to counter the drone menace for effective regulation of their use.

Beyond the Sky: The Rise of Multi-Environment Drones

Drone technology has further evolved to support multi-environment operations, enabling drones to transition from wheeled to airborne modes and from underwater to airborne modes. Waterborne drones, which can operate undetected, pose a significant threat to marine assets such as oil rigs and port infrastructures. They also have the potential to be used as autonomous smuggling pods, transporting contraband such as explosives to intended targets. Advances in automation and computing have significantly enhanced the capabilities of these versatile drones.[5]

Drones Counter-measures: Battling the Threat with Geo-fencing, Jamming, and Nets

Drone countermeasures increasingly rely on geo-fencing, radiofrequency jamming (RF-jamming), and physical capture or destruction. *Geo-fencing*, which depends on software limitations built into drones, is effective if manufacturers integrate the geo-reference coding provided by regulators. This method primarily works for drones that rely on GPS. However, most drones in India, primarily imported from China, are not equipped with geo-fencing capabilities, presenting a significant deficiency in India's emerging drone sector.[6]

Furthermore, geo-fencing can be easily bypassed by not updating the firmware or by hacking the device, a process known as *rooting* or *jail breaking*. Additionally, wrapping aluminium foil around the onboard GPS antenna can disable geo-fencing, though this also limits the piloting capabilities of most drones.[7]

Another significant counter-drone tactic is *RF jamming*, which works on the principle of disrupting radio signals between the drone and its on-ground pilot communication device and GPS signals. RF jamming devices come in various sizes, ranging from handheld (rifle-pattern) to long-range systems mounted on vehicles and buildings. Portable RF jammers are mainly unidirectional, while heavy-duty jammers can be installed with omni-directional protocols.

Radio frequency jammers send out powerful bursts of radio frequencies once unidentified UAVs are detected within their range. These powerful radio-frequency bursts violently interfere with the onboard radio receiver and its systems, disrupting the flight path and causing the UAV to stray. The effectiveness and range of RF-jamming systems vary widely.[8]

Physical counter-measures against drones were the first ones to be used for obvious reasons. They are quite effective if used rightly. Nets and meshing around the targets are the most reliable physical counter-measures that have been increasingly seen in the Ukraine-Russia conflict wherein Russian tanks were covered with physical barriers such as nets to save them from Ukrainian armed drones. Their larger area makes them more effective at catching drones in mid-air by entangling their propellers. Net launchers come in various sizes, from handheld to shoulder-fired, offering a range of options.

Birds of prey were also initially used with specialized training (by operant conditioning involving reinforcement strategies). However, their limitations led to its discontinuation on a large scale. New research explores using trained pigeons attracted to drones and even marine mammals for potential countermeasures, but challenges likely remain.[9]

Drones: The New Battlefield for Asymmetric Warfare

The threats from drones will rise with the development and increased diffusion of emerging technologies. The history of terrorism is a stark reminder of use of dual-use technologies for sinister and insidious designs that terrorists are capable of think. Examples of drone use by ISIS and other armed groups in the middle east and other parts of the world have just opened a Pandora's Box. The ease of use, off-the-shelf availability, 'rooting' and 'jail-breaking' the existing software and hardware configurations are just some of the concerns that need to incorporated in any strategy seeking counter-measures against abuse of UAV technologies.

Drones will be a weapon of choice for targeting critical infrastructure, especially those installations that are vital to the security architecture of any nation. Nations such as India that are witnessing a developmental transformation are at particular risk considering their placement within a geostrategic hotspot onlooked by terrorist organizations well supported by inimical governments.

Recent drone deliveries of contraband materials by Pakistan based terrorists is a warning sign that requires geo-fencing protocols to be installed in every drone that is imported in the country. Imagine multiple simultaneous strikes on vital facilities by swarm of drones that self-destruct after the operation. Such an attack is not only imaginable but possible considering the current advancements in drone technology. In such circumstances, drone counter-measures including 'geo-fencing', 'Rf-jamming' and other counter-drone technologies must be invested in before it is too late. Low cost, high impact, and standoff distance make drones a weapon of choice for future terrorists. The advantage surely lies with attackers; unless effective and pre-emptive countermeasures are invested in and 'free-regime' drone acquisition by individuals should be strictly regulated. Terrorists are already experimenting, and one successful attack could lead to widespread adoption.

From Lab to Weapon: The Rise of Synthetic Biology Threats

Historical examples of terrorist groups employing chemical and biological agents, such as the Aum Shinrikyo cult and ISIS, underscore the potential for catastrophic consequences. While past incidents relied on relatively crude methods, the convergence of biotechnology, DIY revolution, and emerging technologies has significantly lowered the barrier to entry for biological weapons development. The accessibility of advanced equipment, coupled with the growing body of open-source biological information, empowers individuals and small groups to pursue dangerous research with relative anonymity.

It is a common knowledge that terrorist organizations have consistently demonstrated a reckless disregard for human life and a willingness to endure severe consequences in pursuit of their objectives. Groups such as Al Qaeda, Aum Shinrikyo, and ISIS have proven impervious to deterrence, making it unlikely that the threat of retaliation will dissuade them from employing biological weapons.

The democratization of technology has further empowered potential perpetrators. The DIY movement, while predominantly focused on benign innovation, inadvertently creates a breeding ground for the development of dangerous capabilities. The accessibility of scientific knowledge and equipment enables individuals with malicious intent to engage in potentially catastrophic research. This convergence of factors significantly elevates the risk of biological attacks.

The emerging bio-technologies such as using CRISPR-C9 (*Clustered Regularly Interspaced Short Palindromic Repeats* and CRISPR-associated protein 9) which is a gene-editing technology that allows precise, targeted modifications to DNA is revolutionizing genetic research and therapy. This technology can be used to further modify genetic material of a cell to program cells in desired ways, is a powerful tool for editing genomes, allowing researchers to easily alter DNA sequences and modify gene function.

Various biotechnologies have seen promising innovations over the last few decades. Some of these technologies are considered emerging due to their radical approaches to manipulating DNA and other sub-cellular organelles. These technologies alter cellular functions by modifying how cells behave. The following emerging technologies in biological sciences have dual-use potential and could be abused by non-state actors.

CRISPR-Cas9 and Gene Editing

CRISPR-Cas9 is a revolutionary gene-editing technology that allows scientists to precisely alter DNA sequences in living organisms. It uses a guide RNA to direct the *Cas9* enzyme to a specific location in the genome, where Cas9 cuts the DNA, enabling the addition, removal, or modification of genes. CRISPR-Cas9 can be misused to create harmful biological agents by modifying pathogens to be more virulent or resistant to treatment.[10]

Terrorists could potentially engineer viruses or bacteria that evade current vaccines or antibiotics, posing significant public health threats. It could be exploited by terrorists to transform benign bacteria into harmful pathogens. By inserting virulence genes, they could engineer bacteria to produce toxins or evade the immune system. For instance, terrorists could modify E. coli to produce harmful *Shiga* toxin or alter other bacteria to resist antibiotics, making infections difficult to treat. This engineered bacterium could then be released into water supplies, food sources, or as aerosols, targeting specific populations. The ease of access to CRISPR kits and the increasing DIY biohacking movement make this a realistic and concerning threat.[11]

Synthetic Biology

Synthetic biology is revolutionizing how we interact with the living world. By merging biology with engineering, scientists can now design and build entirely new biological systems such as custom-made organisms or cells that perform specific tasks. This ground-breaking technology has vast potential: from creating cleaner biofuels and life-saving drugs to developing bacteria that eat plastic or neutralize toxic waste. But with great power comes serious risk.

In the wrong hands, synthetic biology could be used to build dangerous pathogens or engineer microbes that release deadly toxins—ones we have never seen before and might not be able to quickly detect or treat. The threat is not just science fiction. A malicious actor with the right knowledge and tools could weaponize synthetic organisms to target human populations, destroy crops, or damage ecosystems. These dangers make synthetic biology a growing concern for global security. As the field advances, so must our ability to monitor, regulate, and protect against its misuse. The same tools that promise to heal the world could, if misapplied, cause irreparable harm.[12]

Synthetic biology holds immense promise for humanity, but its misuse, particularly by terrorists, poses significant risks. While some may overstate the threat, the potential for creating and spreading deadly pathogens through synthetic biology is a real concern. The risks are often underestimated due to scientific and financial interests, sometimes fuelled by the belief in the inevitability of technological progress. However, this optimism fails to consider the potential unequal distribution of benefits and burdens. Therefore, a precautionary approach is essential when evaluating advancements in synthetic biology. This principle, which emphasizes the need for strong safety evidence before proceeding, is especially critical given the potential for terrorist groups to exploit these technologies for malicious purposes.[13]

Single-Cell Sequencing

Single-cell sequencing is another biotechnology breakthrough that analyses the genetic material of individual cells. This technology enables detailed insights into cellular diversity, revealing how individual cells contribute to complex biological processes and disease progression. It is crucial for understanding cancer, developmental biology, and tissue heterogeneity at an unprecedented resolution. Single-cell sequencing could be used to develop highly targeted biological weapons that affect specific genetic populations or individuals. By identifying genetic vulnerabilities, terrorists might create agents that exploit these weaknesses.

Organoids and Tissue Engineering

Organoids and tissue engineering emerging fields of biotechnologies that involve creating miniature, simplified versions of organs or tissues in the lab. These 3D structures mimic the functionality of real organs, providing valuable models for disease research, drug testing, and potentially future applications in regenerative medicine and organ transplantation. Organoids and tissue engineering can be abused to grow human tissues for testing biological weapons, ensuring they are effective against human biology. Terrorists might also use these technologies to create organoids for toxicological studies of new bio-weapons.

Microbiome Research

Microbiome research is an emerging field in biotechnology focusing on the study of microbial communities living in and on organisms, especially humans. It aims to understand the complex interactions between these microbes and their hosts, with implications for health, disease treatment, personalized medicine, and the development of probiotic and antimicrobial therapies. Microbiome research could be manipulated to design pathogens that specifically disrupt the human microbiome, leading to severe health issues. Terrorists could also use microbiome data to engineer more virulent and transmissible diseases.

Nanobiotechnology

Nanobiotechnology as an emerging field combines nanotechnology and biology to create nanoscale tools and materials for medical and biological applications. Its benign applications enable the development of targeted drug delivery systems, advanced diagnostic techniques, and innovative treatments, significantly enhancing the precision and effectiveness of healthcare interventions. However, Nanobiotechnology might be exploited to develop nanoscale organismic devices that deliver toxins or pathogens in a highly targeted manner. Terrorists could use nanomaterials to create undetectable delivery systems for biological or chemical agents.

Artificial Intelligence and Machine Learning Applications in Biology

The application of Artificial Intelligence (AI) and machine learning (ML) in biology leverage computational algorithms to analyse complex biological data. These applications enhance research by predicting disease outcomes, identifying new drug targets, and personalizing treatments, thereby accelerating discoveries and improving the accuracy and efficiency of biomedical research. AI and machine learning can be used to optimize the design of biological weapons, predict the spread of diseases, and enhance the effectiveness of bio-terror attacks.

Terrorists might leverage AI to identify new vulnerabilities in biological systems. The possibility was substantiated in a surprising study conducted in 2021 by a group of researchers led by Fabio Urbina from Collaborations Pharmaceuticals that artificial intelligence to generate thousands of potential new toxins. In a proof-of-concept study, they demonstrated how AI, typically used for drug discovery, could be repurposed to design toxic molecules. They used a laptop to modify their drug discovery model, generating 40,000 potential toxic molecules, including some similar to the lethal nerve agent VX, in just six hours.[14]

Metagenomics as a Tool for Bioterrorism

Metagenomics, the study of genetic material extracted from environmental samples, has revolutionized our understanding of microbial ecosystems. By analysing the collective genomes of microbial communities, researchers have made significant discoveries in fields such as medicine and agriculture. However, this powerful technology also carries a dark potential.

In the hands of malicious actors, metagenomics could be exploited to develop novel biological weapons. By studying the genetic makeup of pathogens found in nature, terrorists could identify and enhance their virulence factors, creating highly infectious and lethal strains. Furthermore, metagenomics could be used to design entirely new pathogens with tailored properties, capable of targeting specific populations or evading existing counter-measures. The ability to manipulate microbial communities on a large scale could also be used to disrupt critical ecosystems or infrastructure, causing widespread environmental and economic damage.

Wearable Biosensors: A Double-Edged Sword

Wearable biosensors, designed to monitor and analyse physiological data, have become ubiquitous in modern life. These devices offer numerous benefits, from fitness tracking to disease management. However, they also introduce new vulnerabilities.

In the hands of malicious actors, wearable biosensors can be exploited for nefarious purposes. By hacking these devices, terrorists could gain access to sensitive health information about individuals or entire populations. This data could be used to identify potential targets for biological attacks, tailoring the agent to exploit specific vulnerabilities. Moreover, wearable biosensors could be repurposed to monitor the spread and impact of biological weapons, enabling terrorists to refine their tactics and evade countermeasures. The convergence of wearable technology and biotechnology creates a complex and evolving threat landscape.

Biohacking

Biohacking, a movement characterized by individuals experimenting with biology outside traditional laboratory settings, represents both a frontier of scientific innovation and a potential breeding ground for bioterrorism. While many biohackers are motivated by noble intentions, such as improving human health or understanding biological processes, the democratization of biotechnology carries significant risks.

The accessibility of gene-editing tools like CRISPR-Cas9 has lowered the barrier to entry for genetic manipulation, empowering individuals with limited scientific expertise to undertake complex biological experiments. While this trend has led to remarkable discoveries and applications, it also raises concerns about the potential misuse of these technologies. Terrorist organizations could exploit the open-source nature of biohacking to recruit or inspire individuals to develop biological weapons.

By leveraging the knowledge and techniques shared within the biohacking community, these groups could accelerate their research and development efforts, potentially creating more potent and resilient biological agents. Furthermore, the decentralized nature of biohacking makes it difficult to track and regulate, increasing the likelihood of clandestine activities and the emergence of black markets for dangerous biomaterials.[15]

The convergence of biohacking with other emerging technologies, such as synthetic biology and artificial intelligence, further exacerbates the threat. These technologies could be combined to create highly sophisticated and customizable biological weapons, capable of evading detection and causing widespread devastation.

From Recruitment to Rampage: AI's Potential Role in Terrorism of the Future

Advances in Artificial Intelligence (AI) present numerous opportunities for innovation, but they also pose significant risks if misused by terrorists. AI's capability to process vast amounts of data and identify patterns can be exploited to develop sophisticated cyber-attacks. AI is increasingly being used to create and modify content that cannot be easily differentiated from the real ones. Such content can have harmful effects if used by terrorists to support their narratives. AI can also be used to automate hacking by creating innovative loops that continuously run hacking algorithms until the targeted system gives in.

The Illusion of Truth: Deep Fakes and the Erosion of Trust

It is easy to envisage a scenario where a terrorist group utilises an AI-enabled audio-video application to create a deep fake video of a political leader or military official making inflammatory statements or announcing false policies. This deep fake video could then be disseminated on social media and other online platforms to incite violence, spread disinformation, or create panic among the public. If convincing enough, such a video could undermine trust in public institutions, escalate conflicts, or destabilise regions.

In another hypothetical scenario, a deep fake of a government official falsely declaring a state of emergency or delivering an inflammatory speech against a particular ethnic or religious group could incite unrest and violence. The technology's ability to produce credible yet entirely fabricated content makes it a potent tool for malicious actors seeking to manipulate public perception and destabilise societies.

While this scenario remains hypothetical, the rapid advancement of deep fake technology underscores the importance of developing robust detection methods and public awareness to mitigate the potential misuse of AI for propaganda and other nefarious purposes.

Artificial Intelligence has been misused to create false narratives on social media and to significantly enhance the dissemination of propaganda. Tech-savvy terrorists can exploit AI bots to greatly amplify their online presence, making them appear more formidable than they actually are. These AI-enabled bots can streamline the recruitment process by automating interactions with potential targets on social media platforms. Extremists have utilised AI-generated chatbots to bypass stringent content moderation measures implemented by social media companies. These companies typically employ '*digital fingerprinting*' to track extremist content by scanning for similar messages. However, AI-enabled chatbots can easily circumvent these mechanisms by continuously altering each message and avoiding direct repetitions.

Metaverse Jihad: The Digital Battlefield for Terror

Artificial Intelligence is rapidly becoming an essential and crucial enabling technology for virtual reality (VR) headsets, immersive audio-visual devices, and gaming consoles. Their convergence has evoked unprecedented excitement in their user base and the promise it holds due to its ability to provide an immersive experience for the user which was hitherto not available. A notable example is Apple's VisionPro, which has sold over 200,000 units despite its high $ 3,499 price tag. This technology could be highly advantageous for hackers working with terrorists, enabling them to manipulate critical infrastructure while inconspicuously sitting in public places or on public transportation. Unfortunately, this area of concern has not been extensively researched or highlighted.

Online gamers constantly communicate using both text and voice chats, largely beyond lawful surveillance and content moderation protocols. For terrorists, virtual reality gaming can provide a medium for recruiting impressionable youth and training them. Radicalising content, such as execution videos and doctored materials (using AI to modify audio and video), can be supplied to have a devastating effect on young minds.

Terrorists can construct their own metaverse, presenting a world tailored to a specific ideology. Here, new recruits encounter a modified version of history aligning with the terrorist narrative. They are exposed to various videos, including deep fakes, and interact with mentors via AI-generated avatars – imagine Osama bin Laden's virtual persona persuading recruits to embrace 'the path'. Immersed in this metaverse, recruits are enveloped in a narrative urging them to become 'true followers' (essentially, terrorists). They explore virtual environments showcasing sophisticated weaponry, virtually engaging in attacks against perceived enemies. This immersive experience resembles a video game, allowing recruits to simulate first-person shooter scenarios, targeting and eliminating adversaries. The potential for such manipulation is vast and profoundly unsettling.

From Keyboard to Kill Zone: OSINT-Driven Terrorism

The realm of the traditional state spy has undergone a radical transformation with the increase in surveillance capacities due to advancements in information technology. However, the democratization of the Internet and the anonymity it provides have spawned a new class of investigative individuals who can do the job of a spy better than those employed by the government. The level of motivation and determination plays a crucial role here. A state spy is a government employee who may or may not be as motivated as a determined terrorist whose energies are fuelled by extremist ideologies and pure hate. Social media engagement by common citizens and almost anyone with an internet connection has created a parallel universe in cyberspace, which oftentimes reveals much more than the physical one.

The July 2014 shooting of a Malaysian Boeing 777 flight over Russian airspace was intensely investigated by a group of ordinary civilians who had nothing more than their motivation and an ordinary laptop with a normal internet connection. The investigation far exceeded expectations and revealed details of the attack, including the rocket launcher, the Russian military unit, and the personnel involved in the shooting. With today's freely available online AI algorithms and resources, anyone can do a job much better than state employees who might not be as motivated and determined as a OSINT 'lone wolf'.[16]

A study conducted by Berger and Morgan in 2015 investigated the online presence of ISIS on Twitter, focusing on the demographics, behaviour, and influence of its supporters. Analysing a dataset of 20,000 pro-ISIS accounts, they discovered that these users had a significantly larger following, averaging around 1,000 followers per account, compared to typical Twitter users at the time. These accounts were not only more popular but also considerably more active. Their research highlighted that ISIS's online success stemmed largely from a relatively small yet highly dedicated group of users, estimated at 500 to 2,000, who posted at extremely high volumes to amplify propaganda.[17]

This intense activity helped broaden their reach and enhance their appeal to recruits. Other studies complemented the finding by examining social media behaviour among Western ISIS fighters and found that 70% of their Twitter output consisted of retweets rather than original content. This suggested a calculated communication strategy rather than random expression. Her findings revealed a deliberate blend of seemingly harmless content, like cat images, alongside violent imagery—used to both desensitize audiences and intimidate adversaries, underscoring the manipulative power of ISIS's digital propaganda.

OSINT techniques can also enable a lone wolf or cyber geeks employed by terrorists to reconnoitre targets, publish sensitive personal details about politicians precisely to influence elections, or collect details about their targets from digital footprints across the internet. The craze of leaving online footprints during social events (such as a party, dining out in a fancy restaurant, etc.) can create an interesting digital map of a congregation, which can then be misused by terrorists.

Hypothetically speaking, terrorists can misuse digital footprints left by people visiting a discotheque by analysing the photos and online profiles shared on the venue's social media account. They can identify frequent visitors, their social circles, and personal details. By tracking check-ins, comments, and interactions, they can establish patterns and predict future visits. This information can be exploited to plan targeted attacks, identify and track individuals for kidnapping, or create fake profiles to infiltrate social groups. Additionally, they can use the gathered data to craft personalized phishing attacks or spread propaganda, leveraging the trust and familiarity within the social network.

Narco-terrorists in Latin America are known to have used cyber-tracking to zero in on their targets and then get them kidnapped or, worse, killed. Libyan civil war spawned a whole new group of individual arms dealers who posted their weapons on their Facebook profiles for anyone to buy. Terrorists also use AI-enabled online applications to create fake profiles by generating temporary emails, morphing photographs, and using virtual phone numbers. Such profiles are then used as 'avatars.' Potential recruits can then be lured into their net by reaching out through these avatars and the same profiles are also used for spreading their propaganda.

Terrorists will try their hardest to profit from advances in Machine Learning (ML) in the near future by creating automated software that significantly improves target tracking and propaganda activities. They will use AI to mount impressive and damaging denial of service attacks that quickly learn (in milliseconds) from all possible counter-attack cyber-protocols deployed by their targets. They will engineer fake news and make it viral in seconds using an exponential number of online avatars created by their AI tools. Like recent AI-enabled research on the discovery of new toxins, they will be able to create a significant number of dynamically mutable malware and computer viruses that will attack their targets incessantly.

Taming the AI Beast: A Regulatory Crisis

The global AI market is projected to surpass USD 2.5 trillion within the next decade.[18] AI is transforming banking, healthcare, defence, law enforcement, infrastructure, education, and more. As it becomes embedded in daily life, we may stop noticing its presence—just as we rarely think about the internal combustion engine, incandescent bulbs, or video calls with people across the world. This is how revolutionary technologies become mundane.

Yet, AI is fundamentally different from earlier innovations. Unlike machines or devices of the past, AI systems can engage with humans and mimic sentience. A computer scientist would rightly argue this sentience is only simulated—AI lacks consciousness, emotion, and self-awareness. It performs tasks through algorithms and data, without understanding or subjective experience. Unlike humans, AI cannot act intuitively or empathetically; it remains a sophisticated tool, not a conscious being.

However, this distinction is what makes AI's misuse concerning. Today's AI—encompassing machine learning, natural language processing, computer vision, and expert systems—is not yet Artificial General Intelligence (AGI), but it already offers capabilities that can be exploited by malicious actors, including terrorists. Current regulatory frameworks often suffer from epistemic ambiguity and policy confusion. Developers champion 'freedom of use,' while distancing themselves from responsibility. After all, regulation may hinder adoption—and profit. Ultimately it is an open licence for 'freedom to abuse'.

On the other side, policymakers and regulators often lack the technical depth to respond meaningfully. AI is evolving so rapidly that even insiders struggle to stay updated. Expecting policy executives to craft effective controls in such an environment is unrealistic. This is where an analogy from the arms trade proves helpful.

Imagine a licensed gun dealer sells a firearm to a legal buyer. If that gun is later used in a crime, the dealer typically is not held responsible. But what if the dealer *knew* the buyer had a history of violent extremism, made threats to kill his partner, viewed execution videos, and regularly visited hate sites using a VPN? This context drastically alters the moral—and perhaps legal—responsibility of the seller. The dealer should have alerted authorities.

This analogy mirrors the dilemma facing social media companies (SMCs) and internet service providers (ISPs). These entities collect and analyze massive behavioural data, which they monetize through targeted advertising. If they have the technical ability to detect indicators of violent extremism, why aren't they required to alert law enforcement when a credible threat emerges?

SMCs and ISPs already use AI-based moderation tools to flag policy violations. But these systems often focus on protecting 'community guidelines' (akin to arbitrary company policy) rather than aligning with the laws of the jurisdictions they operate in. This creates a fundamental problem. If businesses can detect a user's inclination toward serious crimes such as terrorism, they should not escape accountability.

Some companies may voluntarily report threats, but this discretion is shaped by internal cost-benefit calculations. Without legal mandates, public safety will always compete with corporate priorities. To be effective, such responsibilities must be embedded in law and firmly fastened on service providers.

For instance, in the United States legal system, 18 U.S. Code § 2258A mandates electronic service providers to report child pornography to the National Centre for Missing & Exploited Children (NCMEC). In the European Union, GDPR allows personal data processing for crime prevention while balancing user privacy. EU member-states also have national laws that may require or permit the reporting of suspicious activity—especially in cases involving terrorism, child exploitation, or other serious crimes.

In sum, as AI continues to evolve and integrate with everyday systems, it is essential to ensure ethical responsibility and regulatory clarity—both for developers and service providers. Without this, the potential misuse of AI could far outpace society's capacity to respond.

The Surveillance Dilemma: Balancing Security and Privacy in the Digital Age

While numerous reports have alleged Orwellian surveillance by intelligence agencies and covert data-sharing arrangements with major social media companies and ISPs (SMC/ISPs), these claims often lack solid evidence. The most notable case remains Edward Snowden's 2013 revelations, which exposed significant overreach by the U.S. National Security Agency (NSA). Snowden, a former NSA contractor, disclosed that the agency was collecting vast amounts of data on American citizens, without consent, including bulk phone metadata that tracked who called whom, when, and for how long.

Snowden also revealed the existence of PRISM, a program that allowed direct access to emails, chats, and other data from major tech firms like Google, Facebook, and Microsoft. Additionally, he exposed NSA operations tapping into global communications infrastructure, enabling surveillance of foreign leaders and massive cross-border data collection. These classified leaks, shared with journalists Glenn Greenwald, Laura Poitras, and Ewen MacAskill, triggered global debates on surveillance, privacy, and state power.

Despite these high-profile disclosures, replicating such technological dominance in developing countries remains improbable. First, most BigTech companies are based in the USA and often resist compliance with laws outside

American jurisdiction. Second, countries like India lack robust institutional frameworks to oversee or regulate the activities of these powerful corporations, weakening their ability to enforce local accountability. Third, a critical knowledge gap exists between the technological sophistication of these companies and the capacity of public policy executives to regulate them effectively.

Compounding this is the persistent narrative from SMC/ISPs that their top priority is to uphold users' 'freedom of expression and privacy.' Yet this stance is deeply contradictory. These same companies systematically extract users' behavioural data—everything from clicks and searches to location and device usage—under the guise of consent, typically via opaque terms of service that offer no real choice but to opt out entirely.

This data, akin to digital 'crude oil,' is meticulously refined through advanced analytics to produce powerful insights into users' preferences, fears, and buying habits. It is then monetized through hyper-targeted marketing strategies, benefiting corporations willing to pay the most. Far from protecting privacy, these practices represent a sophisticated form of digital surveillance and commodification of user behaviour—often without meaningful oversight or transparency.

Artificial Intelligence and Effective Counter-terrorism: Public Policy and the Compliance Conundrum

Rather than being a bane, AI has the potential to be a much-awaited boon for counter-terrorism. Only if policymakers institutionalize the inherent responsibility of SMCs/ISPs through effective legal instrumentation that emphasizes the prevention of terrorist acts can this be achieved. This can be accomplished by legally requiring SMCs/ISPs to implement AI solutions to detect and report suspicious activities and content that significantly discloses terrorist propaganda, malicious activity, or support for terrorism. While SMCs/ISPs raise reasonable concerns about the potential for a sweeping crackdown on dissent and freedom of expression harming their USP of being an 'open' platform, public policy executives should address these concerns by formulating 'red flags' in cooperation with regulators that can be incorporated into algorithms running in these AI-enabled applications.

One of the effective ways to accomplish a convergence between privacy, anonymity, and freedom of expression, and counter-terrorism would be greater synergy between SMC/ISPs, government executives and experts on the subject. SMC/ISPs must offer detection tools and reporting protocols based on algorithms on which inputs regarding 'red-flags' should be incorporated based on mutual understanding rather than one way 'compliance directives' which tend to overshoot and appear to bring 'Orwellian' elephant in the room.

It is concerning that BigTech companies seem to prioritize commercial interests over their potential role in public health and safety. While they often cite concerns about civil liberties, their reluctance to share real time data concerning terror threats and propensities with law enforcement and other relevant agencies raises questions about their commitment to societal well-being. SMCs/ISPs occupy a unique position with the ability to shape public discourse. By seemingly overlooking malicious activities, including support for crime and terrorism, they may be undermining the efforts of governments worldwide to address these pressing issues.

AI has tremendous potential to enable law enforcement agencies to detect significant anomalies in online behaviour suggesting malicious activities such as terrorism and other serious crimes. AI-enabled detection of deviant online behaviour and further zeroing in on possible suspects on the verge of committing terror acts would go a long way in ensuring a terror-free world. BigTech can play a very important role in this regard.

Crypto Currency and Funding of Terrorism: The Dark Web Economy

Cryptography: From Enigma to Bitcoin

Cryptography, the art and science of secure communication, traces back to ancient civilizations. The Egyptians used hieroglyphics for encoding, while Spartans employed the Scytale to encrypt military orders. However, cryptography truly evolved into a sophisticated discipline with the advent of the digital age.

A pivotal moment came during the Second World War when advanced nations such as Germany used advanced encryption machines like the Enigma, a polyalphabetic substitution cipher considered unbreakable. In response, Allied cryptanalysts at Bletchley Park (Britain's wartime SIGINT hub) developed revolutionary techniques and devices. Among their achievements was the *Bombe*, a machine that could systematically test Enigma settings and decipher German messages. Their success is widely credited with shortening the war.

For decades, cryptography remained primarily within military and intelligence domains. This changed in the early 1990s with significant advancements in cryptographic software. In 1998, engineer Wei Dai proposed *b-money*, a concept for anonymous, distributed electronic cash using cryptographic principles. Around the same time, Nick Szabo introduced *Bit Gold*, a precursor to modern crypto currencies, designed to reduce reliance on centralized financial institutions.

These innovations laid the groundwork for *Bitcoin* (BTC), introduced in 2008 by an individual or group using the pseudonym Satoshi Nakamoto. Bitcoin aimed to offer a decentralized financial system, responding in part to the failures exposed by the global financial crisis.

This historical trajectory highlights cryptography's transformative role, from securing wartime secrets to enabling digital currencies. Lessons from WWII and post-war innovations directly shaped today's cryptographic systems. With the rise of computing, cryptographic algorithms became increasingly complex, far beyond the reach of traditional code-breaking. This evolution led to public-key cryptography, a foundation of modern cyber security.

Within this technological context, crypto currencies emerged. They leverage advanced cryptography to secure transactions and rely on blockchain, a decentralized ledger that ensures transparency and immutability. Bitcoin, as the pioneer, exemplifies how cryptography underpins a new era of digital financial systems.

Crypto Currencies and Dark Web: An Enticing Frontier for Financing Terrorism

Crypto currencies operate on decentralized systems, typically without a central bank or administrator. This structure, combined with the pseudonymity offered by cryptographic addresses, makes them attractive for both lawful and unlawful activities. Since Bitcoin's success, a surge of digital currencies has entered the market. While some mirror Bitcoin's ethos, others diverge with distinct use cases. *Ethereum*, for instance—the second most valuable crypto currency,[19] was launched in 2015 to support decentralized applications (dApps) and smart contracts. This expanded blockchain's utility beyond simple transactions.

Crypto currencies such as Bitcoin, Ethereum, and Monero are digital currencies that use cryptography to ensure secure and verifiable transfers. Together with blockchain technology and the Dark Web, they have transformed the digital landscape—offering innovation, but also new vectors for illicit activity. Their inherent anonymity appeals to cybercriminals, money launderers, and terrorist organizations.

Blockchain, the backbone of crypto currencies, is a distributed ledger that records transactions across multiple computers. Each block includes a time stamp, transaction data, and a cryptographic hash of the previous block, making the chain immutable. Despite its transparency, blockchain's pseudonymous nature allows users to obscure their identities—an advantage exploited by malicious actors who can move funds anonymously, complicating investigations.[20]

The Dark Web, accessible only through software such as Tor (The Onion Router), is not indexed by regular search engines and offers high anonymity. This has turned it into a hub for illicit activities, including weapons sales, drug trafficking, and terrorism financing. When combined with onion routing and crypto currency, it offers criminals unprecedented cover from detection.

Terrorist groups have long sought to bypass conventional financial scrutiny. Crypto currencies provide an alternative path. Bitcoin, in particular, serves as an entry point into digital finance due to its popularity. Although all Bitcoin transactions are publicly recorded, user identities are hidden behind cryptographic addresses, making it difficult to trace flows to specific individuals or entities.[21]

The Dark Web now acts as a digital marketplace for illicit trade. Here, terrorist groups find opportunities for fundraising, leveraging crypto currencies' cross-border nature and resistance to asset seizure. Payments are routed through complex address networks, further obscuring their origins.[22]

A notable innovation in this domain is the use of Initial Coin Offerings (ICOs) and crypto donations. Terrorist groups solicit contributions via social media and encrypted messaging apps, often under the guise of humanitarian causes. Once collected, the funds are layered through multiple transactions to mask their origin and use.[23]

ICOs pose serious regulatory challenges. Their pseudonymous nature and decentralized architecture make oversight difficult and make them ideal vehicles for terrorists, fraudsters, and money launderers. These offerings are vulnerable to fraud, misrepresentation, and regulatory evasion. Fake crypto currency apps promising high returns have proliferated, defrauding users and creating complex cases for cyber investigators—made worse by the near-impossible task of tracing anonymous transactions.

Crypto Currency: A Challenge in Tracing Terrorist Financing

The pseudonymous nature of crypto currencies, while technically not entirely anonymous, provides a significant barrier to identification in practice. Advanced technologies and services, such as tumblers or mixers, further complicate the tracking process. Tumblers and mixers are tools used in cyber-fraud to obfuscate the origins and destinations of crypto currencies. They operate by pooling multiple transactions from various sources, mixing them together, and then redistributing the funds to new addresses. This process makes it exceedingly difficult to trace the path of the funds, thereby enhancing anonymity.[24]

Cyber criminals frequently utilise tumblers and mixers to launder money obtained through illicit activities, such as hacking, ransomware, or other online frauds, effectively 'laundering' the digital currency by concealing its illegal origins and facilitating its integration into the legitimate financial system. The same process is now being utilized by a terrorist organization and narco-terrorists to distribute funds collected from variety of sources so as to hide their source and destination while retaining control of all the funds.

Experts in terrorist financing have revealed that the military wing of Hamas was an early adopter of crypto currency, soliciting Bitcoin donations starting in 2019. Hamas assured supporters that these transactions were anonymous; however, all crypto currency exchanges are recorded on a public ledger known as a blockchain. This transparency enabled the Department of Justice, USA, to seize 150 crypto accounts associated with Hamas's *Al-Qassam Brigades* in 2020. There exists an illicit sector of non-compliant crypto currency exchanges worldwide, with many based in Russia, including Chatex, SUEX, and Garantex, all sanctioned (banned) by the U.S. Treasury Department.[25]

The United Nations Counter-Terrorism Committee (CTED) recently revealed its findings that the Syrian Arab Republic, particularly areas controlled by *Hayat Tahrir al-Sham* (HTS), has become a significant hub for crypto currency used by ISIS and al-Qaeda affiliates and their supporters. The report also noted an increase in crypto currency use by ISIS affiliates and their supporters in Asia, with stable coins emerging as the preferred form of crypto currency. Furthermore, it also revealed that terrorist groups are enhancing their operational security.[26]

Victoria Jacobs Case: First Conviction in Crypto-Enabled Terror Financing

In a groundbreaking case, Victoria Jacobs, a New York resident, was convicted in 2024 for providing over $ 5,000 in crypto currency to Malhama Tactical, a militant group linked to the designated terrorist organization Hayat Tahrir al-Sham. This landmark prosecution underscores the growing concern over crypto currency's role in facilitating terrorism financing.

Proponents of crypto currency often highlight its potential for financial inclusion, but critics emphasize its anonymity as a breeding ground for illicit activities. The recent regulatory scrutiny targeting major crypto currency exchanges reflects the intensifying global effort to combat financial crime, including terrorism financing, through this digital frontier.[27]

Unchecked Crypto Use Threatens Global Security

In April 2023, Hamas announced it would cease Bitcoin fundraising efforts. Nonetheless, as evidenced by the US Treasury Department's recent sanctions, terrorist organisations such as Hamas, al-Qaeda, and ISIS continue to exploit crypto currency exchanges to raise and launder money while evading detection. According to TRM Labs (a blockchain intelligence company that provides a suite of tools and services for detecting, investigating, and preventing crypto currency fraud and financial crime) multiple pro-ISIS groups have been identified using crypto currency, including for recruiting fighters to join ISIS's affiliate in Afghanistan (ISKP).[28]

TRM reported many such crypto currency transfers by terrorist organizations such as ISIS one of which turned out to be over 2 million USD. TRM also traces individual involved in such transactions leveraging its large database of KYC controls and reports it to law enforcement authorities for effective countering terrorist financing. In one such action Turkish authorities arrested Shamil Hukumatov, a senior ISIS fundraiser who was behind one such long running campaign. TRM also reported many such suspected persons to law enforcement authorities in Indonesia, Pakistan, Afghanistan, Syria, Iran and India.[29]

In another instance of crypto-abuse the National Bureau of Counterterrorism, an Israeli agency seized significant funds in crypto currency belonging to individuals and outfits associated with Hamas which led to the discovery of their intricate network and exceptionally cleaver ways of transactions reaching millions of dollars.

As the digital world rapidly evolves, so do the methods employed by groups such as ISIS, al-Qaeda and Hamas to finance their operations. However, Israel's counterterrorism efforts are bolstered by significant abilities and experience in advanced computer forensics an exceptionally recondite area. Only a handful of countries such as Israel, UK-USA (the 'Five Eye' countries) and China apparently have such capabilities and required level of expertise. To counter terrorist financing through crypto currency private agencies such as Chainalysis and TRM Labs also provide expertise and use of their systems to law enforcement agencies of those countries where the level of expertise might require outside assistance.

Terrorists have begun employing cyber experts to find new ways to finance their operations. They continually evolve their methods for collecting, transferring, and using funds to support their activities, adapting to technological advancements and changes in global financial systems. The decentralised nature, pseudonymity, and global reach of crypto currencies make them attractive options for illicit transactions. By leveraging crypto currencies, terrorists have learned to bypass traditional banking systems and avoid detection by regulatory authorities.

Crypto Cat and Mouse: Tracking Terrorist Funds

Law enforcement agencies are engaged in a relentless pursuit of terrorist financiers, as these criminal networks adapt their tactics to exploit emerging technologies. While traditional financial systems are subject to increasingly stringent KYC regulations, terrorist organizations are turning to decentralized platforms such as crypto currencies and the Dark Web to obfuscate tracing of their activities.

The use of crypto currency tumblers and mixers, combined with the pseudonymous nature of these digital currencies, significantly hampers financial tracking efforts. Furthermore, the emergence of blockchain-based smart contracts offers new avenues for illicit transactions, automating fund transfers without intermediaries. To counter these evolving threats, law enforcement agencies must invest in advanced analytical tools, international cooperation, and a deep understanding of the evolving technological landscape.

The case of Hamas, which utilized crypto currency donations and crowd funding platforms to finance its activities, highlights the versatility of terrorist financing methods. As technology continues to advance, so too will the tactics employed by these criminal networks.[30]

Printing Terror: The Looming Threat of 3D-Printed Weapons

What is 3D Printing?

3D printing, or additive manufacturing, is the process of creating three-dimensional objects from computer-aided digital models (CAD). The design is created on a computer, and the printer builds the object layer by layer until the final shape is formed. This method supports various materials, plastics, metals, ceramics. It enables the creation of intricate designs that are often expensive or impractical with traditional manufacturing, especially at small scales.

Once niche, 3D printers have become versatile tools. Desktop 3D printers, widely available online without KYC checks or regulatory hurdles, can now produce high-resolution items from advanced materials. Their affordability and user-friendly interfaces have made them popular among hobbyists, makers, and entrepreneurs for creating custom parts, prototypes, and functional items.

The democratization of manufacturing through 3D printing has far-reaching implications. On one hand, it drives innovation and cost-effective production across sectors like medicine, aerospace, automotive, and consumer goods. On the other, it introduces serious security risks. The ease of translating digital blueprints into physical objects empowers small businesses and individuals, but also offers new tools for malicious actors.

One of the most pressing concerns is the production of firearm components, even entire guns—using 3D printers. These so-called 'ghost guns' lack serial numbers, are hard to trace, and bypass traditional firearm regulations, posing significant threats to public safety and law enforcement.

The ability to fabricate complex components, including explosives or weapon parts, with minimal oversight has transformed 3D printing into a potential tool for criminal and terrorist activity. While law enforcement struggles to adapt, the rapid pace of technological advancement continues to widen the threat landscape.

Looking ahead, the convergence of 3D printing with artificial intelligence and robotics may further complicate regulatory and security frameworks, highlighting the urgent need for proactive monitoring and international cooperation.

Ghost Guns and Beyond: The 3D Printing Threat

One of the most alarming developments today is the rise of do-it-yourself (DIY) firearm production. Blueprints for creating functional guns, often referred to as 'ghost guns' due to their lack of serial numbers, are freely available online. With access to a 3D printer, individuals can easily manufacture these untraceable weapons.

Ghost guns exploit a legal loophole: firearm regulations typically require serial numbers only on the frames or receivers, not on individual components. This allows people in some countries to purchase parts or kits online and assemble fully functional firearms at home. As a result, these weapons bypass established gun control measures, raising serious concerns about their potential misuse.

The ease of producing untraceable firearms presents a grave threat, particularly as it enables terrorists and criminals to obtain deadly weapons without detection. By circumventing regulated channels, DIY gun manufacturing significantly lowers the barriers to acquiring firearms, undermining public safety and law enforcement efforts.[31]

The genesis of this development lies with Cody Wilson, a law student from Austin, Texas who in 2012, established an online, open-source hardware and software organization called '*Defence Distributed*', ostensibly to champion the civil liberty of widespread gun ownership. On May 6, 2013, Wilson took a significant step. Under the watchful eye of BBC at a private Austin shooting range, he fired the world's first 3D-printed firearm. The following day, in a move promoting open-source accessibility, he published the gun's design schematics online.

This weapon, dubbed the '*FP-45 Liberator*,' saw its plans downloaded a staggering 100,000 times globally within just 48 hours. This invention, christened the 'wiki weapon,' ignited a fierce debate, fundamentally altering our perspective on both novel manufacturing technologies and the unfettered online dissemination of such designs.[32]

Since then, other firearms enthusiasts have released their own versions of 3D-printed firearms. These weapons have begun to appear in criminal activity. Notably, in 2019, a 27-year-old named Stefan Balliet attacked a synagogue in Halle, Germany, using homemade weapons that resulted in two deaths and multiple injuries. While Balliet claimed he manufactured improvised weapons to demonstrate their lethality, it is believed he utilised online instructions and a 3D printer to create some components (though not the complete firearms) used in the attack.

In another notable instance, in November 2020 FBI arrested Timothy Watson in West Virginia for selling 3D-printed 'drop-in auto sears' online. These small, precisely crafted devices can convert a semi-automatic weapon into a fully automatic one.[33] He was selling his printed weapons to a gang 'Boogaloo boys' who were involved in killing of law enforcement officers.

Ghost Gun Revolution: The fCG-9 MKII

The fCG-9 MKII is the most advanced largely 3D-printed firearm available today. Using 9mm ammunition and primarily made from plastic, it is lightweight and difficult to detect. Its design files are shared online, enabling easy, decentralized production that bypasses traditional gun control measures. Released in 2020 by an individual known as 'JStark' in Germany, reports indicate dedicated factories in Spain, Canada, and the United States manufacture these guns.[34]

The fCG-9 MKII has been used by rebels in Myanmar against the military junta, by narco-terrorists in South America, and by Irish paramilitary groups. This unregulated manufacturing poses significant risks, as the gun can be assembled quickly and discreetly, even in jurisdictions with strict laws. Terrorists and criminals can exploit this anonymity and accessibility. The fCG-9 MKII highlights the urgency to address the emerging threat of 3D-printed firearms.[35]

The DIY Terrorist Toolkit: Drones and 3D Printed Weapons

3D printing has further facilitated the creation of weaponized drones. By combining readily available electronics with custom-printed components, terrorists can now construct drones capable of carrying and deploying explosives or other hazardous materials. Such unmanned aerial vehicles (UAVs) can be programmed for targeted attacks, posing a significant threat to public safety and national security. The lightweight and adaptable nature of 3D-printed parts allows for the production of drones that evade detection and interception, further complicating counter-terrorism efforts.[36]

The threat actually extends beyond firearms and drones. Terrorist organizations can utilize 3D printing to manufacture components for improvised explosive devices (IEDs). The ability to design and print custom parts allows for the creation of more lethal and sophisticated IEDs, potentially incorporating novel designs that challenge bomb disposal teams. The complex shapes and structures achievable through 3D printing present a significant obstacle in defusing such devices.

It would be reasonable to assert that the most immediate threat appears to be the 3D printing of weaponized drones. A concerning precedent occurred in January 2023 when a PhD student in the UK was apprehended for successfully 3D printing a drone capable of delivering a chemical weapon. The student had researched chemical agents, potentially for use by terrorist groups. This case serves as a stark warning of the potential for these groups to exploit additive manufacturing technologies and recruit individuals with the technical skills to weaponize 3D printing.[37]

The proliferation of knowledge concerning 3D printing processes, particularly bioprinting, has become a growing concern within the online DIY communities. These communities not only share theoretical knowledge on 3D printing firearms, but also dispense practical tips on their use. This dissemination of expertise is further amplified by the development of large language models, which act as facilitators by simplifying access to potentially dual-use scientific information.

3D-printed weapons come in a variety of configurations from *fully 3D-printed* (these firearms are constructed entirely from 3D-printed components), *Hybrid* (when pre-printed weapons combines are readily available, unregulated parts with 3D-printed components) and *Kit Completions* (that involve a mix of 3D-printed elements and commercially available, pressure-bearing components (like receivers) specifically purchased for firearm construction. Regulations surrounding such 'kit' weapons vary by jurisdiction; some may require permits for specific parts, potentially rendering them legal.

Criminality is a highly infectious affliction, especially when the returns are overwhelmingly higher than the risks. What could be better for a criminal than a 3D printer and a freely available CAD file that produces a functional gun in a short time? For organized criminals, such as terrorists, emerging technology brings enormous power. The inaccessibility of such weapons is akin to the anonymity of the internet, which is highly valued by terrorists. A 3D printer is a dual-use technology that can be easily bought and installed legitimately, then used part-time for making weapons. Combined with the Dark Web and crypto currencies, there is a fertile market for such weapons, and the inherent anonymity between sellers and buyers ensures perfect cover from law enforcement. This is the new underground.

Conclusion

It would be unwise not to raise an alarm when technological capabilities risk being abused by malicious actors. However, it would be equally unwise to raise the alarm without suggesting potential solutions. Every technology, from the discovery of fire to the development of nuclear science, has been misused by malicious individuals. History is replete with instances where seemingly innocuous and benign technologies have wreaked havoc when placed in the wrong hands.

So, what should our approach be to address these growing concerns? While emerging technologies continue to amaze us with their diverse applications, their misuse poses serious threats. Optimism is valuable, but it must be tempered with rationality. Effective regulation is key to preventing abuse. Not everyone operates with good intentions, and regulatory oversight must involve experts from the corporate entities that develop and deploy such technologies. The responsibility for ensuring their safe and ethical use must be shared across stakeholders; government agencies alone cannot manage this burden, especially when public officials often lack a deep understanding of technologies they were not involved in creating.

To address this, cooperation between corporations and government regulators must be codified into the laws governing the use of emerging technologies. One approach is to ensure that every user is registered and that KYC norms are rigorously enforced. Freedom does not extend to harming others, and liberty cannot justify the acquisition of tools intended for malicious use. The use of emerging technologies should not be banned, but it must be placed under effective oversight to ensure they are used for benign purposes.

For instance, every UAV, 3D printer, and similar device should be required to transmit usage data to a central server monitored by AI-based algorithms designed to detect anomalies. If a significant deviation is detected, a human regulator can investigate further.

Ethical oversight communities, supported by joint public-private funding, can be established to monitor the use of emerging technologies within defined jurisdictions. These communities should be empowered with certain legal authorities, including the ability to subpoena and compel service providers to disclose relevant information. While pervasive surveillance is not the answer, much can be achieved by identifying and addressing anomalous behaviour before it leads to harm.

13

The Psychology of Fear: How Perception Shapes Our Understanding of Terrorism

"Facebook is only 13 years old, Twitter 11, and even Google is but 19. At this moment in the evolution of the auto industry, there were still no seat belts, airbags, emission controls, or mandatory crumple zones."

—**Zeynep Tufekci**, Internet Sociologist
(Discussing the need for social media companies to be responsible)

Public Opinion: The Silent Architect of Counter-terrorism Policy

'Terrorism', a word that evokes fear and outrage, is often shrouded in misunderstanding. Public discourse tends to focus on the violence itself, neglecting the complex motivations and contexts that fuel it. At the end of this book therefore, we are compelled to once again delve into the complex and expansive range of definitions that terrorism can evoke and how these are sometimes if not often, misinterpreted. Despite the expansive cornucopia of definitions and the legal certitude enshrined under various national and international legal instruments, there still appears to be a deficit of clarity regarding what terrorism truly is. This paradox in understanding leads to confusion and a failure to comprehend terrorism accurately.

The events of 9/11 sensationalized the entire spectrum of terrorism as a political instrument. Almost any act, violent or not, against the state is now termed terrorism. Even opinions against the actions of the state, which would not have raised eyebrows a few decades ago, are frequently labelled as 'terrorism' during TV debates, where anchors and 'experts' freely exchange heated barbs over seemingly innocuous political differences.

Beyond the Stereotypes: Understanding the Causes of Terrorism

One of the ways in which terrorism has been misunderstood is in its causal analysis. What causes terrorism to manifest in a polity? Is terrorism a disease akin to cancer, requiring radical surgery or at least a strong dose of concoction of severely deterrent laws that do more harm than good? Does socio-economic deprivation and grievances serve as strong correlation with incident of terrorist acts? These are some of the questions that become a bone of contention between scholars and laymen alike. Terrorism evokes strong emotions in almost everyone. Whether you are directly affected by it or not, there would be almost none who would not have an opinion about the concept. The opinions differ violently, as to the causes that led to terrorism as preferred choice of disgruntled and 'deprived' communities and groups.

Opinions abound, a fact that has become seemingly ubiquitous due to frequent outbursts on social media, where a virtual war of words breaks out as soon as a major terror incident takes place. The recent spate of terror attacks by Hamas on Israel has started another global war of words and opinions. Reason becomes the ultimate casualty, and the fact that the incident was unmistakably a terrorist act gets sidelined. Social media channels appear to have become echo chambers, where polarization becomes exponential and reasonable arguments are repressed by a barrage of hateful speech and counter-attacks on those speaking about facts and figures.

To imagine that policy making and resultant modulation in counter-terrorism efforts are untouched by what circulates on media channels in general, and social media in particular, would be naïve at best. Counter-terrorism policymakers face significant challenges due to the relentless barrage of negativity on social media. This pervasive negativity can undermine their efforts in several ways. Firstly, the spread of misinformation and sensationalist narratives can cause skewed public perception through 'echo chambers,' making it difficult for policymakers to take a definitive stance on issues concerning counter-terrorism.

War-mongering after every terrorist attack, wherein public discourse increasingly leads to recrimination and profound reverberations, especially when non-state actors from neighbouring states are involved, is a frequent phenomenon in India. Almost every terrorist attack emanating from Pakistan has led to heightened state of military tension between two nuclear powers significantly disturbing the fragile geopolitical scene in South Asia.

Such negativity and recrimination make it exceedingly difficult for policymakers to convey accurate information and gain public support for necessary measures, especially when these measures significantly differ from demands for going to war to annihilate the enemy in their stronghold. Understandably, the hostile environment on social media prevents such reasonable courses of action by putting increased pressure on policymakers to follow 'what the public wants,' prompting hasty or overly cautious decisions that may not align with the best strategic interests of the country.

Moreover, the polarization amplified by social media can foster an environment where nuanced discussions are stifled, as they might not be 'politically correct'—another term for the prevailing *zeitgeist* of social media discourse—hindering the development of comprehensive and effective counter-terrorism strategies. The constant influx of negative commentary can also demoralize those working in counter-terrorism, potentially affecting their morale and commitment to their work requiring critical thinking. The narrative is further complicated by the employment of counter-terrorism and security 'experts' by news channels, who are generally long-retired officials. These experts might lack relevant information but nevertheless bolster the recriminations pouring from the public.

In the wake of the Orlando nightclub shooting in June 2016, then U.S. President Barack Obama delivered a widely televised address that underscored the dangers of conflating terrorism with religion. Responding to political pressure from certain quarters demanding the use of the term 'Radical Islam,' Obama firmly rejected the notion that labelling terrorism with religious terminology would enhance national security. He questioned,

> *"What exactly would using this label accomplish? What exactly would it change? Would it make ISIL less committed to trying to kill Americans? Would it bring in more allies? Is there a military strategy that is served by this? The answer is none of the above."*[1]

Obama emphasized that using such phrases was a political distraction rather than a practical strategy. He reiterated that, throughout his presidency, his administration had never been hindered by not using the term '*Radical Islam.*' On the contrary, operational clarity remained intact, as illustrated by actions such as dismantling terrorist networks and the mission to eliminate Osama bin Laden. *"If there is anyone out there who thinks we are confused about who our enemies are, that would come as a surprise to the thousands of terrorists who have been taken out of the battlefield,"* he noted, emphasizing that intelligence and law enforcement professionals were not confused about the enemy's identity.[2]

Concluding his address, Obama warned against adopting language that serves terrorist narratives. He argued that groups such as ISIL and al-Qaeda aim to provoke a war between Islam and the West by falsely claiming to represent the global Muslim population. Using the phrase *"Radical Islam,"* he explained, would only validate extremist propaganda and alienate over a billion Muslims worldwide who reject such ideologies. *"There is no magic to the phrase 'Radical Islam'. It is a political talking point... and the reason I am careful about how I describe this threat has nothing to do with political correctness and everything to do with actually defeating extremism".*[3] His speech served as a critical reminder of the importance of precise language in counterterrorism discourse.

This televised address, available on YouTube, has attracted thousands of comments reflecting a deeply divided public. While some viewers supported President Obama's refusal to conflate Islam with terrorism, many criticized him harshly, accusing him of denial or political correctness. Some comments are emotional and derogatory, yet they offer insight into the public's mood. In the United States, where freedom of speech is a fiercely protected right, such platforms reveal a wide spectrum of perception and sentiment, often raw, conflicting, and uninhibited.

In the digital age, public sentiment can be gauged in real time, but this *immediacy* can also influence policymakers, sometimes subtly and unconsciously. Though online discourse may not instantly reshape counter-terrorism strategies, its cumulative impact over time cannot be ignored. No government can afford to remain out of step with prevailing public attitudes, especially when elections are just round the corner. While social media gives voice to diverse opinions, it also amplifies misinformation and emotional responses, often distorting the reality that policymakers must address.

Therefore, navigating the challenges of modern media ecosystems is critical. Policymakers must remain alert to the distortion risks posed by polarized narratives on cable and social media. Promoting media literacy and encouraging informed, critical engagement is key to resisting manipulation.

Public figures must approach social media with caution, resisting the temptation to treat it as a primary stage for political theatre. Instead of fuelling polarization through inflammatory posts or personal attacks, they should promote critical thinking and open, respectful dialogue. While sensational rhetoric may deliver quick political wins or viral moments, it ultimately weakens the foundations of cooperative governance—particularly in areas as vital as counter-terrorism.

Fragmented discourse hampers the ability to build cohesive strategies, erodes public trust, and distracts from evidence-based solutions. In contrast, a commitment to thoughtful, fact-driven engagement strengthens democratic values and supports the development of policies that are both effective and resilient. Leaders have a responsibility to rise above the noise, model integrity, and encourage a public culture where informed debate is valued over outrage. In doing so, they help foster a united front against threats like terrorism, one built not on fear or division, but on clarity, reason, and collective purpose.

How Bias Guides Notions About Terrorism

The events of 9/11 marked a turning point, transforming terrorism into a truly global threat. The West was forced to confront the dangers of viewing terrorism through narrow, localized lenses and treating it as a distant issue. The attacks were not random, they deliberately targeted iconic symbols of American power and Western dominance, underscoring the perpetrators' intent to strike at the core of U.S. influence. These calculated choices revealed not only tactical precision but also a deeper ideological message aimed at challenging American hegemony, particularly in the Middle East.

Terrorists seek attention, and few things provoke global alarm more effectively than the fear of violent, unexpected death. Their strategy is rooted in the psychological impact of their actions, designed to shock, instil fear, and command international focus. Despite the widespread public revulsion toward terrorism, some voices attempt to rationalize, or worse, glorify these acts under the pretext of addressing global socio-economic or political imbalances. Such narratives, while often couched in ideological critique, dangerously blur the lines between understanding real causes and excusing violence.

This tendency to romanticize or justify terrorism reflects a deeper challenge in the global discourse. Recognizing grievances without condoning violence is crucial. Terrorism must be unequivocally condemned, not only for its brutality but also for its deliberate manipulation of public fear and its exploitation of legitimate concerns to serve illegitimate ends.

The Dangers of False Moral Equivalence: How Terrorists Use 'Othering' to

Justify Violence

Despite widespread and principled condemnation of terrorism, certain dangerous and deceptive narratives continue to gain traction—narratives that attempt to justify or sanitize acts of terror by disguising them as forms of moral resistance. These narratives thrive by cloaking violence in the rhetoric of struggle, casting perpetrators as victims of an unjust system and framing their actions as desperate, even heroic, responses to oppression. Nowhere is this distortion more evident than in the case of Naxalism in India, where acts of terror are persistently rebranded under the romanticized notion of resistance against a so-called exploitative State.

Naxal groups, despite being responsible for decades of brutal violence, continue to rationalize their attacks on security personnel, civilians, and infrastructure as part of an ideological crusade against systemic inequality. Yet this justification ignores the significant welfare measures undertaken by the Indian state in tribal and underdeveloped regions—efforts aimed at inclusion, empowerment, and upliftment. By clinging to outdated Maoist dogma, these groups resist progress not in the name of justice, but to preserve a self-serving narrative that masks terrorism as revolution. In doing so, they reduce complex socio-political realities to a binary of victim and oppressor, conveniently casting themselves as the righteous few standing against tyranny.

Such narratives are not merely misguided; they are dangerously corrosive. They create a false moral equivalence between the legitimate, democratically accountable institutions of the State and the unlawful, violent methods of terror groups. In the process, they attempt to erode the public's ability to distinguish between justice and vengeance, between principled dissent and indiscriminate violence. These portrayals often hinge on tactics of 'othering'—dehumanizing state actors, law enforcement, or entire communities, rendering them faceless agents of oppression. This psychological manoeuvring enables terrorists to appear as underdog heroes in a distorted David-versus-Goliath frame, while victims of their violence are reduced to mere collateral in a supposed war for justice.

This romanticization of violence poses a grave threat not only to national security but also to the moral fabric of democratic societies. When terrorism is narrated as revolution, and death in counter-terror operations as martyrdom, society risks losing the moral clarity required to confront such threats decisively. Recognizing and rejecting these false equivalencies is not only a matter of security—it is a necessary act of intellectual and ethical integrity. Only by dismantling these deceptive narratives can we uphold the principles of justice, truth, and peace in the face of terror's seductive lies.

Take for instance the Israeli Defence Forces (IDF) and Hamas that operate on fundamentally different moral principles. The IDF seeks to minimize civilian casualties, while Hamas deliberately targets innocents and uses civilians as human shields. Hamas even celebrates the deaths of their own citizens to gain international sympathy and fuel anti-Israel sentiment. This contrast underscores a clear lack of moral equivalence between the two groups. By emphasizing this distorted view, such narratives attempt to equate terror with a state's efforts at self-preservation, subtly reframing violence as a justified response to perceived oppression.[4]

This manipulation of the narrative not only obscures the reality of terrorism's destruction, violence, and loss of innocent lives but also shifts the discourse. Instead of condemning atrocities, the focus becomes the supposed grievances of the perpetrators. These justifications weaken counterterrorism efforts and perpetuate a cycle of victimization and retaliation. Terrorist groups exploit these narratives to recruit, fuel violence, and sustain long-standing conflicts. Ultimately, this distorted moral framing undermines the international rule of law and efforts toward peace and justice.[5]

Poverty and Terrorism: A Complex Relationship

While it is almost a received wisdom that poverty and socio-economic disparities lead to terrorism, the evidence tells a more complex story. Socioeconomic hardship may create conditions that foster discontent, but it has no cause-effect relationship with radicalization. In reality, most terrorists come from middle or even upper-class backgrounds, suggesting that ideology, perceived political grievances, identity crises, and perceived injustice play a more important role. Poverty alone cannot explain the motivations behind terrorism. Oversimplifying this relationship risks misdiagnosing the real causes and misguiding policy responses. Effective counterterrorism strategies must look beyond economic conditions and address the deeper political, psychological, and social drivers that lead individuals down extremist paths. Understanding this complexity is essential to developing real, lasting solutions to global terrorism.[6]

Reducing poverty and addressing inequalities are important, but they are not solutions for terrorism. A comprehensive approach is needed, addressing ideological extremism, political grievances, and the resources available to terrorist groups especially through external state sponsorship.

Terrorist groups use poverty and inequality as tools to gain sympathy and justify their actions as anti-establishment responses to socio-political injustice. These organizations exploit social grievances to recruit and radicalize, distorting the realities of socioeconomic conditions to further their agendas.

The Limitations of Profiling and Stereotyping

The view that terrorism is driven solely by psychological factors or socioeconomic conditions is overly simplistic. While individual cases may show certain patterns, these should not form generalized theories of terrorism. Focusing on specific profiles can lead to confirmation bias, where evidence supporting preconceived notions is prioritized, obscuring the complex nature of terrorism and hindering effective counterterrorism efforts.

It is essential to avoid generalizations when analyzing terrorist behaviour. Each case should be examined on its own merits, considering ideological, personal, and socio-political factors. Terrorists are rarely irrational; while psychopathological symptoms are uncommon, they often exhibit dogmatism, helplessness, and excessive tendency to follow someone important. Some studies suggest terrorists share similar traits, but there is no definitive '*common personality profile*'.[7] Terrorists follow their own logic based on their ideology, but they are not irrational.[8]

Thus, when interested parties try to identify the causes of terrorism, they often end up justifying it by blaming the perceived flaws of a specific socio-political system. This is a classic case of justification by explanation, often favoured by 'public-spirited' individuals who aim to highlight societal flaws and incorrectly label them as *the* '*root causes*' of terrorism.

Deconstructing the Terrorism Narrative: Challenging 'Root Cause' Theories

Often, attributing terrorism primarily to socioeconomic factors is a simplistic generalization, and increasingly a fashionable one. While poverty, inequality, and political marginalization may create environments that facilitate radicalization, they are not definitive causes. Involvement in terrorist acts is not confined to the impoverished, history shows that an overwhelming variety from well-educated, privileged backgrounds also engage in terrorism. This highlights that radicalization stems from a mix of ideological, political, and personal factors, challenging the notion that economic hardship alone drives people toward extremist paths.

The common fallacy of equating correlation with causation leads to serious misunderstandings. Although certain social conditions may correlate with terrorism, proving a direct causal link is overly-simplistic and illusory. Psychological predispositions, ideological influences, and the availability of opportunity all play critical roles. Mistaking co-occurrence for causation is a recurring logical error.

Focusing exclusively on root causes can also distract from the urgent need to confront immediate threats. While addressing long-term grievances is important, effective counter terrorism must also prioritize the disruption and dismantling of active terrorist networks. A sound strategy requires tackling both prevention and enforcement in tandem.

Origins of Oppositional Violence

The link between state repression and terrorism is complex and often misunderstood. While the erosion of civil liberties and the rule of law can foster resentment, coercion alone does not predict oppositional violence. Historical patterns show that both repressive regimes and stable democracies often maintain relatively low levels of oppositional violence. A more decisive factor is state weakness. Fragile governments and power vacuums provide fertile ground for terrorist groups to emerge and operate, as seen with the Taliban's rise amid Afghanistan's political instability. Moreover, rapid modernization—particularly driven by sudden economic booms like resource discoveries—can fuel ideological terrorism by unsettling traditional norms and identities. However, this dynamic appears less relevant to ethno-nationalist terrorism, which often stems from distinct historical and territorial grievances.

Alienation of significant groups is also a strong indicator of terrorism driven by ethnic factors. In India, Khalistani terrorism peaked under the leadership of Bhindranwale, a figure who transformed from a religious preacher to a militant leader. However, these correlations are not causative. Terrorism arises from a variety of factors, and searching for definitive 'root causes' is largely futile. While a powerful cause may significantly influence terrorism, it cannot solely explain its emergence.

'Multidimensionality' bandwagon or Obfuscation?

Attributing terrorism to 'multidimensional' causes has become intellectually convenient, yet such broad categorizations often obscure more than they reveal. While it is true that terrorism arises from a complex interplay of factors, explaining it away citing 'multidimensionality' can and does hinder serious analysis by blurring distinctions between contributing conditions and actual causes. It is akin to explaining cancer solely through lifestyle without isolating the carcinogenic agent, misleading and incomplete.

One of the reasons for this obfuscatory tendency is the attempt to explain the causes of terrorism in universal terms, while barely understanding the unique context in which a particular terrorist ecosystem has emerged. While the causes that fuel terrorism in Kashmir differ from those that drive Naxal violence, the tendency to explain them through the vague notion of the 'multidimensionality' of socio-economic and political causes is a weak attempt that borders on intellectual dishonesty.

A more precise analogy is weather forecasting: we can observe patterns and contributing conditions, yet predicting exactly when and where it will rain remains difficult. Likewise, while we can identify social, political, economic, and psychological variables associated with terrorism, conflating correlation with causation leads to flawed conclusions. For example, poverty, repression, or modernization may correlate with terrorism in some contexts but not in others—each case must be unpacked with specificity.

The challenge lies not in acknowledging complexity but in resisting the temptation to hide behind it. A rigorous approach demands identifying proximate drivers, contextual triggers, and enabling conditions of each unique terror ecosystem, rather than invoking vague theoretical catchalls. Only then can we move toward policies and interventions grounded in evidence, not generalities.

Cognitive Bias and Misunderstanding Terrorism

Another significant bias is the unconscious sympathy toward terrorism. Actions such as sharing unverified content on social media creates fear, confusion, and distrust, indirectly supporting terrorist narratives aimed at destabilizing societies. Propagating hate speech or stereotyping groups can amplify extremist ideologies, foster division and enabling violence.

Even well-intended actions can support extremist causes. For example, amplifying extremist content on social media, even with criticism, increases its visibility and reach. Ignoring or trivializing the grievances of marginalized communities can fuel resentment, which extremist groups exploit for recruitment.

Terrorists operate in a marketplace of fear and violence, where biases shape public perceptions. In India, Naxalism has long portrayed its actions as a response to state corruption. However, the reality is that Naxals engage in extortion, denying essential services to vulnerable populations. The 'fight of the oppressed' narrative has lost its credibility as Naxal leaders are increasingly seen as opportunistic and violent. The hypocrisy of Naxals has become evident as they appeal to democratic principles only when pressure from security forces becomes unbearable.

How Emotions such as Motivations Sustain Terrorism

Motivation is a powerful psychological force. It not only predicts behaviour but also explains why harmful actions such as smoking or excessive drinking, persist. Beyond bad habits, long-term behaviours are often driven by core human motivations. According to McClelland's theory of needs, individuals are primarily motivated by achievement, power, and affiliation. Terrorist organizations exploit these basic drives to recruit and retain members.

Groups such as SIS have manipulated all three. They appeal to achievement by offering recruits meaningful roles and ideological 'success.' The need for affiliation is met through a sense of belonging and shared purpose within the group. Power is offered through promises of authority, control, and influence. These motivations form the psychological foundation of recruitment strategies.

Investigations into ISIS's social media campaigns show how their narratives glorified violence while offering connection and identity, filling emotional voids in potential recruits' lives. Initial contact was often made through mainstream social platforms. Then, 'like-minded' individuals—those sympathetic to ISIS's ideology—were funnelled into encrypted apps like Telegram and Threema for more private indoctrination.

Recruits were evaluated for ideological alignment. Dissent or diversity of thought was targeted and smoothed out to enforce groupthink and total subordination. ISIS exploited a key psychological tendency: humans are drawn to those who reflect their own beliefs. Those within the group were considered authentic and worthy; outsiders were branded as *Takfir* (unbelievers) and marked for elimination. By hijacking this basic cognitive bias of 'us vs them', ISIS built a brutal and fanatical movement driven by bloodshed and unwavering loyalty.

Countering Violent Extremism and Emotional Engagement

A sense of belonging is a powerful emotional force, rooted in the human need for affiliation. Social media's deep reach into people's lives gives expression to this inner drive to find personal meaning through connection. The field of Countering Violent Extremism (CVE), which aims to prevent radicalization, emphasizes replicating radicalization pathways in positive ways.

One early proponent of this view was Farah Pandith, the U.S. Special Representative for Muslim Communities. Hailing from Kashmir, Pandith witnessed the radicalization of youth firsthand. She argued that 'only peer-to-peer relations can change minds,' stressing that engaging youth emotionally through positive peer networks is more effective than top-down lectures.[9]

Recognizing social media as a key battleground against radicalization, Farah Pandith developed a grassroots digital strategy akin to forming a 'Dumbledore's Army' from Harry Potter. Her initiatives included the Online Civil Courage Initiative, which united over 100 anti-hate groups across Europe via Facebook; Generation Next, aimed at 'deprogramming' former jihadists by amplifying voices of those who rejected extremism; and Creative Minds for Social Good, which enlisted popular Middle Eastern influencers to promote interfaith dialogue and tolerance online. Together, these efforts emphasized prevention, rehabilitation, and community empowerment to counter extremist narratives and foster resilience in vulnerable digital spaces.

Countering the Venom: Positive Narratives vs. Radicalization

The work of Pandith and others underscores a crucial point: evil cannot be fought with evil. Instead, terrorist narratives must be countered with content that offers hope, authenticity, and community, while exposing the lies of extremist ideologies. Community engagement is key—classroom-style information delivery alone doesn't create the emotional resonance needed for lasting change.

Like affiliation, the needs for power and achievement are potent motivators. ISIS weaponized these, using imagery of fighters achieving 'victory' through battle and gore. These graphic depictions satisfied the need for achievement (via conquest) and power (via destruction). The portrayal of violence as a video-game-like experience drew in recruits by offering them purpose and excitement.

Negative content—especially fear, anger, and shock—goes viral faster than positive messages. This stems from our evolutionary wiring to detect threats (the fight-or-flight response). ISIS's early media campaign succeeded rapidly by exploiting this: videos of beheadings, mass killings, and brutal warfare provoked strong emotional reactions. This virality both shocked the public and fed a sense of power and purpose among potential recruits.

ISIS's strategy also created a vicious cycle: their violent content triggered anti-Muslim backlash, which was then used to fuel further anger among sympathizers, reinforcing their beliefs and drawing more into the fold through fear of missing out (FOMO).

Social Media's Shadow: The Psychology of Violent Extremism

Radicalization is often driven by emotions such as the need for significance, purpose, and belonging. People drawn to terrorism typically seek out like-minded networks that justify violence and offer a sense of identity. Even limited exposure to extremist content online can begin this process.

A powerful concept explaining this is 'identity fusion', a deep connection between the self and a group. When fused with a cause, individuals may go so far as to kill or die for it. Shared experiences amplify this sense of unity. For instance, Pakistani infiltrators involved in attacks in Kashmir often act despite evidence that such violence undermines regional development.[10]

Even a simple act such as 'liking' extremist content on social media platforms can trigger dopamine-opiate responses in the brain. While most who consume such material do not commit violence, a small fraction—perhaps just 0.01%—can be nudged into joining, funding, or otherwise aiding terrorist campaigns. That tiny fraction, in real numbers, is still substantial.[11]

The 'Lone Wolf' Enigma: Psychology of Solo Terrorists

'Lone-wolf' terrorists still remain an enduring puzzle for psychologists and counterterrorism experts. Unlike traditional recruits, 'lone wolves' appear disconnected from typical motivators like belonging or status. They operate without direct organizational support—even if ideologically aligned—and use basic means to attack, making their motivations harder to detect.

A landmark study by Ariel Merari and Boaz Ganor analyzed over 550 'lone-wolf' attacks by Palestinians in Israel (2015–2017), finding diverse motivations: humiliation, a desire for martyrdom, nationalist fervour, religious defence, or the need for validation. These were grouped into three categories—psychopathological, personal, and ideological. The diversity itself illustrates the difficulty of predicting 'lone-wolf' behaviour.[12]

'Lone-wolf' attacks result from a complex decision-making process. Multiple motives—psychological, personal, ideological—are weighed against internal inhibitions such as mental health, crisis-coping skills, and value systems. An attack becomes more likely when the force of motivations outweighs these inhibitions.[13]

The constant ideological incitement from groups like ISIS acts as an accelerant, fertilizing the soil for lone-wolf attacks. Their propaganda glorifies violence, feeds into suicidal or honour-based impulses, and exacerbates perceived injustices. These messages can be the tipping point that transforms isolated intent into action.[14]

Social Media: Propaganda's Perfect Playground

In a now-famous 2005 letter, Ayman al-Zawahiri, then al-Qaeda's deputy leader, acknowledged the critical role of media in their fight. He wrote, *"We are engaged in a battle, and more than half of it unfolds on the media battlefield."* This statement holds true even today, despite the seemingly independent reach of terrorism through the internet.

The so-called Islamic State (IS) stands as a prime example of this media savvy. They were arguably the first terrorist organization to claim dominance in both physical and digital territory. IS's mastery of social media was nothing short of ingenious. They created a virtual space where fighters and supporters could interact, seamlessly disseminating propaganda through over fifty online channels. This content, frequently 'liked' and shared, became viral with incredible speed.

Since then, the Internet has become a key battleground in the modern war of polarization. The 2024 Hamas-Israel conflict exemplifies this trend. Hamas and its supporters poured immense energy into shaping public opinion online, crafting narratives that justified their actions. Hamas sought to garner international sympathy by leveraging international organizations and highlighting the civilian death toll, which exceeded 22,000 in just two and a half months. This shift towards online warfare reflects a recognition by both sides that shaping the digital narrative can be as, if not more, impactful than traditional ground offensives.[15]

New Protestants?

Social media connectivity has fostered a unique flurry of new Protestantism, one that fuels vigorous and oftentimes vituperative protests, dissent, and social movements. This 'networked protest' phenomenon has created a unique digital realm that is distinctly different from traditional demonstrations. Unlike traditional forms of protest, social media provides ease and anonymity, which were sorely lacking earlier. Now, one can mount a 'protest' from the comfort of their home without the obvious danger of tear gas shells and batons from state law enforcement. Social media also empowers participation with lower barriers to entry – mobilization is streamlined, and citizen voices are readily amplified. Additionally, the internet never forgets, and it is extremely resistant to erasing dissent, much less suppressing it.

However, this ease of engagement comes at a cost. Social media can quickly devolve into an echo chamber of opinions, with facts often taking a backseat. Viral posts, regardless of their accuracy, become the foundation for narratives. Trending topics and 'likes' dictate the perceived truth, rather than objective reality. Consequently, online activism often prioritizes readily consumable content, even propaganda—over a nuanced portrayal of reality. Much of it can and does prove to be ready fuel for terrorist organizations to take advantage of. Naxalites, Hamas, and particularly Kashmiri separatists extensively use social media to garner public support by portraying legitimate counter-terrorism operations as 'oppression' by the state.

This online activism nevertheless empowers netizens (however naïve or misinformed) to actively engage with socio-political issues, even with the most bizarre content. They can take sides and express their viewpoints, fostering a collaborative accentuation of 'justification tactics' used by terrorist organizations through the dissemination of twisted and concocted propaganda inserted by terrorists. By leveraging the key advantages social networks hold over traditional media, gullible members of the public are used as fodder to fuel terrorist propaganda.

Social media activism offers an emotional outlet for those troubled by conflicts like the war in Israel and Gaza. It fosters a sense of agency, a feeling of contributing to a cause, even if the actual impact is limited. Platforms such as X (formerly Twitter), Instagram, YouTube, and TikTok prioritize engagement, keeping users glued to their screens. It does not matter if the narrative has any proximate relation to the realities on the ground. The only thing that matters is what most people are talking about. In other words, virality of content is prized rather than its reality. FOMO (fear of missing out) becomes a powerful device to fuel and sustain terrorist propaganda.

Terrorists have long realized that by weaponizing the power of social media they can damage counter-terrorism efforts (at least by maligning them by being violative of human rights) of their adversaries. This is often achieved by feeding ordinary public content that aligns with their concocted propaganda of 'oppression by the state' to triggers outrage. What starts as a counter terrorism operation quickly spirals into much despised activity in the name of violation of human rights. Extensive use of viral devices such as hashtag campaigns, graphic imagery and videos, fake news and misinformation, etc. are used frequently to malign state counter-terrorism efforts.

Naxalites in India often use this tactic whenever security forces mount offensives against their roaming bands of armed cadres. Their deaths in legitimate encounters are then portrayed as the 'killings' of 'innocent' civilians, notwithstanding the recovery of war-like stores and the fact that many in the security forces sustain injuries and long-term privation. Naxal propaganda often uses the supportive ecosystem of so-called civil society activists to instil inimical emotions against the law enforcement machinery. Extensive recriminative discourse on social media channels is then deployed to feed propaganda material, targeted at evoking sympathy. Many are sucked into the narrative of portraying the 'mighty state forces' killing 'innocent' tribals. Consequently, social media feeds become echo chambers, reinforcing existing biases and inflaming emotions rather than introducing new information.

Social Media Warfare: Propaganda in the Israel-Hamas Conflict

The dynamics of social media can be exploited by both sides of a conflict. While often used to disseminate propaganda, these platforms can also serve as tools for state security forces to shape public perception and counter misinformation. However, this dynamic has propensity to be increasingly harmful in a complex and emotionally charged conflict like the Israel-Hamas war, especially in the long-run.

Disinformation campaigns run by Russia, Iran, and China further complicate the situation. For instance, their state agencies have circulated false claims about Israeli bombings and U.S. involvement, despite denials from credible news sources. Social media struggles to handle complex issues effectively. The Israeli-Palestinian conflict, for example, is a political, historical, and moral labyrinth. However, the very nature of social media platforms, designed for brevity, virality, and engagement metrics like likes and shares, is fundamentally at odds with conveying such intricacies.[16]

Consider the common portrayal of Israel as a 'settler colonial' entity forcefully displacing an indigenous Palestinian population. While there may be some truth to this narrative, the reality is far more nuanced. The UN partition decision paved the way for Israel's founding, not a unilateral colonial imposition. Additionally, Jews possess an equally strong claim to indigenous status in the region. However, Israel does maintain settlements, widely regarded as illegal by international law experts, established after the 1967 war.

In essence, Israelis are not solely settlers or colonizers, but they do house settlements with settler populations in the West Bank. On the other hand, many communities within the artificially created Middle Eastern countries were forced to accede to rule under a particular autocratic ruler. These communities now face increased alienation. Middle Eastern countries such as Saudi Arabia, Yemen, Syria, Lebanon, and Qatar have consistent records of severe human rights abuses against their own citizens, which are largely absent from social media discourse, as dissent in any form is severely punished in such countries.[17]

Anti-Social Media: A Toxic Breeding Ground for Misinformation and Extremism?

Social media, instead of fostering critical analysis of complex issues, is optimized for short, catchy, and easily digestible messages. It often promotes a caricature of reality rather than encouraging reflection on historical and moral ambiguity. Here are two clear recommendations for those seeking informed engagement with any ongoing conflict: first, avoid social media as a primary news source. Second, de-emphasize social media activism. It is high time to realize the writing on the wall. These platforms prioritize profit over user education or meaningful activism. What matters is more likes, more subscribers and more advertisements.

Knowledge acquisition thrives on a diverse diet of credible and verified news sources. Effective political engagement requires interaction between real people in the real world, grounded in factual information. Unregulated anonymity breeds irresponsible behaviour. Social media can still play a role in directing users towards reliable news and coordinating real-world political action, but this is rarely the case. Just as junk food harms the body, junk information and hollow social media engagement erode the health of our socio-political discourse. The momentous political events of our time demand a deeper level of intellectual and political commitment.

The Internet is largely unregulated and unrestricted. While this lack of regulation should have allowed fearless yet informed discourse has now allowed terrorist groups and unscrupulous individuals to disseminate misinformation with minimal hindrance. Initially, the unregulated nature of the Internet was seen as an advantage, as social media discourse was hailed for promoting democratic values by encouraging free speech and fearless discussion on social, economic, and political subjects, giving space to the voice of the common individual.

The voices of previously 'ignored' individuals could be heard, and just like in electoral democracy, 'one person, one vote' became 'one person, one voice'. Unlike traditional media outlets where information is vetted, the internet facilitates the instantaneous spread of terrorist messages without any effective pre-screening process, which can mislead readers into believing the veracity of this unverified information.

Thus, slowly and steadily, misinformed and ill-informed opinions have gathered such momentum that sounding reasonable has increasingly fallen out of fashion. The ill-informed opinion, represented by vituperative discourse, became too overwhelming to counter by those who based their opinions solely on reason and knowledge. As a result, reasonable discourse has started receding into the background. Keyboard warriors who side with discourses favouring terrorist propaganda swing into action as soon as a sane voice disagrees with the toxic undercurrent.

Nowadays, any well-informed and knowledgeable individual hesitates to post their opinion on social media for fear of backlash from the vitriolic and toxic majority of social media users, whose only source of 'knowledge' appears to be half-cooked and propaganda-based information on social media. Resultantly, as most in the knowhow do not appear on social media discourse making it more ill-informed and increasingly toxic.

The proliferation of this toxic online environment has empowered terrorist organizations such as ISIS and Hamas to exploit propaganda. These terrorist groups leverage innovative techniques to cultivate favourable narratives and spread them virally. Conversely, voices critical of terrorism are drowned out by a relentless barrage of hate and accusations of bigotry from bots and sympathizers. Consequently, efforts to counter this constantly evolving propaganda face an uphill battle. Shutting down pro-ISIS social media accounts proves a futile exercise, as replacements spring up with alarming speed.

The Perfect Storm: Social Media, Encryption, and Terrorism

What makes the Internet, especially social media, so alluring for terrorist propaganda? The allure lies in the very architecture of the internet. It provides anonymity now supported by numerous encrypted protocols and virtual private networks, making it easy for anyone to operate without strict oversight. This anonymity empowers terrorists in multiple ways. It fosters a climate where support for violence is heightened, emboldening individuals since they cannot be easily traced, and allows terrorists to evade detection through numerous fake online identities. Unlike traditional communication methods like wiretapped phones, these online identities are almost impossible to trace. Tracing an actual identity from social media is a law enforcer's nightmare.[18]

Social media platforms exacerbate the problem further. Terrorists exploit algorithms by bombarding social media with propaganda and hashtags, manipulating search results and boosting their content's visibility. Groups such as ISIS and al-Qaeda have employed bots to automate this process. They tailored their propaganda to target specific individuals, particularly those with extremist leanings, fostering a sense of community and belonging among potential recruits. Additionally, social media allows terrorists to target vulnerable populations, such as teenagers, by portraying their ideology as a solution to personal problems. They can even block those deemed unsuitable, further solidifying their virtual community.

Encryption adds another layer of concern. Encrypted communication channels, increasingly common on websites and smartphones, allow terrorists to operate in secrecy, shielding recruitment efforts and other activities from law enforcement scrutiny. Popular encrypted messaging apps such as WhatsApp, Telegram, and Threema make interception even more challenging compared to platforms like Facebook or Twitter. Furthermore, encryption allows for the unrestricted sharing of extremist content that might be filtered out on other platforms due to its violent nature. Social media operators intensely value these encrypted protocols in the name of 'privacy' and 'freedom of speech,' but this can be seen as a clever device to provide a secret facility for communication while disregarding national security concerns. What is clear is that such facility is an ultimate selling point (USP) of these companies and they know that without encryption these platforms would be useless from marketing point of view.

This online clash of ideologies increasingly risks bleeding into real-world conflicts. Conversely, real-world conflicts morph into online warzones where sides vie for favourable public perception. Unwittingly, we are all soldiers in this digital arena where powerful players seek to control how we perceive the world, our preferences, and even our emotions on every issue. Social media, like it or not, has become an undeniable force in our public and private lives, a constant presence. Big Tech, the dominant players, are unlikely to be tamed in the coming days. Social media and the dominance of the BigTech, a double-edged sword, is here to stay.

BigTech's current approach, characterized by self-proclaimed neutrality and a culture of secrecy, is failing to adequately address this complex challenge. Embracing responsibility, fostering transparency, leveraging data for positive social impact, and actively utilizing AI are crucial steps towards a more proactive and effective approach to countering online terrorism. This fight cannot be waged by BigTech alone. Collaborative efforts with governments, civil society, and academia are essential to create a safer online environment for all.

Social Media and Terrorist Propaganda: Is BigTech Acting Responsibly?

It would be naïve to suggest that social media has not benefited mankind. Democracy has benefited immensely as those who did not have voice in the media controlled by the elites can now 'tweet' their grievances and those who consider it to be their powers to govern are bound to listen. It does not matter how powerful you are, surely you can't be powerful than the power of social media. Its meteoric rise has irrevocably altered the communication landscape, fostering unprecedented levels of connection and information dissemination.

However, as discussed, this very ubiquity has cast a dark shadow, as it is easy for terrorist organizations and malicious actors to exploit these platforms' reach and anonymity to disseminate propaganda, recruit followers, and incite violence. While BigTech appears to have enacted 'content moderation' protocols (another word for censor), it can be argued that it has not done enough since their platforms are being consistently used by non-state and state actors to spread propaganda and harm public interest in variety of ways.

The persistent proliferation of propaganda, orchestrated by both non-state actors and state entities like China and Russia, underscores the ongoing failures of social media giants to fulfil their responsibilities. Given these circumstances, an inescapable question emerges: Has Big Tech, the driving force behind these platforms, abdicated its moral duty in the face of this growing threat?

While it would be imprudent to view BigTech as an insidious force intent on destroying the social fabric or to endorse conspiracy theories suggesting such, it would be equally unwise to consider these companies infallible simply because they claim to uphold democratic values in their carefully crafted public statements. Despite their press briefings filled with lofty promises about free speech and privacy, their primary focus remains profit for shareholders and business protection. Despite their frequent proclamations of commitment to free speech, the reality is that adhering to laws and democratic values is seen as a cost by these companies.

Nevertheless, these companies must demonstrate a proactive and serious approach to consider the political, social, and moral implications of their services. Rather than reacting to crises like ISIS propaganda or foreign election interference, they must anticipate and address problems as they emerge. Facebook's role in the 2016 US presidential election highlighted the company's failure to act on internal warnings about hate speech, harassment, and external research indicating neo-Nazi trolling and Russian disinformation.[19]

There is a consistent tendency of the BigTech of oft-repeating its self-proclaimed stance of neutrality, portraying itself as a mere conduit for communication, devoid of influence on content. This assertion is demonstrably false and a mere garb to avoid costs, as both compliance to regulatory policies and vigilance would involve considerable expenditure. While 'content moderation' by algorithms does work to some extent, on the whole these algorithms, the invisible architects of online experience, curate content, may actively promote specific narratives while burying others. Targeted advertising further exacerbates this manipulation, creating personalized echo chambers that reinforce existing biases. Social media companies are not neutral bystanders; they are active participants in shaping the contours of online discourse.[20]

BigTech's content moderation algorithms, crafted to maximize user engagement, present a Faustian bargain. While they prioritize attention-grabbing content, this very strategy amplifies extremist messages, inadvertently nudging users down a path of radicalization. To counter this, BigTech needs a paradigm shift, acknowledging its role as a responsible steward of the online world.

This necessitates a complete revamp of content moderation strategies. The current, reactive approach relies on removing content only after it violates established rules. This reactive stance allows harmful narratives to flourish before intervention. BigTech must move towards proactive disruption of terrorist propaganda. This requires investment in a combination of human expertise and cutting-edge AI tools capable of nuanced content analysis. This would empower them to identify and neutralize threats before they have a chance to metastasize across the platform.

However, BigTech's culture of silence shrouds its decision-making process in a veil of secrecy, engendering public suspicion and distrust. The delayed acknowledgement of Russian interference in the US election exemplifies this concerning trend. This lack of transparency hinders public understanding of the challenges faced by platforms and impedes collaboration with governments and civil society.

Embracing transparency is paramount. Regular reports detailing content takedown statistics and the rationale behind them would foster public trust and facilitate a constructive dialogue. Establishing independent oversight mechanisms is also crucial for holding BigTech accountable. A regulatory body composed of government officials, technology experts, and civil society representatives could review content moderation policies and ensure compliance.[21]

BigTech: AI led Content Moderation

BigTech possesses a unique advantage in the fight against terrorism: an unparalleled trove of data. Through user activity, social media companies possess an intimate understanding of online communities and potential recruitment patterns. This data, when responsibly analysed, can be invaluable in identifying individuals susceptible to radicalization.

However, ethical concerns and a lack of transparency often surround BigTech's data utilization. To effectively thwart terrorist propaganda, a collaborative effort is essential. BigTech can share anonymized data insights with relevant authorities while ensuring robust privacy safeguards are in place. This collaboration can extend to crafting counter-narratives online. Using its advanced analytical capabilities, BigTech can identify emerging trends in terrorist propaganda and develop counter-narratives that resonate with target audiences. This proactive approach can dismantle the allure of extremist ideology before it takes root.

Social media is no longer a fledgling platform; it has matured significantly. BigTech boasts vast resources and cutting-edge Artificial Intelligence (AI) capabilities. It is high time these resources are actively deployed to combat the threat of online terrorism. AI can be a powerful weapon in identifying and removing terrorist content. Algorithms can be trained to recognize patterns in language, imagery, and user behaviour associated with extremist groups. This allows for faster and more comprehensive content takedown, reducing the reach of terrorist propaganda.

Furthermore, AI can be utilized to personalize counter-narratives. Algorithmic analysis can identify users at risk of radicalization and tailor messages that address their specific vulnerabilities. This personalized approach can be significantly more effective than generic counter-propaganda campaigns run by public agencies or largely government-funded programs. Social media giants must realize that research and development in their capabilities are not commensurate with their increasing responsibility to ensure that their platforms are not used for sinister purposes such as terrorism.[22]

On the question of responsibility, one can also argue that if people themselves are unwilling to contemplate the world around them in responsible ways, what can social media companies do about it? This argument perpetuates the old notion that victims are responsible for their own fate. It is easy to place the blame on the public for the ills that some are forced to endure. It is an old trick of fatalism to accuse the public by saying, 'they deserve it.' Such an argument fails to recognize that the public, as a body politic, chooses educated representatives, and a corporate body can ill afford to behave like a criminal syndicate bent on making profits regardless of societal and moral repercussions of their business models.

Seen in that light, social media companies have an added responsibility to ensure that their platforms not only stop terrorist propaganda effectively but also have enough safeguards to promote an environment of positivity and purposeful debate rather than acrimony and recrimination between communities. Censorship and curation go hand in hand. The veil of anonymity should not become an excuse to spread lies, recrimination, and propaganda on social media. It is high time that social media companies ensure that KYC and due diligence protocols are embedded in their services so that the identity of participants can be disclosed to law enforcement authorities, provided they are requested through a judicial order and not by ordinary executive fiat. On the other hand, they must disclose identities of subscribers who are consistent violators of their community guidelines and indulge in terror propaganda.

Freedom of Dangerous Speech?

The challenge of free speech takes a dangerous turn in the age of social media. We now face a new threat: 'dangerous speech'. Unlike everyday partisan bickering or isolated bigotry, dangerous speech is a calculated weapon. It emerges from studies on what fuels communal violence and takes the form of public pronouncements designed to incite hatred and violence, often against minorities.

Emerging from studies of triggers for communal violence, this term defines public pronouncements designed to incite hatred and violence, often against minorities. It would be naive to suggest that the display of openly communal remarks by hate-mongers is a new phenomenon. Earlier, such hate-mongering was, at best, confined to hushed circles, where voicing frustration was considered acceptable in small groups. What social media has enabled is the over-dissemination of such hate, which affects even those whose minds are otherwise free of prejudices and stereotypes. Our brains have a natural tendency to perceive threats from public discourse. Social media chatter of a communal nature invariably affects those who otherwise wouldn't subscribe to hateful notions.[23]

The Toxic Language of Hate

The insidious nature of hate speech often lies in its subtle and manipulative tactics. This toxic rhetoric typically manifests in five primary ways:

1. *Dehumanization:* This is the most fundamental tactic of hate speech. By stripping victims of their humanity, perpetrators make it easier to justify violence against them. This is often accomplished by comparing targeted groups to animals, insects, or diseases, or by using derogatory

and demeaning language. Such rhetoric fosters a climate of fear and hatred, making it easier for extremists to recruit followers.

2. *Coded Language:* Hate groups often employ coded language to spread their message without explicitly inciting violence. This involves using veiled references, inside jokes, or memes that only have meaning to those within the group. The intent is to create a sense of shared identity and purpose among followers while avoiding detection by law enforcement or social media platforms.
3. *Impunity Claims:* This tactic involves portraying the target group as a threat to society, often using exaggerated or false claims about their behaviour. By casting the target group as a danger, perpetrators can justify discrimination, harassment, or even violence against them. The message is clear: these individuals deserve to be punished for their alleged transgressions.
4. *Opportunistic Victimhood:* This manipulative tactic involves portraying the hate group as the actual victim. By falsely claiming to be oppressed or persecuted, perpetrators can garner sympathy and support for their cause. This strategy often involves accusing the target group of committing acts of violence or discrimination against them, thereby inverting the truth and deflecting blame.
5. *Accusatory Mirroring:* This technique involves projecting the hate group's own behaviours onto the target group. By accusing the target group of the same hateful acts, they themselves are committing, perpetrators can justify their own aggression while simultaneously discrediting their opponents. This tactic is often used to sow discord and division within the community.

These five tactics, when combined, create a potent and dangerous form of communication. When amplified by social media, this toxic rhetoric can rapidly spread, radicalizing individuals and fostering a climate of hate and intolerance. To effectively combat hate speech, it is essential to understand these tactics and to develop strategies to counter their impact.

Safeguarding a peaceful and inclusive society requires a concerted effort to identify, challenge, and dismantle the language of hate. This includes educating the public about the dangers of hate speech, supporting victims, and holding perpetrators accountable for their actions.

The Digital Horde: AI, Perception Control, and Mass Manipulation

The second decade of this century witnessed a dramatic shift. Social media, once seen as innocuous and entertaining, became a battleground for narratives and psychological warfare. Terrorist organizations, such as ISIS, exploited the power of social media with devastating effectiveness. Their content spread such terror that, in some instances, opposing security forces fled before even encountering them.

This tactic bears a chilling resemblance to the methods employed by Genghis Khan in the 13th century AD. He used brutal and extremely violent tactics to instil fear and break enemy morale. Massacres of entire populations, leaving no survivors, and the public display of severed heads served as a horrifying warning. This ruthless strategy shattered resistance and enabled the Mongols' swift conquest of vast territories. Genghis Khan's extreme brutality and public displays of violence were key to the Mongol domination of large swathes of the medieval world. Strategy of perception and propaganda wins by showing your size much bigger than it really is. Quite the similar strategy of extreme violence coupled with psychological warfare through social media was employed by ISIS.

The spectre of Genghis Khan, a symbol of brutal conquest, might seem an incongruous reference in the age of silicon and software. Yet, the parallels between his tactics and the potential misuse of artificial intelligence are chillingly apparent. Like the Mongol hordes, a digitally empowered terrorist group could amass an 'army' far greater than its physical manpower. AI could be the Khan, commanding a digital horde of bots, trolls, and deep fakes. Rather than bows and arrows, this new breed of conqueror would wield disinformation, cyber attacks, and psychological warfare.

The Mongol strategy of terrorizing populations into submission finds an eerie echo in the potential of AI to manipulate public opinion on a massive scale. By crafting hyper-targeted messages of fear, division, and hate, terrorists could sow chaos and destabilize societies from within. Moreover, AI-driven surveillance systems could be used to identify and intimidate potential opponents, creating a climate of fear and self-censorship.

The implications are profound. If not harnessed responsibly, AI could transform terrorism from a localized threat to a global, amorphous enemy.

The challenge for humanity is to ensure that this powerful tool is used for the betterment of society rather than its destruction.

Artificial Intelligence (AI) is a rapidly evolving digital frontier, capable of learning, adapting, and performing tasks once exclusive to humans. By ingesting vast quantities of data, AI systems can recognize patterns, understand language, and even simulate human thought processes. However, while AI excels in specific domains, it often lacks the common sense and intuition inherent to human intelligence.

Artificial Superintelligence: The Next Superpower Race

AI development primarily follows two paths: symbolic and connectionist. Symbolic AI relies on predefined rules, while connectionist AI, inspired by the human brain, learns from data through machine and deep learning. These approaches have given rise to different levels of AI: Narrow Intelligence (ANI), focused on specific tasks; General Intelligence (AGI), possessing human-like capabilities; and Artificial Super Intelligence (ASI), surpassing human intelligence altogether.

The prospect of ASI is both exhilarating and terrifying. While it holds the potential to solve humanity's greatest challenges, it also raises concerns about control, safety, and existential risk. A future where AI systems operate autonomously is not inconceivable, but it is essential to approach this reality with caution and foresight. Overblown apocalyptic narratives may be premature, but a sober assessment of potential risks is crucial as we navigate the uncharted waters of AI development.

There is no denying that terrorists have consistently exploited technological advancements to further their nefarious goals of sowing fear and terror. AI would be latest weapon in their arsenal, employed not only to propagate radical ideologies through propaganda but also to manipulate public opinion on a grand scale.

Generative AI, with its capacity to produce realistic yet fabricated content, has emerged as a potent tool for disinformation. Groups such as al-Qaeda, ISIS, and Hezbollah have already begun leveraging this technology to create deep fakes, manipulated videos, and emotionally charged narratives. By distorting reality and exploiting human emotions, these extremist organizations aim to erode trust in governments, incite violence, and recruit new followers.[24]

The integration of generative AI into terrorist propaganda is a game-changer. It would enable the rapid production of high-quality, emotionally resonant content that can spread like wildfire across social media platforms. This, in turn, makes it increasingly difficult to discern fact from fiction, hindering counter-terrorism efforts.

Moreover, the rise of AI-powered chatbots has transformed the landscape of terrorist recruitment. These automated systems can engage potential recruits in personalized conversations, mimicking human interaction to build rapport and trust. While initially, human recruiters might have played a more significant role, the emergence of advanced language models like ChatGPT has elevated the threat. These models can sustain extended, human-like interactions, making it easier for extremist groups to identify and groom vulnerable individuals.

Exploiting Young Minds: Perceptual Seeding and Gamification of Violence

Children are especially vulnerable to *perceptual seeding* (the ability of attacker to infuse thought patterns towards desired set of behaviours in their targets) and other propaganda tactics. AI can be exploited for desensitising children of strife ridden communities by accentuating '*us versus them*' mentality through cleaver use of videogames in which the opposing community is frequently killed as enemy. Terrorists have already used online gaming spaces to recruit, train, network, communicate, and spread terrorist messaging.

Gamification, a behavioural modification strategy which heavily borrows motivational techniques from games, is being used to drive engagement outside the gaming sphere. Online games foster individual and community connections through interactive play and real-time communication, often in anonymous settings, which may not develop otherwise. This environment, particularly for susceptible youth, can become a gateway to terrorist or extremist content through online gaming platforms and associated features like chat, re-sharing, and live streaming.[25]

Terrorist organizations are turning to the playbook of gamers to spread their message. This disturbing trend involves mimicking popular 'Let's Play' videos, where attackers livestream their atrocities like a video game play through. They incorporate elements of first-person shooter games, with live commentary using the same kind of language gamers use. This tactic appears to target specific online communities where gaming references and lingo are commonplace.

The strategy is not limited to a single ideology. Gamification techniques have proven to not only sustain user engagement but also enhance its enjoyment. Jihadist groups such as ISIS have also adopted gamification techniques. For instance, they created an app designed to indoctrinate children through games, and their propaganda videos often include footage from popular games or mimic the first-person perspective common in shooters. Understanding these gaming technologies empowers public safety officials to improve detection methods, outreach efforts within online communities, and training programs to identify, counter, and respond to potential terrorist attacks.[26]

AI applications using gamification have the potential to increase perceptual modification in young minds, leading to desensitization to violence and deriving pleasure from the suffering of others. The 'killer instinct' embedded in first-person shooter games is exploited by terrorist organizations to attract youngsters to their violent propaganda. Gamification offers psychological incentives to transition from the online world of video games to offline acts of violence, as exemplified by the Christchurch attack in 2019.[27]

All Is Not Lost: AI's Potential in Counter-terrorism

Conversely, AI holds significant untapped potential in counter-terrorism efforts. Advanced AI algorithms can analyse live feeds and online gaming to detect suspicious activities supporting terrorist propaganda, as well as messages promoting bigotry and foul language against other communities. These algorithms can also automatically identify and remove extremist content from online platforms, curbing the spread of terrorist propaganda. Additionally, they can support de-radicalization programs by identifying at-risk individuals and analysing their online behaviour.

AI is reshaping the fight against online terrorism propaganda. By sifting through vast amounts of data, AI can identify extremist content, from text and images to videos, flagging suspicious material for swift removal. It can also track user activity to pinpoint individuals vulnerable to radicalization efforts. Furthermore, AI's ability to understand language nuances helps detect propaganda that uses coded messages or tries to slip through content filters. Predictive analytics even allow authorities to anticipate where propaganda might appear next. Predictive analytics can be used to assess the behaviour of vulnerable communities to identify signs of radicalisation and intervene before such feelings of alienation and perceived injustice is further inflamed by terrorist propaganda.

Predictive analytics, programmed through machine learning, can alert authorities when social media and online discourse reach a critical threshold, prompting corrective measures. It can also predict potential terrorist activities by identifying suspected entities and assessing vulnerable behavioural patterns through data analysis and intelligence gathering. AI can integrate large datasets from various sources such as surveillance footage, digital platforms, and financial transactions, providing comprehensive insights from seemingly innocuous metadata. Critics may argue that this resembles an 'Orwellian State,' but the current technological capabilities already grant this power to Big Tech. The community, represented by the state, should prioritize using AI's predictive power for preventing violent acts over profit-driven private entities.[28]

AI's potential for good is undeniable, but its misuse by terrorist groups such as Hamas, ISIS, and al-Qaeda demands a united front. These organizations explore AI for propaganda and weaponization, making collaboration between policymakers, law enforcement, civil society, and BigTech crucial. Adaptability and vigilance are key to combating this evolving threat. By mitigating the risks of AI exploitation and empowering users to discern real from AI-generated content, we build a safer future. This requires robust regulations incorporating AI protocols for propaganda detection, alongside investment in AI attribution tools – all while safeguarding privacy and human rights.

Where Does All This Leave Us?

When thoughtful reflection follows the ingestion of good information and diverse viewpoints, even confusion can be a springboard for revelation and understanding. Understanding terrorism is a daunting task, even for someone who might claim to be an expert. Like any socio-political issue, there are as many versions as there are people describing them. In one way, this is good. Having only one opinion is totalitarian; having many is democratic. However, if there is one idea that I, as a writer, want the reader to carry, it is to always abhor and condemn violence in the name of settling scores against the civilian population.

Whatever the provocation, civilians should never be subjected to suffering simply because the attacker wants to make a statement. Regardless of the definition of the terrorism that one may subscribe to, human suffering is something one should never be a supporter of.

Terrorism, a scourge on humanity, has evolved in the digital age. No longer confined to physical battlefields, it now wages war in the minds of individuals through the manipulation of information. Social media and online platforms have become potent tools for terrorists to target, radicalize, and inspire violence. The once-distant echo chamber of extremist ideologies has transformed into a personalized assault, exploiting vulnerabilities and shaping perceptions with unprecedented precision.

We have seen how terrorist organizations such as ISIS and Hamas became experts in utilizing psychological warfare to gain support of the gullible over the internet. How manipulation of social media led to constant spate of recrimination against counter terrorism efforts. Emotional manipulation, especially through vivid imagery of victims paid rich dividend to their social media campaign and at least for ISIS it seemed that their strategy was winning.

Terrorist propaganda thrives in a world of confusion. It exploits fear, anger, and a sense of injustice to manipulate people into supporting violence. But we have the power to fight back. Critical thinking is our shield against these manipulative messages. Terrorist propaganda does not come screaming 'Join us!'. It often disguises itself as news, commentary, or religious teachings. It preys on our emotions, uses cherry-picked information, and paints a black-and-white picture of the world. Critical thinking equips us to identify biases as propaganda often presents one side of the story as absolute truth. We must critically look for and be aware of the loaded language, emotional appeals, and demonization of opposing viewpoints. We must question sources such as, who created this message? Are they credible? Are they affiliated with a known extremist group? We must research the source's background and intentions.

We must check facts; there is no need to take everything at face value. Whenever possible, verify information with independent, reputable sources, such as established news outlets or academic journals. Always look for evidence as propaganda uses dramatic claims without solid proof. Ask for evidence to support the claims. Are statistics manipulated? Are images taken out of context?

There is always a need to consider alternatives as propaganda thrives on polarity of limited view. We must constantly ask ourselves. Are there other explanations for events? Can a different solution be found? The dictum, that if something is too good to be true, it probably is, hold true especially in case of terrorist propaganda. Authorities and those that have influence among public due to their image (i.e. celebrities of every type) must make people aware of the pitfall of techniques terrorists use to spread their propaganda.

Some of these techniques we are aware of such as instilling us-vs-them mentality, tendency to show violence as the obvious remedy for political grievances (since the other side is using it why should not we?), conspiracy theories and misinterpreting religious text are frequently abused by terrorist organization to justify their acts of wanton killing of civilians.

We also share a significant responsibility when we habitually click the 'share' and 'like' buttons. Every share and like acts as an endorsement of the message it is attached to. We must become discerning consumers. Every school child should be educated on how to critically evaluate messages and content on social media. Instead of passively consuming information, children must learn how to avoid perpetuating harmful content. If you think a particular piece of content is harmful, report it immediately. Most social media platforms have built-in mechanisms for reporting harmful content. Rather than simply liking and inadvertently sharing these videos, young people must be made aware that their endorsement can perpetuate harm to others and ultimately to themselves.

Toxicity extends beyond its chemical definition and permeates the socio-cultural sphere. Bad news and negative content, unfortunately, often capture our attention more than positive news due to ingrained psychological mechanisms that prioritize information triggering survival instincts. This vulnerability is extensively exploited by organizations that thrive on fear. Terrorist organizations, for example, capitalize on fear within both their supporters and target populations. Our society needs to revitalize offline discourse, which has become increasingly rare.

Nowadays, children (and for that matter, even adults) spend more time online than engaged in face-to-face conversations. However, online interaction cannot replace the warmth and nuance of face-to-face communication. In person, messages cannot easily go viral, and people are generally more cautious about what they say due to the potential for immediate judgment. Authorities should explore ways to encourage mature and genuine debates among informed and reasonable individuals, with the potential for these discussions to then be disseminated on social media platforms.

No One is Entitled to Misinformed Opinions

Opinions matter, but not all opinions are created equal. Opinions based on misinformation and a sense of entitlement to facts without research are a dangerous luxury that can fracture society. It is not productive to be overly polite when faced with poorly informed opinions. These opinions, along with fake news and content that spreads hatred, need to be challenged and refuted. Privacy and freedom of speech cannot be used as excuses for spreading hate or supporting terrorism. Content that is harmful or promotes violence should be flagged, and its source identified for appropriate action.

Law enforcement and other authorities cannot be expected to control the menace of terrorist propaganda unless public supports their counter-propaganda efforts. While their role in dismantling terrorist networks and monitoring online activity is vital, it is insufficient. Effective counter-terrorism requires a powerful ally: the public. Public support for counter-propaganda efforts is crucial in weakening the allure of extremist messages and fostering resilience within communities.

The digital landscape presents a significant hurdle. Terrorist organizations exploit the anonymity and reach of the Internet to disseminate propaganda. Social media platforms, with their echo chambers and targeted algorithms, can amplify these messages, creating a virtual breeding ground for radicalization. Law enforcement's ability to proactively identify and remove this content is limited. Takedown efforts are often a game of whack-a-mole, with extremist groups quickly replacing removed content. Additionally, legal restrictions on freedom of speech further complicate content removal strategies.

This is where public awareness and engagement become crucial. Informed citizens equipped with critical thinking skills can become filters, identifying and deconstructing extremist narratives. Educational initiatives can help communities understand the tactics used in propaganda, such as emotional manipulation, dehumanization of the 'other,' and the distortion of facts. Initiatives that promote media literacy can empower individuals to discern truth from falsehood online.

Furthermore, fostering open dialogue within communities is essential. Public forums that address grievances and foster understanding can help counter extremist narratives that exploit feelings of alienation and disenfranchisement. These dialogues should involve religious leaders, educators, and community influencers who can build trust and provide credible alternative voices.

Public support goes beyond passive awareness. By actively reporting suspicious activity and potential radicalization to authorities, citizens become vital partners in early intervention. Initiatives that encourage this type of reporting, while safeguarding against racial or religious profiling, can disrupt the recruitment process before it progresses.

Perhaps most importantly, public support for counter-propaganda efforts requires a commitment to upholding the values that terrorists seek to destroy. Demonstrating tolerance, inclusivity, and respect for diversity undermines the extremist narrative that paints a polarized world of 'us' versus 'them.' Promoting social justice and addressing underlying grievances that fuel extremism can weaken its appeal.

Collaboration between authorities and the public can also leverage the power of storytelling. Counter-narratives shared by former extremists or family members of victims can have a profound impact. These stories humanize the cost of terrorism and expose the emptiness of extremist ideologies. Additionally, promoting positive narratives that highlight the strength of communities can inspire hope and a sense of belonging, countering the isolating tendencies of extremist ideologies.

Countering terrorist propaganda is a marathon, not a sprint. While law enforcement plays a critical role in dismantling terrorist networks, the battle for hearts and minds ultimately takes place within communities. By fostering a public empowered with critical thinking skills, engaged in open dialogue, and committed to the values of tolerance and social justice, we can build a strong wall of defence against the insidious threat of terrorist propaganda.

NOTES

Chapter 1: Terrorism: Past, Present, and Future

1 Bernard Lewis, *The Assassins: A Radical Sect in Islam*, Basic Books, 2002.

2 Gerard Chaliand and Arnaud Blin, *The History of Terrorism: From Antiquity to Al Qaeda*, University of California Press, 2007.

3 Dash, Mike, *Thug: The true story of India's murderous cult*, 2005.

4 'The History of Terrorism from Antiquity to Al Qaeda'.

5 'Monsters in the Dark: The Discovery of Thuggee and Demographic Knowledge in Colonial India', Palgrave Communications.

6 Philip F. McEldowney, *Pindari Society and the Establishment of British Paramountcy in India.*

7 Sister Nivedita was an Irish social worker, author, teacher, and a dedicated disciple of the renowned Indian spiritual leader, Swami Vivekananda. Born Margaret Elizabeth Noble, she adopted the name Nivedita, meaning "dedicated to God," upon her initiation into the vow of Brahmacharya (vow of lifelong celibacy) by Swami Vivekananda.

8 Rowlatt Report, Para 168: *Government of Bengal, Political Department, Memorandum on the History of Terrorism in Bengal, 1905-1933), West Bengal State Archives, Calcutta), appendix II*; *Report of Committee Appointed to Investigate Revolutionary Conspiracy in India* (London, 1918).

9 Sargon of Akkad (reigned c. 2334–2279 BCE) was a pioneering Mesopotamian king who founded the Akkadian Empire, united city-states, expanded his realm through military conquests, and established one of history's earliest empires.

10 A. Anter, *Max Weber's Theory of the Modern State: Origins, Structure and Significance*, Palgrave Macmillan, 2014.

11 Gérard Chaliand, *The History of Terrorism: From Antiquity to ISIS*, University of California Press, 2016.

12 Andreas Anter, *'Modern State and its Monopoly on Violence': The Oxford Handbook of Max Weber:* pp. 226–236, https://doi.org/10.1093/oxfordhb/9780190679545.013.13.

13 'Why Canada is becoming the focus of India's concerns about the Sikh separatist movement', *CBC News;* https://www.cbc.ca/news/world/canada-india-khalistan-sikh-separatism-1.6983554.

14 Rolph G. Carter, 'Leadership at Risk: The Perils of Unilateralism', *Political Science and Politics*, 2003.

15 A test propounded by Sir Alan Turing that proposed that a machine would be said to display intelligence when responses by it would not be detected to have come from a machine by an ordinary prudent observer.

16 'AI Drug Discovery Systems Might Be Repurposed to Make Chemical Weapons, Researchers Warn', https://www.scientificamerican.com/article/ai-drug-discovery-systems-might-be-repurposed-to-make-chemical-weapons-researchers-warn/.

Chapter 2: The Problem of Defining Terrorism: A Complex Web of Politics, Law, and Ethics

1 League of Nations Doc. 546(1). M.383.1937.V (1938).

2 Daniel Byman, *Deadly Connections: States that Sponsor Terrorism*, Cambridge University Press, 2007; Adèle C. Brown, 'Hard Cases Make Bad Laws: An Analysis of State-Sponsored Terrorism', *Journal of Armed Conflict Law*, Vol. 2, No. 2, Dec. 1997.

3 Jeremy Scahill, *Dirty Wars: The World is a Battlefield*, Bold Type Books, 2013; Matthew P. Taylor, *Pakistan's Kashmir Policy and Strategy Since 1947*, Naval Postgraduate School, 2004.

4 Myra Macdonald, *Defeat is an Orphan: How Pakistan Lost the Great South Asian War*, 2018.

5 'From Biodefence to Cancer Offence: The war on terrorism aids the war on cancer', Synthesis, a publication of UC Davis Cancer Centre, Vol. 7, No 1, 2004; Sui Huang, 'The war on cancer: Lessons from the war on terror', Institute for Systems Biology (ISB) Genomics Washington. https://providence.elsevierpure.com/en/publications/the-war-on-cancer-lessons-from-the-war-on-terror

6 Interlocutory Decision, 2011, para. 85.

7 Martin Scheinin, 'Report of the Special Rapporteur on the promotion and protection of human rights and fundamental freedoms while countering terrorism', A/61/267. https://ap.ohchr.org/documents/alldocs.aspx?doc_id=12600

8 Sir Arnold K., 'Terrorism and International Law: Cure the Underlying Problem, Not Just the Symptom', *Amet, Annual Survey of International & Comparative Law*, 2013.

9 'UNGA Resolution 49/60 Measures to eliminate international terrorism', https://www.legal-tools.org/doc/32083e/

10 'United Nations General Assembly Resolution: https://www.legal-tools.org/doc/32083e/pdf

11 Resolution 1566 (2004), Adopted by the Security Council at its 5053rd meeting, on, 8 October 2004: https://documents.un.org/doc/undoc/gen/n04/542/82/pdf/n0454282.pdf?token=MyOcZHrVfyFWOQmTgK&fe=true

12 Alex P. Schmid, 'Defining Terrorism', *International Centre for Counter-Terrorism Report*, March 2023, https://www.icct.nl/sites/default/files/2023-03/Schmidt%20-%20Defining%20Terrorism_1.pdf; Ben Saul, '*Defining Terrorism in International Law*': Oxford: Oxford University Press; Stella Margariti, '*Defining International Terrorism. Between State Sovereignty and Cosmopolitanism*. Berlin: Springer-Verlag

13 Ben Saul (ed), *Research Handbook on International Law and Terrorism*, Edward Elgar Publishing Ltd, 2020

14 Jean-Marc Sorel, 'Some Questions About the Definition of Terrorism and the Fight Against Its Financing', *EJIL*, 2003, Vol. 14, No. 2, 365-378.

15 Georges Abi-Saab, 'The Proper Role of International Law in Combating Terrorism', *Chinese Journal of International Law*, Volume 1, Issue 1, 2002, pp. 305–313, https://doi.org/10.1093/oxfordjournals.cjilaw.a000424

16 F Megret, 'The Politics of International Criminal Justice', *European Journal of International Law*, Volume 13, Issue 5, December 2002, pp. 1261–1284, https://doi.org/10.1093/ejil/13.5.1261

17 Alex Schmid, *Political Terrorism: A Research Guide to Concepts, Theories, Data Bases and Literature*, Transaction Publishers, 1983.

18 Walter Laqueur, *The Age of Terrorism*, Little Brown & Co, First Published 1987.

19 Bruce Hoffman, *Inside Terrorism*, Columbia University Press, 2006.

20 Carsten Bockstette, 'Taliban and Jihadist Terrorist Use of Strategic Communication', *The Quarterly Journal*, https://web.archive.org/web/20170812001116/http://connections-qj.org/system/files/08.3.01_Bockstette.pdf,

21 Max Abrahms, 'Lumpers versus Splitters: A Pivotal Battle in the Field of Terrorism Studies', 2010. https://www.cato-unbound.org/2010/02/10/max-abrahms/lumpers-versus-splitters-pivotal-battle-field-terrorism-studies/

22 Albert. J. Jongman, *Political Terrorism: A New Guide to Actors, Authors, Concepts, Data Bases, Theories, and Literature*, Transaction Publishers, 1988.

23. Article 1 of the Protocol Additional to the Geneva Conventions, Protection of Victims of Non-International Armed Conflicts (Additional Protocol II, which defines an armed conflict of a non-international character as an armed conflict: 'which takes place in the territory of a High Contracting Party between its armed forces and dissident armed forces or other organized armed groups, which under responsible command, exercise such control over a part of its territory as to enable them to carry out sustained and concerted military operations [....].

24 'A Definition of Terrorism in the Making: Balancing State Interest with Cosmopolitan Ideals', (Defining International Terrorism), *International Criminal Justice Series*, Volume 15, Edited by Stella Margariti, Springer Publication.

Chapter 3: The Invisible Enemy: The Rise of Cyber Terrorism

1 Timothy L. Thomas, 'Al Qaeda and the Internet: The Danger of 'Cyberplanning'', *Parameters*, Vol. 23, Issue 1 Dated: Spring 2003

2 Kyung-shick Choi, 'Spreading Propaganda in Cyberspace: Comparing Cyber-Resource Usage of Al Qaeda and ISIS', *International Journal of Cybersecurity Intelligence and Cybercrime*, 1 (1), 21-39. 2018.

3 William Gibson, *Neuromancer*; Barry C. Collin; *"Moonlight Maze" case; 1998 LTTE cyber-attack; Stuxnet; "OpIsrael"; Cyberterrorism and Cyberwarfare: The Basics*, Routledge.

4 The 'Guardians of Peace,' also known as the Lazarus Group or occasionally as the 'Who is Team', is a hacker collective reportedly tied to the North Korean government and has been linked to various cyber attacks since 2010.

5 https://www.bbc.com/news/articles/cz04m913m49o; https://www.ndtv.com/world-news/hezbollah-israel-war-soon-32-killed-as-walkie-talkies-pagers-explode-across-lebanon-6598300.

6 https://www.theguardian.com/world/2024/sep/17/hezbollah-pager-explosions-if-caused-by-the-mossad-would-be-a-big-escalation.

7 Jordan J. Plotnek, 'Cyber terrorism: A Homogenized Taxonomy and Definition', *Computers & Security*, Vol. 102, March, 2021.

8 Babak Akhgar (Ed.), *Cyber Crime and Cyber Terrorism: Investigator's Handbook*, Syngress, 2014.

9 Janczewski, L.J. and Colarik, A.M. (2008), 'Cyber Warfare and Cyber Terrorism', *IGI Global*, Hershey. https://doi.org/10.4018/978-1-59140-991-5.

10 Laura Mayer Lux, Defining Cyberterrorism, http://dx.doi.org/10.5354/0719-2584.2018.51028.

11 Maura Conway, 'Cyberterrorism', *Journal of Information Warfare*, Vol. 2, No. 2 (2003), pp. 33-42.

12 'Internet Usage Statistics in 2024', *Forbes*.

13 Maura Conway, 'Cyberterrorism: Media Myth or Clear and Present Danger?', *CORE*, https://core.ac.uk/reader/11308380.

14 Ibid.

15 Amanda Floyd, *Common Motivations and Personality Types of Cyber Terrorists*, Virginia Commonwealth University.

16 Dennis Broeders, 'Too Close for Comfort: Cyber Terrorism and Information Security across National Policies and International Diplomacy', *Studies in Conflict and Terrorism*, Vol. 46, Issue 12, 2023, https://doi.org/10.1080/1057610X.2021.1928887.

17 Godwin Udo, 'Analysis of the Growth of Security Breaches: A Multi-Growth Model Approach', *Issues in Information Systems*, Vol. 19, Issue 4, pp. 176-186, 2018.
18 'Alarming Cybersecurity Stats: What You Need to Know in 2024', *Forbes magazine*.
19 https://www.statista.com/statistics/379046/worldwide-retail-e-commerce-sales/.
20 Petra Bayerl, *Social media and its role for LEAs: Cyber Crime and Cyber Terrorism Investigator's Handbook* (pp. 197-220), December 2014: DOI:10.1016/B978-0-12-800743-3.00016-5.
21 Simon Kewin, 'Apple vs. Microsoft: The Innovation, The Power, The Epic Nerd Catfight!', Charlie Miller and Dion Blazakis, *iOS Hacker's Handbook, Apple Inc. (Big Business):* Marcia Amidon Lusted.
22 Babak Akhgar et al., *Cyber Crime and Cyber Terrorism Investigator's Handbook.*
23 '6 Medical Devices Hackers Like to Target and Why', https://www.globalsign.com/en/blog/medical-devices-hackers-target.
24 Priyanka Gandhi and Sonal Pawha, 'All India Institute of Medical Sciences (AIIMS), Delhi: Cyberattack Puts Digitalisation Under Scanner', *IMIB Journal of Innovation and Management*, 2024.
25 Nikita Malik, *Terror in the Dark: How Terrorists Use Encryption, the Darknet, and Cryptocurrency*, Centre for the Response to Radicalization and Terrorism, The Henry Jackson Society*)*.
26 Ibid.
27 Stéphane Coulondre, 'Bouncing Techniques': Encyclopaedia of Cyber-Warfare and Cyber-Terrorism', January, 2007.
28 Bennet Clifford and Helen Powell, 'Encrypted Extremism: Inside the English-Speaking Islamic State Ecosystem on Telegram', *Program on Extremism*, George Washington University, https://extremism.gwu.edu/sites/g/files/zaxdzs5746/files/EncryptedExtremism.pdf.
29 *The Dark Web: Breakthroughs in Research and Practice: Information Resources Management Association.*
30 Dr. Thomas J. Mowbray, *Cybersecurity: Managing Systems, Conducting Testing, and Investigating Intrusions.*
31 Matt Andrews, Lant Pritchett, Michael Woolcock, 'Looking like a state: The seduction of isomorphic mimicry', https://doi.org/10.1093/acprof:oso/9780198747482.003.0003.
32 Nicolas Myers, *Cyber Security: Cyber Crime, Attacks and Terrorism*, Old Dominion University.
33 'A Proposal for an International Convention to Regulate the Use of Information Systems in Armed Conflict, (2006) *47 Harvard International Law Journal.* 179; 'Why States Need an International Law for Information Operations' (2007) 11(4) *Lewis & Clark Law Review*, 1023.
34 James Crawford & John S. Bell, *Cyber Warfare and the Laws of War: Cambridge Studies in International & Comparative Law.*
35 Gabriel Weimann, 'Cyberterrorism: The Sum of All Fears?' *28, Studies in Conflict & Terrorism*, 2005.
36 *A list of Resolutions: 53/70 (1998), 54/49 (1999), 55/28 (2000), 56/19 (2001), 57/239 (2002), A/RES/77/298:, A/RES/77/36, A/77/37, A/77/512: (2022), A/RES/76/19: (2021), A/RES/75/240: (2020), A/RES/74/28; A/RES/74/29: (2019), A/RES/73/266; A/RES/73/27: (2018), A/C.1/72/L.44: (2017), A/RES/71/28: (2016), A/RES/70/237: (2015) and The 8th review of the UN's Global Counter-Terrorism Strategy, UNSC Resolution 2341: (2017).*
37 Agus Nilmada Azmi and Syarah Shabrina, 'Challenges of Universal Adoption of The Budapest Convention on Cybercrime', https://ejurnal.unisri.ac.id/index.php/proictss/article/view/10254/5431.
38 'Why the World Needs a New Cyber Treaty for Critical Infrastructure', https://carnegieendowment.org/research/2024/03/why-the-world-needs-a-new-cyber-treaty-for-critical-infrastructure?lang=en¢er=europe.

39 Jamal Awwad Alkharman, 'Cyberterrorism and Self-Defence in the Framework of International Law', *Journal of Law and Sustainable Development,* DOI: https://doi.org/10.55908/sdgs.v11i8.1430.

40 Peter Flemming & Michael Stohl, *Myths and Realities of Cyber terrorism, in Countering Terrorism Through International Cooperation:* Proceedings of the International Conference.

41 Cédric Dupont & Astrid Skjold, 'Coordination Conundrum in the United Nations Development System: Solutions from Self-Managed Organizations', *Global Perspectives,* University of California Press, December, 2022.

Chapter 4: Protecting the Skies: The Fight against Aviation Terrorism

1 S. Sugimori, 'The role of accident size in the risk-overestimation phenomenon', 1994 Oct. 65(4): 261-9. doi: 10.4992/jjpsy.65.261.

2 K.M. Sweet, *Aviation and Airport Security: Terrorism and Safety Concerns,* CRC Press Taylor & Francis, USA, 2009.

3 F. Robert Van der Linden & Victor J. Seely, 'The Boeing 247: The First Modern Airliner,' p. 83. By 2016, over 100 such attacks had been recorded, resulting in more than 2,500 deaths. (*Aviation Terrorism*', Jin-Tai Choi, pp. 7–8.

4 *India Today,* '1976 Hijack': https://www.indiatoday.in/...819368-2015-04-15.

5 *The Hindu,* https://www.thehindu.com/...62116028.ece.

6 *Indian Express,* https://indianexpress.com/...8071470.

7 *India Today,* https://www.indiatoday.in/...772191-2013-08-27.

8 *Economic Times,* https://economictimes.indiatimes.com/...53363184.cms.

9 *BBC,* https://www.bbc.com/news/uk-england-london-65430030.

10 Inshorts, https://inshorts.com/...1534524545424.

11 *India Times,* https://www.indiatimes.com/...342290.html.

12 *ASN,* https://asn.flightsafety.org/wikibase/325292.

13 *Indian Express,* https://indianexpress.com/...8879192.

14 'Reparation for Injuries Suffered in the Service of the United Nations', https://www.icj-cij.org/case/4.

15 'Convention on International Civil Aviation', https://www.icao.int/publications/documents/7300_orig.pdf.

16 M.E. Fingerman, 'Skyjacking and the Bonn Declaration of 1978 - Sanctions Applicable to Recalcitrant Nations', *California Western International Law Journal,* Vol. 10 Issue 1, Winter 1980, pp. 123-152; James J. Busuttil, 'The Bonn Declaration on International Terrorism: A Non-Binding International Agreement on Aircraft Hijacking', *International & Comparative Law Quarterly,* Vol. 31, Issue 3, July 1982, pp. 474–487.

17 P. Wilkinson & B.M. Jenkins, *Aviation Terrorism and Security,* Frank Cass, London 1999, pp. 11-16.

18 A. Merrari, 'Attacks on Civil Aviation: Trends and Lessons', https://doi.org/10.1080/09546559808427466.

19 Y. Kuriyama, 'Terrorism at Tel Aviv Airport and a 'New Left' Group in Japan', *Asian Survey,* Vol. 13, March 1973, pp. 336–346.

20 'Lockerbie bombing: The ultimate detective story?', https://www.bbc.com/news/uk-scotland-67659046.

21 Detlof von Winterfeldt, 'Should We Protect Commercial Airplanes Against Surface-to-Air Missile Attacks by Terrorists?', *Decision Analysis,* DOI:10.1287/deca.1060.0071.

22 'Defending Civilian Aircrafts from Surface-to-Air Missiles', https://www.airwaysmag.com/legacy-posts/defending-aircraft-sam-missiles.

23 'MANPADS: Combating the Threat to Global Aviation from Man-Portable Air Defence Systems', https://2009-2017.state.gov/t/pm/wra/c62623.htm.

24 Ruwantissa Abeyaratne, *The Illicit Transport of Narcotic Drugs by Air and Narco-terrorism, Aviation Security*, pp. 197–295.

25 J. Choi, *Aviation Terrorism: Historical Survey, Perspectives and Responses*, 1994.

26 Kathleen Sweet, *Aviation and Airport Security: Terrorism and Safety Concerns*, 2nd edn., CRC Press.

27 Pavel Pavlovich Hachikyan, *Countering Air Terrorism*, 2022.

28 'Oplan Bojinka Revisited: The Plot and Its Legacy', https://www.tsi-mag.com/oplan-bojinka-revisited-the-plot-and-its-legacy/.

29 Amy B. Zegart, 'September 11 and the Adaptation Failure of U.S. Intelligence Agencies', *International Security*, MIT Press, Vol. 29, No. 4, Spring 2005, pp. 78–111.

30 Tim Weiner, *Enemies: A History of the FBI.*

31 John David Blom, 'Unmanned Aerial Systems: A Historical Perspective', https://usacac.army.mil/sites/default/files/documents/cace/CSI/CSIPubs/OP37.pdf.

32 Jean-Paul Yaacoub et al., 'Security Analysis of Drone Systems: Attacks, Limitations, and Recommendations', https://doi.org/10.1016/j.iot.2020.100218.

33 Michael Gips, 'A Remote Threat,' *Security Management Online*, October 2002; Sue Mahan and Pamala L. Griset, *Terrorism in Perspective*, Sage Publications, 2008.

34 'Hamas's Cheap, Makeshift Drones Are Outsmarting Israel's High-Tech Military', https://www.bloomberg.com/news/articles/2023-12-19/israel-s-advanced-defenses-are-pierced-by-makeshift-hamas-drones-in-gaza-war.

35 Sameer Patil & Raj Arora, 'Countering Hostile Drone Activity on the India Pakistan Border', Issue Brief, Observer Research Foundation, May 2023, https://www.orfonline.org/public/uploads/posts/pdf/20240610194554.pdf.

36 'Drone Waypoint GPS Navigation Technology and Uses Explained', *DroneZon*, 24 November 2019.

37 Ian GR Shaw, *Predator Empire: Drone Warfare and Full Spectrum Dominance, 2016.*

38 'The Drone Market 2019-2024: 5 Things You Need to Know', *Drone Industry Insight*, 10 April 2019.

39 Robert J. Bunker, 'Terrorist and Insurgent Unmanned Aerial Vehicles: Use, Potential, and Military Implications', Strategic Studies Institute, U.S. Army War College, August 2015.

40 Ritu Sharma, 'Pakistan's "Drone Terrorism" Haunts Indian Border Forces; BSF to Get More Anti-Drone Units to Fight Cross-Border Menace', https://www.eurasiantimes.com/from-lahore-to-amritsar-with-drugs-and-arms-drones/#google_vignette.

41 Jeremy Scahill, *The Assassination Complex: Inside the Government's Secret Drone Warfare Program*, Simon & Schuster, 2017.

42 Medea Benjamin, *Drone Warfare: Killing by Remote Control, 2013*, Verso.

43 Judith Gardam, *Necessity, Proportionality and the Use of Force by States*, Cambridge University Press, 2004.

44 Jameel Jaffer & Amrit Singh, *The Drone Memos: Targeted Killing, Secrecy, and the Law.*

Chapter 5: Counter-Terrorism Legislation in India: Evolution, Issues, and Trends

1 Anil Kalhan et al., *Colonial Continuities: Human Rights, Terrorism, and Security Laws in India.*

2 K.P.S. Gill, 'The Imperatives of National Security Legislation in India', *SEMINAR*, Apr. 2002, http://www.india-seminar.com/2002/512/512%20k.p.s.%20gill.htm.

3 Shylashri Shankar, 'The Legal Framework of Preventive Detention and Anti-Terror Laws'

(Chapter 3), *Scaling Justice: India's Supreme Court, Social Rights and Civil Liberties*, https://doi.org/10.1093/acprof:oso/9780195693201.003.0003.

4 Ujjawal Kumar Singh, 'Mapping Anti-Terror Legal Regimes in India', *Global Anti-terrorism Law and Policy*, Cambridge University Press, 2012, https://doi.org/10.1017/CBO9781139043793.020.

5 *K. S.* Subramanian, 'Response: The Crisis of the IPS, Frontline', Feb. 2-15, 2002.

6 Arushi Sharma & Shivanshi Gupta, 'Origin of Police System in India and the World', *International Journal of Law Management & Humanities*, Vol. 5, Issue 2, 792.

7 Eklavya Vasudev, 'Citizens and the State: Policing, Impunity, and the Rule of Law in India', https://www.thehinducentre.com/incoming/citizens-and-the-state-policing-impunity-and-the-rule-of-law-in-india/article67887312.ece.

8 David Arnold, 'Police Power and the Demise of British Rule in India,' *Policing and Decolonization*, https://doi.org/10.7765/9781526123688.00009; David Anderson et al., *Policing and Decolonization: Politics, Nationalism, and the Police.*

9 V. Balachandran, *Keeping India Safe: The Dilemma of Internal Security*, Harper Collins, 2017.

10 David H. Bayley, *Preventive Detention in India: A Case Study in Democratic Social Control*, Publisher: K.L. Mukhopadhyay, 1962.

11 Anil Kalhan et al., 'Colonial Continuities: Human Rights, Terrorism, and Security Laws in India', *Columbia Journal of Asian Law*, https://www.nycbar.org/pdf/ABCNY_India_Report.pdf.

12 Ibid.

13 He was an Angami Naga who had served as a soldier in the Indian National Army (INA) founded by nationalist leader Subhash Chandra Bose.

14 Vivek Chadha (Editor), 'Armed Forces Special Powers Act: The Debate', *IDSA Monograph Series*, November, 2012.

15 https://www.amnesty.org/en/documents/ASA20/039/1994/en/.

16 Zaidi, S. Hussain (2002), *The True Story of the Bombay Bomb Blasts*. Penguin Books.

17 Law Commission of India, 173rd Report on Prevention of Terrorism Bill, 2000.

18 See POTA Sections 36-48.

19 People's Union for Civil Liberties (AIR 2004 SC 456).

20 A.G. Noorani, 'Repeal of POTA and UPA's Bill', *Economic and Political Weekly*, January 2005.

21 https://digiscr.sci.gov.in/view_judgment?id=Mjg4OTY=.

Chapter 6: Balancing Security and Justice: Procedural Aspects of Anti-Terror Laws

1 'Do not regard De-radicalization as a panacea' (source: https://www.ipinst.org/wp-content/uploads/publications/a_new_approach_epub.pdf), *deradicalization should not be seen as a universal solution.*

2 Emanuel Gross, 'Trying Terrorists - Justification for Differing Trial Rules: The Balance Between Security Considerations and Human Rights', Haifa University, Israel; 'Life Imitates Art on Secret Tribunals,' *New York Law Journal*, November 28, 2001.

3 'More Than 180 Convicts Sentenced to Death by Pakistan's Military Tribunals Since 2015', https://www.voanews.com/a/pakistan-miltary-tribunals/4303596.html.

4 Cynthia Fountaine, 'Complicity in the Perversion of Justice: The Role of Lawyers in Eroding the Rule of Law in the Third Reich', *St. Mary's Journal on Legal Malpractice & Ethics*, Vol. 10, No. 2, 2020.

5 Abdul Khader Kunju S., 'Investigation of UAPA Cases–Does the NIA Act Off end The Federal System?', https://prosecution.kerala.gov.in/images/pdf/20201_Crimes_P_105_HC_092806.pdf; https://lawandotherthings.com/examining-the-legality-of-the-nia-act/; https://

economictimes.indiatimes.com/news/politics-and-nation/nia-act-unconstitutional-repeal-it-congress-ruled-chhattisgarh-to-sc/articleshow/73280865.cms?from=mdr; https://www.humanrightsinitiative.org/programs/aj/police/india/police-reforms/issues_paper_on_the_national_investigation_agency_act_2008.pdf.

6 Vikas Katheria, *The Art of Scientific Criminal Investigation*, Mohan Law House, 2024.

7 Jimmy Gurule, 'Introduction: The Ancient Roots of Modern Forfeiture Law,' 21 J. Legis. 156 (1995). https://scholarship.law.nd.edu/law_faculty_scholarship/888.

8 M. Fourie, 'Tracing the Roots of Forfeiture and the Loss of Property in English and American Law': January 2017, *Fundamina* 23(1): 20-38, 23(1): 20-38, DOI:10.17159/2411-7870/2017/v23n1a2.

9 https://core.ac.uk/download/pdf/82825891.pdf; Jimmy Gurule, 'Introduction: The Ancient Roots of Modern Forfeiture Law', 21 J. Legis. 156 (1995).

10 'Impact Study on Civil Forfeiture': Council of Europe, 2013.

11 Simon Young, *Civil Forfeiture of Criminal Property: Legal Measures for Targeting the Proceeds of Crime*, University of Hong Kong, 2009.

12 Kristin M. Finklea, 'Organized Crime in the United States: Trends and Issues for Congress', Congressional Research Service, 2010, https://sgp.fas.org/crs/misc/R40525.pdf.

13 Soumya Awasthi, 'The Dark Web as Enabler of Terrorist Activities', Observer Research Foundation, https://www.orfonline.org/research/the-dark-web-as-enabler-of-terrorist-activities.

14 Shakir Mir, 'Will Critical Court Verdicts Stem the Misuse of PSA in Kashmir?', *The Quint*, https://www.thequint.com/opinion/will-critical-court-verdicts-stem-the-misuse-of-psa-in-kashmir; Dr. Gopal Krishan, 'Preventive Detention in India: A Legal Perspective', https://anvpublication.org/Journals/HTML_Papers/International%20Journal%20of%20Reviews%20and%20Research%20in%20Social%20Sciences__PID__2019-7-2-29.html.

15 Article 22(4) of the Constitution of India.

16 Durga Das Basu, *Shorter Constitution of India*, 16th Edition, Vol. I, p. 525.

17 *Maneka Gandhi vs. Union of India*, https://digiscr.sci.gov.in/view_judgment?id=NjE1MQ==.

18 *National Investigation Agency vs. Zahoor Ahmad Shah Watali:* https://digiscr.sci.gov.in/view_judgment?id=MTI3MDk=.

19 Jayanth K. Krishnan and C. Rajkumar, 'Delay in Process, Denial of Justice: The Jurisprudence and Empirics of Speedy Trials in Comparative Perspective', Maurer School of Law, Indiana University, 2011.

20 Shikha Pandey, 'Anti-Terrorism Courts and Procedural (In)Justice: The Case of the National Investigation Agency (NIA) Special Courts in South Chhattisgarh, India', *Socio-Legal Review*, Article 5, Vol. 16, Issue 1, 2022.

21 Manisha Sethi, 'Tenuous Legality: Tensions Within Anti-Terrorism Law in India', *Socio-Legal Review*, Vol. 13.

22 Shikha Pandey, 'Anti-Terrorism Courts and Procedural (In)Justice: The Case of the National Investigation Agency (NIA) Special Courts in South Chhattisgarh, India', *Socio-Legal Review*, Article 5, Vol. 16, Issue 1, 2022.

Chapter 7: Counter-Terrorism and Human Rights Law

1 Universal Declaration of Human Rights, Adopted and proclaimed by General Assembly resolution 217 A (III) of 10 December 1948.

2 Durga Das Basu, *Shorter Constitution of India*.

3 'Panel Faults C.I.A. Over Brutality and Deceit in Terrorism Interrogations', https://www.nytimes.com/2014/12/10/world/senate-intelligence-committee-cia-torture-report.html.

4 Christopher J. Einolf, 'The Fall and Rise of Torture: A Comparative and Historical Analysis', University of Virginia, https://www.asanet.org/wp-content/uploads/savvy/images/journals/docs/pdf/st/June07STFeature.pdf.

5 Upinder Singh, *Book 4*, *Kautilya's Arthashastra*, '*The state and violence: perspectives from ancient India*', '*Historians of Asia on Political Violence*', College de France.

6 Sadiq Reza, 'Torture and Islamic Law', *Chicago Journal of International Law*, January, 2007.

7 Robyn Wilson, 'Inside Cellular Jail: the horrors and torture inflicted by the Raj on India's political activists', https://www.independent.co.uk/news/long_reads/cellular-jail-india-integral-country-fight-freedom-independence-british-colony-andaman-and-nicobar-islands-port-blair-sushil-dasguputa-a7883691.html.

8 'Report of the Senate Select Committee on Intelligence Committee Study of the Central Intelligence Agency's Detention and Interrogation Program', https://www.intelligence.senate.gov/sites/default/files/documents/CRPT-113srpt288.pdf.

9 Mark Mazetti, 'Behind Clash Between C.I.A. and Congress, a Secret Report on Interrogations', https://www.nytimes.com/2014/03/08/us/politics/behind-clash-between-cia-and-congress-a-secret-report-on-interrogations.html.

10 Soshana Zuboff, 'The Age of Surveillance Capitalism: The Fight for a Human Future at the New Frontier of Power', *Public Affairs*, 2019.

11 Peter Königs, 'Government Surveillance, Privacy, and Legitimacy', *Philosophy and Technology*, Springer, Vol. 35, 2022.

12 'The Foundation of International Human Rights Law', https://www.un.org/en/about-us/udhr/foundation-of-international-human-rights-law#.

13 'International Legal Protection of Human Rights in Armed Conflict', by the Office of the United Nations High Commissioner for Human Rights in 2011 (New York and Geneva), p. 25.

14 Security Council Resolution 1621(2005), which deals with the protection of children in armed conflict.

15 UN Commission on Human Rights Resolution, 2005/80 (21 April 2005).

16 John Mukum Mbaku, 'African Courts and International Human Rights Law', *Brooklyn Journal of International Law*, Vol. 48, Issue 2, 2023.

17 Gentian Zyberi, 'The Role and Contribution of International Courts in Furthering Peace as an Essential Community Interest', *Promoting Peace Through International Law*, https://doi.org/10.1093/acprof:oso/9780198722731.003.0017.

18 Refer to UN Human Rights Committee, Lopez Burgos v Uruguay, https://juris.ohchr.org/casedetails/298/en-US; Israel facing responsibility for violations in occupied territory. *UN Human Rights Committee, Concluding Observations: Israel*, https://www.un.org/unispal/document/human-rights-committees-concluding-observations-on-fifth-periodic-report-of-israel-ccpr-c-isr-co-5-advance-unedited-version/

19 Ibid., Concluding observations on Germany.

20 Johan Steyn, *The International and Comparative Law Quarterly*, Vol. 53, No. 1, 2004.

21 Andrea Bianchi, *European Journal of International Law*, 2006.

22 Ben Saul, 'Terrorism in International and Regional Treaty Law', *Defining Terrorism in International Law*, Oxford Academic, 2008.

23 Gert Vermeulen & Wendy De Bondt: 'Finding the Right Balance between Effective Measures and Fundamental Human Rights Guarantees', *Dans Revue Internationale de droit Pénal 2008/* 3-4, Vol. 79, pp. 379-402.

24 Patrick F. Larue, 'Judicial Response to Counter Terrorism Law After 9/11', *Democracy and Security*, Vol. 13, 2008, No. 1, 71-95.

25 Shrushti Taori & Tatva Damania, 'Balancing Free Speech and National Security: A Critical

Analysis of Section 152 of the Bhartiya Nyaya Sanhita and Section 124-A of The IPC', *Usage of the Law of Sedition*, Report of the 22nd Law Commission of India, https://cdnbbsr.s3waas.gov.in/s3ca0daec69b5adc880fb464895726dbdf/uploads/2023/06/2023060150.pdf.

26 UN Global Counter-Terrorism Strategies of 2006, Global Counter-Terrorism Strategy, UN General Assembly Res 64/297, 13 October 2010.

27 'Obama Reluctant to Look Into Bush Programs', https://www.nytimes.com/2009/01/12/us/politics/12inquire.html.

28 'Law and Contemporary Problems,' p. 553, Gerhard von Glahn.

29 Laurent Richard & Sandrine Rigaud, *Pegasus: How a Spy in Your Pocket Threatens the End of Privacy, Dignity, and Democracy*: Henry Holt and Co, 2023.

30 'Bank Data is Sifted by U.S. in Secret to Block Terror': https://www.nytimes.com/2006/06/23/washington/23intel.html.

31 Sushana Zuboff, 'The Age of Surveillance Capitalism'.

32 Gautam Bhatia, 'State Surveillance and the Right to Privacy in India: A Constitutional Biography', *National Law School of India Review*, 2014.

33 Kamlesh Shekhar, 'The State of Surveillance in India: National Security at the Cost of Privacy?', Observer Research Foundation, https://www.orfonline.org/expert-speak/the-state-of-surveillance-in-india.

34 Gabriel Weimann, 'Going Dark: Terrorism on the Dark Web', *Studies in Conflict & Terrorism*, Vol. 39, No. 3 (2016): 195-205, https://doi.org/10.1080/1057610X.2015.1119546.

35 Soumya Awasthi, 'The Dark Web as Enabler of Terrorist Activities', https://www.orfonline.org/research/the-dark-web-as-enabler-of-terrorist-activities.

36 Anastasios Giannaros et al., 'Autonomous Vehicles: Sophisticated Attacks, Safety Issues, Challenges, Open Topics, Blockchain, and Future Directions', *J. Cybersecurity Priv.* 2023, 3(3), 493-543; https://doi.org/10.3390/jcp3030025.

37 Yasha Levine, 'Surveillance Valley: The Secret Military History of the Internet', *Public Affairs*, 2018.

38 Virginia Eubanks, 'Automating Inequality: How High-Tech Tools Profile, Police, and Punish the Poor', St. Martin's Press, 2019.

39 Henry Kissinger, Eric Schmidt, and Daniel Huttenlocher, *The Age of AI: And Our Human Future.*

40 David E. Sanger, *The Perfect Weapon: War, Sabotage, and Fear in the Cyber Age*; Bruce Schneier, *Data and Goliath: The Hidden Battles to Collect Your Data and Control Your World*; Shoshana Zuboff, *The Age of Surveillance Capitalism: The Fight for a Human Future at the New Frontier of Power.*

41 Kai Strittmatter, 'We Have Been Harmonized: Life in China's Surveillance State".

42 Paul Scharre, 'Army of None: Autonomous Weapons and the Future of War', WW Norton & Co. 2018.

43 Catarina Fontes et al., 'AI-powered Public Surveillance Systems: Why We (might) Need Them and How We Want Them', https://doi.org/10.1016/j.techsoc.2022.102137.

Chapter 8: Preparatory Acts of Terrorism, Prevention and Counter-Radicalisation

1 Arrya Gangopadhyay, 'Real time big data analytics for predicting terrorist incidents', IEEE, Symposium on Technologies for Homeland Security, 2016.

2 Tanya Mehra et al., 'Trends in the Return and Prosecution of ISIS Foreign Terrorist Fighters in the United States', *ICCT*, 2023, https://www.icct.nl/publication/trends-return-and-prosecution-isis-foreign-terrorist-fighters-united-states#.

3 Matthew Levitt (2015), *The ISIS Economy: War, Finance, and the Rise of a Terrorist State*; William C. Banks & Michael E. Smith (eds.) (2018), *Terrorist Financing: Law, Policy, and Practice*.

4 Joseph Menn (2016), *The Dark Web: Silk Roads, Cyberwarfare, and Scams in the Underground Economy*; Jessica Stern & J. M. Berger (2015), *ISIS: The State of Terror*.

5 Amoore & de Goede, *The State of Preemption: Managing Terrorism Risk Through Counter-Law* (2008).

6 Shylashri Shankar, 'Judicial Restraint in an Era of Terrorism: Prevention of Terrorism Cases and Minorities in India', NLIU, Bengaluru; Xingxing Wei, 'Rule of law or not? A critical evaluation of legal responses to cyber terrorism in the UK', *Computer Law & Security Review*, Vol. 53, July, 2024.

7 Ibid,, Amoore, 2008.

8 M.J. Borgers & E. van Sliedregt, 'The meaning of the precautionary principle for the assessment of criminal measures in the fight against terrorism', *Erasmus Law Review*, 2009.

9 McCullock et al., 'Pre-Crime and Counter-Terrorism: Imagining Future Crime in the War on Terror', *British Journal of Criminology*, 2009.

10 Robert M. Chesney, 'Beyond Conspiracy? Anticipatory Prosecution and the Challenge of Unaffiliated Terrorism', *Southern California Law Review*, 2007.

11 Bowling and Foster, *Policing and the Police: The Oxford Handbook of Criminology*, 2002.

12 'NIA's Terror Crackdown Scales New High in 2023'; *Jihadis, Terror Outfits-Gangsters Operating in Punjab & Naxals Take Brunt of Action*, https://nia.gov.in/writereaddata/Portal/News/1356_1_news.pdf.

13 Rune Ellefsen, 'Everyday Prevention of Radicalization: The Impacts of Family, Peer, and Police Intervention', *Studies in Conflict and Terrorism*, 2022, https://doi.org/10.1080/1057610X.2022.2037185.

14 Christian Leuprecht et al., *Containing the Narrative: Strategy and Tactics in Countering the Storyline of Global Jihad*, Taylor & Francis Online, 2010.

15 Adil Rasheed, *Countering the Radical Narrative*, 2020.

16 Max Erdemandi et al., *Assessing the Effectiveness of Programs to Prevent and Counter Violent Extremism*, 2024.

17 Eric Rosand, *Communities First*, 2016.

18 Etumnu & Williams-Etumnu, *Radicalisation and Extremism on Social Media: What Steps can be taken?*, 2023.

19 Aziz Z. Huq, 'Community-Led Counterterrorism', *Studies in Conflict & Terrorism*, Vol. 40, 2017 Issue 12, Communities and Counterterrorism.

20 Wesam Charkawi, 'Evaluations of countering violent extremism programs: Linking success to content, approach, setting, and participants', *International Journal of Law, Crime and Justice*, Vol. 77, June 2024, 100674.

21 Kaja Prislan et al., '*The Role of Civil Society and Communities in Countering Violent Extremism and Radicalisation*', https://hrcak.srce.hr/file/354347

22 Ibid.

23 Berger and Morgan, 'The ISIS Twitter Census: Defining and describing the population of ISIS supporters on Twitter', Brookings Analysis Paper, https://www.brookings.edu/wp-content/uploads/2016/06/isis_twitter_census_berger_morgan.pdf.

24 'Are Telegram and Signal Havens for Right-Wing Extremists?', https://foreignpolicy.com/2021/03/13/telegram-signal-apps-right-wing-extremism-islamic-state-terrorism-violence-europol-encrypted/.

25 'Paris attacks: Telegram acts after reports that ISIS using app for promotion', https://indianexpress.com/article/technology/tech-news-technology/paris-attacks-telegram-acts-after-reports-that-isis-using-app-for-promotion/.

26 Lauren Vogel, 'Why are doctors joining ISIS?', *CMAJ*. 2016 Feb. 16; 188(3): 177–178.doi: 10.1503/cmaj.109-5217.

27 Alvite Singh Ningthoujam, 'Islamic State of Iraq and Syria (ISIS) and its South Asian Connection: An Indian Perspective', https://www.vifindia.org/sites/default/files/islamic-state-of-iraq-and-syria-isis-and-its-south-asian-connection-an-indian-perspective.pdf.

28 'Hunt on for top ISIS tweeter who works for Bengaluru IT Company', https://timesofindia.indiatimes.com/india/hunt-on-for-top-isis-tweeter-who-works-for-bengaluru-it-company/articleshow/45499463.cms.

29 Shagun Jhaver et al., 'Evaluating the Effectiveness of Deplatforming as a Moderation Strategy on Twitter', *Proceedings of the ACM on Human-Computer Interaction*, Vol. 5, Issue CSCW2, Article No. 381, pp. 1–30, https://doi.org/10.1145/3479525.

30 Amin Mekacher et al., 'The systemic impact of deplatforming on social media', *PNAS Nexus*, Vol. 2, Issue 11, November 2023, https://doi.org/10.1093/pnasnexus/pgad346.

31 Amarasingam, 'Belonging is Just a Click Away: Extremism, radicalisation, and the role of online communities', *The Routledge Handbook on Radicalisation and Countering Radicalisation*.

32 Jhalak M. Kakkar et al., 'Safe Harbour & Content Moderation Regulation in India', *Defeating Disinformation: Advancing Inclusive Growth and Democracy through Global Digital Platform*, https://ccgdelhi.s3.ap-south-1.amazonaws.com/uploads/tufts-paper-454.pdf.

33 Rachel Griffin, 'Algorithmic Content Moderation Brings New Opportunities and Risks', Centre for International Governance Innovation: 2023, https://www.cigionline.org/articles/algorithmic-content-moderation-brings-new-opportunities-and-risks/.

34 Irene González, 'Evidence of Psychological Manipulation in the Process of Violent Radicalization: An Investigation of the 17-A Cell', *Front. Psychiatry*, February 2022, Vol. 13, 2022, https://doi.org/10.3389/fpsyt.2022.789051.

35 'The Nexus between Transnational Organized Crime and Terrorism in Latin America - June 2024', https://unicri.it/Pubblications/Nexus-Transnational-Organized-Crime-Terrorism-Latin-America.

36 Corneliu Bjola and James Pamment, *Countering Online Propaganda and Extremism: The Dark Side of Digital Diplomacy, Routledge New Diplomacy Studies*.

37 Marco Iansiti, Karim Lakhani, *Competing in the Age of AI: Strategy and Leadership When Algorithms and Networks Run the World*, Harvard Business Review Press, 2020.

38 The Best Evidence Rule requires that the original document or recording be produced in court to prove its contents, unless there is a valid reason for the original not to be available. This rule is designed to ensure the accuracy and reliability of evidence.

Chapter 9: The Poppy Fields of Terror: The Narco-Terrorism Threat

1 D. Boyce, 'Narco Terrorism', *FBI Law Enforcement Bulletin*, Vol. 56, No. 11, Special Issue, October 1987, pp. 24–27.

2 Emma Bjornehed, 'Narco-Terrorism: The Merger of the War on Drugs and the War on Terror', *Global Crime*, Vol. 6, Nos. 3 & 4, August–November 2004, pp. 305–324.

3 Ayjaz Wani & Samir Patel, *The Narcoterrorism Challenge to India's National Security*, Observer Research Foundation, https://www.orfonline.org/public/uploads/posts/pdf/20240728170202.pdf.

4 https://indianexpress.com/article/cities/ahmedabad/indian-navy-3300-kg-drugs-seized-gujarat-9185301/.

5 https://www.newindianexpress.com/nation/2023/Dec/30/gujarat-on-a-high-93k-kg-of-drugs-seized-in-5-yrs-no-of-addicts-19l-2646181.html.

6 https://www.thehindu.com/news/national/punjab/punjab-police-bust-international-drug-syndicate/article68121003.ece.

7 https://economictimes.indiatimes.com/news/india/dri-seizes-300-kg-cocaine-worth-rs-2000-crore-at-tuticorin-port-in-tamil-nadu/articleshow/82191478.cms?from=mdr.

8 https://timesofindia.indiatimes.com/city/mumbai/mumbai-police-busts-major-mdma-ecstasy-manufacturing-unit-in-nashik-seizes-drugs-worth-rs-267-crores/articleshow/104219307.cms.

9 Aijaz Wani, 'Pakistan Using Narco-Terrorism in Proxy War against India: Report', https://www.ndtv.com/india-news/pakistan-using-narco-terrorism-in-proxy-war-against-india-report-3305694.

10 Yashasvi Chandra, 'Illicit Drug Trafficking and Financing of Terrorism: The Case of Islamic State, Al Qaeda and their Affiliate Groups', https://idsa.in/system/files/jds/14-2-2020-illicit-drug-financing-of-terrorism-ychandra.pdf.

11 Jonas Hartelius, 'Narcoterrorism', https://www.files.ethz.ch/isn/90550/2008-02-20_Narcoterrorism.pdf.

12 Ehrenfeld R, *Narcoterrorism*, New York: Basic Books, 1990.

13 John Otis, 'FARC and Colombia's Illegal Drug Trade', Wilson Centre, Latin America Program, November 2014.

14 Douglass, J.D. (1990), *Red Cocaine: The Drugging of America*, Atlanta: Clarion House.

15 Daniel Valencia, 'The Evolving Dynamics of Terrorism: The Terrorist-Criminal Nexus of Hezbollah and The Los Zetas Drug Cartel', https://www.utep.edu/liberalarts/nssi/_files/docs/capstone%20projects1/valencia_evolving-dynamics-of-terrorism.pdf.

16 Thomas H. Johnson & Barry Scott Zellen, 'Gangs and Guerrillas: Ideas from Counter-insurgency and Counter-terrorism', 'Iron Triangle of Terror: Iran, Hezbollah, and Los Zetas?', *Analysis Intelligence.*

17 Rohan Gunaratna, 'Funding Terrorism in Southeast Asia: The Financial Network of Al Qaeda and Jemaah Islamiyah', National Bureau of Asian Research, University of California, 2003.

18 Jennifer M. McDowell, *The Terrorist-Criminal Nexus: An Alliance of International Drug Cartels, Organized Crime, and Terror Groups*, CRC Press, 2013; Louise I. Shelley, *Dirty Entanglements: Corruption, Crime, and Terrorism*, Cambridge University Press, 2014.

19 'Cartel-Related Violence in Mexico as Narco-Terrorism or Criminal Insurgency', *Perspectives on Terrorism*, August 2020, Vol. 14, No. 4, pp. 83-98.

20 Shelley, L.I. & Picarelli, J.T. 'Methods not motives: Implications of the convergence of international organized crime and terrorism', *Police Practice and Research*, 2002.

21 Colin P. Clarke & Chad C. Serena, *Terrorism, Inc.: The Financing of Terrorism, Insurgency, and Irregular Warfare*, Oxford University Press, 2015.

22 'Fourteen Drug Traffickers Arrested in "Operation Titan"', https://www.occrp.org/en/news/fourteen-drug-traffickers-arrested-in-operation-titan.

23 Terence Rosenthal, *Loz Zetas and Hezbollah, a Deadly Alliance of Terror and Vice.*

24 Jennifer Hesterman, *The Terrorist-Criminal Nexus: An Alliance of International Drug Cartels, Organized Crime, and Terror Groups*, Taylor & Francis, 2013; Zachary Abuza, 'Funding Terrorism in Southeast Asia: The Financial Network of Al Qaeda and Jemaah Islamiyah', NBR Analysis, Vol. 14, Issue 5, National Bureau of Asian Research, 2003.

25 Jennifer L. Hesterman, *The Terrorist-Criminal Nexus: An Alliance of International Drug Cartels, Organized Crime, and Terror Groups*, CRC Press, 2013.

26 Elijah Wald, *Narcocorrido: A Journey into the Music of Drugs, Guns, and Guerrillas*, Harper Perennial, 2002.

27 Ryan Rashotte, *Narco Cinema: Sex, Drugs, and Banda Music in Mexico's B-Filmography*, University of Arizona Press, 2019.

28 Anabel Hernandez, *Narcoland: The Mexican Drug Lords and Their Godfathers*, Verso, 2012.

29 Manjeet Sehgal, 'How Punjabi filmmakers are back to glorifying Khalistani terrorists,' Dailyo.in., Sept. 2015,

30 Michael Watson, Guns, Drugs, and Thugs: Smuggling in the Golden Crescent, *The International Affairs Review*, 2015, https://www.iar-gwu.org/print-archive/rd6yeppccpud0opgkamoq1uzjz5izy.

31 S. Sen, Heroin Trafficking in the Golden Triangle, *Police Journal*, Vol. 64, Issue 3, July-September 1991, pp. 241-248.

32 Charles H. Kennedy, *Pakistan's Drug Problem: Narcotics, Terrorism and the Limits of the State*, Routledge, 2013.

33 R.E. Kaslow, *Terrorism and Drug Trafficking: An Integrated Response*, Aspen Publishers, 2003; G.E. Rogers, *The New Heroin Chronicles: Narco-terrorism in Afghanistan, Pakistan, and the Taliban*, Praeger Publishing, 2011.

34 'Afghanistan's drug trade is booming under Taliban rule,' https://www.atlanticcouncil.org/blogs/southasiasource/afghanistans-drug-trade-is-booming-under-taliban-rule/.

35 Bruce Zagaris, 'Protecting the Rule of Law from Assault in the War Against Drugs and Narco-Terrorism': *Nova Law Review*, Vol. 15, Issue 2, 1991; Phil Williams & Dimitri Vlassis, 'Combating Transnational Crime: Concepts, Activities, and Responses', Routledge, 2013.

36 Ahmed Rashid, 'Descent into Chaos: The United States and the Failure of Nation Building in Pakistan, Afghanistan, and Central Asia'.

37 Prof. Dr. Gaurav Kataria and Madhvi Gautam 'Exploring Complex Dynamics of Narco-terrorism and its Impact on Human Rights in Indian Context'.

38 'US Congress Report on Pakistan's Politicians and Army's Link with Narco-terrorists' https://irp.fas.org/congress/1994_cr/h941003-terror-pak.htm.

39 Shuja Nawaz, 'Who Controls Pakistan's Security Forces?', United States Institute of Peace, https://www.usip.org/sites/default/files/SR%20297.pdf.

40 Aarish Ullah Khan, 'The Terrorist Threat and the Policy Response in Pakistan', SIPRI Policy Paper No. 11, Stockholm International Peace Research Institute: https://www.sipri.org/sites/default/files/files/PP/SIPRIPP11.pdf.

41 Droogan, J., 'The Perennial Problem of Terrorism and Political Violence in Pakistan', *Journal of Policing, Intelligence and Counter Terrorism* 13, 2018.

42 Murphy, E., *The Making of Terrorism in Pakistan: Historical and Social Roots of Extremism*, Routledge, 2012.

43 Hassan Abbas, *Pakistan's Drift into Extremism: Allah, the Army, and America's War on Terror*, M.E. Sharpe, 2005.

44 Louise I. Shelly, *Dark Commerce: How a New Illicit Economy is Threatening Our Future*, Princeton University Press, 2018; Jeffrey Robinson, *The Laundrymen: Inside the World's Third Largest Business*, Simon & Schuster, UK, 1998.

45 Anabel Hernandez, *Narcoland: The Mexican Drug Lords and Their Godfathers*; Peter Lilley, *Dirty Dealing: The Untold Truth About Global Money Laundering, International Crime and Terrorism*, Kogan Page Publishers, 2003.

46 Ayesha Siddiqa, *Military Inc.: Inside Pakistan's Military Economy*, Pluto Press, 2016.

47 Ahmad Rashid, *Taliban: Militant Islam, Oil and Fundamentalism in Central Asia*, Yale University Publication, 2010; Rohan Gunaratna, *Pakistan: Terrorism Ground Zero*, Reaktion Books, 2010,

48 Gretchen Peters & Thomas Dunne, *Seeds of Terror: How Heroin is Bankrolling the Taliban and Al Qaeda*, 2009.

49 Aneela Rashid, 'The Silent Killer: Booming Billion-Dollar Drug Trade in Pakistan', https://sputniknews.in/20230129/the-silent-killer-booming-billion-dollar-drug-trade-in-pakistan-683060.html.

50 Hein Kiessling, 'Faith, Unity, Discipline: The Inter-Services Intelligence of Pakistan,' C. Hurst & Co Publishers Ltd, 2016; Wadie E. Said, *Crimes of Terror: The Legal and Political Implications of Federal Terrorism Prosecutions*, Oxford University Press, 2015.

51 Hatice Çelik, 'Transformation in Indian Politics after the Pulwama Attack,' *Turkish Journal of Political Science*, Vol. 3, Issue 2, 2020.

52 'Enforcement Directorate finds significant cash pumped into real estate and movie production in Tamil Nadu', https://www.thehindu.com/news/national/drug-cartel-enforcement-directorate-finds-significant-cash-pumped-into-real-estate-and-movie-production-in-tamil-nadu/article68061323.ece; Kshitij Prabha, '*Narco-Terrorism and India's Security*': *Strategic Analysis, IDSA Journal*, https://ciaotest.cc.columbia.edu/olj/sa/sa_jan01prk01.html.

53 Ahmad Rashid, 'Taliban: Militant Islam, Oil and Fundamentalism in Central Asia', Yale University Press, 2010; Rohan Gunaratna, 'Pakistan: Terrorism Ground Zero,' Reaktion Books, 2010.

54 *The Hindu*, 'Enforcement Directorate finds significant cash pumped into real estate and movie production in Tamil Nadu', 13 April, 2014; Kshitij Prabha, 'Narco-Terrorism and India's Security', *Strategic Analysis, IDSA Journal*, https://ciaotest.cc.columbia.edu/olj/sa/sa_jan01prk01.html.

55 Peter Schwarz, 'Money launderers and tax havens: Two sides of the same coin?', *International Review of Law and Economics*, 31(1):37-47, DOI:10.1016/j.irle.2010.12.001.

56 Rachel Ehrenfeld, *Narco-Terrorism: How Governments Around the World Have Used the Drug Trade to Finance and Further Terrorist Activities*, 1992.

57 'Narco-terrorism: International Drug Trafficking and Terrorism: A Dangerous Mix', United States Congress Senate Committee on Judiciary, 2010.

58 Javier F. Pena & Steve Murphy, *Manhunters: How we Took Down Pablo Escobar*, St. Martin's Press.

59 'Dreamland: The True Tale of America's Opiate Epidemic', Sam Quinones, 2015.

60 Daniel Meierrieks, 'Bribes and Bombs: The Effect of Corruption on Terrorism', *American Political Science Review*, Cambridge University Press, 2024.

61 David Teiner, 'Cartel-Related Violence in Mexico as Narco-Terrorism or Criminal Insurgency', *Perspectives on Terrorism*, Vol. 14, No. 4, August 2020, pp. 83-98.

62 Press Release: 'Nicolás Maduro Moros and 14 Current and Former Venezuelan Officials Charged with Narco-Terrorism...', US DOJ, March 26, 2020.

63 https://www.ice.gov/news/releases/15-current-former-venezuelan-officials-charged-narco-terrorism-corruption-drug.

64 https://www.reuters.com/article/idUSKCN1SQ2H6/.

65 Gabriel Ferreyra, 'The Michoacanazo...', *Mexican Law Review*, Vol. 8, July–December 2015, pp. 3–31.

66 American Enterprise Institute, 'Kingpins and Corruption...', http://www.jstor.com/stable/resrep03288.6.

67 Tom Wainwright, 'Narconomics: How to Run a Drug Cartel,' *Public Affairs*, 2016; Jonathan V. Marshall, *The Lebanese Connection*, Stanford University Press, 2012.

Chapter 10: Cashing in on Chaos: The Business of Terror-Funding

1 Singh, Gargi A., *Terrorism Financing: Unravelling Complex Challenges and Crafting Solutions* (November 18, 2023). Available at SSRN, https://ssrn.com/abstract=4637129 or http://dx.doi.org/10.2139/ssrn.4637129.
2 https://www.fbi.gov/investigate/terrorism.
3 https://treaties.un.org/doc/db/terrorism/english-18-11.pdf.
4 Jae-myong Koh, *Suppressing Terrorist Financing and Money Laundering*, Springer, 2006.
5 Matthew Levitt, 'Charitable Organizations and Terrorist Financing: A War on Terror Status-Check', https://www.washingtoninstitute.org/policy-analysis/charitable-organizations-and-terrorist-financing-war-terror-status-check.
6 https://indianexpress.com/article/india/naga-militants-got-funds-from-state-depts-nia-4484611/; https://www.thehindu.com/news/national/In-Nagaland-govt.-wings-pay-%E2%80%98extortion-money%E2%80%99/article17195281.ece.
7 https://2009-2017.state.gov/r/pa/prs/ps/2010/11/151931.htm; https://scroll.in/latest/929346/pakistan-hafiz-saeed-among-jamaat-ud-dawa-leaders-booked-in-terror-financing-cases; https://www.businesstoday.in/pti-feed/story/ed-attaches-over-rs-70l-assets-in-delhi-linked-to-hafiz-saeed-pak-based-group-falah-e-insaniyat-194499-2019-05-02; https://www.thehindu.com/news/national/chargesheet-against-hafiz-saeed-others/article32746904.ece.
8 https://www.fatf-gafi.org/en/countries/black-and-grey-lists.html.
9 Timothy Wittig, *Understanding Terrorist Finance*, Palgrave Macmillan, 2011.
10 Gabriel Weimann, 'Terrorist Migration to the Dark Web', *Perspectives on Terrorism*, Vol. 10, No. 3, June 2016, pp. 40-44; Aditi Kumar & Eric Rosenbach, 'The Truth About Dark Web', https://www.imf.org/en/Publications/fandd/issues/2019/09/the-truth-about-the-dark-web-kumar.
11 Erica Simons, B.S., 'Faith, Fanaticism, and Fear: Aum Shinrikyo—The Birth and Death of a Terrorist Organization', *Forensic Examiner*, Vol. 15 Issue 1, Spring 2006, pp. 37-45.
12 Robert Jay Lifton, *Destroying the World to Save It: Aum Shinrikyo, Apocalyptic Violence, and the New Global Terrorism*, Picador, 2000.
13 Ian Reader, *Religious Violence in Contemporary Japan: The Case of Aum Shinrikyo*, Routledge, 2013.
14 David E. Kaplan, *The Cult at the End of the World: The Terrifying Story of the Aum Doomsday Cult, from the Subways of Tokyo to the Nuclear Arsenals of Russia*, Crown, 1996.
15 'Japan Software Suppliers Linked to Sect', *New York Times*, https://www.nytimes.com/2000/03/02/world/japan-software-suppliers-linked-to-sect.html.
16 Haruki Murakami, *Underground: The Tokyo Gas Attack and the Japanese Psyche*, 2001.
17 James Adams, *The Financing of Terror: How the Groups that are Terrorising the World get the Money to Do It*, 2017.
18 'Trading with the Enemy: Trade-Based Money Laundering is the Growth Industry in Terror Finance', Task Force to Investigate Terrorism Financing of the Committee on Financial Services U.S. House of Representatives, 2017.
19 Valeriia Dyntu & Oleg Dykyj, Cryptocurrency as an Instrument of Terrorist Financing, https://ideas.repec.org/a/bal/journl/2256-07422021758.html.
20 Jennifer L. Hesterman, *The Terrorist-Criminal Nexus: An Alliance of International Drug Cartels, Organized Crime, and Terror Groups*, CRC Press, 2013.
21 'Risk of terrorist abuse in non-profit organisations', https://www.fatf-gafi.org/en/publications/Methodsandtrends/Risk-terrorist-abuse-non-profits.html.

22 Shai Farber, 'Financial Extremism: The Dark Side of Crowd-funding and Terrorism', https://doi.org/10.1080/09546553.2024.2362665.

23 Ajit Lal, 'Fight against terrorism and terror financing', https://economictimes.indiatimes.com/news/defence/view-fight-against-terrorism-and-terror-financing/articleshow/95494654.cms?from=mdr.

24 S.K. Saini, 'Problems and Prospects of Combating Terrorist Financing', *Strategic Analysis*, Vol. 33, 2008.

25 S.K. Jha, 'Digital Jihad: Global Trends, Architecture and Footprints in Kashmir', Manekshaw Paper, No. 87, 2020, Centre for Land Warfare Studies.

26 N.S. Jamwal, 'Terrorist Financing and Support Structures in Jammu and Kashmir', *Strategic Analysis, IDSA*, Jan-March, 2002.

27 Abinav Pandya, *Terror Financing in Kashmir*, Routledge India, 2023.

28 Sushant Sareen & Gautam Chikermane, 'Canada's endorsement of terrorism will come back to haunt it', https://www.orfonline.org/expert-speak/canadas-endorsement-of-terrorism-will-come-back-to-haunt-it.

29 Syed Eesar Mehdi, 'The Complexity of Terror Financing in Kashmir: A Review', International Centre for Peace Studies, https://www.icpsnet.org/comments/The-Complexity-of-Terror-Financing-in-Kashmir.

30 Thomas J. Biersteker & Sue E. Eckert, *Countering the Financing of Terrorism*, Routledge Publication, 2007; Bill Scheppler, 'The USA Patriot Act: Anti-terror Legislation in Response to 9/11', The Library of American Laws and Legal Principles, 2005.

31 Smith, Cary Stacy, & Hung, Li-Ching, *The Patriot Act: Issues and Controversies*, Charles C. Thomas Pub. Ltd., 2010.

32 G. LaFree, *The Handbook of the Criminology of Terrorism*, Wiley Handbooks in Criminology and Criminal Justice, John Wiley & Sons Inc., 2016; 'International Standards on Combating Money Laundering and The Financing of Terrorism & Proliferation', FATF Recommendations, Adopted by FATF Plenary, 2012, updated in November 2023.

33 'High-Risk Jurisdictions subject to a Call for Action - June 2024', https://www.fatf-gafi.org/en/publications/High-risk-and-other-monitored-jurisdictions/Call-for-action-june-2024.html.

34 https://www.fatf-gafi.org/en/countries/black-and-grey-lists.html.

35 'Emerging Terrorist Financing Risks', FATF Publication, https://www.fatf-gafi.org/en/publications/Methodsandtrends/Emerging-terrorist-financing-risks.html#:

36 Sauradeep Bag, *The Use of AI in Arresting Financial Crime*, ORF Article, https://www.orfonline.org/research/the-use-of-ai-in-arresting-financial-crime.

37 Ibid.

38 Sabrina Leo, 'Distributed ledger technology and the future of finance: tracking innovation, regulation and inclusion', *Technology Analysis & Strategic Management*, 37:4, 369-372, DOI: 10.1080/09537325.2025.2464881.

39 'Opportunities and Challenges of New Technologies for AML/CFT,' FATF, July 2021.

40 Dylan Butts, 'Over 60% of illegal crypto activity is tied to sanctioned groups or terrorist organizations, report finds', https://www.cnbc.com/2024/02/29/sanctioned-and-terrorist-entities-receive-most-global-illicit-crypto.html.

41 Robert W. Balch, 'The Rise and Fall of Aryan Nations A Resource Mobilization Perspective', *Journal of Political & Military Sociology*, Vol. 34, No. 1, Summer 2006.

42 'New York Woman Gets 18 Years for Funding Terrorism With Cryptocurrency', https://www.nytimes.com/2024/04/30/nyregion/cryptocurrency-terrorism-victoria-jacobs.html.

43 Noragal Dasni & Lakmalee Hemchandra, 'What do We Know About Self-Finance Terrorism', *The Defence Horizon Journal*, September 2023.

44 'NIA Court Charges Kashmiri Separatist Asiya Andrabi, 8 Others With 'Inciting Mob, Conspiracy Against India', https://www.news18.com/news/india/nia-court-kashmiri-separatist-asiya-andrabi-inciting-mob-conspiracy-against-india-4305569.html.

45 'Understanding the abuse of crowd-funding for terrorism financing purposes', https://www.un.org/securitycouncil/ctc/news/understanding-abuse-crowdfunding-terrorism-financing-purposes.

Chapter 11: The Silent Arsenal: The Menace of CBRN Terror

1 Derrick Tin et al., 'A Descriptive Analysis of the Use of Chemical, Biological, Radiological, and Nuclear Weapons by Violent Non-State Actors and the Modern-Day Environment of Threat', *Prehospital Disaster Medicine*, June 2023, 2023; 38(3): 395–400, doi: 10.1017/S1049023X23000481.

2 Eric Croddy, Clarisa Perez-Armendariz & John Hart, *Chemical and Biological Warfare: A Comprehensive Survey for the Concerned Citizen*, Copernicus Books; Avery Goldstein & Edward D. Mansfield, 'The Nexus of Economics, Security, and International Relations in East Asia', *Stanford Security Studies*, Stanford University Press.

3 Binder, Markus K. & Gary A. Ackerman. (2023). 'CBRN Terrorism', *Oxford Research Encyclopaedia of International Studies* (February). https://doi.org/10.1093/acrefore/9780190846626.013.706.

4 Joseph McDade & David Franz, 'Bioterrorism as a Public Health Threat', *Emerging Infectious Diseases*, Special Issue, Vol. 4, No. 3, July–September 1998.

5 Bill Bryson, *In a Sunburnt Country/Down Under*, Black Swan; Andrea A. Nehorayoff, 'Aum Shinrikyo's Nuclear and Chemical Weapons Development Efforts', *Journal of Strategic Security*, Special Issue, Spring 2016: https://digitalcommons.usf.edu/cgi/viewcontent.cgi?article= 1510&context=jss.

6 Dominik Juling, *Future Bioterror and Biowarfare Threats for NATO's Armed Forces Until 2030*, Marine Corps University, https://doi.org/10.21140/mcuj.20231401005.

7 Leonard A. Cole, *The Anthrax Letters: A Medical Detective Story*, Joseph Henry Press, 2003.

8 Vesselin Nedkov, *57 Hours: A Survivor's Account of the Moscow Hostage Drama*, Penguin Global, 2004.

9 Sanjeev Kumar Shrivastav, Ricin-laced Letter to Obama; Recurring threat calls for long term solutions', *CBW Magazine*, Manohar Parrikar Institute for Defence Studies and Analysis. https://www.idsa.in/cbwmagazine/Ricin-lacedLettertoObama_SanjeevShrivastav.

10 Salama & Hansell, ACLU: https://www.aclu.org/wp-content/uploads/legal-documents/ACLURM002136.pdf.

11 'FBI Millennium Plot': https://www.fbi.gov/history/famous-cases/millennium-plot-ahmed-ressam.

12 Burke, *Foreign Policy*, 2004.

13 Hashim, *Naval War College Review*, 2001.

14 *DIA FOIA:* https://www.dia.mil/FOIA/FOIA-Electronic-Reading-Room/FileId/161443/

15 *Washington Post*, July 11, 2022: https://www.washingtonpost.com/national-security/2022/07/11/isis-chemical-biological-weapons/

16 *IHS Markit*, June 13, 2017.

17 'Senate Staff Report, 1995', https://irp.fas.org/congress/1995_rpt/aum/part04.htm.

18 'US Cost to the War in Afghanistan', Watson Institute, Brown University, https://

watson.brown.edu/costsofwar/figures/2021/human-and-budgetary-costs-date-us-war-afghanistan-2001-2022.

19 Tahir Mahmood Azad, 'Assessing the security of Pakistan's nuclear weapon programme', *Defence & Security Analysis*, Vol. 39, Issue 2, 2023, https://doi.org/10.1080/14751798.2023.2178069.

20 Shaun Gregory, 'Terrorist Tactics in Pakistan Threaten Nuclear Weapons Safety', *CTC Sentinel*, June 2011, Vol. 4, Issue 6, https://ctc.westpoint.edu/terrorist-tactics-in-pakistan-threaten-nuclear-weapons-safety/

21 Qasim Nauman, 'Militants Attack Major Pakistan Air Base; Nine killed', *Reuters*, August 17, 2012 https://www.reuters.com/article/idUSBRE87E1C7.

22 'Pakistan Air Force foils terror attack at Mianwali Air Base', https://www.thehindu.com/news/international/pakistan-air-force-foils-terror-attack-at-mianwali-air-base/article67496605.ece.

23 https://www.brookings.edu/articles/the-agonizing-problem-of-pakistans-nukes/; Albright, D. (2001). *Securing Pakistan's Nuclear Weapons Complex*, http://www.isis-online.org/publications/terrorism/stanleypaper.html; Grossman, E.M. (2011) 'Mullen: Pakistani nuclear controls should avert any insider threat,' *Global Security Newswire*, 8 July. http://www.nti.org/gsn/article/mullen-pakistani-nuclear-controls-should-avert-anyinsider-threat; International Institute for Strategic Studies (2007), *Nuclear Black Markets: Pakistan, A.Q. Khan and the Rise of Proliferation Networks*, London: IISS; Wonacott P. (2007), 'Inside Pakistan's Drive to Guard Its A-bombs', *Wall Street Journal*, 29 November. http://www.wsj.com/public/article/SB119629674095207239.html.

24 Gregory D. Koblentz, *"Emerging Technologies and the Future of CBRN Terrorism," The Washington Quarterly*, Published online: 16 June 2020.

25 Anthony Tu, *Chemical and Biological Weapons and Terrorism*, CRC Press, 2018.

26 Gary A. Ackerman & Lauren E. Pinson, *An Army of One: Assessing CBRN Pursuit and Use by Lone Wolves and Autonomous Cells*, Terrorism and Political Violence, Published Online: 20 Dec 2013.

27 Walter Laqueur, *The New Terrorism: Fanaticism and the Arms of Mass Destruction*, Oxford University Press, 1999.

28 Daniel Byman & Sarah E. Kreps, 'Agents of Destruction? Applying Principal-Agent Analysis to State-Sponsored Terrorism', *International Studies Perspectives*, Vol. 11, No. 1, Oxford University Press, Feb. 2010, pp. 1–18.

29 A.T. Nizami et al., 'Terrorism in Pakistan: the psychosocial context and why it matters', *BJPsych Int.* 2018 Feb, 15(1): 20–22. doi: 10.1192/bji.2017.9.

30 Alexander Kelle, 'The CWC at 25: from verification of chemical-weapons destruction to attribution of their use', https://www.tandfonline.com/doi/full/10.1080/10736700.2023.2180234.

31 'Convention on the Prohibition of the Development, Production and Stockpiling of Bacteriological (Biological) and Toxin Weapons and on their Destruction', 10 April 1972: https://www.un.org/en/genocideprevention/documents/atrocity-crimes/Doc.37_conv%20biolo gical%20weapons.pdf

32 Susan J. Koch, *Proliferation Security Initiative: Origins and Evolution, Centre for the Study of Weapons of Mass Destruction*, National Defence University, https://wmdcenter.ndu.edu/Portals/97/Documents/Publications/Occasional%20Papers/09_Proliferation%20Security%20Initiative.pdf.

33 Walter Isaacson, *The Code Breakers; Jennifer Doudna, Gene Editing, and the Future of the Human Race*, 2021.

34 Nicholas Winstead, 'The Applications and Implications of Nanotechnology', *Security, Innovation and New Technology*, American University, 2020.

35 Kerry Shavez, 'Off the Shelf: The Violent Nonstate Actor Drone Threat', *Air and Space Power Journal*, Fall 2020.

Chapter 12: The Digital Caliphate: Emerging Tech and the Terrorist Nexus

1 Lubna Luxmi Dhirani et al., 'Ethical Dilemmas and Privacy Issues in Emerging Technologies: A Review', *Sensors* (Open Access), 2023.

2 https://www.business-standard.com/india-news/nia-files-charge-sheet-in-cross-border-arms-smuggling-case-in-punjab-123111200375_1.html.

3 'Russia says it killed rebels behind swarm drone attack in Syria, but experts see more such strikes ahead', https://www.cnbc.com/2018/01/12/russia-says-it-eliminated-rebels-behind-swarm-drone-attack-in-syria.html.

4 Thomas G. Pledger, 'The Role of Drones in Future Terrorist Attacks', *Land Warfare, Paper* 137, 2021, The Association of the United States Army.

5 Mikhail Zelenkov et al., 'Maritime terrorism as a threat to confidence in water transport and logistics systems', *X International Scientific Siberian Transport Forum*, ScienceDirect Publication: 2022.

6 Sameer Patil & Zachary Kallenborn, 'Indian drones prepare for flight', https://www.gatewayhouse.in/indian-drones-prepare-for-flight/.

7 Tamraparni Dasu et al., 'Geo-fences in the Sky: Herding Drones with Blockchains and 5G', 26th ACM SIGSPATIAL International Conference on Advances in Geographic Information Systems, DOI:10.1145/3274895.3274914.

8 Arushi Singh, 'Future Counter-measures for Drones and Drone Swarms: India as a Case in Point', https://cove.army.gov.au/article/future-countermeasures-drones.

9 '"Kamikaze pigeons" trained to intercept suspicious drones amid warnings of deepening UAV terror threat', https://inews.co.uk/news/long-reads/kamikaze-pigeons-trained-us-intercept-suspicious-drones-uav-threat-warning-1204561.

10 Margaret E. Kosal, 'Emerging Life Sciences and Possible Threats to International Security', *Orbis*. 2020; 64(4): 599–614 (Published 2020): doi: 10.1016/j.orbis.2020.08.008.

11 Ibid.

12 J. Kenneth Wickiser et al., 'Engineered Pathogens and Unnatural Biological Weapons: The Future Threat of Synthetic Biology', Combating Terrorism Centre at West Point, Vol. 13, Issue 8, August, 2020.

13 Anders Melin, 'Overstatements and Understatements in the Debate on Synthetic Biology, Bioterrorism and Ethics', 2021: https://www.frontiersin.org/journals/bioengineering-and-biotechnology/articles/10.3389/fbioe.2021.703735/full.

14 Fabio Urbina, 'Dual Use of Artificial Intelligence-powered Drug Discovery', https://www.ncbi.nlm.nih.gov/pmc/articles/PMC9544280/.

15 John Wikswo, 'The Biohacker: A Threat to National Security', Combating Terrorism Centre, Vol. 7, Issue 1, , January 2014.

16 P.W. Singer & Emerson T. Brooking, *Like War: The Weaponization of Social Media*, 2018.

17 J.M. Berger & Jonathon Morgan, 'The ISIS Twitter census: Defining and describing the population of ISIS supporters on Twitter', Brookings Institute, 2015.

18 https://www.precedenceresearch.com/artificial-intelligence-market.

19 https://corporatefinanceinstitute.com/resources/cryptocurrency/top-10-cryptocurrencies.

20 Van der Wagen et al., *British Journal of Criminology*, 55(3), 578–595.

21 Shacheng Wang & Xixi Zhu, *Policing: A Journal of Policy and Practice*, Vol. 15, Issue 4, 2021, pp. 2329–2340.

22 Y. Song et al., *Cryptocurrency Technology Revolution*, https://www.ncbi.nlm.nih.gov/pmc/articles/PMC9860235/)

23 Milind Tiwari, 'Crime Law and Social Change', 73(2), DOI:10.1007/s10611-019-09873-2.

24 Nakul. R. Padalkar, 'Unveiling the Digital Shadows: Exploring the Role of Technology in Illicit Financial Flows', https://www.imf.org/-/media/Files/News/Seminars/2023/11th-stats-forum/session-iii-nakul-r-padalkar.ashx.

25 'The role of crypto currency in financing terrorist organizations', *PBS News Weekend*, 4 November, 2023, https://www.pbs.org/newshour/show/the-role-of-cryptocurrency-in-financing-terrorist-organizations#:~:text=Terrorists%20financiers%2C%20like%20any%20other,from%20them%20to%20raise%20funds.

26 'Latest trends in the use of crypto currency by terrorist groups and their supporters', Security Council - Counter-Terrorism Committee (CTC), Counter-Terrorism Committee Executive Directorate (CTED), https://www.un.org/securitycouncil/ctc/news/cted-hosts-insight-briefing-%E2%80%9Clatest-trends-use-cryptocurrency-terrorist-groups-and-their.

27 'Manhattan Woman Convicted of Using Crypto to Fund Terror Groups in Syria', https://www.nytimes.com/2024/02/01/nyregion/nyc-crypto-syria-terrorism.html.

28 'Hamas Militants Behind Israel Attack Raised Millions in Crypto', *The Wall Street Journal*, 10 October, 2023: https://www.wsj.com/world/middle-east/militants-behind-israel-attack-raised-millions-in-crypto-b9134b7a.

29 https://www.trmlabs.com/post/trm-finds-mounting-evidence-of-crypto-use-by-isis-and-its-supporters-in-asia.

30 Kritika Karmakar, 'Terror and Cyber Finance: Use of Crypto Currencies by Terror Organizations', Centre for Security Studies (JSIA), July, 2020, https://jgu.s3.ap-south-1.amazonaws.com/JSIA/Kritika+Karmakar+-+Terrorism+and+Cyber+Finance.pdf.

31 Stefan Schaufelbühl, 'The emergence of 3D-printed firearms: An analysis of media and law enforcement reports', University of Lausanne, *Forensic Science International Synergy*, March 2024, DOI:10.1016/j.fsisyn.2024.100464.

32 Andy Greenberg, *Meet The 'Liberator': Test-Firing The World's First Fully 3D-Printed Gun, Forbes*, May 5, 2013, https://www.forbes.com/sites/andygreenberg/2013/05/05/meet-the-liberator-test-firing-the-worlds-first-fully-3d-printed-gun/?sh=31046d8a52d7; *"Printing Insecurity? The Security Implications of 3D-Printing of Weapons"*: Gerald Walther, *Sci Eng Ethics* (2015) 21:1435–1445, DOI 10.1007/s11948-014-9617-x.

33 '"Boogaloo" far-right extremists have been illegally buying 3D-printed machine gun parts disguised as wall hangers online, FBI says', https://www.businessinsider.com/boogaloo-extremists-buying-3d-printed-gun-parts-2020-11?IR=T.

34 'Spain dismantles workshop making 3D-printed weapons', 19 April 2022, https://www.bbc.com/news/world-europe-56798743.

35 'Myanmar Fighters Continue Improvising in Struggle Against Junta', https://www.thedefensepost.com/2022/07/18/myanmar-fighters-improvised-weapons/; 'Brazil and US Dismantle Ghost Gun Manufacturing Group', https://dialogo-americas.com/articles/brazil-and-us-dismantle-ghost-gun-manufacturing-group/.

36 Dr. Alexander Blanchard & Jonathan Hall, K. C., *Terrorism and Autonomous Weapon Systems: Future Threat or Science Fiction?*, https://cetas.turing.ac.uk/publications/terrorism-and-autonomous-weapon-systems-future-threat-or-science-fiction.

37 Caroline Gall & PA News Agency, 'Coventry student guilty of making IS chemical weapon drone', *BBC News*, West Midlands. https://www.bbc.com/news/uk-england-coventry-warwickshire-66947311.

Chapter 13: The Psychology of Fear: How Perception Shapes Our Understanding of Terrorism

1 'FNN: Obama Talks About Orlando Shooting, Fighting ISIS and Phrase "Radical Islam"', https://www.youtube.com/watch?v=-0e0BxeZhnA.

2 Ibid.

3 Ibid.

4 Emily Green, *Israel and Hamas Are Not Morally Equivalent*, Lincoln Institute: https://www.lincolninstitute.org/israel-hamas-are-not-morally-equivalent/

5 Shekhar Dutt, *The Nexus of Terror and Ideology: Scourge of Naxalism in India*, https://www.vifindia.org/article/2017/august/21/the-nexus-of-terror-and-ideology-scourge-of-naxalism-in-india.

6 Alan B. Krueger & Jitka Maleckova, 'Education, Poverty and Terrorism: Is There a Causal Connection?', *Journal of Economic Perspectives*, Vol. 17, No. 4, Fall 2003.

7 C.E. Stout, 'Social-Psychological Considerations in the Emergence and Growth of Terrorism,' *The Psychology of Terrorism*, Vol. 3, Praeger Publishers.

8 'Understanding Terrorism: Psychosocial Roots, Consequences, and Interventions,' *American Psychological Association*, 2003.

9 'Farah Pandith explores how to defeat the extremist threat', https://www.start.umd.edu/news/farah-pandith-explores-how-defeat-extremist-threat.

10 Angel Gomez et al., 'Why People Enter and Embrace Violent Groups', *Frontiers in Psychology*, January 2021.

11 Neil Shortland et al., 'A Reinforcement Sensitivity Theory of Violent Extremist Propaganda', *Frontiers in Psychology*, May 2022.

12 Boaz Ganor, 'Understanding the Motivations of "Lone Wolf" Terrorists', *Perspectives on Terrorism*, April 2021.

13 Gabriel Weimann, 'Lone Wolves in Cyberspace', *Journal of Terrorism Research*, 2012.

14 'Can Lone Wolves Be Stopped?', Brookings, March 2017.

15 Y. Winter, "The Siege of Gaza: Spatial Violence, Humanitarian Strategies, and the Biopolitics of Punishment," *Constellations*, Vol. 23, 2016, https://onlinelibrary.wiley.com/doi/10.1111/1467-8675.12185.

16 Shannon Bond, *This is what Russian propaganda looks like in 2024*, June, 2024, All Things Considered, https://www.npr.org/2024/06/06/g-s1-2965/russia-propaganda-deepfakes-sham-websites-social-media-ukraine.

17 'Middle East and North African Regional Overview', 2023, Amnesty International, https://www.amnesty.org/en/location/middle-east-and-north-africa/report-middle-east-and-north-africa/.

18 Petra Guasti & Zdenka Mansfeldova, *Perception of Terrorism and Security and the Role of Media*, September, 2013.

19 'Facebook Acted Too Late to Tackle Misinformation on 2020 Election, Report Finds', https://time.com/5949210/facebook-misinformation-2020-election-report/; 'Facebook condemned for hosting neo-Nazi network with UK links': https://www.theguardian.com/technology/2020/nov/22/facebook-condemned-for-hosting-neo-nazi-network-with-uk-links.

20 Jyoti Panday, 'Exploring the problems of content moderation on social media': Internet Governance Project, School of Public Policy, Georgio Institute of Technology, https://www.internetgovernance.org/2020/12/23/exploring-the-problems-of-content-moderation-on-social-media/.

21 Vaishali Gongane, 'Detection and moderation of detrimental content on social media', *Social Network Analysis and Mining* (2022) 12:129, https://doi.org/10.1007/s13278-022-00951-3.

22 Yuliia Kniazieva, *AI Content Moderation for Responsible Social Media Practices*, https://labelyourdata.com/articles/ai-content-moderation.

23 Siddharth Narrain, *Dangerous Speech in Real Time: Social Media, Policing, and Communal Violence*, https://www.epw.in/engage/article/dangerous-speech-real-time-social-media-policing-and-communal-violence.

24 Clarisa Nelu, *Exploitation of Generative AI by Terrorist Groups*' https://www.icct.nl/publication/exploitation-generative-ai-terrorist-groups.

25 Gabriel Weimann, 'Generating Terror: The Risks of Generative AI Exploitation', January 2024, Vol. 17, Issue 1, *CTC Sentinel* : https://ctc.westpoint.edu/generating-terror-the-risks-of-generative-ai-exploitation/.

26 'The Gamification of Violent Extremism & Lessons for P/CVE', Linda Schlegel, RAN External Expert, European Commission. https://home-affairs.ec.europa.eu/system/files/2021-03/ran_ad-hoc_pap_gamification_20210215_en.pdf.

27 Dr. Suraj Lakhani et al., *The Gamification of Violent Extremism: An Exploration of Emerging Trends, Future Threats Scenarios and Potential P/CVE Solutions*, Rand Policy Support: https://home-affairs.ec.europa.eu/system/files/2022-09/RAN%20Policy%20Support-%20gamification%20of%20violent%20extremism_en.pdf.

28 Fahad Ali Khan et al., 'AI-Driven Counter-Terrorism: Enhancing Global Security Through Advanced Predictive Analytics', *IEEE* , https://ieeexplore.ieee.org/stamp/stamp.jsp?tp=&arnumber=10328769.

INDEX

3D printing, 288, 292, 321, 323-24
9/11 attacks, 6, 15, 18, 21, 32, 47, 86-87, 92, 97-99, 101, 130-31, 166, 167, 174-75, 179, 181, 191-92, 195, 201, 209, 227, 249-50, 253, 256-58, 271, 279-80, 282-83, 286-87, 326, 330

Abrahms, Max, 49
Addressing Grievances (immunotherapy), 31
Afghanistan, 19, 105, 117, 122, 192, 216, 222-23, 225, 270-71, 274-75, 279-80, 319, 334
African Court on Human and Peoples' Rights (ACHPR), 172
AFSPA, 120-23, 135
AI-enabled Hardware Systems (AIEHS), 296
Air India Flight 182, 97
AIRCOP, 100
Al Arabiya, 56
Al-Aqsa Martyrs Brigade, 252
Algeria, 15, 18, 166
All-India Institute of Medical Sciences (AIIMS), 57-58, 68
All-India Service, 116
al-Qaeda, 6, 18-19, 29, 43, 55, 69, 105, 217, 239-40, 244, 250, 263-65, 271, 273, 282, 302, 318-20, 329, 339, 344, 352, 355
al-Qaeda in Iraq (AQI), 19
al-Qaeda in the Arabian Peninsula (AQAP), 19
Al-Shahab, 55
AML-CTF, 254, 259
anti-money laundering (AML), 250, 254, 258
AntsP2P, 70
Anushilan Samiti, 5, 10
Apple Approach, 67
Apple's VisionPro, 309
Arab Convention for the Suppression of Terrorism, 40
Arafat, Yasser, 24
Aristotle, 137
Armed Forces (Assam and Manipur) Special Powers Ordinance, 119-20
Armed Forces (Special Powers) Act, 118-21, 135
Armstrong, Karen, *Fields of Blood: Religion and the History of Violence*, 17
Arthashastra, 166
Artificial General Intelligence (AGI), 312
Artificial Intelligence (AI), AI, 19-21, 68, 102, 186-89, 203, 208, 211, 260, 262, 288-89, 292, 297-98, 305, 307-15, 325, 345, 347-48, 351-55
Artificial Intelligence Enabled Hardware Systems (AIEHS), 288
Ashoka, 13
Asia, 318
Associated Press Twitter, 56
Association of Southeast Asian Nations Convention on Counter-Terrorism, 40
Aum Shinrikyo, 102, 240, 252, 269-73, 277, 282-83, 291, 302
Aum Shinsen Association, 240
Australia, 11, 56, 62, 146, 166, 183, 212, 270, 278, 287
Australia, Banjawarn Station, 277

Autonomous Vehicles Based-Improvised Explosive Devices (AVB-IED), 20

Baader-Meinhof Gang, 6
Babbar Khalsa, 252
Bangladesh, 259
Basel Committee on Banking Supervision (BCBS), 257
Behavioural Data Exhaust, 79
Ben Gurion Airport, 98
Bhartiya Nagarik Suraksha Samhita (BNSS), 176
Bhartiya Nyaya Samhita (BNS), 198, 229
BigTech, 79, 181, 296, 313, 315, 345-48, 355
Big-Tech Super-State, 189
bin Laden, Osama, 6, 25, 271, 273-74, 277, 309, 328
Biohacking, 306
Biological Weapons Convention (BWC), 286
Bitcoin, 56, 264, 315-19
Black Internet Tigers, 55
Blockchain, 317
Bodo Security Force, 130
Boliska, Al, 86
Border Security Force (BSF), 104
British Empire, 119
British Raj, 7-8, 14, 115
Bureau of Civil Aviation Security (BCAS), 89, 106
Bush, George W., 102, 236

Canada, 11, 15, 25, 146, 183, 212, 323
Cancer, 32
Capek, Karel, 293
Carsten Bockstette, 49
CCTV, 57, 186
Central Bureau of Investigation (CBI), 142, 161, 228-29, 231
CFT-AML, 258
Chaliand, Gerard, *The History of Terrorism from Antiquity to ISIS*, 14
Chartered Accountant (CA), 232
Chat GPT, 187
Chemical Weapons Convention, 284-85
Chemical, Biological, Radiological, and Nuclear (CBRN) , 268-75, 277-80, 282-84, 287-93
Chicago Convention, 90, 92-93
China, 24, 27, 56, 105, 166, 297, 300, 320, 341, 346
Churchill, Winston, 112
CIA, 167
Clarifying Lawful Overseas Use of Data (CLOUD) Act, 167
Clarke, Richard, 54
Clausewitz, Carl von, *On War*, 215
Collin, Barry C., 55, 60
Communist Party of India (Maoist), 26
Comprehensive Approach, 38
Comprehensive Convention on International Terrorism (CCIT), 36
Computer-aided Digital (CAD), 321
Convention on International Civil Aviation, 90
Convention on the Physical Protection of Nuclear Material (CPPNM), 285
Council of Europe Convention on the Prevention of Terrorism, 40
Counter Terror Financing and Money Laundering (CTF-ML), 236
Countering Violent Extremism (CVE), 337
Counter-terrorism, 63, 105, 113, 115, 136, 141, 194, 199-200, 212, 214, 314, 326-27, 354
Counter-Terrorism Committee (CTC), 172, 251
Counter-Terrorism Financing, 249
Counter-Terrorism Implementation Task Force (CTITF), 172
Counter-terrorist Financing (CFT), 253-54
Criminal Procedure Code (CrPC) , 150, 156, 161, 183, 230
CRISPR-Cas9, 290, 302-03, 307
Crypto Currency, 69, 193, 243, 263, 265, 288, 316-20
Customer Due Diligence (CDD), 256, 262-63, 267

Cyber Attack, 55-56, 63-66, 71-72, 74, 77, 79-80, 82, 84-85, 102, 108, 212, 298, 307, 351
Cyber Crime, 55, 58-60-64, 77, 81, 83, 295
Cyber Technology, 289
Cyber-Forensics, 73-74
Cyber Security, 54-55, 64-65, 69, 71, 73, 75-77, 80, 83-84, 264, 316
Cyber Space, 59, 63, 67, 69, 75-76, 78, 80-85, 187, 310
Cyber Terrorism, 18, 20, 55-56, 58-67, 69-70, 72, 75, 80-82, 84-85, 295
Cyber Warfare, 57, 65, 80-81
Cyprus, 225, 230

Dark Net, 69, 243, 263, 264, 295-96
Dark Web, 69, 204, 208, 288, 293, 315-17, 320, 324
Data Localization, 77
Data Sovereignty, 77
Deep Blue, 19
Deep Thought, 19
DeepSeek, 187
Defence of India Act, 110-11
Designated Authority, 150
Digital Age, 212, 313
Digital Assistants, 73
Digital Dark Matter, 66
Digital Robots, 68
Digital Swarming, 265
Dismantling Networks (Surgery), 31
Disruptive Activities, 124, 127, 129
Distributed Denial-of-Service (DDoS) Attack, 56
Distributed Ledger Technology (DLT), 262
DNS Hijacking, 70
Do-It-Yourself (DIY) , 289, 291, 302-03, 322-24
Domain Name System (DNS), 70
Drones Counter-measures, 300
Drones, 20, 101, 102, 277, 291, 300-01, 323

Egmont Group, 258
Egypt, 93, 97, 259, 285
Electronic Control Units (ECUs), 68
Emperor Ashoka's XIIIth Major Rock Edict, 13
Enforcement Directorate (ED) , 161, 228-29, 231
English Crown, 144
ENIAC, 182
Ethereum, 316
European Court of Human Rights (ECtHR), 174, 180
European Court of Justice (ECJ), 172
European Union (EU) , 41, 51, 251, 313

Facebook, 67, 79, 182, 193, 265, 311, 313, 326, 337, 344, 346
Falah-e-Insaniyat (FIF), 239, 281
FARC, 43, 218
FBI, 55, 62, 101, 146, 240, 263, 269-70, 323
fCG-9 MKII, 323
Federal Bureau of Investigation, 55, 59
Financial Action Task Force (FATF), 253-54, 258, 261, 281
Financial Intelligence Units (FIUs), 256
Financial Sector Assessment Program (FSAP), 256
Financial Times, 56
Foreign Terrorist Fighters (FTFs), 265
FP-45 Liberator, 322
France, 12, 287
Freedom Fighters, 23-24, 26, 46, 52, 110

G-7, 253
Geo-fencing, 104, 300-02
Germany, 2, 5, 30, 138, 173, 287, 315, 322-23
Germany's Red Army Faction, 5
Ghosh, Aurobindo, 11
Gibson, William, 55
Golden Age of Terrorism, 6
Golden Crescent, 222
Google Pay, 247
Google, 79, 167, 313, 326
Government of India Act of 1935, 111-12
GPS, 108, 300

Grey List, 259
Grow AI, 187

Hague Convention, 81, 94
Hamas, 6, 24, 29, 43, 52, 56, 58, 244, 247, 252, 280, 298, 318-20, 327, 332, 339-41, 343, 355-56
Hashashians, 2-3
Hawala Transactions, 226
Hawala, 69, 145, 219, 226, 238-39, 243, 247
Hezbollah Pager Attack, 57
Hezbollah, 6, 29, 52, 56-58, 218-20, 222, 273-74, 279-80, 352
High Court, 111, 154-55, 157-59, 162
Hindustan Socialist Republican Association, 5
Hostages Case, 44-45
Hybrid, 324
Hybrid Approach, 39, 41
Hybrid Crime, 228, 231, 233
Hybrid Nature, 238

IMF, 254, 256-57, 259
Improvised Explosive Devices (IEDs), 103, 323
India, 5, 7-11, 23-24, 28, 36, 43, 58, 62, 64, 87-89, 93, 104-06, 109-25, 129-30, 132-36, 141-42, 145, 150, 153-55, 157, 159-61, 166, 176, 183-85, 194, 196-201, 203, 206, 210, 216-17, 222-24, 226-29, 231-32, 234-35, 239, 246, 257, 274-75, 280-82, 298, 300-01, 314, 319, 327, 331, 334, 336, 341
Indian Army, 123
Indian Constitution, 112, 116-17, 142
Indian Penal Code, 176
India-Pakistan border, 20, 298
Indo-China, 15
Indonesia, 259, 319
Information and Communication Technologies (ICT), 62, 67
Information Technology Enabled Services (ITES), 182
Information Warfare, 60, 70
Initial Coin Offerings (ICOs), 317
Instagram, 67, 79, 265, 340
Inter-American Convention against Terrorism, 40
International Association of Insurance Supervisors (IAIS), 258
International Atomic Energy Agency (IAEA), 286
International Civil Aviation Organization (ICAO) , 92-93, 95-97, 100-01, 106-08
International Covenant on Civil and Political Rights (ICCPR) , 170-72, 178-79
International Covenant on Economic, Social, and Cultural Rights (ICESCR), 170, 172
International Human Rights Law (IHRL) , 169-71, 174, 176
International Organization of Securities Commissions (IOSCO), 258
Internet of Things (IoT), 288-89
Internet Protocol (IP), 70
Internet Service Providers (ISPs), 230, 312, 314-15
INTERPOL, 62, 100, 232, 234
Inter-Service Intelligence (ISI), 117, 129
IP hijacking, 71
Iranian Revolution, 6
Iraq, 19, 167, 192, 269, 274, 279-80, 283, 285
Ireland, 5
Irish Republican Army (IRA), 98
Islamic State (IS), 19, 339
Islamic State of Iraq (ISI), 19
Islamic State of Iraq and Syria (ISIS) , 2, 14, 19, 29, 43, 69, 105, 179, 185, 192-94, 196, 198, 204-07, 223, 240, 244, 263-65, 271-73, 283, 301-02, 310, 318-20, 336-39, 343-44, 346, 351-52, 354-56
Isolegal Mimicry, 75
Isomorphic Mimicry, 75
Israel, 25, 29, 43, 57-58, 104-05, 285, 297-98, 320, 327, 332, 339-42
Israel, Tel Aviv, , 98
Israeli Defence Forces (IDF), 332
Italy, 93, 102, 146, 287

Izz al-Din al-Qassam Cyber Fighters, 56

Jaish-e-Mohammed, 43, 89, 281
Jammu and Kashmir, 117, 122-23, 129-30, 135, 154, 200, 225, 227
Japan, 56, 240, 257
Japan, Kamikuishiki, , 277
Japan's Aum Shinrikyo, 56
Japanese Red Army (JRA), 6, 98
Jeevan Reddy Committee, 122
Judicial Sovereignty, 45
Jugantar, 5, 11

Kamra Air Base, 276
Kathmandu, 89, 93
Kenya, 6, 62, 250, 259
Khalistan Movement, 15
Khalistan Zindabad Force, 252
Khalistani, 15, 87, 117, 334
Khan, A.Q., 282, 287
Khyber-Pakhtunkhwa (KP), 224
Know-Your-Customer (KYC), 76, 258, 260, 319-21, 325, 349

Lang, Timur, 12
Laptops, 73
Laqueur, Walter, *A History of Terrorism*, 18, 48, 278
Lashkar-e-Taiba, 130
Latin America, 5, 100, 219-20, 233-34, 311
Left-Wing Extremism, 200
Letter Rogatory, 72
Liberation Tigers of Tamil Eelam (LTTE), 55, 98, 247, 252
Libya, 98, 222, 250, 274, 280
LiDAR, 103
Liechtenstein, 225
London Bombings, 177
Lone-Wolf, 238, 264, 278, 310, 338-39
Los Zetas, 219-20

Maal-e-Ghanima, 265
Machine Learning (ML), 305, 311
Maintenance of Internal Security Act, 117
Malaysia, 99, 146, 259
Mandela, Nelson, 24, 164
Marathas, 9
Martens Clause, 81, 84
Matrix, 82
MegaSyn, 20
Metrojet Flight 9268, 98
Mianwali Air Force Base, 276
Middle East, 19, 29, 98-100, 219-20, 234, 283, 330
Minhas Air Force Base, 276
Ministry of External Affairs, 228
Ministry of Home Affairs, 231, 233
Modi, Narendra, 190
Monaco, 225, 259
Monero, 316
Mongols, 4, 12, 351
Montreal Convention, 91-92, 94
Moonlight Maze, 55
Mughals, 9
Mumbai attacks, 141
Mumbai Attacks, 199
Mumbai Taj Hotel, 197
Mutual Legal Assistance Treaties (MLATs), 72, 143, 72, 230, 232

Nanotechnology, 279, 288, 290, 305
Narco-terrorism, 100, 215, 217, 219, 222-24, 227-29, 234
Narco-terrorists, 219, 221, 224, 230-31, 234, 311
Narcotics Control Bureau (NCB), 228, 231
National Centre for Missing & Exploited Children (NCMEC), 313
National Investigation Agency (NIA) Act, 135, 139, 141-42, 144, 150, 157, 161-63, 194, 199, 200-01, 206-07, 210, 228-29, 231, 239, 298
Naxalism, 336
Naziris, 3-4
New Zealand, 183, 212
NGOs, 201, 280
Nietzsche, 268
Nightmare, 56

Non-Proliferation Treaty (NPT), 282
North Korea, 56, 259, 280, 285
North West Frontier Province, 224
North-East, 200, 228
Northern Ireland, 5
NotPetya, 56
Nuclear Terrorism, 282, 284-85

Obama, Barack, 105, 177, 270, 328-29
Online Radicalisation, 193, 204
Operation Sindoor, 105
Organization for the Prohibition of Chemical Weapons (OPCW), 285
Organization of African Unity (OAU), 40
Organization of the Islamic Conference (OIC), 40
OSINT, 309, 310
Over Ground Workers (OGWs), 200, 219-20

Pahalgam Attack, 227, 257, 281
Pakistan, 20, 24, 27-29, 43, 53, 62, 87-89, 93, 104-05, 119, 122, 129-30, 138, 191, 216-17, 219-20, 222-29, 232, 234, 239, 257, 259, 273-76, 279-81, 284, 298, 301, 319, 327
Pal, Bipin Chandra, 14
Palestine Liberation Organization (PLO), 6, 24
Palestinian Islamic Jihad, 252
Pan Am Flight 103, 97-98
Paytm, 247
Peace and Tranquillity, 111
Pearl Harbour, 32
Pentagon, Washington, D.C., 19
Phansi, 7
Phansigar, 7
Pindari War, 8-9
Political Terrorism, 48, 209
Popular Front for the Liberation of Palestine (PFLP), 98
Prevention of Money Laundering Act (PMLA), 231
Prevention of Terrorism Act, 2002 (POTA) , 115, 129-33, 135, 149
Prevention of Terrorism Ordinance, 130
Preventive Detention Act (PDA), 117
PRISM, 313
Privacy-enhancing Techniques (PETs), 74
Proceeds of Terrorism, means, 147
Promoting Peace (Prevention), 31
pro-Palestinian Groups, 56
Pure Cyberterrorism, 61
Purpose-based Approach, 38

Racketeer Influenced and Corrupt Organizations (RICO) Act, 146
Radical Islam, 328-29
Rai, Lala Lajpat, 14
Red Army Faction, 6
Red Brigades, 6
Reparation for Injuries Case, 89
RetroShare, 70
Rf-jamming, 302
Roomal, 7
Rowlatt Act, 110-11
Russia, 56, 105, 240, 254, 269, 298, 301, 318, 341, 346

Sandhya, 11
Sanyal, Sachin, 11
Sardesai, G.S., 9
Scheduled Offences, 161
Schmid, Alex, 50
Schmid, Alex, *Political Terrorism: A Research Guide*, 48
Sectoral Approach, 38
Sen, S.N., 9
Sicarii, 1-2, 4, 21
Singh, Bhagat, 5
Singh, Dr. Upinder, *Political Violence in Ancient India*, 13
Smartphones, 68, 73, 344
Smartwatches, 73
Social Media, 265, 266, 338, 339, 341-42, 344-45
Social Media Companies (SMCs), 312, 314-15
Sony Pictures, 56

South Africa, 146, 259
South Asia Association for Regional Cooperation Regional Convention on Suppression of Terrorism, 40
Spanish Civil War, 5
Special Courts, 114, 135, 141, 159-62
StealthNet, 70
STUXNET, 81
Supercop, 113
Supervisory Control and Data Acquisition (SCADA), 55
Supreme Court, 42, 126, 128-29, 132, 135-36, 153-57, 159-60, 181
Surface Web, 263
Surface-to-air Missile (SAM), 99
Swaraj, 11
Switzerland, 225
Synthetic Biology, 279, 288, 290, 303-04, 307
Syria, 4, 19, 27, 103, 192, 259, 265, 272, 285, 299, 319, 342
Syrian Electronic Army (SEA), 56

Taliban-ISI nexus, 224
Tamerlane, 12
Telegram, 72-73, 193, 204-05, 208, 210, 265, 336, 344
Terrorism, 12, 22, 29, 137, 140, 281, 355
Terrorist and Disruptive Activities (Prevention) Act (TADA) , 123-33, 135, 148-49
Terrorist Financing (TF), 236-39
Terrorist Lumpers, 49
Terrorist Splitters, 49
Terrorists, 138, 147
Thatcher, Margaret, 1, 5
The Onion Router (TOR), 317
The Organization for Economic Cooperation and Development (OECD), 83
the Philippines, 146, 259
The Washington Post, 56
Third Anglo-Maratha War, 9
Threema, 205, 336, 344
Thuggee, 8
Thugs, 7, 8
Tilak, Bal Gangadhar, 10-11, 14
Titan Rain, 56
Tokyo Convention, 94
Tokyo Subway Attack, 269
Transnational Criminal Syndicates (TCS), 218
Transportation Security Administration (TSA), 99
Treaty of Westphalia, 16
Tufekci, Zeynep, 326

UK's Terrorism Act, 2000, 63
UN Convention against Transnational Organized Crime (UNTOC), 210
UN Counter-Terrorism Committee, 47
UN Office on Drugs and Crime (UNODC), 100, 232, 234
Uncertainty Principle, 74
United Against Drone Threats, 103
United Airlines Chesterton Crash, 87
United Kingdom (UK), 63, 128, 146, 174, 183, 212, 271, 298, 320, 324
United Nations (UN), 15, 23, 25, 35, 37, 43, 46, 51, 83-84, 90, 106, 133, 136, 165, 171-73, 177-78, 223, 250, 254, 283-84, 318
United Nations Charter, 89
United Nations General Assembly (UNGA), 36
United Nations Security Council (UNSC), 24, 33, 37, 47, 62, 64, 106, 114, 133, 170, 174-75, 177, 223, 250, 252, 284, 287
  Resolution 49/60, 36
  Resolution 1264, 178, 179
  Resolution 1373, 35, 37-38, 62, 174-75, 250-52
  Resolution 1540, 284, 287
  Resolution 1566, 33, 37
  Resolution 1624, 175, 177, 179-80
United States Drug Enforcement Administration (DEA), 215
United States Foreign Intelligence Surveillance Act, 167
Universal Declaration of Human Rights, 139, 165, 170-72, 178

Unlawful Activities (Prevention) Act (UAPA), 115, 122, 125, 131, 133-35, 145, 147-51, 157-59, 162-63, 178, 194, 197, 199, 201, 210, 229-30
Unlawful Activities (Prevention) Act, 132, 144, 162, 178
Unmanned Aerial Vehicles (UAVs) , 101-05, 108, 288, 298, 300-01, 323, 325
Uruguay, 5, 173
US Military Tribunal, 45
US National Security Agency (NSA), 313
US Supreme Court Justice Potter Stewart, 42
USA, 32, 47, 55, 81, 93, 99, 105, 127, 146, 174, 183, 191-93, 201, 219, 227, 252, 257, 259, 269, 274, 280, 282, 313, 318, 320
US-Canada, 95
USS Cole, 6

Vajpayee, Atal Bihari, 88
Venugopal, Arun, 113
Virtual Private Networks (VPNs), 205
Virtual Reality (VR), 308

Wah Cantonment, 275
Waly, Gadha Fathi, 22
WannaCry, 56
War on Terror, 15, 19, 31-32, 47, 177
Warren, Earl, 109
Weapons of Mass Destruction (WMDs), 254-55, 269, 271-73, 279-81, 283-84, 287
Weber, Max, 13
Western Union, 147
WhatsApp, 72, 204, 210, 265, 344
Wiseman, Jon D., *Encyclopaedia of Violence, Peace, & Conflict*, 14
Wolfsberg Group, 258
World Bank, 254, 256-57
World Trade Centre in New York, 18
World War I, 5, 22, 110
World War II, 5, 89, 110, 182, 256

Yemen, 6, 105, 342

Zia-ul-Haq, 275, 280
Zuboff, Soshana, *The Surveillance Capitalism*, 78